Human Interactions, Processes, and Contexts: Reflections on the Past and Envisioning the Future

Human Interactions, Processes, and Contexts: Reflections on the Past and Envisioning the Future

DAVID R. SCHWANDT
ELLEN SCULLY-RUSS
KATHLEEN CROWLEY

authorHOUSE®

AuthorHouse™ LLC
1663 Liberty Drive
Bloomington, IN 47403
www.authorhouse.com
Phone: 1-800-839-8640

Published by AuthorHouse   03/21/2014

ISBN: 978-1-4918-1909-8 (sc)
ISBN: 978-1-4918-1907-4 (hc)
ISBN: 978-1-4918-1908-1 (e)

Library of Congress Control Number: 2013922147

TABLE OF CONTENTS

Part IV: Moving to the Future

Preface

In late 1989 a visiting professor, teaching in The Graduate School of Education and Human Development, explored the feasibility of launching a nontraditional doctoral program as an "experiment" at the George Washington University (GWU). The focus of the program was to be human and organizational development, and it became known as the Executive Leadership Program (ELP). The experiment involved more than just starting a nontraditional doctoral program for working professionals; it included the seeds for building a global learning community that embodied research and "thought experiments" among diverse scholars and organizational practitioners around different lines of inquiry associated with questions concerning how we relate, how we know, and how we remain socially integrated. The founder's vision: "To build a community where scholars and practitioners can come together in the pursuit of learning and gain insight into human and organizational phenomena resulting in the creation of new knowledge that impacts theory, research, and practice. And to do so by continuously creating innovative learning formats that facilitate ongoing dialogue and human development" (David R. Schwandt, 1989, prospectus paper launching the ELP). Almost three decades later, these practitioners and scholars are still exchanging ideas—whether it's through panel presentations at international research conferences, across boardrooms of emerging nonprofits, or in the classrooms at the GWU Ashburn Campus. This book commemorates ELP's learning community and its coevolving discourse that has been shaped by so many thoughtful ELP students, alumni, and invited scholars. Then and now, amazing transdisciplinary collaborations and team-science thinking have emerged from the ELP. The purpose of this preface is to provide the reader a brief background about the nature of the ELP, its national speakers program, and the international conversations that are occurring with and among its students, faculty, alumni, and invited scholars.

The ELP sustains its commitment to creating a learning community with various innovative formats in which experienced practitioners can engage in thoughtful exploration of unsolved organizational puzzles through transdisciplinary approaches. The curriculum is designed around cross-cutting constructs pertinent to the ideas of leadership, change, culture, and learning—and continues to provide a platform for collegial conversation in which "complex people explore complex ideas to solve complex problems" (Tony Sablo, National Geographic, ELP alumnus). Twenty-five years later, Schwandt's experiment has spawned new doctoral programs at other universities, some using blended delivery or full online delivery formats. ELP remains committed to its real-time face-to-face collaborative conversations via its 2½-year one-weekend-a-month and June residency format.

One of the critical components of the ELP vision has been the national scholars program. From ELP's inception, the program faculty envisioned a network of thought-provoking scholars joining the weekend discourse to help build the bridges between the academic campus and the organizational boardroom. Starting with the first cohort, Schwandt began inviting scholars—some of whom have chapters in this book, while others have since departed or retired—including Richard Hackman, Harry Levinson, Elliot Jaques, Peter Vaill, and Martha Rashid. This book is a commemoration of these 25 years of conversation between the scholars, faculty, and alumni, who humbly engaged in mind-thought experiments each weekend. More importantly, this book commemorates the ELP community that transcends any brick-and-mortar.

There are many heartwarming and humorous stories about guest scholars who've visited ELP over the 25 years, from Elliot Jaques' ranting about organizational development practitioners as alchemists to Hackman's barefoot lecture walk-about to Vic Vroom's trumpet playing at a jazz club. There have been philosophical debates, role playing, and much lively banter about the usefulness of theory with scholars such as Henry Mintzberg, Linda Smircich, Ed Lawler, Peter Vaill, Mary Anne Glynn, Jerry Davis, Martin Kilduff, Dan Denison, Dave Whetten, Irv Seidman, Marta Calas, Rob Stones, Colon Eden, and Gareth Morgan. The common experience across all of these scholars' visits was the nature of the conversation. All of them were "in dialogue" with the cohort of students and at times uncertain who was playing the senior scholar and who the student. Sometimes you might see Weick pull out his pocket spiral notepad to write down an idea spawned from a student's insight, and perhaps you'd see Woody Powell chuckle and state that a student had presented an interesting idea that he had not considered but might address in his next article. Each of these national scholars came to the cohort classroom in Ashburn and sat as equals with the ELP students in hopes of cocreating a new insight about these organizational puzzles. There has been much criticism about executive education and the gap between academia and "the real world"; I'd like to think that this national scholars program and ELP's network represent the possibilities for bridging and building ideas. The chapters in this book represent some of these conversations and these insights.

The contributions in this book provide a glimpse into the wonderful conversations that occurred in the ELP over the last 25 years. The scholars selected a piece of their work they felt was significant or representative of their thinking, and in the prologue they shared their reflections about that work. The first section of the book, "Knowledge Creation and Meaning," has contributions from three long-time visiting scholars and friends of ELP: Anne Huff, Karl Weick, and Victoria Marsick. These scholars are exemplars within their own disciplines, noted for their thought-provoking publications, yet within ELP they have been revered for their compassionate engagement with the students concerning human and organizational issues. The second section of the book, "Leadership and Complexity," has contributions from three scholars who have transformed the way many of our students think about chaos and the role of leaders.

Mary Uhl-Bien, Russ Marion, and Bill McKelvey have challenged our cohorts with their discussions of fractals, dissipative structures, and nonlinear systems. The third section of the book, "Dynamics of Organizations," brings forth contributions from four provocative and engaging ELP guest scholars: Jerry Harvey, Jo Hatch, Sid Winter, and Woody Powell. From stories about frog pharms, jazz improvisation, learning in spite of organizational routines, and amphibious organizations, these four scholars and their coauthors share a piece of their work that continues to reshape our thinking about organizing and its dynamics. The final section of the book, "Moving to the Future," includes a contribution from a long-time ELP friend and the father of organizational development, Warner Burke. Warner's perspective on the field of organizational development and change, coupled with the final chapter on moving to the future that's written by ELP faculty, provides a capstone to the book and a path to exploring future issues in human and organizational development.

The GWU Ashburn campus has certainly been a wonderful forum and playground where scholars and practitioners have come together to engage in thought-provoking conversations about human and social dilemmas. This book serves as a tribute to the founding values of the ELP.

Dr. Margaret Delaney Gorman
Northeastern University
Boston, MA
September 2013

Part I
Knowledge Creation and Meaning

Chapter 1

The Coevolving Nature of Human and Organizational Sciences: A Theory-Practice Imperative

David R. Schwandt
Professor of Human and Organizational Learning

Marshall Sashkin
Professor of Human and Organizational Learning, Emeritus

Introduction

The theory-practice relationship. The 25 years from the late 1980s to the early 2000s, spanning the transition from the 20th to the 21st century, has seen increased interest in social interactions and their reciprocal influence on collective outcomes. This interest includes both theory and practice in the human and organizational sciences. With the interest came the realization, and acceptance, that the theoretical explanation of social dynamics requires the inclusion of multiple levels of social analysis, as well as cross-disciplinary contributions. As a result, there is considerable variability among theories in both the human and organizational sciences with respect to context and content. And this variability has, in turn, accentuated the gap between abstract theories and real-time practice in organizations.

As good logic would dictate, we turned to increasing our understanding of the gap by defining the term "theory." However, even the definition of the word *theory* did not help. The Oxford English Dictionary defines the word as a "system of ideas explaining something" or "the sphere of abstract knowledge or speculative thought." These two somewhat differing definitions have in many respects widened the theory-practice gap as opposed to bridging it. The definitions allow two divergent interpretations of how theory is related to practice.

The first definition reflects what may be a false assurance that theory will provide formulas for action. But when formulas are applied without consideration of context or boundary conditions, theory can easily fail, leaving the practitioner with dashed expectations. The second definition reflects the ideas of abstraction and speculation, raising serious questions about the usefulness of theory for practice. Both of these interpretations have allowed practitioners to dismiss the study of theory as nonrelevant or speculative with respect to pragmatic "real-life" situations, and therefore as not useful.

However, with that said, we believe the current reputation of theory in the human and organizational sciences is steadily gaining positive recognition. This change is not due to the ability of theory to accurately predict social outcomes based on relational arrangements of critical variables. On the contrary, it is understanding the inherent variability of the substance of social science theory over time and across contexts that has spurred increased recognition of the importance and relevance of theory. Understanding the variability within social science theory can trigger critical thinking about both the substance of theory and the nature of practice.

No longer do enlightened managers raise their eyebrows at the mention of the word "theory," as though confronted with ideas of fantasy.

Theoretical relationships have become frameworks for explanations that can be tested and modified based on the results of human actions and interactions. This different idea of the theory-practice relationship has been an impetus for developing "scholar-practitioners," individuals who are able to integrate knowledge, skills, and experiences. It is our argument that the tension between theory and practice has allowed the redefining of the gap between them as a positive factor that helps the scholar-practitioner to better understand both the human and organizational sciences and to make better practice decisions.

The present volume. This collection consists of seminal papers written by scholars across various disciplines, including management, the business sciences, social psychology, adult learning, and economics. The papers were published over the 1988 to 2012 time span and represent important additions to our understanding of the social sciences, the practice of membership and leadership in organizations, and the creation of knowledge in the human and organizational sciences. They address the process of creating knowledge and meaning, understanding different conceptualizations of leadership, and explaining organizational dynamics. Each of the papers, to a certain extent, reflects this variability within and between human and organizational theory, the author's insights, and, ultimately, changes in practice over the past 25 years.

While these authors understand the inherent variability within and between human and organizational theories, they have also achieved a connection with practice that makes their contributions not only good science but useful practice. The papers were selected by the authors as significant representations of their thinking over the past 25 years. Each author offers a prologue and/or epilogue that represents current reflections on the paper. In addition, over this time frame, each author has participated with us in the doctoral studies program we initiated 25 years ago aimed at the development of scholar-practitioners in the area of human and organizational studies. They have interacted with doctoral students (who have often been experienced practitioners), presenting their ideas, their theories, and their experiences for discussion and testing in the context of changing environments over time.

This introductory chapter introduces each chapter author's work in the context of the variability of theory—variability in terms of both substance and process. As indicated in each author's prologue or epilogue, building theory is not always a logical, sequential, and linear process. Understanding the history of theoretical thought is important for many theorists, while others place greater weight on observing—and even participating in-practice. Many continuously question their own past thinking and reflect on the meaning of their own worldviews. We believe that this critical reflection process, triggered by the variability of the substance of theory—over time and contexts—is the scholar-practitioner's unique contribution to bridging the gap between theory and practice.

We begin here with a closer examination of the coevolving nature of managerial and organizational science constructs. We present two historical approaches to this coevolution. One is focused on the changing economic context, the other on interaction with the changing human condition. These factors are important for understanding the fluidity of theory, over time and context. We then relate this inherent substantive variation of managerial and organizational science constructs to the process of theory development, emphasizing the critical role for scholar-practitioners of this variation. We conclude with a brief review of the nature of the theory contributions of the chapter authors.

The Coevolving Nature of Human and Organization Theory

Although we might expand our view to include the variability of theory in most social sciences, we limit ourselves here to those theories associated with managerial and organizational sciences. This body of theory does not represent systematically discovered incremental knowledge, but is instead more a set of continuously coevolving explanations of human actions in organizations. In examining these theories, we find some have developed over time while others occur in punctuated processes (Kuhn, 1970). However, in all cases it is "better not to think of science as a quest for timeless truths. Science creates 'effective theories.' These are models—incomplete by definition. They are effective in limited domains and they are approximate" (Gleick, 2013).

To demonstrate the variability of human and organizational theory, we first expand on our premise that theory constitutes an explanation of social phenomena but is not permanent truth. This is, of course, due to the inherent variability in the substance of theory. This variation of theoretical substance can be related to contextual dynamics as well as to variations in basic human assumptions that are grounded in values. One approach to examining how theoretical substance varies with context is through a historical analysis of the coevolution of concepts.

Barley and Kunda (1992) examined managerial discourse, rhetoric, and ideologies across 100 years of published journal papers on managerial theories concerning the control of complex organizations. They found that the evolution of theory was not a linear progression. Instead, they concluded that "managerial discourses appear to have alternated between ideologies of normative and rational control" (p. 364). For example, scientific management ideas were prevalent during the time period 1900 to 1923 and represented a very rational approach to management actions. The subsequent period—1923 to 1955—was dominated by theories of human relations that represented a normative approach to management actions. Figure 1 provides a historical interpretation of the reciprocating normative-rational control theory variation.

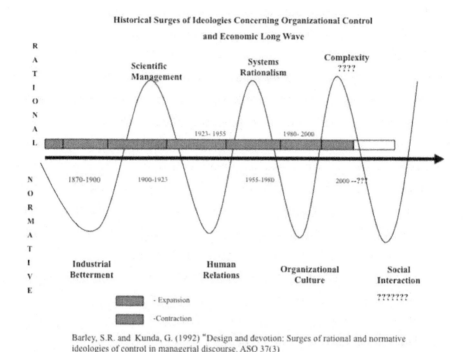

Barley, S.R. and Kunda, G. (1992) "Design and devotion: Surges of rational and normative ideologies of control in managerial discourse. ASQ 37(3)

Figure 1. Interpretation of Barley and Kunda's theory variation.

Barley and Kunda (1992) found two interesting characteristics of this reciprocating variability of managerial theories of control. *First,* none of the five ideologies they identified (shown in Figure 1) disappeared completely over time. At any time in history one could expect to see managerial theories that reflected multiple ideologies characteristic of earlier times. *Second,* periods of rational and normative variation in theory were related to shifts in economic conditions: "New waves of rational and normative theorizing have in turn, been associated with long-term expansions and contractions in the economy" (p. 392). These observations provide a plausible relationship between normative actions of control being employed during times of economic contractions and more rational theories being emphasized during times of economic expansions. We might make judgments on the applicability of this frame for explaining

6

the variability of complexity theories during the expansion and recession period of 2000 to 2012.

The Barley and Kunda contextual explanation of theoretical variance in managerial control was extended by a similar analysis of the same managerial control theories over the same time periods. Eastman and Bailey (1998), however, came to different conclusions. Their study of the evolution of the substance of theory identified a different relationship. Eastman and Bailey characterized the evolution of theoretical substance as efforts to close the "fact-value" conflict or "antinomy." Specifically, they found that a requisite of theoretical rhetoric, regardless of discipline, is to mediate the antinomy between objectively, scientifically ascertainable and formally determined "facts," and subjectively perceived, open ended, and indeterminate "value." (p. 232)

This reduction in antinomy was achieved through time periods during which changes in theory served to mediate the tension between fact and value. In the first part of the 20th century, from 1900 to about 1940, a "mode" of theory change that Eastman and Bailey called "formalism" characterized a shift in theory from a focus on industrial betterment to a concentration on "scientific management" as best expressed in the work and writing of Frederick Winslow Taylor. Over the next 40 years or so, from the 1940s to the 1970s, a new mode of "consensualism" described a shift in theory from a concern with human relations to a concentration on systems rationalism. Finally, from the 1970s through the 1990s, the mode was "value partisanship," involving the move in theory from a focus on systems rationalism to the centrality of organizational culture. Eastman and Bailey concluded:

These modes can all be understood as strategies or devices for dealing with tensions between the contrasting polar positions of "fact" versus "value," "objectivity" versus "subjectivity," or, to use terms more evocative of earlier conceptions of society and human nature, "reason" versus "passion." (p. 239)

We have identified two specific variations in the substance of theory: rational versus normative and fact versus value. These two variations in the substance of managerial theories of control clearly reflect an ideological difference. Even so, as Connell and Nord (1998) observed, they are not mutually exclusive. We have identified, at an abstract level of propositions, 14 social change constructs that have maintained relative stability over the 100 years examined by Barley and Kunda (see Figure 2). For example, power has been, and still is, a crucial element in organizational change. However, when implementing organizational change at the lowest level, the micro level of analysis, one can see the inherent theoretical variability of each of the constructs without changing the names of the phenomena involved. Thus, continuing our example, we are not as interested in power as a personal change lever as much as we are in understanding it as a distributed collective phenomenon affecting (and effecting) change. The micro characteristics of each of these change constructs can be seen as moving from a more rational conceptualization to a more subjective orientation. This combines Barley and Kunda's normative-rational dependence on the context with Eastman and Bailey's human condition migration to value orientations. The complexity of the environments in which organizations must operate, both internal and external, necessitates the need to question the strictly rational worldview.

Evolution of Thoughts Concerning Social Change Constructs

	From	To	To
Constructs:			
Social Structure	Order is Imposed	Structuration/Participation	Self-Organizing
Environment	Internal Reactive to	Enacting on	Coevolving with
Norms	Achieve Equilibrium	Dynamic Homeostasis	Interactive-Adaptive
Nature of Human	Rational Objective	Rational Subjective	Non Linear Interpretive
Knowledge Bases	Natural Sciences	Sociology/ Psychology	Cross-Discipline
Social Actions	Mechanical Response	Motivational Response	Interactive Reciprocations
Basis of Prediction	Cause-Effect	Multiple Cause Effect	Emergence
Power	Concentrated/Control	Empowerment	Distributed
Conflict	Suppress	Constructive Use	Tensions
Social Change	Incremental-Controlled	Planned	Punctuated/ Incremental
Learning	Directed	Experiential	Self Directed/ Collective
Leadership	Trait Based	Behavioral/Situational Based	Interactional
Meaning	Effective/Efficient	Missions/Goals	Reflective/Sensemaking
Organizations	Functional	Systems	Cultures./Dynamic Capability

1920	1930	1940	1950	1960	1970	1980	1990	2000	2013
Early Traditional				*Mid-Contemporary*				*Current*	*Future?*

Figure 2. Coevolution of change constructs.

Thus, although the abstract construct remains relatively stable, its micro definition and measurement reflect a variance in its substance. Turning to another construct that is addressed in this volume, the abstract concept of leadership varied during the mid-20th century in terms of the micro meaning and measurement from rational "trait" to normative "situational-based" indicators. In the latter years of the century, the micro-meaning came to center on relational and interaction dynamics (Uhl-Bien, Marion, & McKelvey, 2007). Over this same period leadership measures moved to incorporate more subjective value-oriented perspectives as opposed to only objective measures.

The construct of social structure provides another example at the organizational change level of analysis. The meaning of this construct moved from imposed order by means of fixed rules, to order through participation, to self-organizing. No one questions the legitimacy of the construct "social structure"; however, over the course of the 20th century, the measures and dynamic relationships within the construct have shifted from objective to subjective orientations.

These examples of variation in the substance of human and organizational theory indicate the fluid nature of explanations concerning the human condition, a point noted by John Dewey in the early 20th century (Dewey, 1922). Social theory does not represent a finite set of natural laws. Rather, it is better thought of as a set of coevolving explanations that are dependent on contexts. We have focused here on contexts referring to economic conditions or to the evolution of human nature, but it is surely likely that other contextual factors could play similar roles. Because of this theoretical fluidity, we must also be aware of the epistemological nature of these explanations and their implications for the process by which theories are formulated. We now turn to the nature of that process.

The Process of Formulating Theory: Theorizing

In an essay intended to give guidance to the authors of research papers in the field of social sciences, Sutton and Staw (1995) provided guidance as to what good human and organizational theory is and is not. They built their argument around "what theory is not—it is not references, data, variables, diagrams, and hypothese" (p. 371). They went on to state that theory "is about the connection among phenomena, a story about why acts, events, structures, and thoughts occur" (p. 378).

Weick (1995a) critiqued Sutton and Staw's analysis of theory, making the case that "What Theory Is Not, Theorizing Is." Although he agreed that Sutton and Staw's five categories of "not theory" are relevant, he pointed to levels of gradation in each of the categories and concluded that most theories are only approximations. Weick saw theory as more of a process than a product and preferred the term "theorizing" rather than "theory." Weick applied a schema developed by Merton (1967) to support his contention. That is, approximations to theory can take one of four forms. Such approximations may consist of broad frameworks that

10

specify the types of variables that should be taken into account. Merton's second form is defined as the analysis of concepts by which concepts are clarified but not related. A third form involves the investigation of ad hoc hypotheses derived from single observations. Finally, the fourth approximation is what Merton called "pure generalization."

Theorizing, according to Weick, is triggered by the inherent variability of the substance of theory within defined contexts. In these contexts, explanations of social phenomena depend on the interactive and interdependent-recursive-valuing of experiences of theoreticians, field researchers, and practitioners as they participate in explaining the social phenomena under study. Like Dewey (1938), Weick argued that research actions should provide a continuity of experience across contexts, time, and value frames defined by the researchers' academic disciplines. Their purpose is to open paths for information to flow, while simultaneously emphasizing the value of theory and practice. Research actions should, in Weick's view, provide for the active integration of concepts through consideration of multiple, and at times competing, explanations of phenomena. As a researcher-scholar one must always listen to the voice that emerges from one's interactions as a practitioner.

The Scholar-Practitioner and the Theory-Practice Imperative

The concept of scholar-practitioner has been used by many professional programs that focus on the development by individuals of the scholarly skills and knowledge that will enable them to create and transfer useful knowledge into and from their practice. The concept has migrated from a clinical orientation to psychology in general and educational policy in particular. The ideal of the scholar-practitioner has become common in the fields of managerial and organizational sciences and adult learning (Kormanik, Lehner, & Winnick, 2009). The goal of these programs is to bring more relevance to theory, more rigor to research, and more effectiveness to practice. The scholar-practitioner approach to developing managers is a means of filling the gaps between theory and practice as well as between research and practice. Many such development programs are founded on propositions that emphasize the emergence of pragmatic knowledge from practice, not unlike Lewin's (1951) action research model. However, unlike Lewin's model, more emphasis has often been placed on filling the practice-research gap, rather than closing the gap between practice and theory, thus shortchanging the latter.

Having spent the last 25 years preparing scholar-practitioners, we concur with the importance of bringing research closer to practice. However, we argue that understanding the theory-practice relationship deserves as much attention as the research-practice component in the development of scholar-practitioners. Unfortunately, the theory-practice gap is often addressed only through models, handbooks, and lists of "steps" associated with rules and equations for success. When this is the case, Weick's concept of theorizing is lost.

By understanding the history of the variance of theory, scholar-practitioners are able to conduct research focused on their own actions, not to verify a theory but to develop theory that more closely approximates the situation. This is what Weick called theorizing. The scholar-practitioner framework enables the interpretation of social science theory not as a body of social laws and rules, but as explanations that depend on the context and on the current states of the coevolving variables contained within the theory's constructs (Bacharach, 1989). For the scholar-practitioner the combination of theory and practice begins to reflect Lewin's idea that "there is nothing so practical as good theory" (Lewin, 1951, p. 169). This enables effective action by turning knowledge into wisdom through critical thinking. In that sense this volume contains 10 Lewinian examples characterized by, and focused on, a cyclic journey between analysis, action, and synthesis—or theorizing.

Significant Theorizing in the Last 25 Years

Our argument establishes an imperative of the theory-practice relationship comprising three crucial elements. First is the inherent and necessary variance in the substance of social theory; that is, such theory can only approximate human and organizational phenomena. Second, theorizing is an ongoing process and a trigger for critical thinking about practice. Finally, the development of the scholar-practitioner requires theorizing *as* practice—over both time and contexts.

In this volume each of the chapter authors' contributions explores, in some way, the theory-practice imperative. The chapters illustrate our argument that the variable nature of managerial and organizational theory provides the tension and triggers for theorizing by scholar-practitioners. We briefly preview these 10 papers that have been important in manifesting the tensions in the theory-practice imperative. They represent theorizing in three change constructs: knowledge creation and meaning making; leadership and complexity; and micro dynamics of organizations. During this period we have seen changes in ideology and movement toward more subjective, value orientations. The papers included in this volume represent these shifts and also demonstrate true theorizing as a mode of progression in our understanding of human and organizational science and its practice.

Change Constructs of Knowledge Creation and Meaning Making

The first three papers that follow this introductory chapter address questions of how knowledge is created at both the micro level of analysis and the macro, collective, or organizational level of analysis. During the last decade of the 20th century there was an emphasis on the process of knowledge creation that was particularly manifested in the study of human learning and the concept of sensemaking (Weick, 1995b). With the advent of the information era and the knowledge society, organizations had to address new questions about goals, purposes, and strategies. One such question focuses on the nature of the "proper" relationship between the organization and its environment. Another concerns how goals relate to success. A third centers on the importance of ethical choices.

The nature and context of the above questions also changed, from the concrete-rational and objective to more subjective-interpretive concerns. Anne Huff, in her 1999 Academy of Management Presidential Address reprinted in chapter 2, makes the case that knowledge creation in the management and organizational sciences must include both knowledge from practice and knowledge from academia, that is, theoretical knowledge. Her "Mode 1.5 of Knowledge Production" concept includes a role for both theory and practice not unlike the scholar-practitioner idea advanced here. Her paper and epilogue reflect the desire of business schools to become more relevant to the practice of management. Huff sets the stage for understanding the implementation of theorizing as knowledge creation. Although she speaks about knowledge creation at a macro level, she acknowledges the importance of learning and sensemaking at the individual level.

Learning can be defined as a process of acquiring knowledge and skills that leads to new abilities or understanding. This definition incorporates the essential elements of knowledge creation and meaning making. Such learning occurs at routine levels of day-to-day cognition such as team learning to accomplish a work task or making sense of one's work context. It also occurs in moments of high emotional stress and radical change that involve issues of changing cultural patterns, as defined by schemata and basic assumptions. In chapter 3, Karl Weick's analysis of the Mann Gulch firefighting catastrophe (Weick, 1993) provides an example of such stress and radical change. His introduction of the human sensemaking construct and its seven characteristics, although theorized in the context of catastrophe, has provided insights into individual judgments and has been extended to other contexts and to collective sensemaking in high-reliability organizations (Weick & Sutcliffe, 2001). In chapter 3 Weick demonstrates the movement of management theory to focus on what one might call "in situ" knowledge creation—or sensemaking. This signifies the move of the field of managerial and organizational sciences from the objective-calculative or purely rational paradigm to a subjective-interpretive judgment orientation. Sensemaking is a focus for understanding the nature of human judgment by observing how managers select cues from their enacted environments. This has enabled Weick—and us—to theorize how environmental cues trigger reflection on action.

In a seminal paper, Victoria Marsick moves away from the behavioral foundations of cognition to a more interpretive reflective model of human learning. She makes observations concerning the differences between learning and training that help explain why many training programs in organizations might not be worth their cost. Learning about oneself in the context of the organization—not just skill-based or problem-oriented training—separates true learning from training. Marsick introduces dialogic learning and self-reflective learning as mechanisms for understanding oneself in the context of organizations. She examines Mezirow's "questioning of assumptions, premises, and schemas" as leading to a reconceptualization of learning in the workplace and its critical importance to the scholar-practitioner concept. Her support of reflective processes favors equally practice and theory building in reciprocating actions of application, analysis, and synthesis. The goal of reflectivity by the individual is to encourage a seamless connection between individuals' actions in practice and their cognitive-emotional schema. The outcome is a clearer understanding of both the phenomena and the human condition (Dewey, 1922). Concerns over the concepts of knowledge, learning, and sensemaking are characteristic of leading-edge 21st century organizations that have started to question the structuring mechanisms associated with culture and leadership.

Change Constructs of Leadership and Complexity

Today's organizations, even with the recognition of growing environmental complexity, still act as though leadership provides order out of chaos, structure instead of anomie, and profitable direction through transformational visions. Such an approach reflects a need for social structure. It also implies that leadership is position-centric and that effective leadership depends on the characteristics, behavior, and attitudes of the individuals in those positions. Most current leadership models encourage "transformational change" or "turnaround" actions. However, there remains an underlying assumption concerning the need for balance and equilibrium.

With the advent of the knowledge society and the realization of the cybernetic importance of information, Mary Uhl-Bien, Russ Marion, and Bill McKelvey argue in chapter 5 that executive leadership must focus less on operational controls and process improvement. Top leadership must now be more concerned with sensemaking, self-reflection, critical inquiry around basic assumptions, and operational and cultural knowledge creation. These authors' complexity leadership concept uses the framework of complex adaptive systems to explore the contextual nature of leadership. Uhl-Bien and her colleagues formulate three mutually dependent leadership roles: adaptive leadership, administrative leadership, and enabling leadership. They use these leadership role constructs in their description of organizations as complex adaptive systems. Complex adaptive systems theory contributes to our understanding of social collective learning processes because it assumes that crucial phenomena emerge from the interaction of independent agents. These emergent phenomena include social structures, cultures, and knowledge. Their theory views the collective as composed of agents that are self-referential and reflexive and who often respond to one another in radical and unpredictable ways (Stacey, Griffin, & Shaw, 2000).

Traditional position-centric executive leadership models encourage the use of planning, direction, control, rational logics, unified messages of vision, and transformational behaviors to provide organization members with a sense of stability. These characteristics have also become the measures and criteria used for judging the success of executive leadership as these leaders confront a complex social environment. That environment is characterized by issues that are more "gray" than "black and white," by events that are full of contradictions not easily solved by "best practices," and by paradoxes that give rise to human tension, doubt, and conflict.

The study of social processes has also increased interest in the application of the complexity sciences, which originated in mathematics and quantum physics, to social interactions in complex adaptive systems. In chapter 6 Bill McKelvey extends the argument he began with Mary Uhl-Bien in chapter 5. McKelvey moves away from the person-in-position approach to executive leadership by incorporating complexity theory "action disciplines" to understand the behavior of Jack Welch when he was CEO of General Electric. Incorporating complexity concepts such as adaptive tensions, scalability, attractor cages, and coevolution, McKelvey shows that Welch's success was dependent on more than personal characteristics. He makes the case that Welch's actions were the catalyst for systems complexity processes to operate effectively. Both McKelvey and Uhl-Bien theorize about the concept of leadership using a nontraditional complexity framework that moves the discussion away from rational-objective measures to interpretive-normative criteria. We are, of course, still confronted with difficult questions concerning human nature. However, these questions are now addressed in a context that is more complex than had been imagined.

Change Constructs of the Dynamics of Organizations

The dynamic interactions of agents and the attempt to make meaning of their context became a primary interest during the early part of our 25-year time span. The earliest efforts to understand macro organizational dynamics were made in an attempt to understand the dynamics of groups and teams. Chapter 7 presents Jerry Harvey's classic paper describing "the road to Abilene." He examines the micro dynamics associated with the interaction of individuals and groups as they participate in decision-making and group consensus. Harvey brings to bear psychological knowledge of phenomena such as separation anxiety, risk awareness, and negative fantasies as they pertain to the paradox of managing agreement within a group.

The interest in human interaction abandoned the traditional notion that collectives, in their pursuit of survival, seek equilibrium positions to stabilize their relationships with their environments. This redefined the concept of "seeking social order" as "continuous social change." Although the system may be "seeking order," its natural state is that of reducing "disorder" or entropy. This important shift in the perception of the nature of social order led to interest in organizational patterns or conditions that described near-stable positions within a time-space continuum. The next three papers address this need to describe micro interactions within an organization and relate them to macro-level social phenomena.

Mary Jo Hatch, early in our time frame, examined the nature of a collective by clarifying and operationalizing the concept of organizational culture. Her paper, in chapter 8, shifted the discussion from organizational theorizing at the macro model level to the micro dynamics level and the subsequent influence on emergent macro cultural phenomena. Up until this paper's publication, cross-level analysis problems had been all but ignored. By conceptualizing and defining the dynamic human processes that influence organizational culture, Hatch adds to the importance we now place on organizational values, basic assumptions, artifacts, and symbols. Her paper establishes the interpretive nature of the dynamics of culture and the subjective nature of theorizing about the latent nature of organizational culture (Parsons & Shils, 1952).

In chapter 9 Michael Jacobides and Sid Winter examine macro organizational phenomena from a framework of organizational capabilities. They move from traditional transaction cost economics to theorizing about the relationship of organizations to their environment. Their focus is on organizational capabilities that incorporate reciprocating relationships between agency and organizational structure. Jacobides and Winter argue for the importance of both context and individual agency. They provide bridges from theory to practice by using their framework to analyze the financial crisis of the first decade of the 21st century. Their paper links economic phenomena to the behaviors of actors in the organization, not to show them as rational actors, but to identify actions that influence an evolutionary process. Organizational capabilities are conceptualized as a multifaceted system of knowledge-creating interactions and, reciprocally, knowledge that generates interactions (Giddens, 1984). This creates a dynamic interacting system that is coevolving with the environment. Three key dynamics that must be simultaneously addressed are those of stability vs. change, exploitation vs. exploration, and control vs. flexibility. Each of these dynamics or "facets" involves a learning process that creates knowledge for the organization, even as the organization shapes the learning process itself.

Buckley's (1998) reformulation of social systems as complex and adaptive systems relied on the collective's capacity to restructure and to change its governing values. Such learning systems, he said, "in turn may rest on specific properties of their members: their capacity for readjustment to new configurations, with renewed complementarity and sustained or renewed communication" (p. 494). Buckley's theorizing about complex adaptive systems had implications not only for social structural change but also for the way the "meaning structures" of collectives and agents are altered. Woody Powell and Jeannette Colyvas's paper, in chapter 10, provides an opportunity to observe scholars as they theorize about the relationships between the dynamics of micro-organizational interactions and those of the macro institution. They define this process as "cobbling together useful, albeit disparate, lines of research and theory" (p. 276). Powell and Colyvas provide applications to existing situations and give scholar-practitioners the research tools to better understand multilevel institutional phenomena. Their work suggests that a collective structure emerges through agent interactions and that such structure has the capacity to adjust its orientation, or value patterns, without a necessary external influence. This is the basic concept of a self-organizing system (Ashby, 1947).

The last two papers in this section by Sid Winter and by Woody Powell exemplify the cross-disciplinary nature of the human and organizational sciences—one coming from the realm of economics and the other from sociology. However, though with differing perspectives, both have theorized about the dynamics of human interactions and their reciprocating relationship with macro social phenomena. Both of these final papers were published in the latter part of our 25-year window, thus pointing to a renewed interest in micro interactions and to unfinished business in understanding these dynamics.

Unfinished Business and the Future

The uncertainty and nonlinearity of the theorizing process is evident in the papers contained in this volume. Although each author has made clear the application of theory to practice, the variability of theory provides the scholar-practitioner with the tension that feeds critical analysis of current practice dilemmas. Despite the progress that has been made in theorizing, new contexts and conditions will always emerge, requiring new understanding for practice. For example, the need for leadership and an emphasis on individual sensemaking and reflection may affect the collective's ability to systematically integrate and self-organize its social patterns with environmental conditions and objects. It would appear that the action of dissolution of related conditions, processes, and knowledge schemata as well as the action of creation of related conditions, processes, and knowledge schemata are both necessary for the effective coevolution of the collective. In chapter 11 Warner Burke creates a fitting summary to the papers included in this volume. His summary is fitting for both theorizing and practice. Burke's extensive background as a scholar-practitioner gives him an excellent foundation for pointing to the unfinished business in the field of organization development. He identifies a need to reconceptualize resistance to change, to include more interpretive frames of reference to help develop the construct of leadership as a more interactive concept, and a need to build our understanding of the organizational dynamics of loosely coupled systems and organizational culture. Each of these areas will require the scholar-practitioner to have a firm grasp on both the theories of the past and the process of theorizing for the future.

The final paper in this volume is written by Ellen Scully-Russ, Andrea Casey, Michael Marquardt, and Diana Burley. They are all members of the Executive Leadership Doctoral Program faculty at The George Washington University. In chapter 12 they provide a fitting summary to this commemorative collection of seminal works by moving into the future and portraying the manifestation of the areas of human and organizational theory in their work with scholar-practitioners. Their paper helps us to better understand the idea of turning knowledge into wisdom, that is, developing critical thinking skills on the part of scholar-practitioners. They examine the work of our guest authors in the context of unfinished organization development work. The discussions in their paper reflect the idea that human and organizational theory variability is a trigger to the theory-practice component of scholar-practitioner development.

Conclusion

This volume's papers and the participation of the authors with us in developing scholar-practitioners over the past 25 years has encouraged us to rethink our understanding of social science theory and its practical applications. We are not discouraged by the fluidity of human and organizational theory. On the contrary, we are energized by its flexibility and its ability to coevolve with a more interpretative social order and subjective human condition. What has emerged is a new emphasis on the importance of micro-macro social relationships in the social sciences, an emphasis that leads to a more interpretive understanding of human cognitive-emotional interactions within the collective (Blau, 1960).

References

Ashby, W. R. (1947). Principles of the self-organizing dynamic system. *Journal of General Psychology, 37,* 125-128.

Bacharach, S. B. (1989). Organizational theories: Some criteria for evaluation. *Academy of Management Review, 14,* 496-515.

Barley, S. R., & Kunda, G. (1992). Design and devotion: Surges of rational and normative ideologies of control in managerial discourse. *Administrative Science Quarterly, 37,* 363-399.

Blau, P. M. (1960). Structural effects. *American Sociological Review, 25,* 178-193.

Buckley, W. (1998). *Society—A complex adaptive system.* Singapore: Gordon and Breach.

Connell, A. F., & Nord, W. R. (1998). Reconsidering the "fact-value" antinomy: A comment on Eastman and Bailey (1998). *Organization Science, 9,* 245-250.

Dewey, J. (1922). *Human nature and conduct: An introduction to social psychology.* Lexington, KY: Filiquarian.

Dewey, J. (1938). *Experience & education.* New York, NY: Kappa Delta Pi.

Eastman, W., &. Bailey, J. R. (1998). Mediating the fact-value antinomy: Patterns in managerial and legal rhetoric. *Organization Science, 9,* 232-245.

Giddens, A. (1984). *The constitution of society.* Los Angeles: University of California Press.

Gleick, J. (2013). Time regained. *The New York Review of Books, LX,* 46-49.

Kormanik, M. B., Lehner, R. D., & Winnick, T. A. (2009). General competencies for the HRD scholar-practitioner: Perspectives from across the profession. *Advances in Developing Human Resources, 11,* 486-506.

Kuhn, T. S. (1970). *The structure of scientific revolutions.* Chicago, IL: University of Chicago Press.

Lewin, K. (1951). Problems of research in social psychology. In D. Cartwright (Ed.), *Field theory in social science: Selected theoretical papers* (pp. 155-169). New York, NY: Harper and Row.

Merton, R. K. (1967). *On theoretical sociology.* New York, NY: Free Press.

Parsons, T., & Shils, E. A. (1952). *Toward a general theory of action.* Cambridge, MA: Harvard University Press.

Stacey, R. D., Griffin, D., & Shaw, P. (2000). *Complexity and management: Fad or radical challenge to systems thinking?* London, UK: Routledge.

Sutton, R. I., & Staw, B. M. (1995). What theory is not. *Administrative Science Quarterly, 40,* 371-384.

Uhl-Bien, M., Marion, R., & McKelvey, B. (2007). Complexity leadership theory: Shifting leadership from the industrial age to the knowledge age. *Leadership Quarterly, 18,* 298-318.

Weick, K. E. (1993). The collapse of sensemaking in organizations: The Mann Gulch disaster. *Administrative Science Quarterly, 38,* 628-652.

Weick, K. E. (1995a). What theory is not, theorizing is. *Administrative Science Quarterly, 40,* 385-390.

Weick, K. E. (1995b). *Sensemaking in organizations.* Newbury Park, CA: Sage.

Weick, K. E., & Sutcliffe, K. M. (2001). *Managing the unexpected: Assuring high performance in an age of complexity.* San Francisco, CA: Jossey-Bass.

Chapter 2

Changes In Organizational Knowledge Production

1999 Academy of Management Presidential Address
Anne Sigismund Huff

Epilogue
Anne Sigismund Huff
University of Ireland Maynooth

Changes In Organizational Knowledge Production

Anne Sigimund Huff [1]

Abstract. The explosion of knowledge production within business and other organizations poses a critical challenge to current modes of teaching and research within our business schools. We need to consider new strategic positions closer to the knowledge production being carried on within the organizations we study, without assuming that immediate relevance is our primary objective. The academic advantage, in my opinion, still lies in generalization and abstraction.

Last year, at the British Academy of Management, I was asked to participate in a workshop with Michael Gibbons, who talked about his coauthored book *The New Production of Knowledge* (Gibbons et al., 1994). His claim was that university life as we have known it is rapidly being eclipsed by knowledge produced collaboratively, in practice. Although the book focuses on changes in science and technology, I recommend it as an introduction to issues that have significant implications for business schools. It has encouraged me to think in new ways about alternative paths that business schools might follow in the near future and to strongly advocate that many schools strategically reposition their research efforts.

TRADITIONAL MODE 1 KNOWLEDGE PRODUCTION

Gibbons et al. (1994) outline the post World War II growth in "Mode 1" production of knowledge. Mode 1 can be summarized as the pursuit of "scientific truth" by "scientists." Although it has been highly positivistic over the last century, Mode 1 includes many epistemic traditions—even the postmodern. The work is discipline based, university centered,

---

[1] Originally Published as: Huff, A. S. (2000). "Changes in organizational knowledge production" Accademy of Management Review **25**(2): 288-293.

and dominated by highly trained individuals. It is primarily cognitive, carefully validated by peer review, and applied later, by others, if it is applied at all.

Since the Carnegie Report advocating disciplinary research came out in the 1950s, most U.S. business schools have been striving earnestly to become Mode 1 producers of knowledge about organizational—especially business—activities. More recently, a worldwide trend in this direction is evident. Schools operating in this mode hire new faculty members on the basis of their university training and promote them on the basis of their research output. The emphasis is on knowledge production certified by publication in a very small number of elite journals.

An extensive infrastructure supports this system. Its roots are centuries old and include a central belief in the importance of "knowledge for knowledge's sake." Disciplinary associations identify specific areas of inquiry as their own and provide opportunities for like-minded groups of individuals to coordinate research agendas. Associated journals promote these fields of study and certify the quality of scholarly output. Even those in "interdisciplinary" subjects can be caught up quickly in the Mode 1 dynamic as they establish new university homes, associations, and journals.

INTERACTIVE. PROBLEM-ORIENTED MODE 2 PRODUCTION

A radically different style of knowledge production, which Gibbons and his colleagues call "Mode 2," has grown up alongside Mode 1 in the last 50 years. In contrast to the production of science by scientists, Mode 2 is characterized as the production of knowledge from application. Its practitioners often have disciplinary training from Mode 1 institutions, but their work tends to be transdisciplinary. Whereas Mode 1 is hierarchical, Mode 2 is heterarchical. It is group based, rather than focused on the work of individuals. Whereas Mode 1 producers of knowledge worry about certification, Mode 2 knowledge is validated in use. Response time is critical. Mode 2 knowledge tends to be transitory.

Gibbons et al.'s book suggests that Mode 1 and Mode 2 exist side by side. At the British Academy of Management, Michael Gibbons was more assertive. I believe his words were that "our golden goose is dead"—killed by overproduction of graduate students in the post World War II period who could not be absorbed by universities and went instead to corporations, governments, think tanks, consulting firms, and their own private practices. Some of these "homes" subscribed to Mode 1 methods; many others were more fluid in their social structure and purpose.

But Mode 2 is not just a supply-side story. Sheltered university work also is being eclipsed because of changes in demand. The shift is most clear in science and technology, but it can be seen in response to many other immediate, market-driven needs. Globalizing competition has necessitated the development and reconfiguration of new knowledge assets. Public policies and funding to promote national competitiveness, around the world, have further fueled the flames.

The scientists who contribute to Mode 2 projects typically move away from Mode 1 disciplines and practices toward a different infrastructure. The speed and vitality of genome research and other Mode 2 work owe a great deal to global electronic connections. Knowledge developments, often shared by virtual groups, tend to generate further reconfigurations of knowledge. Consulting companies and transdisciplinary associations help diffuse these developments before, and sometimes instead of, formal publication.

Similar changes in knowledge work have been identified by many other observers. Although the distinctiveness of new forms of knowledge production is easiest to see in the sciences, a similar revolution appears to have occurred in the social sciences, and even the humanities. In our own field, a conference, "Re-Organizing Knowledge: Transforming Institutions," held at Amherst University in October 1999, had "knowledge in motion" as one of its themes. Organizational scholars from a diverse set of countries and backgrounds discussed, among other things, whether the overall university as a "house of knowledge" has a future.

BUSINESS SCHOOL ALTERNATIVES

The shift in knowledge production outlined by these and other observers is especially relevant for professional schools, and business schools in particular. Professional schools are intentionally positioned at the intersection of theory and practice. Jim March, the Academy of Management's 1999 Scholar of the Year, suggests that this "uneasy tension" has tended to produce pendulum swings in attention.

After 40 years of disciplinary strategies of knowledge production, especially in U.S. business schools, around the world there is a swing back toward the practical concerns that led to establishing the first business schools in the early 1900s. March feels this dramatic redirection is misguided. He urges management scholars to stand back from immediate problems that practitioners have an advantage in understanding, in favor of continuing to draw on disciplinary insights (Huff, 2000).

David Tranfield and Ken Starkey (1998: 352-353), in the *British Journal of Management,* present a contrasting view. They suggest that management research has been overly influenced by an American belief in universal laws. Mode 2 is described as a source of appropriate research guidelines because management is inherently transdisciplinary.

This difference illustrates a larger debate, although it is, in part, a semantic one. I agree with many points made by March, Tranfield, and Starkey. Nonetheless, business schools are faced with real choices, made more salient by public scrutiny, funding restrictions, and expanding opportunities. These alternatives are worth discussing, although, obviously, no single mode of activity will fit all institutions or all members of a given institution.

Remain in Mode 1

I believe that many schools in research universities will make a few gestures toward Mode 2, especially to keep their educational offerings attractive, but will continue in the Mode 1 tradition. They will continue to hire candidates with the best university training they can attract. They will continue to give young faculty modest teaching loads, shelter them from committee work, and focus early promotion decisions primarily on publication.

Sticking with Mode 1 is not just the result of inertia. It is influenced by the strength of the Mode 1 infrastructure. In a world where it is difficult to judge quality and contribution, established procedures and clear standards are reassuring. Professional schools, especially in business and engineering, are the most pressured by the changing world of knowledge production. The rest of the university is more likely to advocate Mode 1, and it will expect business schools to meet these standards.

Nonetheless, I am convinced that Mode 1 will be increasingly seen as "counting angels dancing on the head of a pin" by the public, particularly by the organizations most important to our future. Don Hambrick (1994) asked, when he was president of the Academy of Management, "What if the Academy really mattered?" That question is even more relevant today. Business schools that linger in Mode 1 will have to address new questions about relevance. Indeed, in many western nations the university as a whole is coming under scrutiny. Those who stay with Mode 1 will have to improve their ability to convey the importance of the work they do.

Focus on Our Base Business: Education

Another possibility, being realized more quickly than some of us like, is to attend to an educational mission. In many places, such as the state of Colorado, there is strong public pressure for this focus. It is easy for administrators or legislators to equate education with student contact hours. It is harder to calculate the educational and social benefits of abstract research. Thus, some schools are pressured to do less research and to pay more attention to instruction.

Education, however, is an increasingly competitive business. Corporations now spend more on business education than do business schools. Flexible nonuniversity providers are flourishing. Distance

29

education allows entry into territorially defined markets schools once regarded as their own. Students from developing nations, who help finance many programs, are harder to entice as national and regional schools gain expertise. Tailored programs are attractive to employers, but typically more expensive to provide.

At the same time, effective delivery is changing. Attractive packaging is more important. Web-based materials are expected. Not only global cases but demanding global travel and exchange programs are becoming the norm. It is expensive to play the rating game, and annual reassessments invite escalating investments. Meanwhile, many universities still expect their business schools to be cash cows. In short, we are in a mature industry with all its difficulties: rising product expectations and cost and efficiency pressures.

Working in this industry is worthwhile, but current standards do not emphasize knowledge production. This is a significant change over the last 50 years. Despite the mounting pressures for publication, and despite AACSB and other accreditors' demands that faculty be "intellectually active," faculty in schools that emphasize teaching have to spend much less time in knowledge production.

It is perhaps useful to recognize that this is a "bus" business—we are one link in a value chain that begins when one of our sister providers picks up small children to learn about sand tables and how to wait for juice time in pre-school. These students are moved, in time, to elementary school and on to secondary school. We pick them up for transport to colleges and universities and deliver them, in time, to corporations.

More complex career patterns, which bring a rising proportion of mature students, do not really change the basic picture. Those manning each stop along the way tend to complain about the raw material they receive. In colleges and universities we often disparage the communication and analytic skills even of well-qualified entrants. These complaints are not that different from high school instructors' complaints about middle school students or grade school teachers' desire that preschools provide kindergartners who can wait their turn more quietly. Corporations have some of their own complaints, but the flow continues at least to this point.

Our biggest risk is that an increasingly sophisticated customer base will devalue what we have to offer. I recently heard a rumor that 25 percent of Harvard Business School's MBA class did not return for their second year; most of them elected to move directly to e-commerce instead. This may be an apocryphal story, but it points to a widely recognized decline in the attractiveness of longer educational programs. Students leaving early have perhaps discovered a particularly effective strategy. They are certified as bright as soon as they are accepted. If they stay a short time, they gain recognized training, make some contacts, and have access to a network for more. Leaving might even be a positive signal that they are especially eager for the opportunities business has to offer. It is another sign of a difficult business.

Adopt Mode 2 Methods

We can try to join big science in a Mode 2 world. There are many signs that business schools are aware of, and energized by, these developments. Spurred by several years of discussion, the British Academy of Management urged the Economic and Social Research Council—their primary government funding agency—to develop a new grant program for work with significant industry involvement. At our own Academy of Management meetings, the National Science Foundation announced a very similar program. Both funding sources support a trend to involve industry colleagues that is already evident in management research.

Organizations are also more active partners in teaching programs. Internships, for example, have become a major mode of instruction in undergraduate and MBA programs. Students seek internships because of the practical experience they offer and because they are often a direct route to employment.

These transitions in research and teaching obviously are positive. We have to accept the fact that knowledge production has moved beyond the boundaries of the university. We have to meet Mode 2 producers where they work and where they need new knowledge.

I worry, however, that business schools cannot become significant Mode 2 producers of knowledge about organizations (other than their own). Mode 2 knowledge is rooted in the tasks at hand. Students benefit from direct connections with these tasks. Often, they can make some contribution, even while in school, if they become sufficiently immersed in the organization. To do so invites further employment. The faculty, however, rarely can or should be so involved. Market-driven tasks are predicated on a speedy response that works against the involvement of outsiders like ourselves. That is why key contractors and consultants often have representatives on site.

The scope of organizational problems also limits the faculty's role in Mode 2. As they become more highly networked, more and more players are, of necessity, implicated in problem solving. Globalization increases the complexity. It takes a great deal of effort to know and understand this cast of contributors, the work they do, what they know now, and what they need to know next. We need to be familiar with these complexities, but we have limited resources to develop them in specific contexts to produce immediately useful knowledge.

Furthermore, the major Mode 2 players operate at a scale that dwarfs not only the largest schools of business but also the consortia we are beginning to form. Major multinational companies operate in the billions. Business schools cannot operate at this scale, but our primary competitors—the major consulting firms—do. They are skilled at seeking Mode 2 work and know how to perpetuate it. We are bit players in comparison.

Of course, there are smaller organizations and subunits of larger companies. Business faculty are often welcome participants in knowledge production at these sites, and they can be significant contributors. It might make sense for business schools to establish competency in a few specific areas. In addition to making a real Mode 2 contribution, work done in this collaborative way ensures that we understand the changing nature of organizations. Niche positions are risky, however, because they can only represent a small part of the world we were established to help understand. In a Mode 2 world, the knowledge gained is especially transitory.

MODE 1.5 PRODUCTION OF KNOWLEDGE

Mode 2 rose out of unmet needs and opportunities. Mode 1 is too slow, too inward looking; it gives priority to pedigrees. Although Mode 2 offers improved methods of knowledge production in each of these areas—more timely, more practical, more democratic—I believe it has its own limitations, especially as it moves away from science and technology into management.

In organizing, strategizing, and human relations, Mode 2 methods appear to be too pragmatic, their practitioners too willing to "make do." They tend to make big bets on the basis of limited evidence. "Throw it on the wall and see if it sticks" might make sense in many innovative knowledge production activities. It is more questionable in management arenas.

Recent enthusiasm for reengineering is just one case in point. Few of the productivity gains first promised appear to have been realized. An amazing number of companies followed prescriptions based on compelling stories. The human, and organizational, costs appear to be large in comparison to achievement. These are not issues, however, that seem to be dominating Mode 2 conversations. Their market implications are unclear, even if they engage attention. Surely, management researchers have something to offer.

In the end, I think we need to think about "Mode 1.5" methods of knowledge production. This label is not meant to suggest that business schools are in some kind of transition between Mode 1 and Mode 2. Rather, Mode 1.5 is a difficult but desirable position "above" these modes of production. It is a position we potentially have the competitive advantage to fill, and it provides needed perspective.

My argument for a Mode 1.5 alternative is based on three assumptions:

1. Disciplinary knowledge and theoretic models can continue to constitute a useful knowledge base in novel situations where Mode 2 experimentation is not desirable or not possible.
2. Research institutions, if sheltered from the immediate need to generate significant income from their knowledge production activities, can produce "public goods" that companies and consultants cannot credibly produce.
3. Business schools also offer a desirable, neutral ground on which new, more synthetic knowledge can be generated from the inter-action of individuals with diverse business, consulting, public, and university experience.

The need for Mode 1.5 arises from the limitations of both Mode 1 and Mode 2. Those limitations are most clear, as Jim March and John Reed argued in their session at the 1999 Academy of Management meeting (Huff, 2000), when important but novel situations arise. Mode 2 is often inventive in new situations, such as e-commerce. However, it is not a tradition that lingers over consequences. Mode 1 procedures often focus on consequences, but not in "real time."

I have in mind something that my colleagues in England call a "virtuous circle." The issues of importance to Mode 1.5 typically will rise from practice and will be defined in conversation with those in practice, but other insights should be solicited and integrated. The relevant data will come primarily, but not entirely, from practice. Academic skills will be useful in developing definitions, comparing data across organizational settings, and suggesting generalizable frameworks for further sensemaking. Conversation is not expected to terminate in one round of investigation. The "circle" is actually more of a spiral that generates its own further agenda.

Business school faculty cannot claim a unique Ph.D. advantage in this conversation; many Mode 2 players have PhDs. Yet, our values and experiences are unique. Perhaps most important, we are dedicated to "education"—not the "training" that rightly concerns our colleagues in business and consulting organizations. The aims of education are broad and lifelong. They are not tied to the immediate needs of one employer. These goals are increasingly unique in the hurry-up world that produces such interesting Mode 2 results. Although we will have to work hard to make our case, I believe education—not just experience—continues to be a necessary base for Mode 2 and an interesting foil for Mode 2.

Mode 1.5 should accommodate fault finders as well as facilitators. Critical observations, undertaken more often by scholars outside the United States than within, have a particularly important role to play as nation states and other organizing forces are dwarfed by large global companies. However, the critic's role cannot be undertaken credibly without familiarity with Mode 2 practices. Critics who adopt a Mode 1.5 position add an important element of diversity.

My basic point is that the limited resources of research-oriented business schools should be invested when the stakes appear to be large. We must worry about insufficient scale and scope, when compared with the institutions hosting Mode 2 innovations. Focused, cooperative relationships can address, although perhaps not re-dress, these limitations. Operating either a Mode 1 or a Mode 2 environment squanders our resources. We are uniquely prepared to provide conversational space when market forces do not demand Mode 2 attention. Our tradition of public service gives us a credible voice at the table.

SUMMARY

Many people are thinking about the strategic position of business schools. Three of my own conclusions led to this Presidential address:

1. Public support for traditional, Mode 1 production of knowledge in professional business schools can be expected to continue to decline.
2. A rapidly maturing market for professional education, around the world, will be increasingly competitive.
3. Business schools cannot excel at Mode 2 production of knowledge about practical problems, except in narrowly defined niches.

These observations are made with reluctance. On the one hand, almost all of my work has taken place in the Mode 1 tradition. I do not think the end of that tradition is imminent, but I am not happy to remain in a Mode 1 professional school of decreasing interest and value to the organizations we serve. Conveying information produced by others or facilitating students producing their own knowledge does not require a Ph.D. Becoming a marginal player in Mode 2 efforts feels like poorly paid consulting.

On the other hand, I am excited about the alternative I have tentatively called Mode 1.5. It is based on the belief that Mode 1 training continues to be of value in a world dominated by Mode 2 practices, as long as researchers are familiar with these changes in knowledge production. As I envision it, Mode 1.5 balances not easily remedied weaknesses in both Mode 1 and Mode 2. While Mode 1 is driven by the theoretic agenda of elites, Mode 2 is driven by the market. Business schools cannot dominate, but they can help drive the development of a Mode 1.5 agenda that attempts to redress the limitations of both modes of knowledge production.

References

Gibbons, M., Limoges, C., Nowotny, H., Schwartzman, S., Scott, P., & Trow, M. 1994. *The new production of knowledge: The dynamics of science and research in contemporary societies.* London: Sage.

Hambrick, D. 1994. Presidential address: What if the Academy actually mattered? Academy *of Management Review,* 19: 11-16.

Huff, A. S. (Ed.). 2000. Citigroup's John Reed and Stanford's James March on management research and practice. *Academy of Management Executive.* 14(1): 1-13.

Re-organizing knowledge: Trans-forming organizations. 1999. *http://www. som.umass.edu/som/resource/projects/ conference/conference.html*

Tranfield, D., & Starkey, K. 1998. The nature, social organization and promotion of management research: Towards policy. *British Journal of Management,* 9: 341-353.

Epilogue:

Anne Sigismund Huff

Interactive forms of knowledge creation have become more important but more difficult in the14 years since "Changes in Knowledge Production" was written. This commentary briefly considers three issues: significant changes in the knowledge environment, growing numbers and diversity of problem-solving participants, and suggestions for moving forward that are consistent with work on entrepreneurial effectuation.

The Changing Landscape of Knowledge Creation

While the issues raised in "Changes in Knowledge Production" are still central to my thinking and research, I am amazed by how much has happened since it was written. First and most important, Wikipedia had not been launched. Today it is part of an astonishing range of free resources found on the Internet. The result is that almost all individuals, even children and those in very limited circumstances, can be independent and often quite effective knowledge creators. This democratization of knowledge creation and use has been discussed in academic publications (von Hippel, 2005, 2013), but it is underacknowledged and underutilized in both Mode 1 (traditional academic) and Mode 2 (problem solving, organizationally oriented) activities.

In a quite different but equally powerful change facilitated by the Internet, there have been rapid increases in the collection, storage, and use of 'big data.' I have moved to thinking about knowledge *creation* because 'knowledge production' seems too mechanical to capture the processes that most interest me, but the size and scale of big data activities suggest that move was premature. Collecting, coding, and acting on micro observations have positive and negative consequences that are being equated to the impact of the industrial revolution. On the one hand, concerns about big data increase with demonstrated and potential hacking of information that was thought to be secure, and as the extent of corporate and government use is revealed. On the other hand, intelligent software agents using this resource are rapidly expanding the capacity of human decision-makers. Especially notable is IBM's work on Watson, a supercomputer 'cognitive assistant.' After successfully beating Jeopardy! stars and the world chess champion,

IBM's business agreement with the Memorial Sloan-Kettering Cancer Center in New York and American private healthcare company Wellpoint will see Watson available for rent to any hospital or clinic that wants to get its opinion on matters relating to oncology. Not only that, but it'll suggest the most affordable way of paying for it in America's excessively-complex healthcare market. The hope is it will improve diagnoses while reducing their costs at the same time. (Steadman, 2013)

These expansions in knowledge creation deserve their own commentary; instead I will add a third important shift, the neoliberal reforms across public institutions that were not very obvious in 1999, at least to me. In public universities, movement away from faculty governance toward centralized control is well underway. State and university prescriptions for individual and departmental teaching and research are increasing. Funding for research is also changing, with many opportunities requiring multidisciplinary and cross-sector solutions to 'grand challenges.' These and other changes influence Mode 1 agendas in ways that run counter to the ideals of academic responsibility and freedom established two centuries ago and especially dominant in the period after World War II until very recently (Bresnan & Burrell, 2013).

While research activity is increasingly channeled, teaching faces disruptive fragmentation. The proliferation of online courses, many free, some with course credit, often provided by distinguished professors at elite universities, is alarming my academic colleagues around the world. A small collection of individuals in one institution, no matter how distinguished, cannot match the reputation and content of the best offerings. Scale is not a problem: millions of people have already taken part. There are opportunities to add online courses to programs at brick-and-mortar institutions, but the trajectory into the future is not clear.

More obvious and more revolutionary, in my view, are instructive communications in new, engaging, and compact formats. Academics are the minority in Ted Talks my friends send me. The Khan Academy regularly notifies me that 'a bunch of new content' has been added to its site. The language alone stands in direct contrast to Mode 1. In my college we are experimenting with clickers, tweets, class blogs, online resources, and other innovations to increase engagement. My students are positive but say they also value face-to-face interaction. I still feel that I am falling behind.

It is important to mention one more vector of change significantly affecting professional schools. I did not anticipate in 1999 that ranking schemes and global certification would become the dominant forces they are today. Both have raised the overall quality of research and teaching, which is important for addressing public doubt and even more beneficial for knowledge creation. But in my opinion too much faculty and administrator time is consumed in meeting bureaucratic requirements. Too much attention is given to number of publications and surrogate measures of content quality. My prediction is that new requirements to prove practical impact will have similar benefits and burdens, while focusing still more attention on the bottle rather than the wine.

The result of external control and ranking by those who are relatively far from Mode 1 knowledge creation is homogenization that limits future adaptability and innovation (Huff, 2012). This is a well-known feature of competitive, mature industries and difficult to counteract, especially since similar forces affect many other knowledge creators. On the other side of the coin, however, those relying primarily on Modes 1, 2, and 1.5 have been joined by a much larger set of knowledge producers. The numbers, diversity, and possibilities for connection in this broader setting offer interesting possibilities.

Open Innovation in a Complex Environment

For the past 12 years I have lived and worked in Europe, drawn by unfamiliar environments but also by closer ties among sectors and stronger attention to innovation. From this perspective it has been easier for me to conclude that the simplistic 'virtuous circle' of Mode 1.5 collaborative research described in "Changes in Knowledge Production" has been irrevocably replaced by much more complex problem-solving landscapes illustrated in Figure 1.

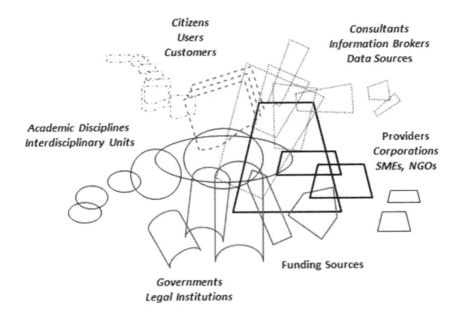

Figure 1. Partially overlapping stakeholders in an action domain.

Attempts to improve the well being of those with a rare disease provide an example.[2] Because of the low profitability of developing treatments for 'orphan' illnesses affecting a very small number of people,

---

[2]   My knowledge in this area comes primarily from descriptions of Project EIVE, http://www.wi1.uni-erlangen.de/node/727, and presentations by Professor Pedro Olivera at Católica Lisbon. See for example, http://www.slideshare.net/romy_momi/visualizing-user-innovation-in-health-care

major pharmaceutical companies and other providers are relatively uninterested in them, but a quick search on the Internet will show a relatively large number of organizations and websites that facilitate interaction among those with different interests in a specific disease. The afflicted can be pictured at the top left of Figure 1. They are motivated to interact with each other to share experiences, observations, and actions that appear to be helpful.

Other actors, working with other forms of knowledge creation and use, are also involved. Sufferers and caregivers are facilitated by information brokers who design websites and maintain databases. While 'big data' may not be required or available, the formats used benefit from this experience. At the middle right of the diagram are pharmaceutical companies and other caregivers. They may not pay a great deal of attention to a specific rare disease, yet they offer needed drugs, devices, and care. Moving down the diagram, some providers may join others, including philanthropic foundations, in offering rewards for promising therapies or new drugs. The activities involved, and especially solutions provided, are subject to government regulation and existing laws, as shown on the lower left. Finally, there are academics interested in various aspects of health care, working in the sciences, social sciences, and various professions, who have a role to play in discovering improvements and solutions.

This is a brief example of open innovation, an approach to knowledge creation used by large diversified companies (Lackner, 2013), startups (van Delden & Wünderlich, 2013), those contributing to Wikipedia, and many others. Problem solving always required more inputs than I described in 2000, but the ideas behind open innovation, a term only formalized in 2005 (Chesbrough, 2005), have led to new forms of interaction. These new approaches are being shared (Bessant & von Stamm, 2013) and new tools are being developed (Möslein, 2013).

Yet significant barriers to solving problems in such a complex knowledge environment are inevitable. Many arise from the distinctive cultures that support knowledge creation and use but result in differences among knowledge creators in goals, tasks, priorities, ways of working, and so on (Gibbons et al., 1994). NIH ("not invented here") resistance often stands in the way of adoption and further improvement of promising solutions that should be expected in such rich environments. It seems we must be more entrepreneurial in dealing with these and other intractable issues.

An Entrepreneurial Way Forward

The biggest changes in my thinking about knowledge creation are due to Saras Sarasvathy and her colleagues (Sarasvathy, 2001, 2008; Sarasvathy & Dew, 2005). Their development of 'effectual' logic, as opposed to casual logic, is summarized at www.effectuation.org. The growing group of researchers involved in this discussion has found that experienced entrepreneurs typically do not start with well-defined objectives; instead they gradually discover both means and ends. I heard a compelling example of moving from causal to effectual thinking from a social entrepreneur who described starting a nongovernmental organization in South Africa dedicated to serving AIDS patients. She found she had to switch course when her patients convinced her that they needed medical support for the whole family, not just a patient with one problem, no matter how difficult.

As summarized in Figure 2, research has shown, in short, that successful entrepreneurs often begin with relatively vague ideas about what is possible. They assess their knowledge and contacts and then discover what is possible by involving others. As goals and means are discovered, further activities gradually take on characteristics of the classic problem-solving model where objectives are stated and alternatives compared. But this is a midpoint, not a starting point, and problem solving circles back to effectual thinking and activities when difficult issues arise and remain unresolved.

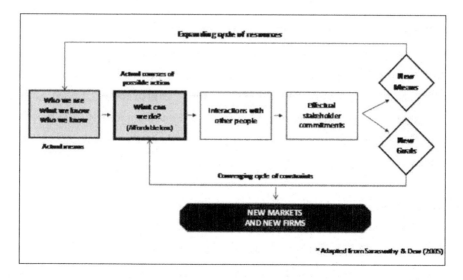

Figure 2. Dynamics of the effectual network.

The growing body of evidence in this area resonates with my own experience and with what I have observed in open innovation. The idea of effectuation has changed the way I and others teach entrepreneurship (Read, Sarasvathy, Dew, Wiltbank, & Ohlsson, 2010). It has informed the way I think about opportunity discovery in my research and more specifically my ideas about Mode 1.5.

Knowledge creators in different settings are able to solve many problems, aided by the development of a problem-solving culture that fits their circumstances. Interesting new methods of sharing and using knowledge are unfolding on the Internet. I am especially intrigued by the Khan Academy,[3] which appears to be a clear example of effectuation success.

However, difficult problems do arise and some resist local experimentation. I believe that something like the genuinely collaborative Mode 1.5 is more necessary than ever as attempts are made to draw on

---

[3]   http://www.youtube.com/user/khanacademy.

inputs from very different settings. The basic premise of this book is therefore timely and important.

References

Bessant, J., & von Stamm, B. (2013). Opening innovations for innovation. In A. S. Huff, K. M. Möslein, & R. Reichwald (Eds.), *Leading open innovation*. Cambridge, MA: MIT Press.

Bresnan, M., & Burrell, G. (2013). Journals à la mode? Twenty years of living alongside Mode 2 and the new production of knowledge. *Organization, 20,* 25-37.

Chesbrough, H. W. (2005). *Open innovation: The new imperative for creating and profiting from technology.* San Francisco, CA: Jossey-Bass.

Gibbons, M., Limoges, C., Nowotny, H., Schwartzman, S., Scott, P., & Trow, M. (1994). *The new production of knowledge: The dynamics of science and research in contemporary societies.* London, UK: Sage.

Huff, A. (2000). 1999 Presidential address: Changes in organizational knowledge production. *Academy of Management Review, 25,* 288-293.

Huff, A. (2012). *Global trends in doctoral education.* Presented at the EFMD Doctoral Programmes Conference, Cranfield, UK.

Lackner, T. (2013). Open innovation at Siemens AG. In A. S. Huff, K. M. Möslein, & R. Reichwald (Eds.), *Leading open innovation.* Cambridge, MA: MIT Press.

Möslein, K. M. (2013). Open innovation: Actors, tools and tensions. In A. S. Huff, K. M. Möslein, & R. Reichwald (Eds.), *Leading open innovation.* Cambridge, MA: MIT Press.

Read, S., Sarasvathy, S., Dew, N., Wiltbank, R., & Ohlsson, A-V. (2010). *Effectual entrepreneurship.* Abington, Oxon, UK: Routledge.

Sarasvathy, S. D. (2001). Causation and effectuation: Toward a theoretical shift from economic inevitability to entrepreneurial contingency. *Academy of Management Review, 26*, 243-263.

Sarasvathy, S. D. (2008). *Effectuation: Elements of entrepreneurial expertise*. Cheltenham, UK: Edward Elger.

Sarasvathy, S. D., & Dew, N. (2005). New market creation through transformation. *Journal of Evolutionary Economics, 15*, 533-565.

Steadman, I. (2013, February 11). IBM's Watson is better at diagnosing cancer than human doctors. *Wired Magazine*. Retrieved from http://www.wired.co.uk/news/archive/2013-02/11/ibm-watson-medical-doctor

van Delden, C., & Wünderlich, N. (2013). Viral marketing and Facebook for a new innovation platform. In A. S. Huff, K. M. Möslein, & R. Reichwald (Eds.), *Leading open innovation*. Cambridge, MA: MIT Press.

von Hippel, E. (2005). Democratizing innovation. Cambridge, MA: MIT Press.

von Hippel, E. (2013). User innovation. In A. S. Huff, K. M. Möslein, & R. Reichwald (Eds.), *Leading open innovation*. Cambridge, MA: MIT Press.

Chapter 3

Prologue

Karl E. Weick
Professor Emeritus
University of Michigan

The Collapse of Sensemaking in Organizations: The Mann Gulch Disaster

Karl E. Weick

Prologue:
Vulnerability and Entrapment: Contingencies at Mann Gulch

Karl E. Weick

Why did I pick this article for inclusion in the Executive Leadership Program volume? Partially because readers sometimes say, "Mann Gulch is a little obvious, isn't it?" They imply that there is no way they would find themselves in a similar predicament. But just what is it in the Mann Gulch[4] incident that is so 'obvious'? Why weren't the context and the unfolding drama obvious to the foreman, Wagner Dodge? Aren't there times when you fail to explain yourself, see the solution to problems as tools you need to drop, foresee conditions that could entrap people, build a strong mutual understanding in advance of tough times, and keep your cool when everyone else is startled? People sometimes say, "We already do these things" but then struggle with follow-up queries such as: Where does it go off the tracks? Would other team members agree that you do these things? and Have you even asked them?

But I also picked this article because it continues to raise durable questions and remind us of durable answers. For example, a durable question is: Would you have jumped into a fire lit in front of you by an unfamiliar foreman if you were already trying to outrun a wall of fire that was closing in on you from behind? The answer is not obvious because the fire that foreman Wagner Dodge lit was not perceived as an "escape" fire until later. If we reverse roles, the question is just as troubling: Would people who work with you jump into an "escape" fire that you lit if they were fleeing imminent danger? In either case the answer would probably be, "It depends."

Depends on what? That's the hook! Compiling a list of what it "depends on" draws one deeper into this story and closer to the present.

---

4   For a virtual tour of Mann Gulch, see http://formontana.net/gulch.html.

Candidates for that list begin to connect events in 1949 that were filtered by a literature professor with expertise in tragic forms (Norman Maclean), and filtered a second time by a student of sensemaking under pressure (Karl Weick), with current events that have similar contingencies. For example, you might jump into the fire of a high-credibility foreman but not one with low credibility, just as you might jump into the fire if you thought it was a good idea but not if you thought it was a bad one. But, what if a person with high credibility is paired with a bad idea or a person with low credibility with a good idea? Both dilemmas are possible at Mann Gulch, just as they are possible in everyday life. We begin to reflect more deeply and more broadly as we feel our way into the events at Mann Gulch.

From slightly more distance there is Norman Maclean's durable question: "What the structure of a small outfit should be when its business is to meet sudden danger and prevent disaster" (1992, p. 65). Consider the phrase "meet sudden danger." That phrase has contemporary relevance in the context of the crash of Air France 447 on June 1, 2009 (see Bureau d'Enquêtes et d'Analyses, 2012). While cruising at 37,000 feet, the pilot flying was "startled" by a sudden shift from automatic control to manual control during turbulence and made exactly the wrong continuing response. The aircraft entered a sustained stall and crashed into the ocean. The small outfit of an aircraft crew, Crew Resource Management notwithstanding, was vulnerable to sudden danger just as was true for the firefighters at Mann Gulch. But why? One interpretation of this vulnerability, but only one, lies in the relationship between structure and sense. Those two variables constitute a feedback loop that can either amplify a change in one of them or control and reverse that change. Deviations amplify when both variables move in the same direction (e.g., less sense leads to less structure, and less structure leads to less sense) or deviations are reversed when one of the two variables moves in an opposite direction (e.g., less sense leads to more structure, and more sense leads to less structure). I argue that the Mann Gulch fire became a disaster because of an amplifying loss of sense and structure which created a "cosmology episode." Sense collapsed as did the means to restore it.

A partial safeguard against such collapse and a durable reminder is found in Donald Campbell's (1990) discussion of respectful interaction. The basic idea is that we all use our own experience to get a better idea of what is going on, and we also rely on the experience of others. This is all well and good until those experiences seem to conflict, as they did at Mann Gulch. Then we have the problem of what weights to put on our own viewpoint and what weights to put on others' viewpoints. Since our viewpoints have their limits, we can't afford to ignore completely what others think is happening. Therefore, if we want to combine our observations with those of other people, and maintain our ability to adapt to change, we have to have to do three things: (1) we have to *trust* the reports of others and be willing to base our beliefs and actions on them; (2) we have to report *honestly*, so that others can use our observations in coming to valid beliefs; and (3) we have to maintain *self-respect*, which means we have to respect our own perceptions and beliefs and seek to integrate them with the reports of others without belittling either them or ourselves. What's crucial here is that trust alone is not enough, even though it has become fashionable to diagnose most collective problems as mainly a lack of trust. Trust, however, is not a standalone issue.

If I were to rewrite the Mann Gulch paper I'd rethink several things. I would question my description of firefighters as "panic'd" people (e.g., Clarke, 2002 suggests that we replace the idea of panic, for which there is little evidence, with the idea that people fail with varying degrees of gracefulness). Instead of the description of 'contextual rationality' as a replacement for conventional rational actor theory, I would use a form of rationality that appears closer to sensemaking, namely, 'situational rationality' (Townley, 2008, pp. 113-152). My use of the holograph metaphor grounds the discussion in the 1990s. That usage needs an update in terms of the language of fractals, which would embed Mann Gulch more explicitly in complexity theory (e.g., Topper & Lagadec, 2013; Dekker, Cilliers, & Hofmeyr, 2011).

The style of my analysis bothers some people because it seems to move among empiricism, allegory, tragedy, social science, theory-building, prescription, and public sensemaking. Talk about "blurred genres"! But blurring can add thoroughness to an analysis. John Dewey addressed this issue when he commented on the misleading dichotomy between theory and practice.

> Flights of fancy and inventions of the imagination are not theories. A theory in a particular case is simply a thoroughgoing analysis of it . . . . The alternative to theory as "thoroughgoing analysis" is not practice, but sentimentality, instinct, authority, laziness, stupidity, or, perhaps more positively, flight of fancy. That there is practice that relies on such substitutes for thoroughgoing analysis, however, is a notorious fact. (as cited in Hickman, 1992, p. 112)

> Or, as Bruno Latour (1988, p. 170) put it, "Just offer the lived world, and write."

References

Bureau d'Enquêtes et d'Analyses. (2012, July). *Final report.* Summary retrieved from http://www.skybrary.aero/index.php/A332,_en-route,_Atlantic_Ocean,_2009_(LOC_HF_AW_WX)

Campbell, D. T. (1990). Asch's moral epistemology for socially shared knowledge. In I. Rock (Ed.), *The legacy of Solomon Asch: Essays in cognition and social psychology* (pp. 39-52). Hillsdale, NJ: Erlbaum.

Clarke, L. (2002). Panic: Myth or reality? *Contexts, 1*(3), 21-26.

Dekker, S., Cilliers, P., & Hofmeyr, J.-H. (2011). The complexity of failure: Implications of complexity theory for safety investigations. *Safety Science, 49*, 939-945.

Hickman, L. A. (1992). *John Dewey's pragmatic technology.* Bloomington, IN: Indiana University Press.

Latour, B. (1988). The politics of explanation: An alternative. In S. Woolgar (Ed.), *Knowledge and reflexivity: New frontier in the sociology of knowledge* (pp. 155-176). London, UK: Sage.

Maclean, N. (1992). *Young men and fire.* Chicago, IL: University of Chicago Press.

Topper, B., & Lagadec, P. (2013). Fractal crises: A new theory for crisis theory and management. *Journal of Contingencies and Crisis Management, 21*(1), 4-16.

Townley, B. (2008). *Reason's neglect: Rationality and organizing.* New York, NY: Oxford.

The Collapse of Sensemaking in Organizations: The Mann Gulch Disaster[5]

Karl E. Weick

Abstract. The death of 13 men in the Mann Gulch fire disaster, made famous in Norman Maclean's *Young Men and Fire*, is analyzed as the interactive disintegration of role structure and sensemaking in a minimal organization. Four potential sources of resilience that make groups less vulnerable to disruptions of sensemaking are proposed to forestall disintegration, including improvisation, virtual role systems, the attitude of wisdom, and norms of respectful interaction. The analysis is then embedded in the organizational literature to show that we need to reexamine our thinking about temporary systems, structuration, nondisclosive intimacy, intergroup dynamics, and team building.

The purpose of this article is to reanalyze the Mann Gulch fire disaster in Montana described in Norman Maclean's (1992) award-winning book *Young Men and Fire* to illustrate a gap in our current understanding of organizations. I want to focus on two questions: Why do organizations unravel? And how can organizations be made more resilient? Before doing so, however, I want to strip Maclean's elegant prose away from the events in Mann Gulch and simply review them to provide a context for the analysis.

THE INCIDENT

As Maclean puts it, at its heart, the Mann Gulch disaster is a story of a race (p. 224). The smokejumpers in the race (excluding foreman "Wag" Wagner Dodge and ranger Jim Harrison) were ages 17-28, unmarried, seven of them were forestry students (p. 27), and 12 of them had seen military service (p. 220). They were a highly select group (p. 27) and often described themselves as professional adventurers (p. 26).

---

[5]   Originally Published as: Weick, K. (1993). "The collapse of sensemaking in organizations: The Mann Gulch disaster." Administrative Science Quarterly **38**(4)

A lightning storm passed over the Mann Gulch area at 4PM on August 4, 1949 and is believed to have set a small fire in a dead tree. The next day, August 5, 1949, the temperature was 97 degrees and the fire danger rating was 74 out of a possible 100 (p. 42), which means "explosive potential" (p. 79). When the fire was spotted by a forest ranger, the smokejumpers were dispatched to fight it. Sixteen of them flew out of Missoula, Montana at 2:30PM in a C-47 transport. Wind conditions that day were turbulent, and one smokejumper got sick on the airplane, didn't jump, returned to the base with the plane, and resigned from the smokejumpers as soon as he landed ("his repressions had caught up with him," p. 51). The smokejumpers and their cargo were dropped on the south side of Mann Gulch at 4:10PM from 2000 feet rather than the normal 1200 feet, due to the turbulence (p. 48). The parachute that was connected to their radio failed to open, and the radio was pulverized when it hit the ground. The crew met ranger Jim Harrison who had been fighting the fire alone for four hours (p. 62), collected their supplies, and ate supper. About 5:10 (p. 57) they started to move along the south side of the gulch to surround the fire (p. 62). Dodge and Harrison, however, having scouted ahead, were worried that the thick forest near which they had landed might be a "death trap" (p. 64). They told the second in command, William Hellman, to take the crew across to the north side of the gulch and march them toward the river along the side of the hill. While Hellman did this, Dodge and Harrison ate a quick meal. Dodge rejoined the crew at 5:40Pm and took his position at the head of the line moving toward the river. He could see flames flapping back and forth on the south slope as he looked to his left (p. 69).

At this point the reader hits the most chilling sentence in the entire book: "Then Dodge saw it!" (p. 70). What he saw was that the fire had crossed the gulch just 200 yards ahead and was moving toward them (p. 70). Dodge turned the crew around and had them angle up the 76-percent hill toward the ridge at the top (p. 175). They were soon moving through bunch grass that was two and a half feet tall and were quickly losing ground to the 30-foot-high flames that were soon moving toward them at 610 feet per minute (p. 274). Dodge yelled at the crew to drop their tools, and then, to everyone's astonishment, he lit a fire in front of them and ordered them to lie down in the area it had burned. No one did, and they all ran for the ridge. Two people, Sallee and Rumsey, made it through a crevice in the ridge unburned, Hellman made it over the ridge burned horribly and died at noon the next day, Dodge lived by lying down in the ashes of his escape fire, and one other person, Joseph Sylvia, lived for a short while and then died. The hands on Harrison's watch melted at 5:56 (p. 90), which has been treated officially as the time the 13 people died.

After the fire passed, Dodge found Sallee and Rumsey, and Rumsey stayed to care for Hellman while Sallee and Dodge hiked out for help. They walked into the Meriwether ranger station at 8:50Pm (p. 113), and rescue parties immediately set out to recover the dead and dying. All the dead were found in an area of 100 yards by 300 yards (p. 111). It took 450 men, five more days to get the 4,500-acre Mann Gulch fire under control (pp. 24, 33). At the time the crew jumped on the fire, it was classified as a Class C fire, meaning its scope was between 10 and 99 acres.

The Forest Service inquiry held after the fire, judged by many to be inadequate, concluded that "there is no evidence of disregard by those responsible for the jumper crew of the elements of risk which they are expected to take into account in placing jumper crews on fires." The board also felt that the men would have been saved had they "heeded Dodge's efforts to get them to go into the escape fire area with him" (quoted in Maclean, p. 151). Several parents brought suit against the Forest Service, claiming that people should not have been jumped in the first place (p. 149), but these claims were dismissed by the Ninth Circuit U.S. Court of Appeals, where Warren E. Burger argued the Forest Service's case (p. 151).

Since Mann Gulch, there have been no deaths by burning among Forest Service firefighters, and people are now equipped with backup radios (p. 219), better physical conditioning, the tactic of building an escape fire, knowledge that fires in timber west of the Continental Divide burn differently than do fires in grass east of the Divide, and the insistence that crew safety take precedence over fire suppression.

THE METHODOLOGY

Among the sources of evidence Maclean used to construct this case study were interviews, trace records, archival records, direct observation, personal experience, and mathematical models.

Since Maclean did not begin to gather documents on Mann Gulch until 1976 (p. 156) and did not start to work in earnest on this project until his seventy-fourth birthday in 1977, the lapse of almost 28 years since the disaster made interviewing difficult, especially since Dodge had died of Hodgkin's disease five years after the fire (p. 106). Maclean located and interviewed both living witnesses of the blaze, Sallee and Rumsey, and persuaded both to accompany him and Laird Robinson, a guide at the Smokejumper base, on a visit back to the site on July 1, 1978. Maclean also knew Dodge's wife and had talked to her informally (p. 40). He attempted to interview relatives of some who lost their lives but found them too distraught 27 years later to be of much help (p. 154). He also attempted to interview (p. 239) a member of the Forest Service inquiry team, A. J. Cramer who, in 1951, had persuaded Sallee, Rumsey, and ranger Robert Jansson to alter their testimony about the timing of key incidents. Cramer was the custodian of seven or eight watches that had been removed from victims (p. 233), only one of which (Harrison's) was released and used as the official time of the disaster (5:56PM). To this day it remains unclear why the Forest Service made such a strong effort to locate the disaster closer to 6:00PM than to 5:30, which was suggested by testimony from Jansson, who was near the river when the fire blew up, and from a recovered watch that read 5:42. Maclean had continuing access to two Forest Service insiders, Bud Moore and Laird Robinson (p. 162). He also interviewed experts on precedents for the escape fire (p. 104) and on the nature of death by fire (p. 213).

56

The use of trace records, or physical evidence of past behaviors, is illustrated by the location during a 1979 trip to the gulch, of the wooden cross that had been placed in 1949 to mark the spot where Dodge lit his escape fire (p. 206). The year before, 1978, during the trip into the gulch with Sallee and Rumsey, Maclean located the rusty can of potatoes that had been discarded after Hellman drank its salty water through two knife slits Rumsey had made in the can (p. 173). He also located the flat rocks on which Hellman and Sylvia had rested while awaiting rescue, the juniper tree that was just beyond the crevice Sallee and Rumsey squeezed through on the ridge (p. 207), and Henry Thol, Jr.'s flashlight (p. 183). Considering the lapse of time, the destructive forces of nature over 28 years, and the power of a blowup fire to melt and displace everything in its path, discovery of these traces is surprising as well as helpful in reconstructing events.

Archival records are crucial to the development of the case, although the Forest Service made a considerable effort after its inquiry to scatter the documents (p. 153) and to classify most of them "Confidential" (p. 158), perhaps fearing it would be charged with negligence. Records used by Maclean included statistical reports of fire suppression by smokejumpers in Forest Service Region 1 (e.g., p. 24); the report of the Forest Service Board of Review issued shortly after the incident (dated September 29, 1949, which many felt was too soon for the board to do an adequate job); statements made to the board by people such as the C-47 pilot, parents of the dead crew (p. 150), and the spotter on the aircraft (p. 42); court reports of litigation brought by parents of smokejumpers against the Forest Service; photographs, virtually all of which were retrieved for him by women in the Forest Service who were eager to help him tell the story (p. 160); early records of the smokejumpers organization, which was nine years old at the time of the disaster; reports of the 1957 task force on crew safety (p. 221); and contemporary reports of the disaster in the media, such as the report in the August 22, 1949 issue of *Life* magazine.

Direct observation occurred during Maclean's three visits to Mann Gulch in 1976, 1977, and 1978 (p. 189), trips made much more difficult because of the inaccessibility of the area (pp. 191-192). The most important of these three visits is the trip to the gulch with Sallee and Rumsey, during which the latter pair reenacted what they did and what they saw intermittently through the dense smoke. When their accounts were matched against subsequent hard data (e.g., their estimation of where Dodge lit his escape fire compared against discovery of the actual cross planted in 1949 to mark the spot), it was found that their reconstruction of events prior to the time they made it to safety through the crevice is less accurate than their memory for events and locations after they made it to safety. This suggests to Maclean that "we don't remember as exactly the desperate moments when our lives are in the balance as we remember the moments after, when the balance has tipped in our favor" (p. 212). Direct observation also occurred when Maclean and Robinson themselves hiked the steep slopes of Mann Gulch under summer conditions of heat and slippery, tall grass that resembled the conditions present in the disaster of 1949. The two men repeatedly compared photos and maps from 1949 with physical outcroppings in front of them to see more clearly what they were looking at (e.g., photos misrepresent the steepness of the slope, p. 175). There were also informal experiments, as when Rod Norum, an athlete and specialist on fire behavior, retraced Dodge's route from the point at which he rejoined the crew, moved as fast as possible over the route Dodge covered, and was unable to reach the grave markers as fast as the crew did (p. 67). During these trips, Maclean took special note of prevailing winds by observing their effect on the direction in which rotted timber fell. These observations were used to build a theory of how wind currents in the gulch could have produced the blowup (p. 133).

Personal experience was part of the case because, in 1949, Maclean had visited the Mann Gulch fire while it was still burning (p. 1). Maclean also was a Forest Service firefighter (not a smokejumper) at age 15 and nearly lost his life in the Fish Creek fire, a fire much like the one in

Mann Gulch (p. 4). Maclean also reports using his practical experience as a woodsman to suggest initial hypotheses regarding what happened at Mann Gulch (e.g., he infers wind patterns in the gulch from observations of unusual wave action in the adjacent Missouri River, p. 131).

Having collected data using the above sources, but still feeling gaps in his understanding of precisely how the race between fire and men unfolded, Maclean taught himself mathematics and turned to mathematical modeling. He worked with two mathematicians, Frank Albini and Richard Rothermel, who had built mathematical models of how fires spread. The group ran the predictive models in reverse to see what the fire in Mann Gulch must have been like to generate the reports on its progress that were found in interviews, reports, and actual measurements. It is the combination of output from the model and subjective reports that provide the revealing time line of the final 16 minutes (pp. 267-277).

If these several sources of evidence are combined and assessed for the adequacy with which they address "sources of invalidity," it will be found that they combat 12 of the 15 sources listed by Runkel and McGrath (1972: 191) and are only "moderately vulnerable" to the other three. Of course, an experienced woodsman and storyteller who has "always tried to be accurate with facts" (p. 259) would expect that. The rest of us in organizational studies may be pardoned, however, if we find those numbers a good reason to take these data seriously.

COSMOLOGY EPISODES IN MANN GULCH

Early in the book (p. 65), Maclean asks the question on which I want to focus: "what the structure of a small outfit should be when its business is to meet sudden danger and prevent disaster." This question is timely because the work of organizations is increasingly done in small temporary outfits in which the stakes are high and where foul-ups can have serious consequences (Heydebrand, 1989; Ancona and Caldwell, 1992). Thus, if we understand what happened at Mann Gulch, we may be able to learn some valuable lessons in how to conceptualize and cope with contemporary organizations.

Let me first be clear about why I think the crew of smokejumpers at Mann Gulch was an organization. First, they have a series of interlocking routines, which is crucial in Westley's (1990: 339) definition of an organization as "a series of interlocking routines, habituated action patterns that bring the same people together around the same activities in the same time and places." The crew at Mann Gulch have routine, habituated action patterns, they come together from a common pool of people, and while this set of individual smokejumpers had not come together at the same places or times, they did come together around the same episodes of fire. Westley's definition suggests it doesn't take much to qualify as an organization. The other side is, it also may not take much to stop being one.

Second, the Mann Gulch crew fits the five criteria for a simple organizational structure proposed by Mintzberg (1983: 158). These five include coordination by direct supervision, strategy planned at the top, little formalized behavior, organic structure, and the person in charge tending to formulate plans intuitively, meaning that the plans are generally a direct "extension of his own personality." Structures like this are found most often in entrepreneurial firms.

And third, the Mann Gulch crew has "generic subjectivity" (Wiley, 1988), meaning that roles and rules exist that enable individuals to be interchanged with little disruption to the ongoing pattern of interaction. In the crew at Mann Gulch there were at least three roles: leader, second in command, and crewmember. The person in the lead sizes up the situation, makes decisions, yells orders, picks trails, sets the pace, and identifies escape routes (pp. 65-66). The second in command brings up the rear of the crew as it hikes, repeats orders, sees that the orders are understood, helps the individuals coordinate their actions, and tends to be closer to the crew and more of a buddy with them than does the leader. And finally, the crew clears a fire line around the fire, cleans up after the fire, and maintains trails. Thus, the crew at Mann Gulch is an organization by virtue of a role structure of interlocking routines.

I want to argue that the tragedy at Mann Gulch alerts us to an unsuspected source of vulnerability in organizations. Minimal organizations, such as we find in the crew at Mann Gulch, are susceptible to sudden losses of meaning, which have been variously described as fundamental surprises (Reason, 1990) or events that are inconceivable (Lanir, 1989), hidden (Westrum, 1982), or incomprehensible (Perrow, 1984). Each of these labels points to the low probability that the event could occur, which is why it is meaningless. But these explanations say less about the astonishment of the perceiver, and even less about the perceiver's inability to rebuild some sense of what is happening.

To shift the analytic focus in implausible events from probabilities to feelings and social construction, I have borrowed the term "cosmology" from philosophy and stretched it. Cosmology refers to a branch of philosophy often subsumed under metaphysics that combines rational speculation and scientific evidence to understand the universe as a totality of phenomena. Cosmology is the ultimate macro perspective, directed at issues of time, space, change, and contingency as they relate to the origin and structure of the universe. Integrations of these issues, however, are not just the handiwork of philosophers. Others also make their peace with these issues, as reflected in what they take for granted. People, including those who are smokejumpers, act as if events cohere in time and space and that change unfolds in an orderly manner. These everyday cosmologies are subject to disruption. And when they are severely disrupted, I call this a cosmology episode (Weick, 1985: 51-52). A cosmology episode occurs when people suddenly and deeply feel that the universe is no longer a rational, orderly system. What makes such an episode so shattering is that both the sense of what is occurring and the means to rebuild that sense collapse together.

Stated more informally, a cosmology episode feels like vu jade—the opposite of déjà vu: I've never been here before, I have no idea where I am, and I have no idea who can help me. This is what the smokejumpers may have felt increasingly as the afternoon wore on and they lost what little organization structure they had to start with. As they lost structure they became more anxious and found it harder to make sense of what was happening, until they finally were unable to make any sense whatsoever of the one thing that would have saved their lives, an escape fire. The disaster at Mann Gulch was produced by the interrelated collapse of sensemaking and structure. If we can understand this collapse, we may be able to forestall similar disasters in other organizations.

Sensemaking in Mann Gulch

Although most organizational analyses begin and end with decision making, there is growing dissatisfaction with this orthodoxy. Reed (1991) showed how far the concept of decision making has been stretched, singling out the patching that James G. March has done in recent discussions of decision making. March (1989: 14) wrote that "decision making is a highly contextual, sacred activity, surrounded by myth and ritual, and as much concerned with the interpretive order as with the specifics of particular choices." Reed (1991: 561) summarized March this way: "decision making preferences are often inconsistent, unstable, and externally driven; the linkages between decisions and actions are loosely-coupled and interactive rather than linear; the past is notoriously unreliable as a guide to the present or the future; and . . . political and symbolic considerations play a central, perhaps overriding, role in decision making." Reed wondered aloud whether, if March is right in these descriptions, decision making should continue to set the agenda for organizational studies. At some point a retreat from classic principles becomes a rout.

There have been at least three distinct responses to these problems. First, there has been a shift, reminiscent of Neisser and Winograd's (1988) work on memory, toward examining naturalistic decision making (Orasanu and Connolly, 1993), with more attention to situational assessment and sensemaking (Klein, 1993). Second, people have replaced an interest in decision making with an interest in power, noting, for example, that "power is most strategically deployed in the design and implementation of paradigmatic frameworks within which the very meaning of such actions as 'making decisions' is defined" (Brown, 1978: 376). And third, people are replacing the less appropriate normative models of rationality (e.g., Hirsch, Michaels, and Friedman, 1987) based on asocial "economic man" (Beach and Lipshitz, 1993) with more appropriate models of rationality that are more sophisticated about social relations, such as the model of contextual rationality (White, 1988).

Reed (1991) described contextual rationality as action motivated to create and maintain institutions and traditions that express some conception of right behavior and a good life with others. Contextual rationality is sensitive to the fact that social actors need to create and maintain intersubjectively binding normative structures that sustain and enrich their relationships. Thus, organizations become important because they can provide meaning and order in the face of environments that impose ill-defined, contradictory demands.

One way to shift the focus from decision making to meaning is to look more closely at sensemaking in organizations. The basic idea of sensemaking is that reality is an ongoing accomplishment that emerges from efforts to create order and make retrospective sense of what occurs. Recognition-primed decision making, a model based in part on command decisions made by firefighters, has features of sensemaking in its reliance on past experience, although it remains grounded in decision making (Klein, 1993). Sensemaking emphasizes that people try to make things rationally accountable to themselves and others. Thus, in the words of Morgan, Frost, and Pondy (1983: 24), "individuals are not seen as living in, and acting out their lives in relation to, a wider reality, so much as creating and sustaining images of a wider reality, in part to rationalize what they are doing. They realize their reality, by reading into their situation patterns of significant meaning."

When the smokejumpers landed at Mann Gulch, they expected to find what they had come to call a 10:00 fire. A 10:00 fire is one that can be surrounded completely and isolated by 10:00 the next morning. The spotters on the aircraft that carried the smokejumpers "figured the crew would have it under control by 10:00 the next morning" (Maclean, p. 43). People rationalized this image until it was too late. And because they did, less and less of what they saw made sense:

1. The crew expects a 10:00 fire but grows uneasy when this fire does not act like one.
2. Crewmembers wonder how this fire can be all that serious if Dodge and Harrison eat supper while they hike toward the river.
3. People are often unclear who is in charge of the crew (p. 65).
4. The flames on the south side of the gulch look intense, yet one of the smokejumpers, David Navon is taking pictures, so people conclude the fire can't be that serious, even though their senses tell them otherwise.
5. Crewmembers know they are moving toward the river where they will be safe from the fire, only to see Dodge inexplicably turn them around, away from the river, and start angling upslope, but not running straight for the top. Why? (Dodge is the only one who sees the fire jump the gulch ahead of them.)
6. As the fire gains on them, Dodge says, "Drop your tools," but if the people in the crew do that, then who are they? Firefighters? With no tools?
7. The foreman lights a fire that seems to be right in the middle of the only escape route people can see.
8. The foreman points to the fire he has started and yells, "Join me," whatever that means. But his second in command sounds like he's saying, "To hell with that, I'm getting out of here" (p. 95).
9. Each individual faces the dilemma, I must be my own boss yet follow orders unhesitatingly, but I can't comprehend what the

orders mean, and I'm losing my race with the advancing fire (pp. 219-220).

As Mann Gulch loses its resemblance to a 10:00 fire, it does so in ways that make it increasingly hard to socially construct reality. When the noise created by wind, flames, and exploding trees is deafening; when people are strung out in a line and relative strangers to begin with; when they are people who, in Maclean's words, "love the universe but are not intimidated by it" (p. 28); and when the temperature is approaching a lethal 140 degrees (p. 220), people can neither validate their impressions with a trusted neighbor nor pay close attention to a boss who is also unknown and whose commands make no sense whatsoever. As if these were not obstacles enough, it is hard to make common sense when each person sees something different or nothing at all because of the smoke.

The crew's stubborn belief that it faced a 10:00 fire is a powerful reminder that positive illusions (Taylor, 1989) can kill people. But the more general point is that organizations can be good at decision making and still falter. They falter because of deficient sensemaking. The world of decision making is about strategic rationality. It is built from clear questions and clear answers that attempt to remove ignorance (Daft and Macintosh, 1981). The world of sensemaking is different. Sensemaking is about contextual rationality. It is built out of vague questions, muddy answers, and negotiated agreements that attempt to reduce confusion. People in Mann Gulch did not face questions like where should we go, when do we take a stand, or what should our strategy be? Instead, they faced the more basic, the more frightening feeling that their old labels were no longer working. They were outstripping their past experience and were not sure either what was up or who they were. Until they develop some sense of issues like this, there is nothing to decide.

Role Structure in Mann Gulch

Sensemaking was not the only problem in Mann Gulch. There were also problems of structure. It seems plausible to argue that a major contributor to this disaster was the loss of the only structure that kept these people organized, their role system. There were two key events that destroyed the organization that tied these people together. First, when Dodge told Hellman to take the crew to the north side of the gulch and have it follow a contour down toward the river, the crew got confused, the spaces between members widened appreciably, and Navon—the person taking pictures (p. 71)—made a bid to take over the leadership of the group (p. 65). Notice what this does to the role system. There is now no one at the end of the line repeating orders as a check on the accuracy with which they are understood. Furthermore, the person who is leading them, Hellman, is more familiar with implementing orders than with constructing them or plotting possible escape routes. So the crew is left for a crucial period of time with ill-structured, unacknowledged orders shouted by someone who is unaccustomed to being firm or noticing escape routes. Both routines and interlocking are beginning to come apart.

The second, and in some way more unsettling threat to the role system occurred when Dodge told the retreating crew "throw away your tools!" (p. 226). A fire crew that retreats from a fire should find its identity and morale strained. If the retreating people are then also told to discard the very things that are their reason for being there in the first place, then the moment quickly turns existential. If I am no longer a firefighter, then who am I? With the fire bearing down, the only possible answer becomes, An endangered person in a world where it is every man for himself. Thus, people who, in Maclean's words, had perpetually been almost their own boss (p. 218) suddenly became completely their own boss at the worst possible moment. As the entity of a crew dissolved, it is not surprising that the final command from the "crew" leader to jump into an escape fire was heard not as a legitimate order but as the ravings of someone who had

66

"gone nuts" (p. 75). Dodge's command lost its basis of legitimacy when the smokejumpers threw away their organization along with their tools.

Panic In Mann Gulch

With these observations as background, we can now look more closely at the process of a cosmology episode, an interlude in which the orderliness of the universe is called into question because both understanding and procedures for sensemaking collapse together. People stop thinking and panic. What is interesting about this collapse is that it was discussed by Freud (1959: 28) in the context of panic in military groups: "A panic arises if a group of that kind [military group] becomes disintegrated. Its characteristics are that none of the orders given by superiors are any longer listened to, and that each individual is only solicitous on his own account, and without any consideration for the rest. The mutual ties have ceased to exist, and a gigantic and senseless fear is set free." Unlike earlier formulations, such as McDougall's (1920), which had argued that panic leads to group disintegration, Freud, reversing this causality, argued that group disintegration precipitates panic. By group disintegration, Freud meant "the cessation of all the feelings of consideration which the members of the group otherwise show one another" (p. 29). He described the mechanism involved this way: "If an individual in panic fear begins to be solicitous only on his own account, he bears witness in so doing to the fact that the emotional ties, which have hitherto made the danger seem small to him, have ceased to exist. Now that he is by himself in facing the danger, he may surely think it greater."

It is certainly true in Mann Gulch that there is a real, palpable danger that can be seen, felt, heard, and smelled by the smokejumpers. But this is not the first time they have confronted danger. It may, however, be the first time they have confronted danger as a member of a disintegrating organization. As the crew moved toward the river and became more spread out, individuals were isolated and left without explanations or emotional support for their reactions. As the ties weakened, the sense of danger increased, and the means to cope became more primitive. The world rapidly shifted from a cosmos to chaos as it became emptied of order and rationality.

It is intriguing that the three people who survived the disaster did so in ways that seem to forestall group disintegration. Sallee and Rumsey stuck together, their small group of two people did not disintegrate, which helped them keep their fear under control. As a result, they escaped through a crack in the ridge that the others either didn't see or thought was too small to squeeze through. Wag Dodge, as the formal leader of a group he presumed still existed, ordered his followers to join him in the escape fire. Dodge continued to see a group and to think about its well-being, which helped keep his own fear under control. The rest of the people, however, took less notice of one another. Consequently, the group, as they knew it, disintegrated. As their group disintegrated, the smokejumpers became more frightened, stopped thinking sooner, pulled apart even more, and in doing so, lost a leader-follower relationship as well as access to the novel ideas of other people who are a lot like them. As these relationships disappeared, individuals reverted to primitive tendencies of flight. Unfortunately, this response was too simple to match the complexity of the Mann Gulch fire.

What holds organization in place may be more tenuous than we realize. The recipe for disorganization in Mann Gulch is not all that rare in everyday life. The recipe reads, Thrust people into unfamiliar roles, leave some key roles unfilled, make the task more ambiguous, discredit the role system, and make all of these changes in a context in which small events can combine into something monstrous. Faced with similar conditions, organizations that seem much sturdier may also come crashing down (Miller, 1990; Miles and Snow, 1992), much like Icarus who overreached his competence as he flew toward the sun and also perished because of fire.

FROM VULNERABILITY TO RESILIENCE

The steady erosion of sense and structure reached its climax in the refusal of the crew to escape one fire by walking into another one that was intentionally set. A closer look at that escape fire allows us to move from a discussion of what went wrong at Mann Gulch, to a discussion of what makes organizations more resilient. I want to discuss four sources of resilience: (1) improvisation and bricolage, (2) virtual role systems, (3) the attitude of wisdom, and (4) respectful interaction.

Improvisation and Bricolage

The escape fire is a good place to start in the search for sources of resilience simply because it is clear evidence that, minimal though the organization of the crew might have been, there still was a solution to the crisis inside the group. The problem was, no one but Dodge recognized this. The question then becomes, How could more people either see this escape fire as a solution or develop their own solution? This is not an easy question to answer because, from everything we know, Dodge's invention of burning a hole in a fire should not have happened. It should not have happened because there is good evidence that when people are put under pressure, they regress to their most habituated ways of responding (e.g., Barthol and Ku, 1959). This is what we see in the 15 people who reject Dodge's order to join him and who resort instead to flight, a more overlearned tendency. What we do not expect under life-threatening pressure is creativity.

The tactic of lighting a fire to create an area where people can escape a major prairie fire is mentioned in James Fenimore Cooper's 1827 novel *The Prairie*, but there is no evidence Dodge knew this source (Maclean, p. 104). Furthermore, most of Dodge's experience had been in timbered country where such a tactic wouldn't work. In timber, an escape fire is too slow and consumes too much oxygen (p. 105). And the fire that Dodge built did not burn long enough to clear an area in which people could move around and dodge the fire as they did in the prairie fire. There was just room enough to lie down in the ashes where the heat was less intense (p. 104).

While no one can say how or why the escape fire was created, there is a line of argument that is consistent with what we know. Bruner (1983: 183) described creativity as "figuring out how to use what you already know in order to go beyond what you currently think." With this as background, it now becomes relevant that Dodge was an experienced woodsman, with lots of hands-on experience. He was what we now would call a bricoleur, someone able to create order out of whatever materials were at hand (e.g., Levi-Strauss, 1966; Harper, 1987). Dodge would have known at least two things about fires. He would have known the famous fire triangle—you must have oxygen, flammable material, and temperature above the point of ignition to create a fire (Maclean, p. 35). A shortage of any one of these would prevent a fire. In his case, the escape fire removed flammable material. And since Dodge had been with the Forest Service longer than anyone else on the crew, he would also have known more fully their four guidelines at that time for dealing with fire emergencies (p. 100). These included (1) start a backfire if you can, (2) get to the top of a ridge where the fuel is thinner, (3) turn into the fire and try to work through it, and (4) don't allow the fire to pick the spot where it hits you. Dodge's invention, if we stretch a bit, fits all four. It is a backfire, though not in the conventional sense of a fire built to stop a fire. The escape fire is lit near the top of a ridge, Dodge turns into the main fire and works through it by burning a hole in it, and he chooses where the fire hits him. The 15 who tried to outrun the fire moved toward the ridge but by not facing the fire, they allowed it to pick the spot where it hit them.

The collapse of role systems need not result in disaster if people develop skills in improvisation and bricolage (see Janowitz, 1959: 481). Bricoleurs remain creative under pressure, precisely because they routinely act in chaotic conditions and pull order out of them. Thus, when situations unravel, this is simply normal natural trouble for bricoleurs, and they proceed with whatever materials are at hand. Knowing these materials intimately, they then are able, usually in the company of other similarly skilled people, to form the materials or insights into novel combinations.

While improvised firefighting may sound improbable, in fact, Park Service firefighters like those stationed at the Grand Canyon approximate just such a style. Stephen Pyne (1989), a Park Service firefighter, observed that people like him typically have discretion to dispatch themselves, which is unfathomable to the Forest Service crews that rely on dispatchers, specialization, regimentation, rules, and a conscious preference for the strength of the whole rather than the versatility and resourcefulness of the parts. Forest Service people marvel at the freedom of movement among the Park people. Park Service people marvel at how much power the Forest Service is able to mobilize on a fire. Pyne (1989: 122) described the Park Service fire operations as a nonstandard "eclectic assembly of compromises" built of discretion and mobility. In contrast to the Forest Service, where people do everything by the book, "The Park Service has no books; it puts a premium on the individual. Its collective behavior is tribal, and it protects its permanent ranks." If improvisation were given more attention in the job description of a crew person, that person's receptiveness to and generation of role improvisations might be enhanced. As a result, when one organizational order collapses, a substitute might be invented immediately. Swift replacement of a traditional, order with an improvised order would forestall the paralysis that can follow a command to "drop your tools."

Virtual Role Systems

Social construction of reality is next to impossible amidst the chaos of a fire, unless social construction takes place inside one person's head, where the role system is reconstituted and run. Even though the role system at Mann Gulch collapsed, this kind of collapse need not result in disaster if the system remains intact in the individual's mind. If each individual in the crew mentally takes all roles and therefore can

71

then register escape routes and acknowledge commands and facilitate coordination, then each person literally becomes a group (Schutz, 1961). And, in the manner of a holograph, each person can reconstitute the group and assume whatever role is vacated, pick up the activities, and run a credible version of the role. Furthermore, people can run the group in their head and use it for continued guidance of their own individual action. It makes just as much sense to talk about a virtual role system as it does to talk about a virtual anything else (e.g., Bruner, 1986: 36-37). An organization can continue to function in the imagination long after it has ceased to function in tangible distributed activities. For the Mann Gulch fire, this issue has bearing on the question of escape routes. In our research on accidents in flight operations off nuclear carriers (Weick and Roberts, 1993), Karlene Roberts and I found that people who avoid accidents live by the credo, "never get into anything without making sure you have a way out." At the very last moment in the Mann Gulch tragedy, Dodge discovered a way out. The point is that if other people had been able to simulate Dodge and/or his role in their imagination, they too might have been less puzzled by his solution or better able to invent a different sensible solution for themselves.

The Attitude of Wisdom

To understand the role of wisdom (Bigelow, 1992) as a source of resilience, we need to return to the crew's belief that all fires are 10:00 fires. This belief was consistent with members' experience. As Maclean put it, if the major purpose of your group is to "put out fires so fast they don't have time to become big ones" (p. 31), then you won't learn much about fighting big fires. Nor will you learn what Maclean calls the first principle of reality: "little things suddenly and literally can become big as hell, the ordinary can suddenly become monstrous, and the upgulch breezes can suddenly turn to murder" (p. 217). To state the point more generally, what most organizations miss, and what explains why most organizations fail to learn (Scott, 1987: 282), is that "Reality backs up while it is approached by the subject who tries to understand it. Ignorance and knowledge grow together" (Meacham, 1983: 130). To put it a different way, "Each new domain of knowledge appears simple from the distance of ignorance. The more we learn about a particular domain, the greater the number of uncertainties, doubts, questions and complexities. Each bit of knowledge serves as the thesis from which additional questions or antithesis arise" (Meacham, 1983: 120).

The role system best able to accept the reality that ignorance and knowledge grow together may be one in which the organizational culture values wisdom. Meacham (1983: 187) argued that wisdom is an attitude rather than a skill or a body of information:

> *"To be wise is not to know particular facts but to know without excessive confidence or excessive cautiousness. Wisdom is thus not a belief, a value, a set of facts, a corpus of knowledge or information in some specialized area, or a set of special abilities or skills. Wisdom is an attitude taken by persons toward the beliefs, values, knowledge, information, abilities, and skills that are held, a tendency to doubt that these are necessarily true or valid and to doubt that they are an exhaustive set of those things that could be known".*

In a fluid world, wise people know that they don't fully understand what is happening right now, because they have never seen precisely this event before. Extreme confidence and extreme caution both can destroy what organizations most need in changing times, namely, curiosity, openness, and complex sensing. The overconfident shun curiosity because they feel they know most of what there is to know. The overcautious shun curiosity for fear it will only deepen their uncertainties. Both the cautious and the confident are closed-minded, which means neither makes good judgments. It is this sense in which wisdom, which avoids extremes, improves adaptability.

A good example of wisdom in groups is the Naskapi Indians' use of caribou shoulder bones to locate game (Weick, 1979). They hold bones over a fire until they crack and then hunt in the directions to which the cracks point. This ritual is effective because the decision is not influenced by the outcomes of past hunts, which means the stock of animals is not depleted. More important, the final decision is not influenced by the inevitable patterning in human choice, which enables hunted animals to become sensitized to humans and take evasive action. The wisdom inherent in this practice derives from its ambivalence toward the past. Any attempt to hunt for caribou is both a new experience and an old experience. It is new in the sense that time has elapsed, the composition of the hunter band has changed, the caribou have learned new things, and so forth. But the hunt is also old in the sense that if you've seen one hunt, you've seen them all: There are always hunters, weapons, stealth, decoys, tracks, odors, and winds. The practice of divination incorporates the attitude of wisdom because past experience is discounted when a new set of cracks forms a crude map for the hunt. But past experience is also given some weight, because a seasoned hunter "reads" the cracks and injects some of his own past experience into an interpretation of what the cracks mean. The reader is crucial. If the reader's hunches dominate, randomization is lost. If the cracks dominate, then the experience base is discarded. The cracks are a lot like the four guidelines for fire emergencies that Dodge may have relied on when he invented the escape fire. They embody experience, but they invite doubt, reassembly, and shaping to fit novelties in the present.

Respectful Interaction

The final suggestion about how to counteract vulnerability makes explicit the preceding focus on the individual and social interaction. Respectful interaction depends on intersubjectivity (Wiley, 1988: 258), which has two defining characteristics: (1) Intersubjectivity emerges from the interchange and synthesis of meanings among two or more communicating selves, and (2) the self or subject gets transformed during interaction such that a joint or merged subjectivity develops. It is possible that many role systems do not change fast enough to keep up with a rapidly changing environment. The only form that can keep up is one based on face-to-face interaction. And it is here, rather than in routines, that we are best able to see the core of organizing. This may be why interaction in airline cockpit crews, such as discussed by Foushee (1984), strikes us so often as a plausible microcosm of what happens in much larger systems. In a cockpit under crisis, the only unit that makes sense (pun intended) is face-to-face synthesis of meaning.

Intersubjectivity was lost on everyone at Mann Gulch, everyone, that is, but Sallee and Rumsey. They stuck together and lived. Dodge went his own individual way with a burst of improvisation, and he too lived. Perhaps it's more important that you have a partner than an organization when you fight fires. A partner makes social construction easier. A partner is a second source of ideas. A partner strengthens independent judgment in the face of a majority. And a partner enlarges the pool of data that are considered. Partnerships that endure are likely to be those that adhere to Campbell's three imperatives for social life, based on a reanalysis of Asch's (1952) conformity experiment: (1) Respect the reports of others and be willing to base beliefs and actions on them (trust); (2) Report honestly so that others may use your observations in coming to valid beliefs (honesty); and, (3) Respect your own perceptions and beliefs and seek to integrate them with the reports of others without deprecating them or yourselves (self-respect) (adapted from Campbell, 1990: 45-46).

Earlier I noted a growing interest in contextual rationality, understood as actions that create and maintain institutions and traditions that express some conception of right behavior and a good life with others (Reed, 1991). Campbell's maxims operationalize this good life with others as trust, honesty, and self-respect in moment-to-moment interaction. This triangle of trust, honesty, and self-respect is conspicuously missing (e.g., King, 1989: 46 /18) in several well-documented disasters in which faulty interaction processes led to increased fear, diminished communication, and death. For example, in the Tenerife air disaster (Weick, 1990), the copilot of the KLM aircraft had a strong hunch that another 747 airplane was on the takeoff runway directly in front of them when his own captain began takeoff without clearance. But the copilot said nothing about either the suspicions or the illegal departure. Transient cockpit crews, tied together by narrow definitions of formal responsibilities, and headed by captains who mistakenly assume that their decision-making ability is unaffected by increases in stress (Helmreich et al., 1985), have few protections against a sudden loss of meaning such as the preposterous possibility that a captain is taking off without clearance, directly into the path of another 747.

Even when people try to act with honesty, trust, and self-respect, if they do so with little social support, their efforts are compromised. For example, linguists who analyzed the conversations at Tenerife and in the crash of Air Florida flight 90 in Washington concluded that the copilots in both cases used "devices of mitigation" to soften the effects of their requests and suggestions:

A mitigated instruction might be phrased as a question or hedged with qualifications such as "would" or "could." . . . (I)t was found that the speech of subordinate crew members was much more likely to be mitigated than the speech of captains. It was also found that topics introduced in mitigated speech were less likely to be followed-up by other crew members and less likely to be ratified by the captain. Both of these effects relate directly to the situation in which a subordinate crew member makes a correct solution that is ignored. The value of training in unmitigated speech is strongly suggested by these results. (O'Hare and Roscoe, 1990: 219)

If a role system collapses among people for whom trust, honesty, and self-respect are underdeveloped, then they are on their own. And fear often swamps their resourcefulness. If, however, a role system collapses among people where trust, honesty, and self-respect are more fully developed, then new options, such as mutual adaptation, blind imitation of creative solutions, and trusting compliance, are created. When a formal structure collapses, there is no leader, no roles, no routines, no sense. That is what we may be seeing in Mann Gulch. Dodge can't lead because the role system in which he is a leader disappears. But what is worse, Dodge can't rely on his crewmembers to trust him, question him, or pay attention to him, because they don't know him and there is no time to change this. The key question is, When formal structure collapses, what, if anything, is left? The answer to that question may well be one of life or death.

STRUCTURES FOR RESILIENCE

While the answer to that question is not a matter of life or death for organizational theorists, they do have an interest in how it comes out. A theorist who hears Maclean's question, "what the structure of a small outfit should be when its business is to meet sudden danger and prevent disaster," might come back with a series of follow-up questions based on thinking in organizational studies. I look briefly at four such questions to link Mann Gulch with other concepts and to suggest how these linkages might guide further research.

First, there is the follow-up question, Is "small" necessarily a key dimension, since this group is also young and transient? Maclean calls the 16-person smokejumper crew "small," except that it is conventional in the group literature to treat any group of more than 10 people as large (Bass, 1990: 604). Because there is so little communication within the crew and because it operates largely through obtrusive controls like rules and supervision (Perrow, 1986), it acts more like a large formal group with mediated communication than a small informal group with direct communication.

It is striking how little communication occurred during the three and a half hours of this episode. There was little discussion during the noisy, bumpy plane ride, and even less as individuals retrieved equipment scattered on the north slope. After a quick meal together, people began hiking toward the river but quickly got separated from one another. Then they were suddenly turned around, told to run for the ridge, and quickly ran out of breath as they scaled the steep south slope. The minimal communication is potentially important because of the growing evidence (e.g., Eisenhardt, 1993: 132) that nonstop talk, both vocal and nonverbal, is a crucial source of coordination in complex systems that are susceptible to catastrophic disasters.

The lack of communication, coupled with the fact that this is a temporary group in the early stages of its history, should heighten the group's vulnerability to disruption. As Bass (1990: 637) put it, "Groups that are unable to interact easily or that do not have the formal or informal structure that enables quick reactions are likely to experience stress (Bass, 1960). Panic ensues when members of a group lack superordinate goals—goals that transcend the self-interests of each participant." While the smokejumpers have the obvious superordinate goal of containing fires, their group ties may not be sufficiently developed for this to be a group goal that overrides self-interest. Or Bass's proposition itself may be incomplete, failing to acknowledge that unless superordinate goals are overlearned, they will be discarded in situations of danger.

Second, there is the follow-up question, Is "structure" what we need to understand in Mann Gulch, or might structuring also be important? By structure, I mean "a complex medium of control which is continually produced and recreated in interaction and yet shapes that interaction: structures are constituted and constitutive . . . of interpersonal cognitive processes, power dependencies, and contextual constraints" (Ranson, Hinings, and Greenwood, 1980: 1, 3). Structuring, then, consists of two patterns and the relationships between them. The first pattern, which Ranson et al. variously described as informal structure, agency, or social construction, consists of interaction patterns that stabilize meaning by creating shared interpretive schemes. I refer to this pattern as shared provinces of meaning, or meaning. The second pattern, variously described as configuration, contextual constraints, or a vehicle that embodies dominant meanings, refers to a framework of roles, rules, procedures, configured activities, and authority relations that reflect and facilitate meanings. I refer to this second pattern as structural frameworks of constraint, or frameworks.

Meanings affect frameworks, which affect meaning. This is the basic point of the growing body of work on structuration (e.g., Riley, 1983; Poole, Seibold, and McPhee, 1985), understood as the mutual constitution of frameworks and meanings (Ranson, Hinings, and Greenwood, 1980) or relations and typifications (DiMaggio, 1991) or structures and structuring (Barley, 1986). Missing in this work is attention to reversals of structuration (Giddens, 1984). The use of descriptive words in structuration theory such as "continually produced," "recreated in interaction," "constituted," and "constitutive" directs attention away from losses of frameworks and losses of meaning. For example, Ranson, Hinings, and Greenwood (1980: 5) asserted that the "deep structure of schema which are taken for granted by members enables them to recognize, interpret, and negotiate even strange and unanticipated situations, and thus continuously to create and reenact the sense and meaning of structural forms during the course of interaction." The Mann Gulch disaster is a case in which people were unable to negotiate strangeness. Frameworks and meanings destroyed rather than constructed one another.

This fugitive quality of meaning and frameworks in Mann Gulch suggests that the process of structuring itself may be more unstable than we realized. Structuring, understood as constitutive relations between meaning and frameworks, may be a deviation-amplifying cause loop (Maruyama, 1963; Weick, 1979) capable of intensifying either an increase or decrease in either of the two connected elements. Typically, we see instances of increase in which more shared meanings lead to more elaborate frameworks of roles, which lead to further developments of shared meaning, etc. What we fail to realize is that, when elements are tied together in this direct manner, once one of them declines, this decline can also spread and become amplified as it does so. Fewer shared meanings lead to less elaborate frameworks, less meaning, less elaborate frameworks, and so on. Processes that mutually constitute also have the capability to mutually destroy one another.

If structuration is treated as a deviation-amplifying process, then this suggests the kind of structure that could have prevented the Mann Gulch disaster. What people needed was a structure in which there was both an inverse and a direct relationship between role systems and meaning. This is the only pattern that can maintain resilience in the face of crisis. The resilience can take one of two forms. Assume that we start with an amplifying system like the one in Mann Gulch. The role system lost its structure, which led to a loss of meaning, which led to a further loss of structure, and so on. This is the pattern associated with a deviation-amplifying feedback loop in which an initial change unfolds unchecked in the same direction. One way to prevent this amplification is to retain the direct relation between structure and meaning (less role structure leads to less meaning, more structure leads to more meaning) but create an inverse relation between meaning and structure (less meaning, more structure, and vice versa). This inverse relationship can be understood as follows: When meaning becomes problematic and decreases, this is a signal for people to pay more attention to their formal and informal social ties and to reaffirm and/or reconstruct them. These actions produce more structure, which then increases meaning, which then decreases the attention directed at structure. Puzzlement intensifies attentiveness to the social, which reduces puzzlement.

The other form of control arises when a change in structure, rather than a change in meaning, is responsible for counteracting the fluctuations in sensibleness. In this variation, less structure leads to more meaning, and more meaning then produces more structure. The inverse relationship between structure and meaning can be understood this way: When social ties deteriorate, people try harder to make their own individual sense of what is happening, both socially and in the world. These operations increase meaning, and they increase the tendency to reshape structure consistent with heightened meaning. Alienation intensifies attentiveness to meaning, which reduces alienation.

What is common to both of these controlled forms is an alternation between attention to frameworks and attention to meanings. More attention to one leads to more ignorance of the other, followed by efforts to correct this imbalance, which then creates a new imbalance. In the first scenario, when meaning declines, people pay more attention to frameworks, they ignore meaning temporarily, and as social relations become clearer, their attention shifts back to meanings. In the second scenario, when social relations decline, people pay more attention to meaning, they ignore frameworks temporarily, and as meanings become clearer, attention shifts back to frameworks. Both scenarios illustrate operations of wisdom: In Meacham's words, ignorance and knowledge grow together. Either of these two controlled patterns should reduce the likelihood of disaster in Mann Gulch. As the smokejumpers begin to lose structure they either also lose meaning, which alerts them to be more attentive to the structure they are losing, or they gain individual meaning, which leads them to realign structure. The second alternative may be visible in the actions taken by Dodge and Rumsey and Sallee. This may seem like a great deal of fretting about one single word in Maclean's question, "structure." What I have tried to show is that when we transform this word from a static image into a process, we spot what looks like a potential for collapse in any process of social sensemaking that is tied together by constitutive relations. And we find that social sensemaking may be most stable when it is simultaneously constitutive and destructive, when it is capable of increasing both ignorance and knowledge at the same time. That seems like a fair return for reflecting on a single word.

Third, there is the follow-up question, Is "outfit" the best way to describe the smokejumpers? An outfit is normally defined as "a group associated in an undertaking requiring close cooperation, as a military unit" (Random House, 1987: 1374). The smokejumpers are tied together largely by pooled interdependence, since the job of each one is to clear adjacent portions of a perimeter area around a blaze so that the fire stops for lack of fuel. Individual efforts to clear away debris are pooled and form a fire line. What is significant about pooled interdependence is that it can function without much cohesion (Bass, 1990: 622). And this is what may have trapped the crew. Given the constantly changing composition of the smokejumping crews, the task largely structured their relations. Simply acting in concert was enough, and there was no need to know each other well in addition. This social form resembles what Eisenberg (1990: 160) called nondisclosive intimacy, by which he meant relationships rooted in collective action that stress "coordination of action over the alignment of cognitions, mutual respect over agreement, trust over empathy, diversity over homogeneity, loose over tight coupling, and strategic communication over unrestricted candor." Nondisclosive intimacy is a sufficient ground for relating as long as the task stays constant and the environment remains stable.

What the Mann Gulch disaster suggests is that nondisclosive intimacy may limit the development of emotional ties that keep panic under control in the face of obstacles. Closer ties permit clearer thinking, which enables people to find paths around obstacles. For example, when Rumsey squeezed through a crevice in the ridge just ahead of the fire, he collapsed "half hysterically" into a juniper bush, where he would have soon burned to death. His partner Sallee stopped next to him, looked at him coldly, never said a word, and just stood there until Rumsey roused himself, and the two then ran together over the ridge and down to a rock slide where they were better able to move around and duck the worst flames (Maclean, p. 107). Sallee's surprisingly nuanced prodding of his partner suggests the power of close ties to moderate panic.

One might expect that the less threatening the environment, the less important are relational issues in transient groups, but as Perrow (1984) emphasized in his normal accident theory, there are few safe environments. If events are increasingly interdependent, then small unrelated flaws can interact to produce something monstrous. Maclean saw this clearly at Mann Gulch: The colossal fire blowup in Mann Gulch was "shaped by little screwups that fitted together tighter and tighter until all became one and the same thing—the fateful blowup. Such is much of tragedy in modern times and probably always has been except that past tragedy refrained from speaking of its association with screwups and blowups" (Maclean, 1992: 92).

Nondisclosive intimacy is not the only alternative to "outfit" as a way to describe the smokejumpers. Smith (1983) argued that individual behaviors, perceptions of reality, identities, and acts of leadership are influenced by intergroup processes. Of special relevance to Mann Gulch is Smith's reanalysis of the many groups that formed among the 16 members of the Uruguayan soccer team who survived for 10 weeks in an inaccessible region of the Chilean Andes mountains after their aircraft, carrying 43 people, crashed (see Read, 1974 for the original account of this event). Aside from the eerie coincidence that both disasters involved 16 young males, Smith's analysis makes the important point that 16 people are not just an outfit, they are a social system within which multiple groups emerge and relate to one another. It is these intergroup relationships that determine what will be seen as acts of leadership and which people may be capable of supplying those acts. In the Andes crash, demands shifted from caring for the wounded, in which two medical students took the lead, to acquiring food and water, where the team captain became leader, to articulating that the group would not be rescued and could sustain life only if people consumed the flesh of the dead, to executing and resymbolizing this survival tactic, to selecting and equipping an expeditionary group to hike out and look for help, and finally to finding someone able to explain and rationalize their decisions to the world once they had been rescued.

What Smith shows is that this group of 16 forms and reforms in many different directions during its history, each time with a different coherent structure of people at the top, middle, and bottom, each with different roles. What also becomes clear is that any attempt to pinpoint the leader or to explain survival by looking at a single set of actions is doomed to failure because it does not reflect how needs change as a crisis unfolds, nor does it reflect how different coherent groupings form to meet the new needs.

The team in the Andes had 10 weeks and changing threats of bleeding, hygiene, starvation, avalanche, expedition, rescue, and accounting, whereas the team in Mann Gulch had more like 10 minutes and the increasingly singular threat of being engulfed in fire. Part of the problem in Mann Gulch is the very inability for intergroup structures to form. The inability to form subgroups within the system may be due to such things as time pressure, the relative unfamiliarity of the smokejumpers with one another compared with the interdependent members of a visible sports team, the inability to communicate, the articulation of a common threat very late in the smokejumpers' exposure to Mann Gulch, and ambiguity about means that would clearly remove the threat, compared with the relative clarity of the means needed by the soccer players to deal with each of their threats.

The point is, whatever chance the smokejumpers might have had to survive Mann Gulch is not seen as clearly if we view them as a single group rather than as a social system capable of differentiating into many different sets of subgroups. The earlier discussion of virtual role systems suggested that an intergroup perspective could be simulated in the head and that this should heighten resilience. Smith makes it clear that, virtual or not, intergroup dynamics affect survival, even if we overlook them in our efforts to understand the group or the "outfit."

As a fourth and final follow-up question, If there is a structure that enables people to meet sudden danger, who builds and maintains it? A partial answer is Ken Smith's intergroup analysis, suggesting that the needed structure consists of many structures, built and maintained by a shifting configuration of the same people. As I said, this perspective makes sense when time is extended, demands change, and there is no formal leader at the beginning of the episode. But there is a leader in Mann Gulch, the foreman. There is also a second in command and the remaining crew, which means there is a top (foreman), middle (second in command), and bottom (remaining crew). If we take this a priori structure seriously, then the Mann Gulch disaster can be understood as a dramatic failure of leadership, reminiscent of those lapses in leadership increasingly well documented by people who study cockpit/crew resource management in aircraft accidents (e.g., Wiener, Kanki, and Helmreich, 1993).

The captain of an aircrew, who is analogous to a player-coach on a basketball team (Hackman, 1993: 55), can often have his or her greatest impact on team functioning before people get into a tight, time-critical situation. Ginnett (1993) has shown that aircraft captains identified by check airmen as excellent team leaders spent more time team building when the team first formed than did leaders judged as less expert. Leaders of highly effective teams briefed their crewmembers on four issues: the task, crew boundaries, standards and expected behaviors (norms), and authority dynamics. Captains spent most time on those of the four that were not predefined by the organizational context within which the crew worked. Typically, this meant that excellent captains did not spend much time on routinized tasks, but less-excellent captains did. Crew boundaries were enlarged and made more permeable by excellent captains when, for example, they regarded the flight attendants, gate personnel, and air traffic controllers as members of the total flight crew. This contrasts with less-excellent captains, who drew a boundary around the people in the cockpit and separated them from everyone else.

Excellent captains modeled norms that made it clear that safety, effective communication, and cooperation were expected from everyone. Of special interest, because so little communication occurred at Mann Gulch, is how the norm, "communication is important," was expressed. Excellent crews expect one another to enact any of these four exchanges: "(1) I need to talk to you; (2) I listen to you; (3) I need you to talk to me; or even (4) I expect you to talk to me" (Ginnett, 1993: 88). These four complement and operationalize the spirit of Campbell's social imperatives of trust, honesty, and self-respect. But they also show the importance of inquiry, advocacy, and assertion when people do not understand the reasons why other people are doing something or ignoring something (Helmreich and Foushee, 1993: 21).

Issues of authority are handled differently by excellent captains. They shift their behaviors between complete democracy and complete autocracy during the briefing and thereafter, which makes it clear that they are capable of a range of styles. They establish competence and their capability to assume legitimate authority by doing the briefing in a rational manner, comfortably, with appropriate technical language, all of which suggests that they have given some thought to the upcoming flight and have constructed a framework within which the crew will work.

Less autocratic than this enactment of their legitimate authority is their willingness to disavow perfection. A good example of a statement that tells crewmembers they too must take responsibility for one another is this: "I just want you guys to understand that they assign the seats in this airplane based on seniority, not on the basis of competence. So anything you can see or do that will help out, I'd sure appreciate hearing about it" (Ginnett, 1993: 90). Notice that the captain is not saying, I am not competent to be the captain. Instead, the captain is saying, we're all fallible. We all make mistakes. Let's keep an eye on one another and speak up when we think a mistake is being made.

Most democratic and participative is the captain's behavior to engage the crew. Briefings held by excellent captains last no longer than do those of the less-excellent captains, but excellent captains talk less, listen more, and resort less to "canned presentations."

Taken together, all of these team-building activities increase the probability that constructive, informed interactions can still occur among relative strangers even when they get in a jam. If we compare the leadership of aircraft captains to leadership in Mann Gulch, it is clear that Wag Dodge did not build his team of smokejumpers in advance.

Furthermore, members of the smokejumper crew did not keep each other informed of what they were doing or the reasons for their actions or the situational model they were using to generate these reasons. These multiple failures of leadership may be the result of inadequate training, inadequate understanding of leadership processes in the late '40s, or may be attributable to a culture emphasizing individual work rather than group work. Or these failures of leadership may reflect the fact that even the best leaders and the most team-conscious members can still suffer when structures begin to pull apart, leaving in their wake senselessness, panic, and cosmological questions. If people are lucky, and interpersonally adept, their exposure to questions of cosmology is confined to an episode. If they are not, that exposure stretches much further. Which is just about where Maclean would want us to end.

References

Ancona, Deborah G., and David F. Caldwell 1992 "Bridging the boundary: External activity and performance in organizational teams." Administrative Science Quarterly, 37: 634-665.

Asch, Solomon 1952 Social Psychology. Englewood Cliffs, NJ: Prentice-Hall.

Barley, Stephen R. 1986 "Technology as an occasion for structuring: Evidence from observations of CT scanners and the social order of radiology departments." Administrative Science Quarterly, 31: 78-108.

Barthol, R. P., and N. D. Ku 1959 "Regression under stress to first learned behavior." Journal of Abnormal and Social Psychology, 59: 134-136.

Bass, Bernard M. 1960 Leadership, Psychology, and Organizational Behavior. New York: Harper. 1990 Bass and Stogdill's Handbook of Leadership. New York: Free Press.

Beach, Lee R., and Raanan Lipshitz 1993 "Why classical decision theory is an inappropriate standard for evaluation and aiding most human decision making." In Gary A. Klein, Judith Orasanu, Roberta

Calderwood, and Caroline E. Zsambok (eds.), Decision Making in Action: Models and Methods: 21-35. Norwood, NJ: Ablex.

Bigelow, John 1992 "Developing managerial wisdom." Journal of Management Inquiry, 1: 143-153.

Brown, Richard Harvey 1978 "Bureaucracy as praxis: Toward a political phenomenology of formal organizations." Administrative Science Quarterly, 23: 365-382.

Bruner, Jerome 1983 In Search of Mind. New York: Harper. 1986 Actual Minds, Possible Worlds. Cambridge, MA: Harvard University Press.

Campbell, Donald T. 1990 "Asch's moral epistemology for socially shared knowledge." In Irwin Rock (ed.), The Legacy of Solomon Asch: Essays in Cognition and Social Psychology: 39-52. Hillsdale, NJ: Erlbaum.

Daft, Richard L., and Norman B. Macintosh 1981 "A tentative exploration into the amount and equivocality of information processing in organizational work units." Administrative Science Quarterly, 26: 207-224.

DiMaggio, Paul 1991 "The micro-macro dilemma in organizational research: Implications of role-system theory." In Joan Huber (ed.), Micro-macro Changes in Sociology: 76-98. Newbury Park, CA: Sage.

Eisenberg, Eric M. 1990 "Jamming: Transcendence through organizing." Communication research, 17: 139-164.

Eisenhardt, Kathleen M. 1993 "High reliability organizations meet high velocity environments: Common dilemmas in nuclear power plants, aircraft carriers, and microcomputer firms." In Karlene H. Roberts (ed.), New Challenges to Understanding Organizations: 117-135. New York: Macmillan.

Foushee, H. Clayton 1984 "Dyads and triads at 35,000 feet." American Psychologist, 39: 885-893.

Freud, Sigmund 1959 Group Psychology and the Analysis of the Ego. (First published in 1922.) New York: Norton.

Giddens, Anthony 1984 The Constitution of Society. Berkeley: University of California Press.

Ginnett, Robert C. 1993 "Crews as groups: Their formation and their leadership." In Earl L. Wiener, Barbara G. Kanki, and Robert L. Helmreich (eds.), Cockpit Resource Management: 71-98. San Diego: Academic Press.

Hackman, J. Richard 1993 "Teams, leaders, and organizations: New directions for crew-oriented flight training." In Earl L. Wiener, Barbara G. Kanki, and Robert L. Helmreich (eds.), Cockpit Resource Management: 47-69. San Diego: Academic Press.

Harper, Douglas 1987 Working Knowledge: Skill and Community in a Small Shop. Chicago: University of Chicago Press.

Helmreich, Robert L., and Clayton Foushee 1993 "Why crew resource management? Empirical and theoretical bases of human factors training in aviation." In Earl L. Wiener, Barbara G. Kanki, and Robert L. Helmreich (eds.), Cockpit Resource Management: 3-45. San Diego: Academic Press.

Helmreich, Robert L., Clayton H. Foushee, R. Benson, and W. Russini 1985 "Cockpit resource management: Exploring the attitude-performance linkage." Paper presented at Third Aviation Psychology Symposium, Ohio State University.

Heydebrand, Wolf V. 1989 "New organizational forms." Work and Occupations, 16: 323-357.

Hirsch, Paul, Stuart Michaels, and Ray Friedman 1987 "'Dirty hands' vs. 'clean models': Is sociology in danger of being seduced by economics?" Theory and Society, 16: 317-336.

Janowitz, Morris 1959 "Changing patterns of organizational authority: The military establishment." Administrative Science Quarterly, 3: 473-493.

King, Jonathan B. 1989 "Confronting chaos." Journal of Business Ethics, 8: 39-50.

Klein, Gary A. 1993 "A recognition-primed decision (RPD) model of rapid decision making." In Gary A. Klein, Judith Orasanu, Roberta Calderwood, and Caroline E. Zsambok (eds.), Decision Making in Action: Models and Methods: 138-147. Norwood, NJ: Ablex.

Lanir, Zvi 1989 "The reasonable choice of disaster: The shooting down of the Libyan airliner on 21 February 1973." Journal of Strategic Studies, 12:479-493.

Levi-Strauss, Claude 1966 The Savage Mind. Chicago: University of Chicago Press.

Maclean, Norman 1992 Young Men and Fire. Chicago: University of Chicago Press.

March, James G. 1989 Decisions and Organizations. Oxford: Blackwell.

Maruyama, Magorah 1963 "The second cybernetics: Deviation-amplifying mutual causal process." American Scientist, 51: 164-179.

McDougall, William 1920 The Group Mind. New York: Putnam.

Meacham, John A. 1983 "Wisdom and the context of knowledge." In D. Kuhn and J. A. Meacham (eds.), Contributions in Human Development, 8: 111-134. Basel: Karger.

Miles, Ray E., and Charles C. Snow 1992 "Causes of failure in network organizations." California Management Review, 34(4): 53-72.

Miller, Danny 1990 The Icarus Paradox. New York: Harper.

Mintzberg, Henry 1983 Structure in Fives: Designing Effective Organizations. Englewood Cliffs, NJ: Prentice-Hall.

Morgan, Gareth, Peter J. Frost, and Louis R. Pondy 1983 "Organizational symbolism." In L. R. Pondy, P. J. Frost, G. Morgan, and T. C. Dandridge (eds.), Organizational Symbolism: 3-35. Greenwich, CT: JAI Press.

Neisser, Ulric, and Eugene Winograd 1988 Remembering Reconsidered: Ecological and Traditional Approaches to the Study of Memory. New York: Cambridge University Press.

O'Hare, David, and Stanley Roscoe 1990 Flightdeck Performance: The Human Factor. Ames, IA: Iowa State University Press.

Orasanu, Judith, and Terry Connolly 1993 "The reinvention of decision making." In Gary A. Klein, Judith Orasanu, Roberta Calderwood, and Caroline E. Zsambok (eds.), Decision Making in Action: Models and Methods: 3-20. Norwood, NJ: Ablex.

Perrow, Charles 1984 Normal Accidents. New York: Basic Books.1986 Complex Organizations, 3rd ed. New York: Random House.

Poole, M. Scott, David R. Seibold, and Robert D. McPhee 1985 "Group decision-making as a structurational process." Quarterly Journal of Speech, 71:74-102.

Pyne, Stephen 1989 Fire on the Rim. New York: Weidenfeld & Nicolson.

Random House 1987 Dictionary of the English Language, 2d ed.: Unabridged. New York: Random House.

Ranson, Stewart, Bob Hinings, and Royston T. Greenwood 1980 "The structuring of organizational structures." Administrative Science Quarterly, 25: 1-17.

Read, P. P. 1974 Alive. London: Pan Books.

Reason, James 1990 Human Error. New York: Cambridge University Press.

Reed, M. 1991 "Organizations and rationality: The odd couple." Journal of Management Studies, 28: 559-567.

Riley, Patricia 1983 "A structurationalist account of political culture." Administrative Science Quarterly, 28: 411 137.

Runkel, Phillip J., and Joseph E. McGrath 1972 Research on Human Behavior. New York: Holt, Rinehart, and Winston.

Schutz, William C. 1961 "The ego, FIRO theory and the leader as completer." In Louis Petrullo and Bernard M. Bass (eds.), Leadership and Interpersonal Behavior: 48-65. New York: Holt, Rinehart, and Winston.

Scott, W. Richard 1987 Organizations: Rational, Natural, and Open Systems. Englewood Cliffs, NJ: Prentice-Hall.

Smith, Ken K. 1983 "An intergroup perspective on individual behavior." In J. Richard Hackman, Edward E. Lawler, and Lyman M. Porter (eds.), Perspectives on Behavior in Organizations: 397-408. New York: McGraw-Hill.

Taylor, Shelby E. 1989 Positive Illusions. New York: Basic Books.

Weick, Karl E. 1979 The Social Psychology of Organizing, 2d ed. Reading, MA: Addison-Wesley. 1985 "Cosmos vs. chaos: Sense and nonsense in electronic contexts." Organizational Dynamics, 14(Autumn): 50-64. 1990 "The vulnerable system: Analysis of the Tenerife air disaster." Journal of Management, 16: 571-593.

Weick, Karl E., and Karlene H. Roberts 1993 "Collective mind in organizations: Heedful interrelating on flight decks." Administrative Science Quarterly, 38: 357-381.

Westley, Frances R. 1990 "Middle managers and strategy: Microdynamics of inclusion." Strategic Management Journal, 11: 337-351.

Westrum, Ron 1982 "Social intelligence about hidden events." Knowledge, 3: 381-400.

White, S. K. 1988 The Recent Work of Jurgen Habermas: Reason, Justice, and Modernity. Cambridge: Cambridge University Press.

Wiener, Earl L., Barbara G. Kanki, and Robert L. Helmreich 1993 Cockpit Resource Management. San Diego: Academic Press.

Wiley, Norbert 1988 "The micro-macro problem in social theory." Sociological Theory, 6: 254-261.

Chapter 4

Prologue

Victoria J. Marsick
Professor of Adult Learning and Continuing Education
Columbia Teachers College

Learning in the Workplace: The Case for Reflectivity and Critical Reflectivity

Victoria J. Marsick

Prologue:

Victoria J. Marsick

Overview

I selected this article for inclusion in this volume because it presages many views that I have researched and written about in my own career that I believe represent an early articulation of how the terms "work," "organization," and "workplace learning" are understood today. In this article I reviewed the near ubiquitous behaviorist lens for designing training. I discussed why behaviorism was suited to the industrial era, but *not* the knowledge era. I examined learning-theory alternatives to behaviorism that are based on constructivism, postmodernism, and critical theory. I emphasized the shifting balance in workplace learning towards informal learning, reflective practice, and critical reflection (or double-loop learning) oriented to changing assumptions, mindsets, and ways of thinking about work.

In this prologue, I show how these views have influenced practice and thinking about learning in the workplace today. I discuss trends in the organization and workplace context; elaborate on current learning theories based on constructivism, postmodernism, and critical theory; and focus on recognition of the shift to informal learning at the individual, group, and system level at work.

Workplace Context and Trends

In the article that follows, I discussed the organizational transition toward "entrepreneurship and intrapreneurship, decentralization, networking, participatory management, flattening of middle management, and a culture of empowerment" (p. 189), as well as internationalization (now termed "globalization") and use of intelligent technology. These trends continue today (Perrin & Marsick, 2012).

Further influencing learning—including informal learning in the workplace since my writing—it is clear that globalization has greatly amplified the business drive toward change and forced a reevaluation of the very nature of what it means to be competitive. Customers often want more choice among, and influence over, the products and services they buy. Businesses seek their input, implementing mechanisms to respond quickly to changing preferences and customize products for niche markets. Organizations seek talent around the world and value employees who are diverse, global, more highly educated and skilled. The workforce is smaller in number and often offshored, outsourced, and virtually connected. Suppliers, vendors, and a range of business partners work more frequently across organizational boundaries, sometimes needing to both cooperate and compete in their various business arrangements to get work done.

Technology, too, has driven innovation in the marketplace and changed the way we think about work and learning (Gephart, Marsick, & Shiotani, 2010). Technology enables just-in-time learning, often using mobile devices. Gaming, and other forms of interactive immersive learning, shape new patterns of thinking and engagement. Collaboration is frequently powered by online social networking. Karen Watkins also writes about the way that templates and tools embedded in new technologies democratize the ability to design interactive learning.

Along with generational shifts in habits and preferences, these trends have been altering the way in which architects design space for collaborative vs. focused work, learning, and socializing. A new survey of knowledge workers by Gensler Architects (2013), for example, "examines the design factors that create an effective workplace; how design can better support knowledge worker engagement, satisfaction, and performance; and the influence of the workplace on organizational culture." Informal learning can be enhanced by these new space configurations. Recently, for example, I visited a newly designed employee café space in a hotel chain business headquarters. Light and airy, it offered many different configurations, table and seating arrangements, and circular pods that were technology-enabled for hosting of different kinds of work-related meetings. These relaxed, collaborative spaces appeal to a new generation of mobile, technology-proficient workers who eschew rows of cubicles for environments that mirror Google or Apple offices where work and relaxation are intertwined, and formerly formal lines are crossed in meeting both personal and professional lifestyle needs.

Learning Theory Emphases Today

While behaviorism is (and always will be) valued for many kinds of workplace training, there has also been a rising interest in cognitive and affective dimensions of learning—fueled in part by cognitive science research and social interaction (Perrin & Marsick, 2012) and by acknowledgment of the role that emotional intelligence (Goleman, 1995) plays in work and learning outcomes.

These developments favor alternative learning theories that recognize learning as holistic, situated, and shaped as much by people as agents of their own interests as it is by the organization. There has always been a tension between individual goals and preferences and those of the organization—as Kurt Lewin observed in creating his well-known heuristic equation that posits behavior as a function of the interaction between a person and his/her environment (Weisbord, 2004). In the industrial era the balance of power was concentrated in the organization, and in many cases, it is still in these hands. However, knowledge workers are frequently intrinsically motivated and guided by loyalty to professional or other knowledge-based principles and norms in ways that make them unwilling to cede so much control to corporations. Alignment of goals and directions in work and in increasing learning requires negotiation—explicitly or implicitly—as to whose goals and preferences dominate in getting work done and learning new capabilities to support these demands.

Rhodes and Scheeres (2004) examined the ways that learning at work can be differently interpreted through the paradigm lenses of premodernism, modernism, and postmodernism. They pointed out that today's workplace is often characterized by postmodernism, which grew in opposition to the linear, rational, modern mindset I described in this article. They characterized postmodern organizations as having "flatter hierarchies, decentralized decision making, greater capacity and tolerance for ambiguity, permeable internal and external boundaries, empowerment of employees, capacity for renewal, self-organizing units, and self-integrating coordination mechanism" (Rhodes & Scheeres, 2004, p. 177). Rhodes and Scheeres pointed out that the rhetoric of change does not always match the reality of how learning is designed and supported. Their framing points to the need to engage new learning theories and reinterpret current theories—many of which were conceived, implemented, and codified under modernist workplace conditions. It is no coincidence that Malcolm Knowles subtitled his at-the-time revolutionary "bible" of adult learning as "The Modern Practice of Adult Education." Andragogy and other learning theories stand in need of reinterpretation and reconstruction to better serve and suit today's adults and workplace learners (Marsick, Nicolaides, & Watkins, in press).

Informal Learning at the Individual, Group, and System Level

In my article, I emphasized implications for growing reliance on informal and incdental learning through experience and reflection in/on action. What does this trend mean for workplace learning? Informal learning, and an awareness of its central role in group and organizational learning, is assuming an increasingly central role in the ways in which learning at work is designed and delivered (Marsick & Watkins, in press).

Many organizations follow what is known as the 70-20-10 rule for learning architecture, a heuristic first identified by the Center for Creative Leadership that suggests that 70% of learning occurs informally on the job, 20% through relationships, and 10% through formal training (Perrin

& Marsick, 2012). The 70-20-10 rule describes where or when people learn but does not focus on how people learn informally. Building on this insight, Perrin and Marsick (2012) conceptualized a "20-80 rule"—that is, as much as 20% of learning might be structured in some way and thus more formal whereas at least 80% is informal and incidental. These figures have wide support in research on workplace learning (Marsick, 2012). Framing the *how* of learning in this way can help in informal learning design and support, including ways that formal training can build in needed skills that will faciltate and strengthen informal learning back on the job.

Informal and incidental learning provide opportunities for individual sensemaking, experimentation, and following one's own goals and interests—though, without the benefit of guidance, feedback, coaching, and support, informal and incidental learning can also lead to errors in thinking and conclusion.

Informal learning is often enhanced through collaboration, joint problem solving, and knowledge sharing that can be described as group or organizational learning. Even though the idea of a "learning organization" is not as frequently invoked today as it was 10 years ago, it is widely recognized that individuals and organizations learn better when there is a culture that fosters conditions for group learning so that learning gains can be sustained and facilitated.

Closing

I concluded my earlier article by outlining characteristics of a "new paradigm" for workplace learning:

a broadening of the instrumental focus of learning, integration of personal and job-related development, an organizational model that functions as a learning system, a focus on group as well as individual learning, a concern for critical reflectivity and for problem setting as well as problem solving, emphasis on informal learning, and development of the organization as a learning environment.

I believe these insights not only hold today, but also have grown stronger, as reflected by the evidence and trends described above.

References

Gensler Architects. (2013). *2013 U.S. workplace survey: Executive summary.* New York, NY: Author.

Gephart, M A., Marsick, V. J., & Shiotani, A. K. (2010). *Institutionalizing a performance-based learning perspective* [Research report]. New York, NY: J. M. Huber Institute for Learning in Organizations, Teachers College, Columbia University.

Goleman, D. (1995). *Emotional intelligence: Why it can matter more than IQ.* New York, NY: Random House.

Marsick, V. J. (2012). How organizations can support and facilitate informal workplace learning. In *Knowledge management and organizational development: Training and corporate training* [Proceedings, II EDO International Congress, Autonomous University of Barcelona].

Marsick, V. J., Nicolaides, A., & Watkins, K. E. (in press). Adult learning theory and application in human resource and organization development. In N. Chalofsky, T. Rocco, & L. Morris (Eds.), *The handbook of human resource development: Theory and application.* San Francisco, CA: Jossey-Bass.

Marsick, V. J., & Watkins, K. E. (in press). Informal learning in learning organizations. In R. Poell, T. Rocco, & G. Roth (Eds.), *The Routledge companion to human resource development.* New York, NY: Routledge.

Perrin, C., & Marsick, V. J. (2012). *The reinforcement revolution: How informal learning makes training real* [White paper]. Tampa, FL: AchieveGlobal.

Rhodes, C., & Scheeres, H. (2004, July). Developing people in organizations: Working (on) identity. *Studies in Continuing Education, 26,* 175-193.

Weisbord, M. R. (2004). *Productive workplaces revisited.* San Francisco, CA: Jossey-Bass.

Learning in the Workplace: The Case for Reflectivity and Critical Reflectivity

Victoria J. Marsick

Abstract. Learning in the workplace has traditionally been understood primarily in terms of behaviorism, a perspective compatible with the machine-like design of organizations when training and development emerged as a field of practice. Adult educators have not challenged the desirability of that perspective directly, although various theorists suggest its modification through greater learner participation, problem-centeredness, experience basing, and concern for different learning styles. This article raises questions about the universal valuing of behaviorism in workplace learning based on a review of trends in organizations in the post-industrial era and analysis of theorists within and outside the field who emphasize the importance of reflectivity and critical reflectivity in learning. The author then describes emerging characteristics of a new paradigm for understanding workplace learning and concludes with a discussion of its limits.

Workplace training and development is a field of practice that is rapidly moving toward an identity of its own. The American Society for Training and Development (ASTD) (1986) notes that "employee training is by far the largest delivery system for adult education" (p. 7). ASTD estimates that approximately $30 billion is spent annually by employers for formal training and $180 billion for informal training, while the Government spends an additional $5 billion for training.

While adult educators often lay claim to the professional preparation of trainers, many such programs are based on theory from a variety of disciplines other than adult learning (ASTD, 1981). If any discipline has dominated theory-building in training, it has been psychology, particularly the school of behaviorism (Goldstein, 1980). This article questions this continued primary reliance on behaviorism. It argues that behaviorism does not foster the reflective abilities needed to assist people at all levels to learn in the workplace, particularly in their informal interactions, although such training might successfully develop specific skills.

The article begins with a brief description of how behaviorism manifests in workplace training as well as a discussion of some modifications by adult educators. The next section is a review of trends in organizations that suggest the need for a new paradigm for understanding workplace learning in the post-industrial era. Scholars concerned with learning that emphasizes reflectivity and critical reflectivity are then examined in terms of their "fit" with workplace learning. Finally, the author discusses the emerging characteristics and limits of a new paradigm for workplace learning.

BEHAVIORISM AND SOME MODIFICATIONS

Most descriptions of, and prescriptions for, workplace learning are based in a behavioristic paradigm. The term "paradigm" is here used to mean a fundamental world view that influences the way in which its adherents define reality and locate and solve problems within it. Behaviorism, while interpreted somewhat differently by its adherents, is defined as that educational philosophy which emphasizes environmental conditioning of responses. Marsick (1987) summarizes characteristics of the current behavioristic paradigm for workplace learning as follows:

1. It is behaviorally-oriented with performance outcomes that can be observed, quantified and criterion-referenced.
2. Personal and work-related development are separated.
3. The organizational ideal for which training is designed is a well-functioning machine with clear, hierarchical lines of authority, jobs that do not overlap, and rational systems of delegation and control.
4. Training is designed to meet needs of individuals, not groups.
5. Learning is designed on a "deficit" model that measures individuals against standard, expert-derived norms.

6. Problem-solving emphasizes objectivity, rationality, and step-by-step procedures.

7. Training typically consists of classroom-based, formal group activities.

8. Trainers focus on "pure" learning problems, with support provided to the organization to manipulate the environment to sustain outcomes. (pp. 1-2)

Some training models depart from this purely behavioristic paradigm. Two examples are andragogy and experiential learning. Andragogy (Knowles, 1980) departs from the behaviorist paradigm in that the learner takes a more active role in controlling learning objectives and the means to attain them. Andragogy is increasingly used in workplace training design, although there is, to date, little empirical evidence assessing its usefulness in business and industry. Another modification is experiential learning theory with its concern for differences in learning style (Kolb, 1984). Kolb's work also departs from behaviorism in that it is first concerned with the experience of the learner, not the intent of the experts designing the activity. Knowles and Kolb have substituted a degree of learner-centeredness for the expert control of behaviorism. However, the trainer using these models seldom advocates substituting learner preferences for those of the organization.

The behavioristic models of practice developed as the field emerged to meet the needs of organizations after World War II were based on a production orientation unlike today's service economy, an educational level of the workforce far below today's norm, and technology considered primitive by today's standards. Much of the early theory came from military experience prior to guerrilla warfare, and was well-suited to organizations whose predominant mode of operation might be described by the metaphor of a machine (Morgan, 1986). Characteristics of the social organization of the workplace included logic, rationality, linear cause-effect relationships, clear demarcation of responsibilities, hierarchical control, and forged unification of the movement of parts into a whole which minimized duplication and overlap. In tandem, training was developed to prepare people for machine-like work according to their levels in the hierarchy much as in an assembly line. Workers' deficits would be systematically filled or fixed as they passed along the organizational conveyor belt until they reached the point where the organization decided they could go no further. They had either acquired the prescribed skills to fill the prescribed slot or were matched to a different line to which they were considered more suited.

Two points must be made about the behaviorist paradigm before proceeding with a discussion of an alternative viewpoint. First, there are times when behavioristic training is entirely appropriate to the task at hand, particularly when workers are learning a precise technique that allows no variation. As will be argued later, however, even in these cases there are often good reasons for mediating this instrumental focus. Second, alternatives to the behaviorist paradigm have always existed, particularly in management development or organization development (OD) where answers are not as clear-cut (e.g., interpersonal communications, team building, decision making in a turbulent environment, group dynamics). OD has based much of its learning design on the action research strategies of Kurt Lewin, a philosophy of pragmatism grounded in John Dewey's experiential learning, and on a systems approach. However, trainers have never fully adopted these strategies for learning, perhaps because their mandate does not typically extend beyond instruction to the wider-scale organizational interventions advocated by OD.

Behaviorism has thus become a dominant force in workplace training. The next section reviews changing trends in organizations that challenge this perspective in the post-industrial era.

CHANGES IN ORGANIZATIONS

A group of popular writers have examined trends and pockets of innovation in successful businesses: entrepreneurship and intrapreneurship, decentralization, networking, participatory management, flattening of middle management, and a culture of empowerment (Kanter, 1983; Naisbitt & Aburdene, 1985; Peters & Waterman, 1982; Toffler, 1985). While each holds a somewhat different focus, these authors collectively call for new forms of organization if business is to survive and flourish in this post-industrial technological era. At the heart of their arguments is concern for *intangible* factors not always factored into the bottom line: human values, new forms of social interaction, commitment, a service orientation, risk-taking, independent thinking, integration among units within the organization as well as in external interfaces, and creativity. These authors essentially argue that productivity must be redefined; short-run profit taking must be mediated by a longer-term perspective on productivity that capitalizes on the creativity of its human resources.

Pressures to change come from both the external world of business, particularly the technological revolution and the increase in international competition, and the nature of the workforce itself. Carnevale and Goldstein (1983) highlight some of these factors: the impact of the baby boom and of women entering the market in large numbers, a larger pool of both more highly-educated white middle class workers and less well-educated minorities and immigrants, and the mid-career glut.

Change, however, requires far more than tinkering with the latest management fad, re-writing policies and procedures, or providing a training course in techniques, as both advocates and critics learned with respect to Japanese models of management. Change requires a fundamental shift in thinking. Lincoln (1985) suggests that, in fact, a paradigm revolution is taking place in almost all fields of human endeavor. She draws on the analysis of Schwarz and Ogilvy (1979) of many formal disciplines to highlight the following characteristics of such a shift: from simplicity to complexity, from hierarchy to heterarchy, from a mechanical model to a holographic one in which people can play multiple roles (just as the whole can be recreated from any of its parts in the laser-created photograph called a hologram), from predictability to ambiguity, from direct to mutual causality, from planned assembly of complex systems to their spontaneous creation through interaction, and from objectivity to an awareness of multiple perspectives.

To summarize, organizations are changing rapidly due to changes in the external environment, technology, and the workforce. New models are required to understand, function within, and learn in today's organizations. These models suggest a move away from the mechanistic orientation which fostered and encouraged tightly controlled behavioristic learning. In order to develop a new model for understanding workplace learning in the organization of today and/ or tomorrow, the next section reviews learning theorists who advocate reflection and critical reflectivity in practice.

LEARNING THEORY AND THE WORKPLACE

Carr and Kemmis (1983) also analyze paradigm shifts, their focus being teaching and learning. They identify a dominant technical paradigm based on logical positivism. Practitioners under this paradigm are urged to master and apply an objective body of knowledge, developed over time through controlled experiments and theory building. Education under this paradigm emphasizes transmission of pre-defined knowledge and skills. The role of the educator is to select the best technology to meet these ends.

One alternative to this technical emphasis is the interpretative paradigm, derived from humanism and phenomenology, in which learning is seen as a process of interaction leading to a better understanding of the meaning of experiences. From this viewpoint, education is a practical art in which the educator makes judgments based on his/her experience about how best to facilitate learning in personalized situations. While Carr and Kemmis find this paradigm more suited to learning in today's organizational contexts, they develop a third paradigm that goes one step further: the strategic paradigm, influenced by the critical social science of Habermas. Habermas (1971) suggested people learn differently when they pursue tasks than when they learn social norms or try to understand themselves. Key to learning in this paradigm is understanding the way in which social, cultural, historic, and economic forces shape meaning, and through this understanding, becoming empowered to act on these forces.

Yet training frequently emphasizes job-related knowledge and skills as if it is possible to divorce them from the rest of the worker's life. However, for learning to be effective, one must consider two deeper levels in which job skills are embedded: the social unit that shapes the individual's reactions at work, i.e., the organization and the immediate work group; and the individual's perception of self vis-à-vis the job and organization. Thus, learning for organizational productivity cannot be separated from learning for personal growth, as is often done. Nor can the burden of change be placed primarily on the individual in isolation from the organization.

Mezirow (1981, 1985) has developed a theory of learning, based on the critical social science of Habermas, that simultaneously accounts for the need to develop job skills and the fact that this learning is intertwined with learning about the organization and the self. Mezirow differentiates among three domains of learning: instrumental, dialogic, and self-reflective. He notes that instrumental learning refers to task-oriented problem solving, dialogic learning to the way in which people come to understand consensual norms in society, and self-reflective learning the way in which we learn to understand ourselves. Instrumental learning is what commonly takes place when people learn how to do their job better, and is thus frequently the focus of technical learning. People identify a problem, formulate a hypothetical course of action, try it out, observe the effects and assess results. Learning is generally prescriptive.

Dialogic learning, however, takes place in work settings when people learn about the culture of the organization or when they interpret policies, procedures, goals and objectives. Self-reflective learning, in turn, is directed at personal change. Its emphasis is critical reflection about oneself as a member of larger social units in order to ask fundamental questions about one's identity and the need for self-change. This change usually involves a transformation in "meaning perspectives," which are integrated psychological structures having dimensions of thought, will, and feeling, and which represent the way a person looks at self and relationships.

Instrumental, dialogic and self-reflective learning cannot easily be separated in any given situation. This is perhaps most obvious in managerial training. Technique, while very valuable, cannot be slavishly followed when dealing with people and "psyching out" unspoken norms and rules that influence applications. Here, the manager must balance the technically correct solution with the humanly viable one. While it is true, for example, that managers need skills in delegating tasks, frequently the reasons for non-delegation are embedded more deeply in the culture of the organization that rewards individual achievement and visibility or in the individual's personal working style.

People become most aware of the connections among learning in all three domains when they become critically reflective; that is, they bring their "assumptions, premises, criteria, and schemata into consciousness and vigorously critique them" (Mezirow, 1985, p. 25). Critically reflective learners are continually sensitive to why things are being done in a certain way, the values these reflect, the discrepancies that exist between what is being said and what is being done, and the way in which forces below the surface in the organization shape actions and outcomes. Critically reflective learners will not automatically follow an "expert's" recipe for solving what has been defined for them as a problem. They will determine whether or not they see the problem and proposed solution in the same way, probe the organizational context to ferret out facets of the culture that influence action, and attempt to understand how suggested solutions fit with their own image of themselves.

To summarize, all workplace learning cannot be explained by the technical paradigm. Some learning is best facilitated through interpretative strategies to assist people in understanding the meaning of their experience or through the strategic paradigm with an emphasis on changing consensual norms. By becoming critically reflective, people can better see the way in which task-related learning is often embedded in norms that also impact on one's personal identity. The next section further explores this concept of reflective and critically reflective learning from the perspective of workplace theory, particularly as it relates to the dynamics of informal learning.

INFORMAL LEARNING: REFLECTION-IN-ACTION

Being critically reflective means that one probes for assumptions, values and beliefs underlying actions. All learning in the workplace does not call for this depth of analysis, nor is it always encouraged or even tolerated. At the least, however, learning calls for some level of simple reflection, that is, the regular examination of one's experience to assess its effectiveness. While training can include reflection and critical reflection, it may be easier to examine these phenomena where they more naturally occur, that is, through informal learning while on-the-job. Training and education are delivery systems. By contrast, learning is the way in which individuals or groups acquire, interpret, reorganize, change or assimilate a related cluster of information, skills and feelings. It is also primary to the way in which people construct meaning in their personal and shared organizational lives.

Carnevale and Goldstein (1983) point out that a large percentage of learning takes place on-the-job (p. 37). A Honeywell study (Zemke, 1985) found that 50% of the ways in which managers learned to manage came from challenging job experiences, 30% from relationships with others in the organization, and only 20% from training (pp. 50-51). While important, training was helpful primarily when it was specifically timed to meet pressing job demands and because it increased the development of significant relationships with colleagues. These findings are reinforced by Kaplan, Drath, and Kofodimos (1985) in a study of effective executive self-development and McCauley (1986) in a literature review of managers' development.

There is less information on how people actually do learn informally. Schon's (1983) analysis of "reflection-in-action" sheds some light on this process. Schon critiques the relevance of scientific problem-solving models centered around "technical rationality" to the world of practice he calls "the swamp." In this world of practice, more attention must be paid to problem setting, an interactive process of naming the focus of our attention and framing the context in which a problem is understood. Schon depicts this process of problem setting as a reflective conversation with the situation in which the practitioner draws on his or her experience to understand the situation, attempt to frame the problem, suggest action, and then re-interpret the situation in light of the consequences of action.

Schon has worked with Argyris (1974, 1978) to develop the notion of single and double loop learning to explain what happens when people fail to produce desired results. In single loop learning, a person continues to try out the same strategy or variations on it, and continues to fail because his or her solutions are based in a set of undiscussible governing values that frustrate success, such as remaining in control and avoiding what are perceived as negative feelings. These values are tied to the culture of the organization and are counterproductive in part because they prevent critical inquiry into the reasons for failure. To get out of this bind, a person must get past the single loop into a double loop of learning— that is, become critically reflective and dig below the surface for the unstated values, assumptions, judgments, and attributions that govern one's actions and create the learning block. One must also become skilled at communicating this information to others as the basis for dialogue. Double loop learning is thus based on the generation of valid information, free and informed choice, and internal commitment to outcomes.

For example, a woman may find she typically fails to make her opinions heard in group meetings with male colleagues. She might conclude that the problem is a sexist attitude on the part of her colleagues. She may attempt to correct the problem in a single loop by asserting the authority of her position, but finds she still fails to achieve desired results. While the problem may indeed be her colleagues' attitudes, it may also be the result of other factors. Typically, however, neither party in the situation will explore the meaning of such an interaction. As Argyris and Schon note, in these situations, feelings are kept hidden and rationality invoked, in part out of embarrassment, and someone attempts to keep the situation in control so he or she can win. The result is a closed environment in which people cannot learn because too many strong feelings and opinions are kept undiscussible.

Single loop learning does not involve critical reflectivity, while double loop learning does. The latter also typically draws on all three learning domains described by Mezirow. In single loop learning, reflection takes place on the surface level of means and ends. In the above example, the woman learns instrumentally and in a single loop when she counters being ignored by asserting the authority of her position. Reflection in dialogic learning involves intersubjective agreement. The woman learns dialogically by attempting to understand norms governing the conversation, the most obvious of which might be gender roles. However, perhaps she has less seniority or is a non-engineer in a company of engineers. Self-reflective learning does not always cross over into the dialogic domain, but it is more powerful when it does because assumptions may be based on internalized, unexamined social norms. In the above example, colleagues might point out that her language is laced with question marks at times when she wishes to convey certainty or that her quietness is interpreted by some as an attempt to control. Self-reflection in the workplace, frequently prompted by unsuccessful behavior, is often linked to changes in instrumental action. In the above example, the woman might both watch her own style of delivery as well as begin to inquire into the data behind assertions made by her colleagues in order to move the meetings more toward the ideal of exchange of valid information.

In summary, many training solutions are only partially successful in solving learning problems. Training may be divorced from the context in which people work. Even when steps are taken to assist in transfer of learning to the job, people are left much on their own to figure out how these skills relate to real-life problems. Workers need more than a set of techniques; they must be able to analyze a situation to determine the nature of the problem being addressed and derive their own solutions to these problems, often on-the-job. The next section builds on the above learning frameworks to address this need.

A NEW PARADIGM

If behaviorism is being challenged, what are the elements of a contrasting paradigm for understanding and designing workplace learning? This author suggests that a new paradigm is emerging that includes some of the following characteristics: a broadening of the instrumental focus of learning, integration of personal and job-related development, an organizational model that functions as a learning system, a focus on group as well as individual learning, a concern for critical reflectivity and for problem setting as well as problem solving, emphasis on informal learning, and development of the organization as a learning environment.

To elaborate, work-related learning includes instrumental action for which behavioral models are often suited, but goes beyond it to include dialogic and self-reflective learning. Individuals are most productive when they can participate fully in negotiating meaningful contributions to shared organizational goals and norms. It follows that personal development is not considered either as separate from the job, antagonistic to it, or an "add-on" that is nice but not essential. Persons learn best about the job when their own identity and growth are recognized as integral to that learning.

To facilitate this kind of learning, the organization cannot function strictly as a machine. One option would be the holographic model in which all employees are encouraged to learn many aspects of the work, participate jointly in appropriate decentralized decision making, and continually monitor actions and results to keep the organization flexible. The holographic model may go too far in the direction of participation for many organizations. However, learning in today's era cannot easily take place when employees are confined to individual, pre-determined actions that are collectively orchestrated to minimize overlap or any duplication of abilities or functions.

When looked on in this manner, it is clear that the unit for learning is not only the individual, but groups within the organization joined together to create their working goals and relationships. The emphasis is on teamwork, not solely to meet pre-defined goals, but to modify these and create new goals. A new paradigm would acknowledge that learning takes place at many levels, from the individual on up through groups to, at times, the entire organization. To fully understand learning under a new paradigm, one would look at the way in which individual learning is shaped by and contributes to collective learning, and vice versa.

Learning design under a new paradigm would encourage reflectivity and critical reflectivity. The organization should provide a clear picture of its desired outcomes, but training would not solely consist of a lock-step process of inculcating these pre-defined objectives. Individuals would be encouraged to develop a habit of reflectivity in both formal and informal learning modes in which they continually probe their experience to determine why they are or are not effective and how they can learn to become so. Through such reflection, problems would be continually reformulated as old data are re-evaluated. Participation in setting the problems thus becomes as important in this paradigm as is finding and implementing the best solutions. Problem setting is a creative, non-linear process of probing that can be aborted by a demand for closure before participants have reached consensus on the nature of the problem.

This paradigm emphasizes informal learning because so much of today's formal training is focused on behaviors and skills alone. Informal learning is an opportunity for reflection-in-action. Formal training would still be needed under a new paradigm, some of which would still be aimed primarily at productivity in the instrumental domain. However, training would be designed to link learning in all three domains and timed by the individual in consultation with the organization to take advantage of those turning points in which individuals are more naturally reflective. Self-directed learning, coaching, mentoring and group learning would be encouraged. The organization thus becomes a learning environment for the growth of individuals and groups vis-à-vis work, not primarily a factor to be manipulated to produce desired behavior. As a learning environment, it must provide opportunities for experimentation, risk-taking, dialogue, initiative, creativity, and participation in decision-making.

Limits of a New Paradigm

There are limits to who can best learn under this new paradigm and to the conditions within an organization that facilitate or impede it. These are discussed in the following terms:

1. Workplace learning will always be governed to some extent by an instrumental focus because the primary purpose for such organizations is productivity.
2. All individuals are not ready to participate more fully in decision-making and self-directed learning.
3. Organizations cannot always change conditions such as hierarchy and centralized decision-making even when they wish to do so.

First, workplace learning is informed by its instrumental focus. A number of implications follow. Learning in the dialogic and self-reflective domains must take place primarily for purposes of productivity. However, productivity needs to be redefined in longer-range terms so that the current emphasis on short-term results does not force continual sacrifices in individual and collective learning that require time before results appear. While emphasizing the critical importance of organizations as learning environments, a balance must be maintained between time for learning and time for producing or else the organization will go out of business. Finally, while learning must acknowledge the legitimacy of self-reflection and personal growth, the organization cannot take on the role of therapist. This does not mean that organizations should de-value the importance of personal growth nor should they drop financial or other allowances to facilitate therapy when obviously needed. However, learning under a new paradigm can acknowledge and work with feelings associated with personal identity and growth without, for example, becoming a substitute for psychoanalysis.

The second set of limits deals with individual readiness for this kind of learning. The new paradigm depends on increased participation of all individuals in decision-making and in dialogue about shared goals, norms, values, and procedures. Central to the new paradigm on an individual level are autonomy, initiative, independent judgment, self-direction, and a reservoir of experience and knowledge appropriate to the tasks being faced. Many workers are quite happy with jobs that are clearly defined and that do not require ongoing reflection. Reflection, whether simple or critical, requires extensive dialogue and personal change that might not be desired by the individual or feasible in many organizational contexts.

The third set of limits are organizational. The new paradigm suggests that a structure must be evolved that allows for participation and empowerment without sacrificing its primary purpose for existence. In some businesses, hierarchy and centralized decision-making are probably essential. Kanter (1983) sums up the dilemmas of participation around initiating such programs, managing them, choosing issues on which to focus, working on teams, linking teams to their environments, and evaluating success. She concludes that "managing participation is a balancing act" (p. 275).

The organization develops and reflects conditions and a culture that facilitates or impedes learning. Managers are often allowed greater leeway in such learning than are workers at the lower end of the hierarchy, perhaps because managers must exercise judgment under ambiguous conditions. Currently, judgment is frequently limited the further down one goes in the hierarchy as the nature of work becomes increasingly dependent on carrying out the decisions of others and on complex interaction among groups and work units. Learning likewise is often increasingly limited to routine procedures and prescribed behaviors. Hence, rapid and total change in the direction of a new organizational paradigm may not be desirable or feasible. Likewise, people cannot be expected to learn autonomy and autonomously overnight.

CONCLUSION

Training has been dominated by behaviorism. This article reviews trends in organizations that suggest a new paradigm for understanding and facilitating workplace learning in the post-industrial era and discusses learning theories that contribute to this conceptual framework. Reflectivity and critical reflectivity are at the heart of these perspectives. The framework addresses both formal and informal learning, but encourages a stronger emphasis on informal learning Instrumental learning about the job is not separated from relevant dialogic or self-reflective learning. Since this kind of learning assumes a level of employee participation that is seldom found, productivity under this framework must be redefined and conditions within the organization re-examined if such learning is to take place.

Both organizations and unions are faced with crises that call for a different way of doing business. Such changes will probably come slowly. Nonetheless, some organizations are experimenting with new ways of involving employees in decisions about goals and work procedures. A

116

perspective on learning in the workplace that helps employees engage differently in setting and solving problems seems helpful in these circumstances. All learning does not necessarily involve the dialogic and self-reflective domains. However, a theory of learning in the workplace should include provisions for helping adults understand and interpret the meaning of the full range of events that occur in that setting.

References

Argyris, C. & Schon, D. (1974). *Theory in practice: Increasing professional effectiveness.* San Francisco: Jossey-Bass.

Argyris, C. & Schon, D. (1978). *Organizational learning: A theory of action perspective.* Reading, MA: Addison-Wesley.

American Society for Training & Development. (1981). *Models and concepts for T & D/HRD academic programs* (Paper No. 6, ASTD Research Series). Washington, D.C.: Author. American Society for Training & Development. (1986). *Serving the new corporation.* Alexandria, VA: Author.

Carnevale, A. P., & Goldstein, H. (1983). *Employee training: Its changing role and an analysis of new data.* Washington, D.C.: ASTD Press.

Carr, W. and Kemmis, S. (1983). *Becoming critical: Knowing through action research.* Victoria, Australia: Deakin University Press.

Goldstein, I. L. (1980). Training in work organizations. *Annual Review of Psychology, 31,* 229-272.

Habermas, J. (1971). *Knowledge and human interests.* Boston: Beacon Press.

Kanter, R. M. (1983). *The changemasters: Innovation for productivity in the American corporation.* New York: Simon & Schuster.

Kaplan, R. E., Drath, W. H. & Kofodimos, J. R. (1985). *High hurdles: The challenge of executive self-development* (Technical Report No. 25). Greensboro, NC: Center for Creative Leadership.

Knowles, M. *The modern practice of adult education* (rev. ed.). (1980). Cambridge, NY.

Kolb, D. (1984). *Experiential learning: Experience as the source of learning and development.* Englewood Cliffs, NJ: Prentice-Hall.

Lincoln, Y. S. (1985). *Organizational theory and inquiry: The paradigm revolution.* Beverly Hills: Sage.

Marsick, V. J. (Ed.). (1987). *Learning in the workplace.* Beckenham, Kent, U.K.: Groom Helm.

McCauley, C. D. (1986). *Developmental experiences in managerial work: A literature review* (Technical Report No. 26). Greensboro, NC: Center for Creative Leadership.

Mezirow, J. (1981). A critical theory of adult learning and education. *Adult Education, 32,* 3-24.

Mezirow, J. (1985). A critical theory of self-directed learning. In S. Brookfield (Ed.), *Self-directed learning: From theory to practice* (pp. 17-30). San Francisco: Jossey-Bass.

Morgan, G. (1986). *Images of organization.* Beverly Hills: Sage.

Naisbitt, J. & Aburdene, P. (1985). *Re-inventing the corporation.* New York: Warner.

Peters, T. J., & Waterman, R. H. (1982). In search of excellence: *Lessons from America's best-run companies.* New York: Warner.

Schon, D. (1983). *The reflective practitioner.* New York: Basic Books.

Schwarz, P. & Ogilvy, J. (1979). *The emergent paradigm: Changing patterns of thought and belief.* Menlo Park, CA: Stanford Research Institute.

Toffler, A. (1985). *The adaptive corporation.* New York: Bantam.

Zemke, R. (1985). The Honeywell studies: How managers learn to manage. *Training, 22* (8), 46-51.

Part II
Leadership and Complexity

Chapter 5

Prologue
Mary R. Uhl-Bien
Professor, Howard Hawks Chair in Business Ethics and Leadership
University of Nebraska-Lincoln

Complexity Leadership Theory: Shifting Leadership from the Industrial Age to the Knowledge Era

Mary Uhl-Bien, Russ Marion, and Bill McKelvey

Prologue:
A Brave New *Complex* World

Mary Uhl-Bien

In the late 1990s I was becoming disillusioned with leader-member exchange (LMX) research. I realized that it had serious methodological flaws, but more importantly I was finding that it had limited value for practice. Not only did it not capture the realities facing managers/leaders in the workplace, but it was largely wrong in its prescriptions to managers regarding how to be more effective leaders. LMX, like other traditional leadership theories, purports that, to achieve effectiveness, managers should devote their time and energy to building high-quality one-on-one relationships with subordinates. But when I tried to use this with executives, what I learned was: *That's not really their job.* The pressures and demands placed on managers and organizational leaders were much too complex to be explained by the overly simplified solutions being offered in leadership research. Don't get me wrong: Of course, building relationships is important, and without effective relationships a lot of problems can occur in the workplace. But having effective relationships was not enough. *There was something missing in our understanding of leadership.*

I was deep in the journey of trying to figure this out when in 2001 Jerry Hunt, then editor of *The Leadership Quarterly*, introduced me to Russ Marion and asked us to work together on a paper for the journal's annual review issue. I had never heard of complexity theory and told Jerry as much. But in typical Jerry fashion, his response was, "That's okay. Get Russ's book and go read about it."

I know it sounds cliché to say that my world changed when I read that book (Marion, 1998), but the truth is, that's what happened. In my own search for a better way to study leadership, I had been playing around with the idea that relational theory might hold a clue for a new way of thinking about leadership. But I was still mired in my LMX training and was approaching relational thinking from the standpoint of social exchange and relationship building. When I read about complexity, I was introduced to a whole other dimension of relational thinking—one grounded in *relationality* rather than interpersonal *relationships* (see Uhl-Bien & Ospina, 2012).

Complexity offered an entirely new way to approach leadership, starting with the idea of interactive dynamics and a world that operates *in relation*. It helped me see how we could bring context into leadership in ways that were not available using a postpositive lens. Complexity does not dismiss the importance of relationships; it offers us a way to better understand how and why they are so important in the workplace. Of course I now know that complexity is entirely consistent with strong relational theory (see Drath, 2001). But at the time, this was a profound revelation for me. It offered the answers I had been seeking.

The first paper Russ and I published in 2001 was relatively easy (only because Russ had spent the decade prior extensively researching complexity science). But the journey to the 2007 paper was a much more difficult one. We had been challenged to push beyond metaphor to develop a strong theoretical framework. And while complexity offered a tremendous foundation from which to build, it had limits in its assumptions of self-organization and irreducibility. It was only by bringing Bill McKelvey in to work with us that we were finally able to achieve the breakthrough that resulted in the Complexity Leadership Theory (CLT) framework you see in the paper presented in this book. The CLT framework offers a way to think about organizations from the standpoint of *both* bureaucratic structures and complex adaptive systems. It represents a starting point for a new way to engage in leadership research and practice.

Since the publication of the paper in 2007, we have been engaged in intensive empirical work to ascertain whether our theorizing was on track.[6] This empirical research program has resulted in major discoveries and exciting new breakthroughs that we are just now beginning to write up for publication. Iterations of the findings against practice indicate that our newer, more informed CLT framework is resonating powerfully with practitioners. They are pushing us for more, and they want it quickly.

But advancing leadership research and practice for a complex world is not a "quick and dirty" proposition. It can't be accomplished through simplistic research studies reducing complexity down to a set of survey items. Nor can it be delivered through simple provision of a new set of analytical tools or prepackaged leadership practices. Its promise lies in the new understanding it provides about interactive dynamics and the nature of an interconnected world. What complexity leadership helps us see is that, contrary to "ordered responses" associated with traditional management principles, we need "adaptive responses" appropriate to a complex world.

My belief is that we are on the verge of exciting new developments in leadership and complexity. But I also don't fool myself into thinking the necessary changes will come easily. We are deeply mired in our bureaucratic managerial mindsets, and traditional academic research infrastructures work against multiparadigmatic approaches like complexity. It is only through deep commitment, from both academics and practitioners working in strong partnership with one another, that we will be able to advance the understanding needed to embrace new ways of researching and practicing leadership for today's world. It is coming. I am confident it will happen—if for no other reason than our complex world will demand it of us.

---

[6]   Members of the research/practice team include Russ Marion, Michael Arena, Craig Schreiber, David Sweetman, Bill Hanson, Ivana Milosevic, Jude Olson, Dana Baugh, Anne Harbison, and Debra France.

References

Drath, W. (2001). *The deep blue sea: Rethinking the source of leadership.* San Francisco, CA: Jossey-Bass & Center for Creative Leadership.

Marion, R. (1998). *The edge of organization: Chaos and complexity theories of formal social organizations.* Newbury Park, CA: Sage.

Marion, R., & Uhl-Bien, M. (2001). Leadership in complex organizations. *Leadership Quarterly, 12,* 389-418.

Uhl-Bien, M., & Ospina, S. (2012). *Advancing relational leadership research: A dialogue among perspectives.* Charlotte, NC: Information Age.

Complexity Leadership Theory: Shifting Leadership from the Industrial Age to the Knowledge Era[7]

Mary Uhl-Bien, Russ Marion, and Bill McKelvey

Abstract. Leadership models of the last century have been products of top-down, bureaucratic paradigms. These models are eminently effective for an economy premised on physical production but are not well-suited for a more knowledge-oriented economy. Complexity science suggests a different paradigm for leadership—one that frames leadership as a complex interactive dynamic from which adaptive outcomes (e.g., learning, innovation, and adaptability) emerge. This article draws from complexity science to develop an overarching framework for the study of Complexity Leadership Theory, a leadership paradigm that focuses on enabling the learning, creative, and adaptive capacity of complex adaptive systems (CAS) within a context of knowledge-producing organizations. This conceptual framework includes three entangled leadership roles (i.e., adaptive leadership, administrative leadership, and enabling leadership) that reflect a dynamic relationship between the bureaucratic, administrative functions of the organization and the emergent, informal dynamics of complex adaptive systems (CAS).

As we advance deeper in the knowledge economy, the basic assumptions underlining much of what is taught and practiced in the name of management are hopelessly out of date . . . Most of our assumptions about business, technology and organization are at least 50 years old. They have outlived their time. (Drucker, 1998, p. 162)

We're in a knowledge economy, but our managerial and governance systems are stuck in the Industrial Era. It's time for a whole new model. (Manville & Ober, 2003, Jan., p. 48).

According to Hitt (1998), "we are on the precipice of an epoch," in the midst of a new economic age, in which 21st century organizations are

---

[7] Originally Published as: Uhl-Bien, M., R. Marion, and McKelvey, B. (2007). "Complexity leadership theory: Shifting leadership from the industrial age to the knowledge age" The Leadership Quarterly **18**: 298-318.

facing a complex competitive landscape driven largely by globalization and the technological revolution. This new age is about an economy where knowledge is a core commodity and the rapid production of knowledge and innovation is critical to organizational survival (Bettis & Hitt, 1995; Boisot, 1998). Consistent with these changes, much discussion is taking place in the management literature regarding challenges facing organizations in a transitioning world (Barkema, Baum, & Mannix, 2002; Bettis & Hitt, 1995; Child & McGrath, 2001).

Yet, despite the fact that leadership is a core factor in whether organizations meet these challenges, we find little explicit discussion of leadership models for the Knowledge Era. As noted by Davenport (2001), while it has become clear that the old model of leadership was formed to deal with a very different set of circumstances and is therefore of questionable relevance to the contemporary work environment, no clear alternative has come along to take its place. Osborn, Hunt, & Jauch (2002) argue that "a radical change in perspective" about leadership is necessary to go beyond traditionally accepted views, because ". . . the context in which leaders operate is both radically different and diverse. The world of traditional bureaucracy exists but it is only one of many contexts" (p. 798).

We begin to address this shortcoming by developing a framework for leadership in the fast-paced, volatile context of the Knowledge Era (Marion & Uhl-Bien, 2001; Schneider & Somers, 2006). Our model extends beyond bureaucracy premises by drawing from complexity science, the "study of the behaviour of large collections of . . . simple, interacting units, endowed with the potential to evolve with time" (Coveney, 2003, p. 1058). Using the concept of complex adaptive systems (CAS), we propose that leadership should be seen not only as position and authority but also as an emergent, interactive dynamic—a complex interplay from which a collective impetus for action and change emerges when heterogeneous agents interact in networks in ways that produce new patterns of behavior or new modes of operating (cf. Heifetz, 1994; Plowman et al., 2007-this issue; Plowman & Duchon, in press).

125

Complex adaptive systems (CAS) are a basic unit of analysis in complexity science. CAS are neural-like networks of interacting, interdependent agents who are bonded in a cooperative dynamic by common goal, outlook, need, etc. They are changeable structures with multiple, overlapping hierarchies, and like the individuals that comprise them, CAS are linked with one another in a dynamic, interactive network. Hedlund (1994) describes a generally similar structure relative to managing knowledge flows in organizations that he called "temporary constellations of people and units" (p. 82). CAS emerge naturally in social systems (cf. Homans, 1950; Roy, 1954). They are capable of solving problems creatively and are able to learn and adapt quickly (Carley & Hill, 2001; Carley & Lee, 1998; Goodwin, 1994; Levy, 1992).

The leadership framework we propose, which we call Complexity Leadership Theory, seeks to take advantage of the dynamic capabilities of CAS. Complexity Leadership Theory (CLT) focuses on identifying and exploring the strategies and behaviors that foster organizational and subunit creativity, learning, and adaptability when appropriate CAS dynamics are enabled within contexts of hierarchical coordination (i.e., bureaucracy). In CLT, we recognize three broad types of leadership: (1) leadership grounded in traditional, bureaucratic notions of hierarchy, alignment and control (i.e., administrative leadership), (2) leadership that structures and enables conditions such that CAS are able to optimally address creative problem solving, adaptability, and learning (referring to what we will call, enabling leadership); and (2) leadership as a generative dynamic that underlies emergent change activities (what we will call, adaptive leadership).

The Complexity Leadership perspective is premised on several critical notions. First, the informal dynamic we describe is embedded in context (Hunt, 1999; Osborn et al., 2002). Context in complex adaptive systems is not an antecedent, mediator, or moderator variable; rather, it is the ambiance that spawns a given system's dynamic persona—in the case of complex system personae, it refers to the nature of interactions and interdependencies among agents (people, ideas, etc.), hierarchical divisions, organizations, and environments. CAS and leadership are socially constructed in and from this context—a context in which patterns over time must be considered and where history matters (Cilliers, 1998; Dooley, 1996; Hosking, 1988; Osborn et al., 2002).

Second, a complexity leadership perspective requires that we distinguish between leadership and leaders. Complexity Leadership Theory will add a view of leadership as an emergent, interactive dynamic that is productive of adaptive outcomes (which we call adaptive leadership, cf. Heifetz, 1994). It will consider leaders as individuals who act in ways that influence this dynamic and the outcomes. Leadership theory has largely focused on leaders—the actions of individuals. It has not examined the dynamic, complex systems and processes that comprise leadership. Because of this, earlier models have been criticized for being incomplete and impractical (Gronn, 1999; Osborn et al 2002; see also Hunt, 1999). Rost (1991) refers to this as the problem of focusing on the "periphery" and "content" of leadership with disregard for the essential nature of what leadership is—*a process* (cf. Hunt, 1999; Mackenzie, 2006).

Third, complexity leadership perspectives help us to distinguish leadership from managerial positions or "offices" (a bureaucratic notion, see Heckscher, 1994). The vast majority of leadership research has studied leadership in formal, most often managerial, roles (Bedeian & Hunt, 2006; Rost, 1991) and has not adequately addressed leadership that occurs throughout the organization (Schneider, 2002). To address this, we will use the term administrative leadership to refer to formal acts that serve to coordinate and structure organizational activities (i.e., the bureaucratic function), and introduce the concept of *adaptive leadership* to refer to the leadership that occurs in emergent, informal adaptive dynamics throughout the organization (cf. Heifetz, 1994; Heifetz & Linsky, 2002).

Finally, complexity leadership occurs in the face of adaptive challenges (typical of the Knowledge Era) rather than technical problems (more characteristic of the Industrial Age). As defined by Heifetz (1994; Heifetz & Laurie, 2001), adaptive challenges are problems that require new learning, innovation, and new patterns of behavior. They are different from technical problems, which can be solved with knowledge and procedures already in hand (Parks, 2005). Adaptive challenges are not amenable to authoritative fiat or standard operating procedures, but rather require exploration, new discoveries, and adjustments. Day (2000) refers to this as the difference between management and leadership development. Management development involves the application of proven solutions to known problems, whereas leadership development refers to situations in which groups need to learn their way out of problems that could not have been predicted (e.g., disintegration of traditional organizational structures).

In the sections below we lay out the framework and dynamics we call Complexity Leadership Theory. This framework describes how to enable the learning, creative, and adaptive capacity of complex adaptive systems (CAS) within a context of knowledge-producing organizations. Complexity Leadership Theory seeks to foster CAS dynamics while at the same time enabling control structures for coordinating formal organizations and producing outcomes appropriate to the vision and mission of the organization. We begin by describing the leadership requirements of the Knowledge Era and the limitations of current leadership theory for meeting these requirements. We then describe why CAS dynamics are well suited for the needs of the Knowledge Era, and how leadership can work to enable these dynamics. We conclude with a presentation of the Complexity Leadership Theory framework and a description of the three key leadership functions and roles that comprise this framework: adaptive leadership, enabling leadership, and administrative leadership.

1. Leadership in the Knowledge Era

The Knowledge Era is characterized by a new competitive landscape driven by globalization, technology, deregulation, and democratization (Halal & Taylor, 1999). Many firms deal with this new landscape by allying horizontally and vertically in "constellations" (Bamford, Gomes-Casseres, & Robinson, 2002). In the process, they actively interconnect the world, creating what some have called a "connectionist era" (Halal, 1998; Miles, 1998; see Hogue & Lord, 2007 for an extensive discussion). Through multinational alliances, firms in developing countries now find themselves engaging increasingly in manufacturing activities as producers or subcontractors, while firms in developed economies focus more on information and services (Drucker, 1999). The latter face the need to exhibit speed, flexibility, and adaptability, with the organization's absolute rate of learning and innovation and the pace of its development becoming critical to competitive advantage (Eisenhardt, 1989; Jennings & Haughton, 2000; Prusak, 1996). In other words, firms in developed economies sustain superior performance in the Knowledge Era by promoting faster learning (Child & McGrath, 2001).

This new age creates new kinds of challenges for organizations and their leaders (Barkema et al., 2002; Schneider, 2002). In this post-industrial era, the success of a corporation lies more in its social assets—its corporate IQ and learning capacity—than in its physical assets (McKelvey, 2001; Quinn, Anderson, & Finkelstein, 2002; Zohar, 1997). In the industrial economy, the challenge inside the firm was to coordinate the physical assets produced by employees. This was mainly a problem of optimizing the production and physical flow of products (Boisot, 1998; Schneider, 2002). In the new economy, the challenge is to create an environment in which knowledge accumulates and is shared at a low cost. The goal is to cultivate, protect, and use difficult to imitate knowledge assets as compared to pure commodity—instigated production (Nonaka & Nishiguchi, 2001). It is a problem of enabling intellectual assets through distributed intelligence and cellular networks (Miles, Snow, Matthews, &

Miles, 1999) rather than relying on the limited intelligence of a few brains at the top (Heckscher, 1994; McKelvey, in press). Moreover, the focus is on speed and adaptability (Schilling & Steensma, 2001). Rather than leading for efficiency and control, appropriate to manufacturing (Jones, 2000), organizations find themselves leading for adaptability, knowledge and learning (Achtenhagen, Melin, Mullern, & Ericson, 2003; Volberda, 1996).

To achieve fitness in such a context, complexity science suggests that organizations must increase their complexity to the level of the environment rather than trying to simplify and rationalize their structures. Ashby (1960) refers to this as the law of requisite variety; McKelvey & Boisot (2003) customized this law for complexity theory and call it the Law of Requisite Complexity. This law states simply that it takes complexity to defeat complexity—a system must possess complexity equal to that of its environment in order to function effectively. Requisite complexity enhances a system's capacity to search for solutions to challenges and to innovate because it releases the capacity of a neural network of agents in pursuit of such optimization. That is, it optimizes a system's capacity for learning, creativity, and adaptability.

As Cilliers (2001) observed, traditional approaches to organization have done the opposite: they have sought to simplify or to rationalize the pursuit of adaptation. He argues that simplifying and rationalizing strategies lead to structures that define fixed boundaries, compartmentalized organizational responses, and simplified coordination and communication (e.g., Simon, 1962). However, such approaches are limited because they do not represent reality—boundaries are not fixed perimeters, but rather, are sets of functions that dynamically interpenetrate one another (Cilliers, 2001). To meet the needs of requisite complexity, Knowledge Era leadership requires a change in thinking away from individual, controlling views, and toward views of organizations as complex adaptive systems that enable continuous creation and capture of knowledge. In short, knowledge development, adaptability, and innovation are optimally enabled by organizations that are complexly adaptive (possessing requisite complexity).

1.1. Limitations of current leadership theory

Despite the needs of the Knowledge Era, much of leadership theory remains largely grounded in a bureaucratic framework more appropriate for the Industrial Age (Gronn, 1999). One such element of the bureaucratic concept is the traditional assumption that control must be rationalized. Much of leadership theory is developed around the idea that goals are rationally conceived and that managerial practices should be structured to achieve those goals. As Chester Barnard (1938) framed it, the role of leadership is to align individual preferences with rational organizational goals. Philip Selznick (1948) observed that irrational social forces tend to subvert the formal goals of an institution.

Consistent with this, the dominant paradigm in leadership theory focuses on how leaders can influence others toward desired objectives within frameworks of formal hierarchical organizational structures (Zaccaro & Klimoski, 2001). This paradigmatic model centers on issues such as motivating workers toward task objectives (House & Mitchell, 1974), leading them to produce efficiently and effectively (Zaccaro & Klimoski, 2001) and inspiring them to align with and commit to organizational goals (Bass, 1985). Macro-level theories, such as those that address "upper echelon leadership," are further premised in bureaucratic notions (Heckscher, 1994) that likewise mute uncontrolled behaviors; other models advocate a charismatic, visionary approach that is said to cascade down from the CEO to lower levels (Conger, 1999; Yukl, 2005). Leadership research has explored the implementation of these top-down organizational forms by drilling deeper and deeper into human relations models (aimed at alignment and control; Gronn, 1999; Huxham & Vangen, 2000).

Without realizing it, the inability to move beyond formal leaders and control inherent in traditional bureaucratic mindsets (Heckscher,

1994) limits the applicability of mainstream leadership theories for the Knowledge Era (Stacey, Griffin, & Shaw, 2000; Streatfield, 2001). There seems to be a contradiction between the needs of the Knowledge Era and the reality of centralized power (Child & McGrath, 2001) that leadership theory has not yet addressed. "The dominant paradigms in organizational theory are based on stability seeking and uncertainty avoidance through organizational structure and processes . . . . We believe that those paradigms are inadequate for global, hyper-competitive environments, although their replacements are not clear yet" (Ilinitch, D'Aveni, & Lewin, 1996, p. 217). As noted by Child & McGrath (2001), "Scholars, managers, and others face a widespread challenge to bureaucracy's central benefit, namely, its utility as a vehicle for strong economic performance in the new era" (p. 1136). Leadership scholars face the same challenge:

The . . . challenge is to identify alternatives [to bureaucracy] and develop theories that account for them. It is not trivial. How can we improve upon, even replace, such a painstakingly well-developed concept of how human beings collectively best accomplish their objectives? (Child & McGrath, 2001, p. 1136)

We address this challenge by developing a model of leadership grounded not in bureaucracy, but in complexity. This model focuses on leadership in contexts of dynamically changing networks of informally interacting agents. As will be elaborated below, the premise of complexity leadership is simple: Under conditions of knowledge production, managers should enable, rather than suppress or align, informal network dynamics. Early researchers, such as Lewin (1952) and Homans (1950), glimpsed the potential of such informal dynamics (however vaguely, by complexity theory standards); but the thrust of many follow-up studies of their findings assumed that such informal dynamics were problematic for achieving organizational goals (Roy, 1954; Selznick, 1957). Several recent initiatives have explored the potential of decentralized authority

132

or leadership, including Pearce & Conger's (2003) work with shared leadership, Gronn's (2002) work on distributed leadership, and Fletcher (2004) and Volberda (1996) on flexible forms. None, however, have developed a model that addresses the nature of leadership for enabling network dynamics, one whose epistemology is consistent with *connective, distributed, dynamic,* and *contextual* views of leadership.

We propose such a model in this article, one that we call, Complexity Leadership Theory. This new perspective is grounded in a core proposition: Much of leadership thinking has failed to recognize that leadership is not merely the influential act of an individual or individuals but rather is embedded in a complex interplay of numerous interacting forces.

There are several orienting assumptions that underlie the complexity leadership model; these assumptions will be developed further in this article:

- Complexity Leadership Theory (CLT) is necessarily enmeshed within a bureaucratic superstructure of planning, organizing, and missions. CLT seeks to understand how enabling leaders can interact with the administrative superstructure to both coordinate complex dynamics (i.e., adaptive leadership) and enhance the overall flexibility of the organization (Marion & Uhl-Bien, 2007).
- Complexity Leadership Theory presumes hierarchical structuring and differing enabling and adaptive functions across levels of the hierarchy.
- The unit of analysis for Complexity Leadership Theory is the CAS. The boundaries of CAS are variously defined depending on the intent of the researcher, but however identified, they are, without exception, open systems.
- Leadership, however it is defined, only exists in, and is a function of, interaction.

Before we elaborate these ideas in our framework below, however, we first must understand why complex adaptive systems are well suited for the Knowledge Era and the dynamics that drive these systems. Therefore, we turn next to an overview of CAS dynamics that will serve as a basis for discussion in subsequent sections.

1.2. The argument for Complexity Leadership Theory: CAS dynamics

Earlier we defined complex adaptive systems (or CAS) as open, evolutionary aggregates whose components (or agents) are dynamically interrelated and who are cooperatively bonded by common purpose or outlook. We also introduced Complexity Leadership Theory as a model for leadership in and of complex adaptive systems (CAS) in knowledge-producing organizations. We now ask, "What is so unique about complex adaptive systems theory that it fosters a fresh look at leadership?" and "Why would we want to enable CAS dynamics anyway?"

To answer these questions we need to better understand the structure of CAS and how they are different from systems perspectives offered previously in the organizational literature. As described by Cilliers (1998), complex adaptive systems are different from systems that are merely complicated. If a system can be described in terms of its individual constituents (even if there are a huge number of constituents), it is merely complicated; if the interactions among the constituents of the system, and the interaction between the system and its environment, are of such a nature that the system as a whole cannot be fully understood simply by analyzing its components, it is complex (e.g., a jumbo jet is complicated, but mayonnaise is complex, Cilliers, 1998).

Dooley (1996) describes a CAS as an aggregate of interacting agents that "behaves/evolves according to three key principles: order is emergent as opposed to predetermined, the system's history is irreversible, and the system's future is often unpredictable." In CAS, agents, events, and ideas bump into each other in somewhat unpredictable fashion, and change emerges from this dynamic interactive process. Because of this randomness, and the fact that complex dynamics can exhibit sensitivity to small perturbations (Lorenz, 1993), CAS are rather organic and unpredictable (Marion & Uhl-Bien, 2001). Change in complex adaptive systems occur nonlinearly and in unexpected places, and, as Dooley (1996) observed, their history cannot be revisited (one cannot return a system to a previous state and rerun its trajectory).

Complexity science has identified a number of dynamics that characterize the formation and behaviors of CAS. For example, complexity science has found that interactive, adaptive agents tend to bond in that they adapt to one another's preferences and worldviews (Marion & Uhl-Bien, 2001). From this, they form aggregates (i.e., clusters of interacting agents engaged in some measure of cooperative behavior). Mature social systems are comprised of a complex of hierarchically embedded, overlapping and interdependent aggregates, or CAS (Kauffman, 1993). Complexity science has also found that the behaviors of interactive, interdependent agents and CAS are productive of emergent creativity and learning. Emergence refers to a nonlinear suddenness that characterizes change in complex systems (Marion, 1999; see also Plowman et al. in this edition). It derives from the collapse (or, more technically, dissipation) of built up tensions (Prigogine, 1997), sudden mergers (or divergences) of formerly separate CAS (Kauffman, 1993), or a cascade of changes through network connections (Bak, 1996). Creativity and learning occur when emergence forms a previously unknown solution to a problem or creates a new, unanticipated outcome (i.e., adaptive change).

CAS are unique and desirable in their ability to adapt rapidly and creatively to environmental changes. Complex systems enhance their capacity for adaptive response to environmental problems or internal demand by diversifying their behaviors or strategies (Holland, 1995; McKelvey, in press). Diversification, from the perspective of complexity science, is defined as increasing internal complexity (number and level of interdependent relationships, heterogeneity of skills and outlooks within

CAS, number of CAS, and tension) to the point of, or exceeding, that of competitors or the environment (i.e., "requisite variety," Ashby, 1960 or "requisite complexity," McKelvey & Boisot, 2003). Adaptive responses to environmental problems include counter-moves, altered or new strategies, learning and new knowledge, work-around changes, new allies, and new technologies. By increasing their complexity, CAS enhance their ability to process data (Lewin, 1992), solve problems (Levy, 1992), learn (Carley & Hill, 2001; Levy, 1992), and change creatively (Marion, 1999).

Certain conditions will affect the capacity of CAS to emerge and function effectively in social systems. Agents must, for example, be capable of interacting with each other and with the environment. Agents must be interdependently related, meaning that the productive well being of one agent or aggregate is dependent on the productive well being of others. Moreover, they must experience tension to elaborate.

This capacity to rapidly explore solutions can be illustrated with a problem solving scenario called annealing, which is found in the evolution and simulation complexity literature (Carley, 1997; Carley & Lee, 1998; Kauffman, 1993; Levy, 1992; Lewin, 1999). In this scenario, multiple agents struggle with localized effects created by a given environmental perturbations (or tension; this is called localized because an agent cannot usually perceive a problem as a whole nor do they typically have the capacity to deal with an environmental problem in its entirety). As these agents develop localized solutions, work-arounds, or related responses, they affect the behaviors of other interdependently related agents, who subsequently build on the original response to create higher-order responses. This process extends to broader network levels, to the fabric of interdependent agents, and to the CAS that define the system or subsystem. In this process interdependent agents and CAS experiment, change, combine strategies, and find loopholes in other strategies—and, occasionally, unexpected solutions emerge that address the problem at some level.

Information flows in the annealing process are not necessarily efficient and agents are not necessarily good information processors. Nor does annealing imply that structural adaptations are embraced as official strategy by upper echelon administrators or that the process finds perfect solutions. The annealing process is imperfect and somewhat messy—as Carley (1997) puts it, "it may not be possible for organizations of complex adaptive agents to locate the optimal form, [but] they can improve their performance by altering their structure" (p. 25). The annealing process (and other processes described in the complexity literature; e.g., McKelvey, in press; Prigogine, 1997)[8] does, however, find solutions that individuals, regardless of their authority or expertise, could not find alone. Levy (1992), for example, describes bottom-up simulations that out-performed humans at finding solutions to mazes. Marion (1999) argued that technological and scientific advances inevitably emerge from a movement involving numerous individuals rather than from the isolated minds of individuals.

In sum, complexity describes the interdependent interactions of agents within CAS, agents with CAS, and CAS with CAS. The primary unit of analysis in these interactive dynamics is, however, the CAS itself, and the behaviors of agents are always understood within the context of CAS. CAS are unique and desirable in that their heterogeneous, interactive, and interdependent structures allow them to quickly explore and consolidate solutions to environmental pressures. They require new models of leadership because problem solving is performed by appropriately structured social networks rather than by groups coordinated by centralized authorities. As Mumford & Licuanan (2004) put it, effective leadership influence in conditions requiring creativity occurs through indirect mechanisms and through interaction.

---

[8]   There are other problem-solving approaches in the literature. Complex systems can, for example, respond to the accumulation of tension with phase transitions to new states (McKelvey, in press; Prigogine, 1997). All problem-solving strategies, however, are, in some fashion, driven by tension.

Complexity is a science of mechanisms and interaction and is embedded in context. Mechanisms can be described as the dynamic behaviors that occur within a system such as a complex adaptive system. As defined by Hernes (1998), mechanisms are "a set of interacting parts—an assembly of elements producing an effect not inherent in any of them" (p. 74). They are "not so much about 'nuts and bolts' as about 'cogs and wheels' . . .—the "wheelwork" or agency by which an effect is produced" (Hernes, 1998, p. 74). Contexts are structural, organizational, ideational, and behavioral features—the ambiance of interactions among agents (people, ideas, etc.), hierarchical divisions, organizations, and environments—that influence the nature of mechanism dynamics. Examination of mechanisms and contexts will pry back the cover on leadership, so to speak, and help us to understand how and under what conditions certain outcomes occur.

To further explain this, we turn next to presentation of our framework for Complexity Leadership Theory. Complexity Leadership Theory is about setting up organizations to enable adaptive responses to challenges through network-based problem solving. It offers tools for knowledge-producing organizations and subsystems dealing with rapidly changing, complex problems. It also is useful for systems dealing with less complex problems but for whom creativity is desired.

2. Complexity Leadership Theory

Complexity Leadership Theory is a framework for leadership that enables the learning, creative, and adaptive capacity of complex adaptive systems (CAS) in knowledge-producing organizations or organizational units. This framework seeks to foster CAS dynamics while at the same time enabling control structures appropriate for coordinating formal organizations and producing outcomes appropriate to the vision and mission of the system. It seeks to integrate complexity dynamics and bureaucracy, enabling and coordinating, exploration and exploitation, CAS and hierarchy, and informal emergence and top-down control.

138

Accomplishing this balance poses unique challenges for leadership, however: *How can organizations enable and coordinate CAS dynamics and informal emergence (where appropriate) without suppressing their adaptive and creative capacity?*

As described above, complex adaptive systems are intensely adaptive and innovative (Cilliers, 1998; Marion, 1999). CAS obtain the flexibility to adapt that has been attributed to loose coupling (Weick, 1976) and the capacity to coordinate from a more interdependent structure that is best described as moderately coupled (Kauffman, 1993; Marion, 1999). Moderately coupled interdependency (the actions of one agent are dependent on or limited by those of another) imposes restrictions on behavior. Thus flexibility and what might be called, auto-coordination, derives from informal but interdependent structures and activities (auto-coordination emerges from the nature of system dynamics and is not imposed by authorities). Complexity theorists refer to such informal interactive interdependency as bottom-up behavior, defined as behaviors and changes that emerge spontaneously from the dynamics of neural-like networks. However, the term bottom-up evokes images of hierarchy in organizational studies, so we will substitute the term informal emergence to describe these CAS dynamics in social systems (Lichtenstein et al., 2006; Plowman et al., 2007-this issue, 2007; Plowman & Duchon, in press).

Informal emergence and auto-coordination are seemingly incompatible with administrative coordination, but in reality it depends on the nature of the coordination. In complex adaptive systems, coordination comes from two sources: from informal emergent constraints imposed by interdependent relationships themselves (auto-coordination) and from constraints imposed by actions external to the informal dynamic, including environmental restrictions (Kauffman, 1993; Marion, 1999) and administrative controls (McKelvey, Marion, & Uhl-Bien, 2003). Internal controls are imposed by a sense of common purpose that defines complex adaptive systems and from an inter-agent accountability that is inherent in interdependent systems (Marion & Uhl-Bien, 2001; Marion & Uhl-Bien, 2003; Schneider & Somers, 2006). Hunt and Osborn evocatively describe internal coordination elsewhere in this special issue in their discussion of the Highlander tribes of New Zealand. External constraints and demands are imposed by environmental exigencies and relationships; indeed the core of Stuart Kauffman's (1993) influential descriptions of complex activities in biological evolution involves the inter-influence of multiple interacting species.

In organizational systems, administrators in formal positions of authority likewise influence complex adaptive systems by imposing external coordinating constraints and demands. Such constraints are valuable for (among other things) controlling costs, focusing efforts, allocating resources, and planning. However, authority imposed (top-down) coordination is not necessarily responsive to the potent dynamics of interdependent learning, creativity, and adaptability inherent in complex adaptive systems, and it tends to impose the understanding of a few on the "wisdom" of a neural network (Heckscher, 1994; McKelvey, in press). That is, top-down control (i.e., administrative leadership) can hamper the effective functioning of complex adaptive systems. This is particularly evident in systems with only top-down, hierarchical chains of authority, in systems with closely monitored, centralized goals, or in systems whose dominant ideology is authoritarian.

How, then, can organizations capitalize on the benefits of administrative coordination and of complex adaptive dynamics? Complexity Leadership Theory suggests that the role of managers should not be limited to aligning worker preferences with centralized organizational goals. Rather, managers, particularly under conditions of knowledge production, should act to enable informal emergence and to coordinate the contexts within which it occurs.

3. A framework for Complexity Leadership Theory

This leads us to our overarching framework for Complexity Leadership Theory. This framework envisions three leadership functions that we will refer to as adaptive, administrative, and enabling. Adaptive leadership refers to adaptive, creative, and learning actions that emerge from the interactions of CAS as they strive to adjust to tension (e.g., constraints or perturbations). Adaptive activity can occur in a boardroom or in workgroups of line workers; adaptive leadership is an informal emergent dynamic that occurs among interactive agents (CAS) and is not an act of authority. Administrative leadership refers to the actions of individuals and groups in formal managerial roles who plan and coordinate activities to accomplish organizationally-prescribed outcomes in an efficient and effective manner. Administrative leadership (among other things) structures tasks, engages in planning, builds vision, allocates resources to achieve goals, manages crises (Mumford, Bedell-Avers, & Hunter, in press) and conflicts, and manages organizational strategy (see Yukl, 2005). Administrative leadership focuses on alignment and control and is represented by the hierarchical and bureaucratic functions of the organization. Enabling leadership works to catalyze the conditions in which adaptive leadership can thrive and to manage the entanglement (described below) between the bureaucratic (administrative leadership) and emergent (adaptive leadership) functions of the organization. Managing entanglement involves two roles: (1) creating appropriate organizational conditions (or enabling conditions) to foster effective adaptive leadership in places where innovation and adaptability are needed, and (2) facilitating the flow of knowledge and creativity from adaptive structures into administrative structures. Enabling leadership occurs at all levels of the organization (as well as within the adaptive dynamic), but the nature of this role will vary by hierarchical level and position.

In Complexity Leadership Theory, these three leadership functions are intertwined in a manner that we refer to as entanglement

(Kontopoulos, 1993). Entanglement describes a dynamic relationship between the formal top-down, administrative forces (i.e., bureaucracy) and the informal, complexly adaptive emergent forces (i.e., CAS) of social systems. In organizations, administrative and adaptive leadership interact and may help or oppose one another. Administrative leadership can function in conjunction with adaptive leadership or can thwart it with overly authoritarian or bureaucratic control structures. Adaptive leadership can work to augment the strategic needs of administrative leadership, it can rebel against it, or it can act independently of administrative leadership. The enabling leadership function helps to ameliorate these problems; it serves primarily to enable effective adaptive leadership, but to accomplish this it must tailor the behaviors of administrative and adaptive leadership so that they function in tandem with one another.

In formal organizations, one cannot disentangle bureaucracy from CAS. Earlier we stated that CAS are the basic unit of analysis in a complex system. However, as all organizations are bureaucracies (there are no such things as "post-bureaucratic" organizations, see Hales, 2002), CAS necessarily interact with formal bureaucratic structures in organizations. Moreover, there are times and conditions in which rationalized structure and coordination (e.g., hierarchical authority) need to be emphasized in subunits (e.g., when the environment is stable and the system seeks to enhance profits). At other times or conditions, firm may prefer to emphasize complexity and CAS (e.g., when environments are volatile or the competition's flexibility is threatening).

A role of enabling leadership at the strategic level (Jaques, 1989), then, is to manage the coordination rhythms, or oscillations, between relative importance of top-down, hierarchical dynamics and emergent complex adaptive systems (Thomas, Kaminska-Labbé, & McKelvey, 2005). Ultimately, neither can be separated from the other in knowledge—producing organizations, for such firms must nurture both creativity and exploitation to be fit. Based on this, we can summarize the main points we have developed thus far as follows:

- Complexity Leadership Theory provides an overarching framework that describes administrative leadership, adaptive leadership and enabling leadership; it provides for entanglement among the three leadership roles and, in particular, between CAS and bureaucracy.

- *Adaptive leadership* is an emergent, interactive dynamic that is the primary source by which adaptive outcomes are produced in a firm. *Administrative leadership* is the actions of individuals and groups in formal managerial roles who plan and coordinate organizational activities (the bureaucratic function). *Enabling leadership* serves to enable (catalyze) adaptive dynamics and help manage the entanglement between administrative and adaptive leadership (by fostering enabling conditions and managing the innovation-to-organization interface). These roles are entangled within and across people and actions.

We now expand the elements introduced by Complexity Leadership Theory, beginning with administrative leadership and then moving into the adaptive and enabling roles.

3.1. Administrative leadership

Administrative leadership refers to the actions of individuals in formal managerial roles who plan and coordinate organizational activities (e.g., the bureaucratic function). Administrative leaders (among other things) structure tasks, engage in planning, build vision, acquire resources to achieve goals (Dougherly & Hardy, 1996; Shalley & Gilson, 2004), manage crises (Mumford & Licuanan, 2004) and personal conflicts (Jehn, 1997), and manage organizational strategy. The nature of this administrative leadership varies within the hierarchical level of the system. Administrators at Jaques' (1989) strategic level engage in planning, coordination, resource acquisition (Osborn & Hunt, 2007-this issue), and structuring conditions related to strategy (Marion & Uhl-Bien,

143

2007). At Jaques' organizational level, administrators implement more focused planning and coordination of creative operations, manage resource allocation, and structure conditions within which adaptive leadership occurs.

Administrative leadership is a top-down function based on authority and position, thus it possess the power to make decisions for the organization. However, within the structure described by Complexity Leadership Theory, administrative leadership is advised to exercise its authority with consideration of the firm's need for creativity, learning, and adaptability (i.e., adaptive leadership), for its actions can have significant impact on these dynamics. A decision, for example, to exercise profitable efficiency in a volatile environment could deprive a firm of much needed adaptive capacity.

3.2. Adaptive leadership

Adaptive leadership is an emergent, interactive dynamic that produces adaptive outcomes in a social system. It is a collaborative change movement that emerges nonlinearly from interactive exchanges, or, more specifically, from the "spaces between" agents (cf. Bradbury & Lichtenstein, 2000; Drath, 2001; Lichtenstein et al., 2006). That is, it originates in struggles among agents and groups over conflicting needs, ideas, or preferences; it results in movements, alliances of people, ideas, or technologies, and cooperative efforts. Adaptive leadership is a complex dynamic rather than a person (although people are, importantly, involved); we label it leadership because it is a, and, arguably, the, proximal source of change in an organization.

Adaptive leadership emerges from asymmetrical interaction (the notion of complexity and asymmetry is developed by Cilliers, 1998). We propose two types of asymmetry: that related to authority and that related to preferences (which include differences in knowledge, skills, beliefs, etc.). If an interaction is largely one-sided and authority-based, then the leadership event can be labeled as top-down. If authority asymmetry is

144

less one-sided and more preference oriented, then the leadership event is more likely based on interactive dynamics driven by differences in preferences.

Struggles over asymmetrical preference differences foster adaptive change outcomes (thus the earlier statement that change emerges from the spaces between agents). Adaptive change is produced by the clash of existing but (seemingly) incompatible ideas, knowledge, and technologies; it takes the form of new knowledge and creative ideas, learning, or adaptation. A familiar form of this change occurs when two interdependent individuals who are debating conflicting perceptions of a given issue suddenly, and perhaps simultaneously, generate a new understanding of that issue—this can be considered an "aha" moment. The "aha" is a nonlinear product of a combination of the original perceptions, of the discarding of untenable arguments and the fusion of what is tenable, or perhaps of the rejection of original ideas as untenable and the creation of a totally new idea. It represents a process of seeing beyond original assumptions to something not bounded by those assumptions. Moreover, it cannot be claimed by any one individual, but rather is a product of the interactions among individuals (i.e., it is produced in the "spaces between"; Bradbury & Lichtenstein, 2000).

Adaptive leadership is recognized as such when it has significance and impact—significance is the potential usefulness of new, creative knowledge or adaptive ideas and impact refers to the degree to which other agents external to the generative set embrace and use the new knowledge or idea. The significance of an adaptive moment is related to the expertise of the agents who generate that moment (Mumford, Scott, Gaddis, & Strange, 2002; Weisburg, 1999) and to their capacity for creative thinking (Mumford, Connelly, & Gaddis, 2003). Expertise and creativity are not necessarily co-resident in an adaptive event, of course. Quite obviously, creative individuals without training in physics are not going to advance that field, but neither are, one might argue, two physicists who are unable or unwilling to break out of their paradigmatic assumptions. Complex systems depend on the former (expertise) and stimulate the latter (creativity).

Impact can be independent of significance because impact is influenced by (among other things) the authority and reputation of the agents who generated the idea, the degree to which an idea captures the imagination or to which its implications are understood, or whether the idea can generate enough support to exert an impact (see Arthur, 1989, for discussion). Thus an insignificant idea can have considerable circulation.

Complexity Leadership Theory describes conditions in which adaptive dynamics emerge and generate creative and adaptive knowledge that exhibits sufficient significance and impact to create change. Adaptive leadership is not an act of an individual, but rather a dynamic of interdependent agents (i.e., CAS). To exhibit significance and impact, adaptive leadership must be embedded in an appropriately structured, neural-like network of CAS and agents (within the context of CAS; i.e., network dynamics) and exhibit significance and impact that generate change in the social system.

3.2.1. Network dynamics

Network dynamics refer to the contexts and mechanisms that enable adaptive leadership. As defined above, context is the interactive ambiance within which complex dynamics occur, and mechanisms are the dynamic patterns of behavior that produce complex outcomes. In interactive and interdependent networks, adaptive ideas, whether small or large, emerge and interact in much the same way that pairs or groups of agents interact. The contexts that shape those ideas include networks of interaction, complex patterns of conflicting constraints, patterns of tension, interdependent relationships, rules of action, direct and indirect feedback loops, and rapidly changing environmental demands. The mechanisms that emerge include resonance (i.e., correlated action; see below) and aggregation of ideas, catalytic behaviors (behaviors that speed or enable certain activities; Kauffman, 1993), generation of both dynamically stable and unstable behaviors, dissipation of built up tension as phase transitions (Prigogine, 1997), nonlinear change, information flow and pattern formation, and accreting nodes[9] (ideas that rapidly expand in importance and which accrete related ideas) (see Fig. 1). In complex networks, ideas emerge, combine, diverge, become extinct, conflict with one another, adapt and change, and increase in complexity. The primary outputs of this complex dynamic are adaptability, creativity, and learning.

Adaptive leadership emerges within this complex milieu of contexts and mechanisms—it exists in complex network contexts and produces (and is produced by) complex mechanisms. There are two interactive and interdependent levels of pertinent activity: (1) the interaction of agents and CAS that produce ideas and knowledge, and (2) the interaction of the ideas and knowledge to produce even more complex ideas and knowledge. Loosely adapting Cohen, March, & Olsen's (1972) garbage can metaphor, we can envision this as a complex garbage can in which agents and CAS and contexts and mechanisms and ideas and knowledge swirl. The end result is emergent creativity, learning, and adaptability at all levels of the system and at multiple scales of importance.

---

[9] The notion of accreting nodes is derived from related work in fractal geometry; see, for example, (Mandelbrot, 1983).

The Emergence Dynamic

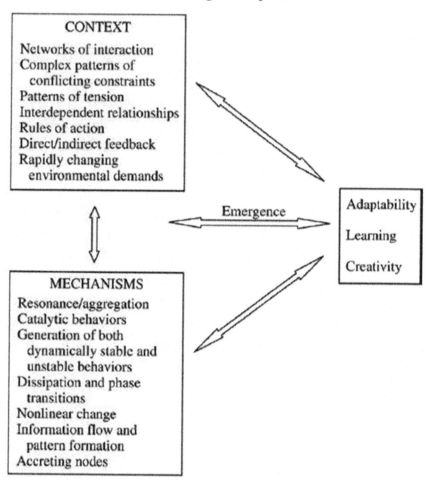

Fig. 1. The emergence dynamic.

3.2.2. Emergence

Earlier we defined the complex change process in terms of "spaces between" and struggles over diverse ideas. We now define it more precisely in terms of emergence. Emergence involves two, interdependent mechanisms: (1) the reformulation of existing elements to produce outcomes that are qualitatively different from the original elements; and (2) self-organization. Reformulation competes with theories of natural selection or human intelligence as a source of unique change (but, importantly, it does not preempt the involvement of other such dynamics; see Kauffman, 1993, for example). Reformulation is defined as the expansion, parsing, amplification, transformation, and combination of multiple interacting, often conflicting, elements under conditions of tension and asymmetrical information. It is produced by complex (as opposed to complicated) interactive mechanisms within appropriately structured contexts; thus reformulation is intimately linked to the random nature of interaction in complex networks and outcomes can be unpredictable and nonlinear. The essence of the original elements is transformed in a manner that gives new meaning or interpretation to the resulting outcome. That is, the system changes in a fundamental way.

Wikipedia defines self-organization as a process in which the "internal organization of a system, normally an open system, increases in complexity without being guided or managed by an outside source" (Wikipedia, n.d.) This phenomenon is well documented in physics, biology, and the social sciences (see the above Wikipedia entry on self-organization for examples). We modify this definition for leadership studies, defining it in terms of resonating reformulation events (Marion & Uhl-Bien, 2001). Resonance is defined as acting in concert; it refers more specifically to situations in which the behaviors of two or more agents are interdependent. Thus clusters of cars speeding down a highway are resonating together. Self-organization, then, is a movement in which different reformulation activities find common cause. The modern terrorist movement, for example, is a self-organized event (Marion & Uhl-Bien, 2003). Importantly, human volition (e.g., managerial coordination) can play important roles in our definition of self-organization; however, volition is not necessarily determinative of self-organizing behaviors but is rather an actor in this dynamic

We now formally define adaptive leadership:

Definition. Adaptive leadership is defined as emergent change behaviors under conditions of interaction, inter-dependence, asymmetrical information, complex network dynamics, and tension. Adaptive leadership manifests in CAS and interactions among agents rather than in individuals, and is recognizable when it has significance and impact.

3.2.3. Multi-level adaptive leadership

CAS occur in all hierarchical levels of an organization. The emergent outcomes and the significance and impact of adaptive behaviors differ across hierarchical levels of course (Boal, Whitehead, Phillips, & Hunt, 1992; Hunt & Ropo, 1995; Phillips & Hunt, 1992). Broadly addressed, the adaptive outputs for the upper level of a hierarchy (what Jaques, 1989, called, the strategic level) relate largely to emergent planning, resource acquisition, and strategic relationships with the environment (for discussion, see Marion & Uhl-Bien, 2007; see also Child & McGrath, 2001, for a useful discussion of interdependency among organizations). Adaptive outputs for the middle hierarchical levels (middle management, or what Jaques, 1989, called, the organizational level) relate to emergence of focused planning, resource allocation, etc. That for the lower levels (Jaques' production level) relates to development of the core products of the organization; for knowledge-producing organizations, this includes knowledge development, innovation, and adaptation (Osborn & Hunt, 2007-this issue, provide an extensive discussion of complexity and the levels perspective).

3.3. Enabling leadership

The role of enabling leadership in the CLT framework is to directly foster and maneuver the conditions (e.g., context) that catalyze adaptive leadership and allow for emergence. Middle managers (Jaques, 1989) are often in a position to engage in enabling behaviors because of their access to resources and their direct involvement in the boundary conditions for the system's production level (see Osborn & Hunt, 2007-this issue). However, enabling leadership can be found anywhere. Its role seemingly overlaps, at times, that of administrative leadership in that it may be performed by agents acting in more managerial capacities. Moreover, a single agent or aggregate can perform either adaptive or enabling roles by merely changing hats as needed.

The roles of enabling leadership can be summarized as follows:

- Enabling leadership enables effective CAS dynamics by fostering enabling conditions that catalyze adaptive leadership and allow for emergence.
- Enabling leadership manages the entanglement between administrative and adaptive leadership; this includes (1) managing the organizational conditions in which adaptive leadership exists, and (2) helping disseminate innovative products of adaptive leadership upward and through the formal managerial system (i.e., the innovation-to-organization interface, Dougherty & Hardy, 1996).

3.3.1. Enable conditions that catalyze adaptive leadership

One function of enabling leadership is to catalyze CAS dynamics that promote adaptive leadership. Catalyzing refers to activities that bring together the enabling conditions (mechanisms and contexts) necessary for adaptive leadership to emerge. As described earlier, complex networks conducive to adaptive leadership are (among other things) interactive, moderately interdependent, and infused with tension. Enabling leadership, then, fosters complex networks by (1) fostering interaction, (2) fostering interdependency, and (3) injecting adaptive tension to help motivate and coordinate the interactive dynamic.

3.3.1.1. Interaction. Effective network conditions are catalyzed first by interaction. Interaction produces the network of linkages across which information flows and connects. Enabling leaders cannot create the sophisticated dynamic linkages that characterize complex networks, nor can they accurately pre-calculate what constitutes the right amount of coupling. Rather, such networks are self-organizing. They can, however, create the general structure of complex networks and the conditions in which sophisticated networks can evolve. For example, from an organizational level (Jaques, 1989), enabling leadership can foster interaction through such strategies as open architecture work places, self-selected work groups, electronic work groups (email, etc.), and by management-induced scheduling or rules structuring.

Moreover, the interactive imperative is not bounded to the immediate work group, but extends to interactions with other groups (CAS) and with the environment. Interaction with other CAS fosters cross-group initiatives, possible aggregation of different ideas into larger ideas, a degree of coordination across efforts, and the importation of information that may inform the target work group.

Further, at Jaques' (1989) strategic level, enabling leadership helps foster interactions of organizational CAS with environmental dynamics. This serves at least two purposes: it enables importation of fresh information into the creative dynamic (Boisot, 1998), and it broadens the organization's capacity to adapt to environmental changes and conditions beyond the adaptive capacity of strategic leadership acting alone. Marion & Uhl-Bien (2007) propose that organizational adaptability should even be a significant element of strategic planning because of its capability to adapt quickly and competently to environmental changes; a particularly potent example is evident in the adaptive strategies of terrorist networks (see Marion & Uhl-Bien, 2003). For a more extensive discussion of complexity and strategic leadership, see the Boal & Schultz (2007-this issue).

Individual agents in adaptive networks can act in an enabling role by adopting behaviors that enhance their interactive contributions. For example, they can enlarge their personal networks to increase the amount of access and network resources they can bring to the table. Moreover, they can contribute to the flow of information across CAS by keeping themselves informed and knowledgeable on issues important to the firm and their field and by framing issues appropriate to the perspectives of the others with whom they are interacting. They can also monitor the environment (e.g., political, economic, social, national, international, technological) to understand the nature of the forces that are influencing the adaptive dynamic.

3.3.1.2 Interdependency. Interaction alone is insufficient for complex functioning; the agents in a system must also be interdependent. While interaction permits the movement and dynamic interplay of information, interdependency creates pressure to act on information. Interdependency's potency derives from naturally occurring (emergent) networks of conflicting constraints. Conflicting constraints manifest when the well-being of one agent is inversely dependent on the well-being of another, or when the information broadcasted by one agent is incompatible with that broadcasted by another agent. Such constraints pressure agents to adjust their actions and to elaborate their information.

At the organizational level (Jaques, 1989) there are a number of ways to manage conditions that catalyze interdependency mechanisms. One useful tool for promoting interdependency is to allow measured autonomy for informal behavior (see also Shalley & Gilson, 2004). Autonomy permits conflicting constraints to emerge and enables agents to work through those constraints without interference from formal authorities. Nordstrom illustrates this approach in a statement in their employee handbook:

> We also encourage you to present your own ideas. Your buyers have a great deal of autonomy, and are encouraged to seek out and promote new fashion directions at all times . . . and we encourage you to share your concerns, suggestions and ideas. (Pfeffer, 2005, p. 99)

A major function of leaders has historically been to solve problems, to intervene when dilemmas arise or when individuals differ on task-related activities. Such action, however, can stifle interdependency and limit adaptive mechanisms. Complexity Leadership Theory proposes circumspection by administrative leaders in such matters, to resist the temptation to create an atmosphere in which workers bring their work problems to management (see Alvesson & Sveningsson, 2003). Enabling leaders fosters such circumspection by mediating this issue with administrative leaders who are overly involved, by stifling one's own desire in administrative roles to act in this way, or even by implementing policy regarding the resolution of problems and task conflicts (see, for example, Snyder's, 1988, description of such implementation).

At the strategic level enabling leaders can foster interdependency with rules—not limiting bureaucratic rules but rules or conditions that apply pressure to coordinate (Eisenhardt, 1989; McKelvey et al., 2003). Microsoft's™ strategy for developing software, for example, is built on interactive work groups and rule-enabled interdependencies (Cusumano, 2001). Programmers operate independently and in small groups, but are periodically required to run their code against the code of other programmers. If there are problems, the team must repair the incompatibility before moving on. Microsoft calls this "sync and stabilize." The process imposes interdependency that can create cascading changes and elaboration in Microsoft's software. Microsoft gains the benefit of flexibility, adaptability, speed, and innovation while maintaining coordinated action.

At the individual level, agents engaging in enabling leadership recognize the importance of interdependency and they can function to foster coordinated efforts. Enabling agents refine or realign their information relative to the information of the other agents (Kauffman, 1993; Marion & Uhl-Bien, 2001) in ways that contribute to co-evolution or co-elaborating of ideas and information such that new, sometimes surprising information can emerge (Kauffman, 1993).

3.3.1.3 Tension. Finally, since tension creates an imperative to act and to elaborate strategy, information, and adaptability, enabling leadership also works to foster tension. Internal tension can be enhanced by heterogeneity, a stimulus of interdependency and conflicting constraints. Heterogeneity refers to differences among agents in such things as skills, preferences, and outlooks (McKelvey, in press; Schilling & Steensma, 2001). When couched within a context of interdependency, heterogeneity pressures agents to adapt to their differences. At the upper echelon and organizational levels, enabling leadership promotes heterogeneity by (among other things) building an atmosphere in which such diversity is respected, with considered hiring practices, and by structuring work groups to enable interaction of diverse ideas. Enabling leadership also fosters internal tension by enabling an atmosphere that tolerates dissent and divergent perspectives on problems, one in which personnel are charged with resolving their differences and finding solutions to their problems (cf. Heifetz & Laurie, 2001).

Enabling leadership not only fosters internal tension, it judiciously injects tension as well—tension that derives externally in that it is not a natural function of informal dynamics. Upper—and mid-level enabling leaders inject tension with managerial pressures or challenges, by distributing resources in a manner that supports creative movements, and by creating demands for results. Enabling leaders can impose tension by dropping "seeds of emergence" (Marion & Uhl-Bien, 2001; McKelvey et al., 1999), or perturbations that have the potential of fostering learning and creativity. Such "seeds" include ideas, information, judiciously placed resources, new people, and the capacity to access unspecified resources (i.e., gateways that permit exploration; access to the internet is an obvious example). Seeds are intended to stimulate the networked system, and their impact may be unpredictable.

At the individual level, agents can engage in enabling leadership by recognizing the creative value of tension and using it to foster productive discussions and interaction. They would not look to authority for answers, but rather commit to engaging in the process of adaptive problem solving. Enabling agents recognize the difference between task (or ideational) conflict (which can produce creative outcomes; Jehn, 1997), and interpersonal conflict (which is disruptive to social dynamics) and work to promote productive, task conflicts (Heifetz, 1994; Jehn, 1997; Lencioni, 2002). They contribute ideas and opinions, they play devil's advocate, and they address the "elephants on the table" that others try to ignore (Parks, 2005). They also recognize when a group is bogged down by consensus (Lencioni, 2002) that comes from lack of diversity, and expose the group to heterogeneous perspectives, bringing other people and ideas into the dynamic as necessary.

Enabling leadership can also emerge from within the adaptive function. Schreiber (2006), in a study of complexity leadership and risk factors, identified several interesting enabling dynamics in work groups (measurements from these observations were used in a follow-up multi-agent based simulation). Certain agents emerged, for example, who tended to induce interactions and establish interdependencies. Others were boundary spanners, or "agent[s] who most likely connect . . . to otherwise disjoint groups" (p. 136). Some agents emerged who were "likely to have the most interactions and to learn more knowledge" (p. 136). There were also agents "who can most quickly communicate to the organization at large" (p. 136). Lastly, some agents were "most likely to communicate new knowledge" (p. 136). Such agent-roles represent nodes in a neural network of agents (see, for example, Carley & Ren, 2001) and serve to enable (and operationalize) interaction, interdependency, and learning within CAS.

3.3.2. Managing the entanglement between adaptive and administrative structures

A second function of the enabling leadership role is to manage the entanglement between CAS dynamics and formal administrative systems and structures. This involves using authority (where applicable), access to resources, and influence to keep the formal and informal organizational systems working in tandem rather than counter to one another (Dougherty, 1996). In this function, enabling leaders:

1) work to prevent administrative leaders from stifling or suppressing beneficial interactive dynamics and foster adaptive dynamics that are consistent with the strategy and mission of the organization (the administrative-adaptive interface); and
2) Facilitate the integration of creative outcomes into the formal system (i.e., the innovation-to-organization interface, Dougherty & Hardy, 1996).

3.3.2.1. Managing the administrative-adaptive interface.

Regarding the first of these roles, enabling leaders help protect the CAS from external politics and top-down preferences. They serve to influence the policies and decisions of administrative leadership, including planning and resource allocation, to accommodate the needs of adaptive structures (Dougherty & Hardy, 1996). They also help align organizational strategy to the needs of CAS dynamics and convince administrative leadership when CAS dynamics are important for organizational strategy (Marion & Uhl-Bien, 2007).

Managing the conditions for adaptive leadership requires a different focus on planning and resource allocation. With regard to planning, Mumford et al. (in press) note a lack of consensus in the leadership literature about whether creativity is enabled or hampered by administrative planning (Bluedorn, Johnson, Cartwright, & Barringer, 1994; Finkelstein & Hambrick, 1996). Some scholars argue that planning provides the resources and structure that creative initiatives require while others argue that administrators cannot anticipate and plan the directions in which creative dynamics will flow (Mumford et al., in press). Complexity Leadership Theory (CLT) has similar concerns about planning. On the one hand, emergence is the product of informal adaptive behavior that would be hampered by top-down restrictions (Krause, 2004). On the other hand, the need to focus creative behaviors is legitimate; indeed unrestrained adaptive behavior would be expensive to support and could compromise rather that enhance the organization's strategic mission.

Framing the question for Complexity Leadership Theory, we ask: Does planning enable or inhibit nonlinear emergence? Our short answer is: It depends on the nature of the plan. Planning for creativity must deal with significant uncertainties, including the fact that creativity by definition involves development of ideas that are currently unknowable (Popper, 1986), changing future environmental uncertainties, and uncertainty about whether creative ideas will become viable market solutions. Mumford et al. (in press; see also Mumford, Schultz & Osborn 2002) propose evolving and flexible plans to deal with such uncertainties. They divide their planning model into five stages: 1) scanning, 2) template planning, 3) plan development, 4) forecasting, and 5) plan execution. These stages can be summarized as idea identification (scanning and template planning), plan development (including forecasting), and plan execution. Mumford et al. (2002) argue that plans should be adapted to the needs of each stage and that planning within these stages should be a continuous process in order to adjust for changes and unknowns that are certain to arise. Mumford et al. (in press) further argue that R&D programs must be understood in the long term and that leaders of R&D are managers of systemic dynamics rather than of day-to-day details.

Mumford et al. (in press) propose that organizational plans should impose limits that assure creative emergence is consistent with the core competencies (or themes) of the system. This focuses creativity around practical constraints without unduly dampening the creative spirit. We further propose that planners separate the creative process from the structure in which it occurs: The creative process itself (e.g., adaptive behaviors) should not be unduly managed or constrained by administrative planning and coordination; however that process should be couched within a larger planning structure similar to that proposed (above) by Mumford et al.

Therefore, our framework proposes that enabling leadership, in general, assumes a systemic relationship with complex dynamics, one in which the responsibility is to provide the framework and conditions within which enabling and adaptive leadership function. At Jaques' (1989) strategic level enabling leaders plan a trajectory for the adaptive process and have a long-term outlook (Marion & Uhl-Bien, 2007). Enabling leaders at Jaques' (1989) organizational level, in contrast, plan the context surrounding work; their function is more short-term than that of strategic leaders and is focused on the given stage of a plan at any given time.

With regard to resources, the literature on creativity has noted the importance of increasing the availability of information resources (Reiter-Palmon & Illies, 2004). Similarly, complex adaptive systems depend on flows of information resources, and when such flows are hindered, they do not operate effectively. Therefore, enabling leaders provide resources that enhance access to information (e.g., access to electronic databases). They coordinate acquisition and allocation of resources (money, supplies, information, personnel, etc.) that support creative, learning, and adaptive behaviors of CAS. Bonabeau & Meyer (2001) add that leaders can enhance the adaptive process by allowing physical resources (e.g., money, supplies, etc.) to follow emergent ideas (see also Dougherty & Hardy, 1996). This fosters motivation and creates tension related to scarce resources. Since personnel are resources, and diversity of personnel skills and preferences are important to the creative and adaptive functions of CAS, enabling leaders also promote diversity in hiring practices and policy actions.

Enabling leadership manages conditions consistent with the strategy and mission of the organization by articulating the mission of a project (e.g., Kennedy's mission to put Americans on the moon by 1970; see, for example, Jaussi & Dionne, 2003). Complexity Leadership Theory adds (as does Mumford et al., in press), however, that such missions should not be so specific that they restrict the creative process. They should be sufficiently flexible to change with changing conditions.

Strategy and mission consistency is fostered by discouraging non-useful adaptations. Adaptive leadership is, by design, unpredictable, and its emergent activities can evolve in directions that are contrary to the strategic mission of the organization. Enabling leaders help realignment of non-useful adaptations by (for example) periodically evaluating adaptive outputs for a given stage of development relative to organizational mission-themes (see Mumford et al., in press), by clearly articulating the mission (described above), or by offering technical support that is consistent with organizational themes.

Enabling leaders promote behavior that advances strategic goals by dealing with crises that threaten to derail adaptive functions (Mumford et al., in press); by protecting the creative process from forces (e.g., boards or directors, other administrators, environmental pressures) that would limit the capacity of the organization or its subsystems to engage in creativity, learning, and adaptation; and by structuring conditions such as missions, physical conditions, crises, personal conflicts, and external threats in ways that support creative adaptive behaviors.

3.3.2.2. Managing the innovation-to-organization interface. In the second role identified above, enabling leaders help in the innovation-to-organization interface. Howell & Boies (2004) refer to this as championing. They argue, describing creative ideas, that:

To overcome the social and political pressures imposed by an organization and convert them to its advantage, champions demonstrate personal commitment to the idea, promote the idea . . . through informal networks, and willingly risk their position and reputation to ensure its success . . . [They] establish . . . and maintain . . . contact with top management, to keep them informed and enthusiastic about the project . . . . [A] new venture idea require[s] a champion to exert social and political effort to galvanize support for the concept. (p. 124)

As noted by Dougherty & Hardy (1996), formal organizational systems are often not structured to foster internal dissemination of innovation—rather, they tend to inhibit it. Because formal structures present obstacles for innovation-to-organization transference, power is needed to facilitate, orchestrate, and share innovative ideas and outcomes throughout the organization. "Unless product innovation has an explicit, organization-wide power basis, there is no generative force, no energy, for developing new products continuously and weaving them into ongoing functioning" (Dougherty & Hardy, 1996, p.1146). They suggest that organizations adopt a "pro-innovation" approach by moving beyond reliance on networks of personal power (a focus on individuals) and toward an organization-system base of power. Such a system would foster processes that "link the right people" and "emphasize the right criteria," as well as "allow resources to begin to flow to the right places" (Dougherty & Hardy, 1996, p.1149). Enabling leaders can play an integral role in helping design and protect such a "pro-innovation" organizational system.

Enabling leadership also works with adaptive and administrative leadership to decide which creative outputs of the adaptive subsystem are the most appropriate to move forward into the broader bureaucratic structure. In conducting this function, Mumford et al. (in press) caution administrators to avoid assessing the creative output itself and to instead focus on assessing the degree to which activities are accomplishing the functions of the given stage of development. "Evaluation," they argue, "should be viewed as a developmental exercise with multiple cycles of evaluation and revision occurring in any stage before planning progresses to the next stage" (in press). Therefore, enabling leadership helps coordinate the interface between adaptive and administrative leadership by working for policies and strategies that enable complex dynamics and by adopting a "pro-innovation" environment that facilitates innovation-to-organization transference.

3.3.3. Summary

Complexity Leadership Theory (CLT), then, is a framework for studying emergent leadership dynamics in relationship to bureaucratic superstructures. CLT identifies three types of leadership, adaptive, enabling, and administrative, and proposes that they differ according to where they occur in the larger organizational hierarchy. A basic unit of analysis of CLT is complex adaptive systems (or CAS), which exist throughout the organization and are entangled with the bureaucratic functions such that they cannot be separated. CLT proposes that CAS, when functioning appropriately, provide an adaptive capability for the organization, and that bureaucracy provides an orienting and coordinating structure. A key role of enabling leadership is to effectively manage the entanglement between administrative and adaptive structures and behaviors in a manner that enhances the overall flexibility and effectiveness of the organization (Marion & Uhl-Bien, 2007). By focusing on emergent leadership dynamics, CLT implies that leadership only exists in, and is a function of, interaction; despite this, there are roles for individual leaders in interacting with (i.e., enabling) this dynamic.

4. Conclusion

As described by Rost (1991), leadership study has been bogged down in the periphery and content of leadership, and what is needed is "a new understanding of what leadership is, in a post-industrial school of leadership" (Rost, 1991, p. 181). In the present article we attempt to move toward such an understanding by developing a model of leadership based in complexity science. Complexity science is a modern "normal" science, the assumptions of which fit the dynamics of social, managerial, and organizational behavior in high velocity, knowledge-type environments (Henrickson & McKelvey, 2002). Complexity science allows us to develop leadership perspectives that extend beyond bureaucratic assumptions to add a view of leadership as a complex interactive dynamic through which adaptive outcomes emerge. This new perspective, which we label Complexity Leadership Theory, recognizes that leadership is too complex to be described as only the act of an individual or individuals; rather, it is a complex interplay of many interacting forces.

Complexity Leadership Theory focuses primarily on the complex interactive dynamics of CAS and addresses how individuals interact with this dynamic to enable adaptive outcomes. CAS are the basic unit of analysis in Complexity Leadership Theory. CAS are comprised of agents, however, and their roles in the CAS dynamic is important. Further, individuals (particularly those in positions of authority) can influence the CAS function and are likewise of interest in Complexity Leadership Theory.

Research on CAS in Complexity Leadership Theory should examine the dynamic (i.e., changing, interactive, temporal), informal interactive patterns that exist in and among organizational systems. This generates interesting questions for leadership research. For example, what patterns of behavior (what Allen, 2001, calls, structural attractors) do organizational CAS gravitate to and are there 'patterns to those patterns' across systems? What is the specific generative nature of asymmetry and how does it function within a network dynamic? What enabling functions emerge from a complex network dynamic (such as those found by Schreiber, 2006)? What psycho-social dynamic occurs in the "spaces between agents" emergent dynamic? What are the mechanisms by which a social system moves from one stable pattern to another? What contexts are conducive to given patterns of interaction and how do enabling and administrative leaders help foster or stifle those contexts?

A complexity leadership approach adds to leadership research a consideration of the mechanisms and contexts by which change occurs and systems elaborate rather than a predominant focus on variables. To understand mechanisms requires methodology that is capable of analyzing the interactions of multiple agents over a period of time (see Hazy, 2007-this issue). Developing an understanding of the mechanisms that underlie Complexity Leadership Theory and the conditions in which such mechanisms will emerge is critical as we move our theorizing forward into embedded context approaches in leadership (Osborn et al., 2002). There can be any number of mechanisms underlying the Complexity Leadership Theory function. In this article we focus on such mechanisms as interaction among heterogeneous agents, annealing, requisite variety, information flows, catalyzing activities, and nonlinear emergence.

Research regarding complexity dynamics needs to capture the nature of mechanisms, which are nonlinearly changeable, unpredictable in the long term (and sometimes in the short term), temporally based, and interactively and causally complex. We suggest two methodological strategies for doing this. First, qualitative procedures allow temporal evaluations and have been used in complexity studies (Bradbury & Lichtenstein, 2000). Second, various computer modeling procedures have been utilized for complexity research (see Hazy, 2007-this issue), the most common being agent based modeling (Carley & Svoboda, 1996) and system dynamic modeling (Sterman, 1994).

In agent based modeling, individual, computerized agents are programmed to interact according to certain defined rules of sociological and organizational engagement (Carley & Svoboda, 1996). Systems dynamics model the interaction of more global variables and dynamics with equations that define their relationships. In either case, a common approach is to measure certain characteristics of a social group (e.g., organizational work groups) and to use those data as initial conditions in a simulation. This obviates the need to make detailed, onsite observations across time and permits the researcher to experiment with "what-if" scenarios (e.g., what if hierarchical centralization is increased). Jim Hazy has provided an excellent review of simulation procedures elsewhere in this edition; see also Guastello's article (2007-this issue) for a statistics-based, research strategy, and Plowman et al. (2007-this issue, 2007) for a qualitative methodology.

In sum, in this article we develop and outline key elements of Complexity Leadership Theory. We argue that while the Knowledge

Era calls for a new leadership paradigm, much of leadership theory still promotes an approach aimed at incentivizing workers to follow vision-led, top-down control by CEOs (Bennis, 1996; Zaccaro & Klimoski, 2001). Though this approach fits recent trends toward performance management and accountability, it can stifle a firm's innovation and fitness (Marion & Uhl-Bien, 2001; Schneider & Somers, 2006). We propose that Complexity Leadership Theory offers a new way of perceiving leadership—a theoretical framework for approaching the study of leadership that moves beyond the managerial logics of the Industrial Age to meet the new leadership requirements of the Knowledge Era.

References

Achtenhagen, L., Melin, L., Mullern, T., & Ericson, T. (2003). Leadership: The role of interactive strategizing. In A. Pettigrew R. Whittington L. Melin C. Sanchez-Runde F. A. J. Van Den Bosch W. Ruigrok & T. Numagami (Eds.), Innovative forms of organizing: International perspectives (pp. 49-71). London: Sage Publications.\\Allen, P. (2001). A complex systems approach to learning in adaptive networks. International Journal of Innovation Management, 5, 149-180.

Alvesson, M., & Sveningsson, S. (2003). The great disappearing act: Difficulties in doing "leadership". The Leadership Quarterly, 14, 359-381.

Arthur, W. B. (1989). The economy and complexity. In D. L. Stein (Ed.), Lectures in the sciences of complexity, vol. 1 (pp. 713-740). Redwood City, CA: Addison-Wesley.

Ashby, W. R. (1960). Design for a brain, (2nd Ed.). New York: Wiley.

Bak, P. (1996). How nature works. New York: Copernicus.

Bamford, J. D., Gomes-Casseres, B., & Robinson, M. S. (2002). Mastering alliance strategy. San Francisco, CA: Jossey Bass.

Barkema, H. G., Baum, J. A. C., & Mannix, E. A. (2002). Management challenges in a new time. Academy of Management Journal, 45(5), 916-930.

Barnard, C. I. (1938). The functions of the executive. Cambridge, MA: Harvard University Press.

Bass, B. M. (1985). Leadership and performance beyond expectations. New York: Free Press.

Bedeian, A. G., & Hunt, J. G. (2006). Academic amnesia and vestigial assumptions of our forefathers. The Leadership Quarterly, 17(2), 190-205.

Bennis, W. G. (1996). Becoming a leader of leaders. In R. Gibson (Ed.), Rethinking the future. London: Brealey.

Bettis, R. A., & Hitt, M. A. (1995). The new competitive landscape. Strategic Management Journal, 7(13), 7-19.

Bluedorn, A. C., Johnson, R. A., Cartwright, D. K., & Barringer, B. R. (1994). The interface and convergence of the strategic management and organizational environment domains. Journal of Management, 20(2), 201-262.

Boal, K., & Schlultz, P. (2007). Storytelling, time, and evolution: The role of strategic leadership in complex adaptive systems. The Leadership Quarterly, 18, 411-428 (this issue). doi:10.1016/j/leaqua.2007.04.008.

Boal, K., Whitehead, C. J., Phillips, R., & Hunt, J. (1992). Strategic leadership: A multiorganizational-level perspective. Westport, CT: Quorum.

Boisot, M. H. (1998). Knowledge assets: Securing competitive advantage in the information economy. Oxford: Oxford University Press.

Bonabeau, E., & Meyer, C. (2001). Swarm intelligence: A whole new way to think about business. Harvard Business Review, 79(5), 107-114.

Bradbury, H., & Lichtenstein, B. (2000). Relationality in organizational research: Exploring the space between. Organization Science, 11, 551-564.

Carley, K. (1997). Organizational adaptation. Annals of Operation Research, 75, 25-47.

Carley, K., & Hill, V. (2001). Structural change and learning within organizations. In A. Lomi & E. R. Larsen (Eds.), Dynamics of organizational societies (pp. 63-92). Cambridge, MA: AAAI/MIT Press.

Carley, K., & Lee, J. S. (1998). Dynamic organizations: Organizational adaptation in a changing environment. Advances in Strategic Management: A Research Annual, 15, 269-297.

Carley, K., & Ren, Y. (2001). Tradeoffs between performance and adaptability for c3i architectures (part of the A2C2 project supported in part by the Office of Naval Research).: Carnegie Mellon University.

Carley, K., & Svoboda, D. M. (1996). Modeling organizational adaptation as a simulated annealing process. Sociological Methods and Research, 25 (1), 138-168.

Child, J., & McGrath, R. G. (2001). Organizations unfettered: Organizational form in an information-intensive economy. The Academy of Management Journal, 44(6), 1135-1149.

Cilliers, P. (1998). Complexity and postmodernism: Understanding complex systems. London: Routledge.

Cilliers, P. (2001). Boundaries, hierarchies and networks in complex systems. International Journal of Innovation Management, 5, 135-147.

Cohen, M. D., March, J. G., & Olsen, J. P. (1972). A garbage can model of organizational choice. Administrative Science Quarterly, 17, 1-25.

Conger, J. A. (1999). Charismatic and transformational leadership in organizations: An insider's perspective on these developing streams of research. The Leadership Quarterly, 10(2), 145-179.

Coveney, P. (2003). Self-organization and complexity: A new age for theory, computation and experiment. Paper presented at the Nobel symposium on self-organization. Stockholm: Karolinska Institutet.

Cusumano, M. (2001). Focusing creativity: Microsoft's "synch and stabilize" approach to software product development. In I. Nonaka & T. Nishiguchi (Eds.), Knowledge emergence: Social, technical, and evolutionary dimensions of knowledge creation. Oxford: Oxford University Press.

Davenport, T. H. (2001). Knowledge work and the future of management. In W. G. Bennis G. M. Spreitzer & T. G. Cummings (Eds.), The future of leadership: Today's top leadership thinkers speak to tomorrow's leaders (pp. 41-58). 2001 San Francisco: Jossey-Bass.

Day, D. V. (2000). Leadership development: A review in context. The Leadership Quarterly, 11(4), 581-613.

Dooley, K. J. (1996, 10.26.96). Complex adaptive systems: A nominal definition. Retrieved September, 2006, from http://www.eas.asu.edu/~kdooley/ casopdef.html

Dougherty, D. (1996). Organizing for innovation. In S. R. Clegg C. Hardy & W. Nord (Eds.), Handbook of organization studies (pp. 424-439). London: Sage.

Dougherty, D., & Hardy, C. (1996). Sustained product innovation in large, mature organizations: Overcoming innovation-to-organization problems. Academy of Management Journal, 39, 1120-1153.

Drath, W. (2001). The deep blue sea: Rethinking the source of leadership. San Francisco: Jossey-Bass and Center for Creative Leadership.

Drucker, P. F. (1998). Management's new paradigms (cover story). Forbes, 162(7), 152-170.

Drucker, P. F. (1999). Management challenges for the 21st century. New York: HarperCollins.

Eisenhardt, K. (1989). Making fast strategic decisions in high-velocity environments. Academy of Management Journal, 32, 543-576.

Finkelstein, S., & Hambrick, D. C. (1996). Strategic leadership: Top executives and their effects on organizations. St. Paul, MN: West Publishing Co.

Fletcher, J. K. (2004). The paradox of postheroic leadership: An essay on gender, power, and transformational change. Leadership Quarterly, Vol. 15 (pp. 647-661).: Elsevier Science Publishing Company, Inc.

Goodwin, B. (1994). How the leopard changed its spots: The evolution of complexity. New York: Charles Scribner's Sons.

Gronn, P. (1999). A realist view of leadership. Paper presented at the educational leaders for the new millenium-leaders with soul. ELO-AusAsia On-line Conference.

Gronn, P. (2002). Distributed leadership as a unit of analysis. The Leadership Quarterly, 13, 423-451.

Guastello, S. (2007). Nonlinear dynamics and leadership emergence. The Leadership Quarterly, 18, 357-369 (this issue). doi:10.1016/j.leaqua.2007.04.005.

Halal, W. E. (Ed.). (1998). The infinite resource: Mastering the boundless power of knowledge. New York: Jossey-Bass.

Halal, W. E. & Taylor, K. B. (Eds.). (1999). Twenty-first century economics: Perspectives of socioeconomics for a changing world. New York: Macmillan.

Hales, C. (2002). 'bureaucracy-lite' and continuities in managerial work. British Journal of Management, vol. 13: Blackwell Publishing Limited, 51. pp.

Hazy, J. (2007). Computer models of leadership: Foundations for a new discipline or meaningless diversion? The Leadership Quarterly, 18, 391-410 (this issue). doi:10.1016/j/leaqua.2007.04.007.

Heckscher, C. (1994). Defining the post-bureaucratic type. In C. Heckscher & A. Donnellon (Eds.), The post-bureaucratic organization: New perspectives on organizational change. Thousand Oaks: Sage.

Hedlund, G. (1994). A model of knowledge management and the N-form corporation. Strategic Management Journal, 15, 73-90.

Heifetz, R. A. (1994). Leadership without easy answers.: Cambridge Harvard University Press.

Heifetz, R. A., & Laurie, D. L. (2001). The work of leadership. Harvard Business Review, 79(11), 131-141.

Heifetz, R. A., & Linsky, M. (2002). Leadership on the line: Staying alive through the dangers of leading. Boston: Harvard University Press.

Henrickson, L., & McKelvey, B. (2002). Foundations of new social science: Institutional legitimacy from philosophy, complexity science, postmodernism, and agent-based modeling. Proceedings of the National Academy of Sciences, 99(Supp. 3), 7288-7297.

Hernes, G. (1998). Real virtuality. In P. Hedström & R. Swedberg (Eds.), Social mechanisms: An analytical approach to social theory (pp. 74-101). Cambridge: Cambridge University Press.

Hitt, M. A. (1998). Presidential address: Twenty-first century organizations: Business firms, business schools, and the academy. The Academy of Management Review, 23, 218-224.

Hogue, M., & Lord, R. G. (2007). A multilevel, complexity theory approach to understanding gender bias in leadership. The Leadership Quarterly, 18, 370-390.

Holland, J. H. (1995). Hidden order. Reading, MA: Addison-Wesley Publishing Company.

Homans, G. C. (1950). The human group. New York: Harcourt, Brace and World.

Hosking, D. M. (1988). Organizing, leadership and skilful process. Journal of Management Studies, 25, 147-166.

House, R. J., & Mitchell, T. (1974). A path-goal theory of leader effectiveness. Journal of Contemporary Business, 81-97.

Howell, J. M., & Boies, K. (2004). Champions of technological innovation: The influence of contextual knowledge, role orientation, idea generation, and idea promotion on champion emergence. The Leadership Quarterly, 15(1), 123-143.

Hunt, J. (1999). Transformational/charismatic leadership's transformation of the field: A historical essay. The Leadership Quarterly, 10(2), 129-144.

Hunt, J., & Ropo, A. (1995). Multi-level leadership-grounded theory and mainstream theory applied to the case of general motors. The Leadership Quarterly, 6(3), 379-412.

Huxham, C., & Vangen, S. (2000). Leadership in the shaping and implementation of collaboration agendas: How things happen in a (not quite) joined-up world. Academy of Management Journal, 43(6), 1159-1175.

Ilinitch, A. Y., D'Aveni, R. A., & Lewin, A. (1996). New organizational forms and strategies for managing in hypercompetitive environments. Organization Science, 7, 211-220.

Jaques, E. (1989). Requisite organization. Arlington, VA: Cason Hall.

Jaussi, K. S., & Dionne, S. D. (2003). Leading for creativity: The role of unconventional leadership behavior. The Leadership Quarterly, 14, 475-498.

Jehn, K. A. (1997). A qualitative analysis of conflict types and dimensions in organizational groups. Administrative Science Quarterly, 42, 530-557.

Jennings, J., & Haughton, L. (2000). It's not the big that eat the small . . . it's the fast that eat the slow. New York: HarperBusiness.

Jones, G. R. (2000). Organizational theory, (3rd ed.). Reading, MA: Addison-Wesley.

Kauffman, S. A. (1993). The origins of order. New York: Oxford University Press.

Kontopoulos, K. M. (1993). The logics of social structure. Cambridge: Cambridge University Press.

Krause, D. E. (2004). Influence-based leadership as a determinant of the inclination to innovate and of innovation-related behaviors: An empirical investigation. The Leadership Quarterly, 15(1), 79-102.

Lencioni, P. (2002). The five dysfunctions of a team: A leadership fable. San Francisco: Jossey-Bass.

Levy, S. (1992). Artificial life: The quest for new creation. New York: Random House.

Lewin, A. (1952). Group decision and social change. In G. E. Swanson T. M. Newcomb & E. L. Hartley (Eds.), Readings in social psychology, rev. ed. (pp. 459-473). New York: Holt.

Lewin, R. (1992). Complexity: Life at the edge of chaos. New York: Macmillan Publishing Company.

Lewin, A. (1999). Complexity: Life at the edge of chaos, (2nd ed.). Chicago: University of Chicago Press.

Lichtenstein, B., Uhl-Bien, M., Marion, R., Seers, A., Orton, D., & Schreiber, C. (2006). Complexity Leadership Theory: An interactive perspective on leading in complex adaptive systems. Emergence: Complexity and Organization, 8(4), 2-12.

Lorenz, E. (1993). The essence of chaos. Seattle: University of Washington Press.

Mackenzie, K. (2006). The LAMPE theory of organizational leadership. In F. Yammarino & F. Dansereau (Eds.), Research in multi-level issues, vol. 5. Oxford, UK: Elsevier Science.

Mandelbrot, B. B. (1983). The fractal geometry of nature. New York: W.H. Freeman.

Manville, B., & Ober, J. (2003, Jan.). Beyond empowerment: Building a company of citizens. Harvard Business Review, 48-53.

Marion, R. (1999). The edge of organization: Chaos and complexity theories of formal social organizations. Newbury Park, CA: Sage.

Marion, R., & Uhl-Bien, M. (2001). Leadership in complex organizations. The Leadership Quarterly, 12, 389-418.

Marion, R., & Uhl-Bien, M. (2003). Complexity theory and Al-Qaeda: Examining complex leadership. Emergence: A Journal of Complexity Issues in Organizations and Management, 5, 56-78.

Marion, R., & Uhl-Bien, M. (2007). Complexity and strategic leadership. In R. Hooijberg J. Hunt J. Antonakis K. Boal & N. Lane (Eds.), Being there even when you are not: Leading through structures, systems, and processes. Amsterdam: Elsevier.

McKelvey, B. (2001). Energizing order-creating networks of distributed intelligence. International Journal of Innovation Management, 5, 181-212.

McKelvey, B. (in press). Emergent strategy via Complexity Leadership: Using complexity science and adaptive tension to build distributed intelligence. In M. Uhl-Bien & R. Marion (Eds.), Complexity and leadership volume I: Conceptual foundations. Charlotte, NC: Information Age Publishing.

McKelvey, B., & Boisot, M. H. (2003). Transcendental organizational foresight in nonlinear contexts. Paper presented at the INSEAD Conference on Expanding Perspectives on Strategy Processes, Fontainebleau, France.

McKelvey, B., Marion, R., & Uhl-Bien, M. (2003). A simple-rule approach to CEO leadership in the 21st century. Paper presented at the University of Lecce Conference on New Approaches to Strategic Management, Ostuni, Italy.

McKelvey, B., Mintzberg, H., Petzinger, T., Prusak, L., Senge, P., & Shultz, R. (1999). The gurus speak: Complexity and organizations. Emergence: A Journal of Complexity Issues in Organizations and Management, 1(1), 73-91.

Miles, R. E. (1998). The spherical network organization. In W. E. Halal (Ed.), The infinite resource: Creating and leading the knowledge enterprise (pp. 111-121). San Francisco: Jossey-Bass.

Miles, R. E., Snow, C. C., Matthews, J. A., & Miles, G. (1999). Cellular-network organizations. In W. E. Halal & K. B. Taylor (Eds.), Twenty-first century economics (pp. 155-173). New York: Macmillan.

Mumford, M., Bedell-Avers, K. E., & Hunter, S. T. (in press). Planning for innovation: A multi-level perspective. In M.D. Mumford, S.T. Hunter and K.E. Bedell (Eds.), Research in multi-level issues. Oxford, GB: Elsevier.

Mumford, M., Connelly, S., & Gaddis, B. (2003). How creative leaders think: Experimental findings and cases. The Leadership Quarterly, 14(4/5, Pt.1), 411-432.

Mumford, M. D., & Licuanan, B. (2004). Leading for innovation: Conclusions, issues, and directions. The Leadership Quarterly, 15(1), 163-171.

Mumford, M. D., Schultz, R. A., & Osborn, H. K. (2002). Planning in organizations: Performance as a multi-level phenomenon. In F. J. Yammarino & F. Dansereau (Eds.), Research in multi-level issues: The many faces of multi-level issues (pp. 3-35). Oxford, GB: Elsevier.

Mumford, M. D., Scott, G. M., Gaddis, B., & Strange, J. M. (2002). Leading creative people: Orchestrating expertise and relationships. The Leadership Quarterly, 13(6), 705-750.

Nonaka, I., & Nishiguchi, T. (2001). Introduction: Knowledge emergence. In I. Nonaka & T. Nishiguchi (Eds.), Knowledge emergence: Social, technical, and evolutionary dimensions of knowledge creation (pp. 3-9). Oxford: Oxford University Press.

Osborn, R., & Hunt, J. (2007). Leadership and the choice of order: Complexity and hierarchical perspectives near the edge of chaos. The Leadership Quarterly, 18, 319-340 (this issue). doi:10.1016/j.leaqua.2007.04.003.

Osborn, R., Hunt, J. G., & Jauch, L. R. (2002). Toward a contextual theory of leadership. The Leadership Quarterly, 13, 797-837.

Parks, S. D. (2005). Leadership can be taught: A bold approach for a complex world. Boston: Harvard Business School Press.

Pearce, C. L., & Conger, J. A. (2003). Shared leadership: Reframing the hows and whys of leadership. Thousand Oaks: Sage.

Pfeffer, J. (2005). Producing sustainable competitive advantage through the effective management of people. The Academy of Management Executive, 19(4), 95-108.

Phillips, R. & Hunt, J. (Eds.). (1992). Strategic leadership: A multiorganizational-level perspective. Westport, CT: Quorum Books.

Plowman, D., Baker, L. T., Beck, T., Kulkarni, M., Solansky, S., & Travis, D. (2007). Radical change accidentally: The emergence and amplification of small change. Academy of Management Journal, 50(3).

Plowman, D., Baker, L. T., Beck, T., Kulkarni, M., Solansky, S., & Travis, D. (2007). The role of leadership in emergent, self-organization. The Leadership Quarterly, 18, 341-356 (this issue). doi:10.1016/j.leaqua.2007.04.004.

Plowman, D., & Duchon, D. (in press). Dispelling the myths about leadership: From cybernetics to emergence. In M. Uhl-Bien & R. Marion (Eds.), Complexity and leadership volume I: Conceptual foundations. Charlotte, NC: Information Age Publishing.

Popper, K. R. (1986). The poverty of historicism. London: Routledge.

Prigogine, I. (1997). The end of certainty. New York: The Free Press.

Prusak, L. (1996). The knowledge advantage. Strategy & Leadership, 24, 6-8.

Quinn, J. B., Anderson, P., & Finkelstein, S. (2002). Managing professional intellect: Making the most of the best. In S. Little P. Quintas & T. Ray (Eds.), Managing knowledge: An essential reader (pp. 335-348). London: Sage.

Reiter-Palmon, R., & Illies, J. J. (2004). Leadership and creativity: Understanding leadership from the creative problem-solving perspective. The Leadership Quarterly, 15, 55-77.

Rost, J. C. (1991). Leadership for the twenty-first century. London: Praeger.

Roy, D. (1954). Efficiency and 'the fix': Informal intergroup relations in a piecework machine shop. American Journal of Sociology, 60, 255-266.

Schilling, M. A., & Steensma, H. K. (2001). The use of modular organizational forms: An industry level analysis. Academy of Management Journal, 44(6), 1149-1168.

Schneider, M. (2002). A stakeholder model of organizational leadership. Organization Science, 13(2), 209-220.

Schneider, M., & Somers, M. (2006). Organizations as complex adaptive systems: Implications of complexity theory for leadership research. The Leadership Quarterly, 17(4), 351-365.

Schreiber, C. (2006). Human and organizational risk modeling: Critical personnel and leadership in network organizations. Unpublished Dissertation, Carnegie Mellon, Pittsburgh, PA.

Selznick, P. (1948). Foundations of the theory of organizations. American Sociological Review, 13, 25-35.

Selznick, P. (1957). Leadership in administration. New York: Harper and Row.

Shalley, C. E., & Gilson, L. L. (2004). What leaders need to know: A review of social and contextual factors that can foster or hinder creativity. The Leadership Quarterly, 15(1), 33-53.

Simon, H. A. (1962). The architecture of complexity. Proceedings of the American Philosophical Society, 106, 467-482.

Snyder, R. C. (1988). New frames for old: Changing the managerial culture of an aircraft factory. In M. O. Jones M. D. Moore & R. C. Snyder (Eds.), Inside organizations: Understanding the human dimension (pp. 191-208). Newbury Park, CA: Sage Publications.

Stacey, R. D., Griffin, D., & Shaw, P. (2000). Complexity and management: Fad or radical challenge to systems thinking. London and New York: Routledge.

Sterman, J. D. (1994). Learning in and about complex systems. System Dynamics Review, 10, 291-330.

Streatfield, P. J. (2001). The paradox of control in organizations. London: Routledge.

Thomas, C., Kaminska Labbé, R., & McKelvey, B. (2005). Managing the MNC and exploitation/exploration dilemma: From static balance to dynamic oscillation. In G. Szulanski Y. Doz & J. Porac (Eds.), Advances in strategic management: Expanding perspectives on the strategy process, Vol. 22 (pp. 213-250). Amsterdam, NL: Elsevier.

Volberda, H. W. (1996). Toward the flexible form: How to remain vital in hypercompetitive environments. Organization Science, 7(4), 359.

Weick, K. E. (1976). Educational organizations as loosely coupled systems. Administrative Science Quarterly, 21, 1-19.

Weisburg, R. (1999). Creativity and knowledge: A challenge to theories. In R. J. Sternberg (Ed.), Handbook of creativity (pp. 226-259). Cambridge, GB: Cambridge University Press.

Wikipedia. (n.d.). Self organization [Electronic Version]. Retrieved 2006 from http://en.wikipedia.org/wiki/Self-organization

Yukl, G. (2005). Leadership in organizations, (6th ed.). Englewood Cliffs, NJ: Prentice Hall.

Zaccaro, S. J., & Klimoski, R. J. (2001). The nature of organizational leadership: An introduction. In S. J. Zaccaro & R. J. Klimoski (Eds.), The nature of organizational leadership (pp. 3-41). San Francisco: Jossey Bass.

Zohar, D. (1997). Rewiring the corporate brain. San Francisco: Berrett-Koehler.

Chapter 6

Prologue
Bill McKelvey
Professor of Strategic Organizing and Complexity Science
UCLA Andersen School of Management

Complexity Leadership: The Secret of Jack Welch's Sucess

Bill McKelvey

Prologue:

Bill McKelvey

My trek down the path leading to *Complexity Science: The Secret of Jack Welch's Success* began with my reading of Stuart Kauffman's book, *The Origins of Order* (1993), which was my introduction to complexity science. My application of complexity theory to organization science first appeared in my 1995 article, "Quasi-Natural Organization Science." Weird, you think? Consider the following titles of a few of my "complexity" publications (often with coauthors; complete references are available on my website: http://www.billmckelvey.org/):

- 1999: "Complexity vs. Selection Among Coevolutionary Firms"
- 1999: "Self-Organization, Complexity Catastrophes, and Microstate Models at the Edge of Chaos"
- 2003: "Emergent Order in Firms: Complexity Science vs. the Entanglement Trap"
- 2004: "Toward a 0th Law of Thermodynamics: Order-Creation Complexity Dynamics from Physics and Biology to Bioeconomics"
- 2004: "Situated Learning Theory: Adding Rate and Complexity Effects via Kauffman's *NK* Model"
- 2008: "'Smart Parts' Supply Networks Systems as Complex Adaptive Systems"
- 2009: "Redefining Strategic Foresight: 'Fast' and 'Far' Sight via Complexity Science"

The foregoing titles reflect the ontology of complexity science, which consists of interdependent agents (e.g., employees, departments, firms) existing in far-from-equilibrium states created by imposed tensions and changing internal and external environmental conditions.

These agents are sensitive to initial conditions and positive or negative feedback effects; they can self-organize toward emergent new order (i.e., structures, networks, objectives) and self-organized criticality (i.e., continuous efforts to maintain an efficaciously adaptive state in a changing niche) via interactions, demands, and coevolving causes and structures. The outcomes are often best characterized by fractal geometry and non-Gaussian power-law distributions.

As my study of complexity science evolved, a series of publications (usually with coauthors) focusing on leadership emerged:

- 2002: "Complexity and Leadership"
- 2004: "'Simple Rules' for Improving Corporate IQ: Basic Lessons from Complexity Science"
- 2004: "Toward a Complexity Science of Entrepreneurship"
- 2005: "Managing the MNC and Exploitation/Exploration Dilemma: From Static Balance to Dynamic Oscillation"
- 2006: "Using Coevolutionary and Complexity Theories to Improve IS Alignment"
- 2007: "Leadership in Four Stages of Emergence"
- 2007: "Complex Leadership: Shifting Leadership from the Industrial Age to the Knowledge Era"
- 2008: "Emergent Strategy via Complexity Leadership: Using Complexity Science and Adaptive Tension to Build Distributed Intelligence"
- 2010: "Avoiding Extreme Risk Before It Occurs: Scalability Lessons from Complexity Science"
- 2010: "Complexity Leadership: The Secret of Jack Welch's Success"
- 2011: "Managing in a Pareto World Calls for New Thinking"
- 2012: "When Organizations and Ecosystems Interact: Toward a Law of Requisite Fractality in Firms"

- 2013: "Extreme Outcomes, Connectivity, and Power Laws: Towards an Econophysics of Organization"
- 2013: "Toward an Econophysics View of Intellectual Capital Dynamics: From Self-Organized Criticality to the Stochastic Frontier"

My challenge leading up to the Welch article was to find better ways of applying complexity science—which started in physics and biology—to management. It came as a surprise to me to discover that Welch's success at GE from 1981 to 2001 could be so readily explained via complexity theory. As we discuss in our 2005 chapter, it is difficult for leaders to shift from top-down to bottom-up (complexity-created) influence streams or vice versa. It is easy for pathological leaders to totally shut down bottom-up emergent complexity dynamics and bottom-up influence—Bob Nardelli was a good example of this when he was CEO of The Home Depot.

Drawing on short descriptions of 12 action disciplines (complexity scientists call them "*simple rules*" that generate complexity dynamics—but they are not so simple in the management arena), my Welch article then shows how his use of the various action disciplines led to a ~7000% increase in GE shareholder value, including five stock splits. It also shows that Welch's value-adding success was vastly better than the two most successful CEOs who were "trained" by Welch at GE (Larry Bossidy and Jim McNerney), who show more value-added than all of the other CEOs trained under Welch at GE. This evidence suggests that Welch's success was due to his use of complexity dynamics rather than what he writes about in his several books—otherwise the complexity message would have been passed on to his trainees who then would have showed much more success as CEOs than their company's stock charts indicate.

While the Chaos Society originally focused on fractals, complexity scientists at the Santa Fe Institute mostly ignored fractals and power-law distributions, even though Per Bak's early research on power laws dates back to 1987. Since then research about fractals and power laws has blossomed. My publications written after the Welch article reflect my increasing focus on the facts that (1) a CEO is positioned at the top of the rank/frequency distribution of employees within a firm; (2) the CEO's firm has to contend with the rank/frequency distribution of competing firms within its industry; (3) the number and size of organizational changes within the CEO's firm, whether top-down or bottom-up, are likely to be fractal, i.e., power-law distributed; and (4) movement up or down the industry ranking of competing firms means creating fractal designs within the CEO's firm that help it adapt and compete efficaciously within the fractal structure of its industry. Papers yet to be written will focus on fractal and scalability leadership.

Given the fractal structures of firms and industries, there is a final message and concern that is emerging from works I have written (all with coauthors):

- 2005: "Why Gaussian Statistics Are Mostly Wrong for Strategic Organization"
- 2007: "Beyond Gaussian Averages: Redirecting Organization Science Toward Extreme Events and Power Laws"
- 2009: "From Gaussian to Paretian Thinking: Causes and Implications of Power Laws in Organizations"
- 2011: "From Skew Distributions to Power Law Science"
- 2011: "Using Scale-Free Processes to Explain Punctuated-Change in Management-Relevant Phenomena"
- 2011: "Introduction to Econophysics: Correlated Trader Behaviours, Bubbles and Crashes, Scalability Dynamics, Power Laws and Scale-Free Theories"
- 2011: "Explaining What Leads Up to Stock Market Crashes: A Phase Transition Model and Scalability Dynamics"

- 2013: "Strategic Implications of Power-Law Distributions in the Creation and Emergence of New Ventures: Power-Law Analyses in Three Panel Studies"
- 2013: "Identifying the Transition from Efficient-Market to Herding Behavior: Using a Method from Econophysics" [Working paper, UCLA Anderson School of Management]

Complexity Leadership: The Secret of Jack Welch's Sucess[10]

Bill McKelvey

Abstract. Leadership theory still focuses on vision and charisma and is stuck at the bottom of hierarchies. What style of leadership did Jack Welch actually use to manage the 350 business units comprising GE to increase its stock value 1,000s of percentage points higher than the Dow Jones Stock Index, stay in office for 20 years when most CEOs are 'temp workers', and produce some $480 billion in shareholder wealth. Welch is an instinctively great manager, but not well clued in on the action-specifics of why he did so well. Complexity science offers 12 'action-disciplines' that appear to be the means by which Welch was able to enable and steer GE to produce incredible wealth. He put complexity theory into practice. Put more dramatically, Welch replaced old-style, top-down 'management by objectives' with 'management by tension'. Evidence is offered to show that Welch's methods were not learned by all the GE-trained managers who became CEOs of other firms. But some outstanding CEOs of major firms appear to be using the complexity action-disciplines as well. This article explains the secret of his success.

Key words: leadership; management; complexity science; tension; emergence; innovation; CEOs; Jack Welch; GE; stock value; shareholder wealth.

1 Introduction

Over the years, there has been a constant plethora of writings making clarifications to traditional leadership theory (e.g., Hogan et al., 1994; Bennis, 1996; Dansereau and Yammarino, 1998a, 1998b). Bolden et al. (2003) suggest that nothing in leadership theory has changed since mid 20th century, except for the appearance of transformational/transactive

---

[10]   Originally Published as: McKelvey, B. (2010). "Complexity leadership: The secret of Jack Welch's success." International Journal of Complexity in Leadership and Management 1(1): 4-35.

leadership (Burns, 1978; Bass, 2002) and distributed/dispersed leadership (Gibb, 1954; Bryman, 1996; Gronn, 2002). Writing in the early 1990s, Rost observes that the 130+ books on leadership published in the 1980s substantiate the orthodox message that 'leadership is basically doing what the leader wants done' (1993, p.70). Writing in 2003, Marion and Uhl-Bien say that leadership theory is still vision-driven, top down, consensus and control oriented, with direct influence attempts by the leader. Leadership theory is still mostly stuck at the bottom of hierarchies; it is mostly about how 'heroic or charismatic' superiors [Bennis, (2007), p.3], who have 'wisdom, intelligence, and creativity' [Sternberg, (2007), p.34] should 'lead' followers in a face-to-face context. While they say the foregoing are still appropriate, Marion and Uhl-Bien point out that leadership also involves ". . . creating the conditions that enable productive, but largely unspecified, future states" (2001, p.391).

Because of the failure of leadership and leadership theory at the CEO level, we see a recent focus on CEO churning (Bennis and O'Toole, 2000; *The Economist,* 2001; Lucieret al., 2003). Lucier et al. (2005) go so far as to call CEOs *'temp workers'*. In short, the more aggressively CEOs pursue their visionary leadership from top-down, the more damage they create most of the time. Why? *The Economist* (2001) says that firms are now much more difficult to manage for reasons such as flattened hierarchies, globalisation, the digital age, and mega-mergers. We also see that 'celebrity CEOs' brought in from outside do well at first—by cutting costs—but then fail in the second half of their tenure (Lucier et al., 2005). Agreeing with Avolio et al. (2001), Brown and Gioia (2002) say that ". . . leadership is not solely a set of characteristics possessed by an individual, but an emergent property of a social system, in which 'leaders' and followers' share in the process of enacting leadership" [quote taken from Parry and Bryman, (2006), p.455, my italics]. The idea of emergent, distributed leadership is further developed by Marion and Uhl-Bien (2001, 2003), McKelvey (2001, 2008), Uhl-Bien et al. (2008) and other 'complexity leadership' writers in the edited volumes by Hazy et al.

(2007) and Uhl-Bien and Marion (2008). Bluntly put, there is much more to good leadership that what is offered by psychologists.

For this article, I am taking a 'reverse' logic. Instead of propounding more 'academic theory' about what aspiring CEOs should do, I go back to 'square one' of leadership at the top of giant firms: I am going to zero in on Jack Welch, CEO of GE from 1981 to 2001 (when he retired)—no 'churning' here. Instead of more regurgitated chatter by academics about what good leadership is, lets start from Fortune Magazine's 'Manager of the Century' and rebuild leadership theory from the ground up by studying what Welch actually did that produced some $480 billion in GE shareholder value. Instead of statistically sound empirical studies about 'average' leadership, let us focus on the business leader with the best performance in the 20th century! And he did it with the oldest member of the Dow Jones Stock Index.

I argue that it was Welch's ability to carry out 'complexity leadership' that produced such amazing results. In what follows, I first try to substantiate this by connecting key elements [I will call them 'action-disciplines' (A-Ds)] of complexity theory to actions he took at GE. Second, by making some market-capitalisation (stock-performance) comparisons with other GE-spin-off CEOs, I argue that Welch did not really know why he was so good at managing GE; the records of almost all 'spin-off CEOs' suggest that they learned virtually nothing from Welch or their experiences at GE. Also, there is little evidence that any of the CEOs and top-management teams 'educated' by visiting the GE Training Institute, or by reading Welch's several books (or other books about Welch at GE) replicated Welch's leadership performance at GE. Finally, I will show that a substantial number of top performing firms, CEOs, and turnaround events appear to be based on the presence of the most critical A-Ds, as opposed to attributions of learning and success to existing books by or about Jack Welch.

Given inadequacies in leadership theory, I turn to Welch for a new approach. After a brief review of leadership and complexity theories,

I suggest 12 complexity-based A-Ds as the basis of Welch's unique managerial success. The success of GE-trained CEOs is then shown to be inferior to Welch's. Finally, I present some evidence that other highly successful CEOs used the complexity A-Ds.

2 Brief review of leadership theory

In a changing world full of diverse political, economic systems and competitors, corporate leaders must be able to create cellular networks[1] (Miles et al., 1999) and complex adaptive systems (Marion and Uhl-Bien, 2001, 2003). They need to learn how to promote agent heterogeneity and enable connectionist networking, self-organisation, and adaptive learning, in search of improved agent and collective fitness. Most leadership theories go opposite to this. And they need to know how to constructively use 'management by tension' to get their complex system into phase-transition mode.

Traditional leadership theory focuses on attributes and skills of leaders and the subsequent impact of leaders on individuals and groups of followers within an organisation (Bennis and Nanus, 1985; Bennis and Biederman, 1996; Hogan et al., 1994; Dansereau and Yammarino, 1998a, 1988b). Klein and House (1998, p.3) say that, "charisma is a fire that ignites followers' energy, commitment, and performance". Their approach focuses on 'mythic', 'heroic', 'visionary', leaders. Building from House (1977) and Nanus (1992), Bennis (1996) describes the visionary leadership school of thought:

"Leaders need to have a strongly defined sense of purpose. A sense of vision Leading means doing the right things . . . creating a compelling, overarching vision. The capacity clearly to articulate a vision. It's about *living* the vision, day in day out—embodying it—and empowering every other person . . . to implement and execute that vision. The vision has to be shared. And the only way that it can be shared is for it to have meaning for the people who are involved in it. Leaders have to specify the steps that behaviorally fit into that vision, and then reward people for following those steps." (pp.154-156; his italics)

Drawing from tradition, Bennis and O'Toole (2000) attribute the recent increase in CEO turnover to lack of charisma and vision. Leadership scholars stress the importance of the 'mythic', 'heroic', 'visionary' leader for creating strong cultures (Peters and Waterman, 1982; Schein, 1992) and leading culture change (Kotter and Heskett, 1992). Sorensen (2002), however, shows that strong cultures are assets in stable environments but liabilities in changing times. Willmott (1993) claims that 'culture management' is a new form of managerial control.

Finkelstein (2003) suggests that 'normal' explanations such as leadership failures are inadequate to explain CEO dismissal. Supporting *The Economist's* view, Finkelstein (2003) concludes that "CEOs fail to carryout standard strategic essentials competently". He does not attribute CEO failure to board processes in selection as it would be hard to imagine a modern board hiring a CEO who did not include the 'strategic basics' in his/her 'vision'. Who would hire a CEO who is 'against' entrepreneurship, innovation, synergies from M&A, and understanding the competition? Since all CEOs have this vision, he argues, especially in a boom economy and at the so-called Dawn of the New Age, this focus on strategic essentials takes 'vision' out of the mix—the 'vision' variable does not separate good from bad CEOs.

A partial movement beyond tradition is based on the *transformational leadership* concept (Burns, 1978; Bass, 1985; Bass and Avolio, 1994) which consists of four components: vision and charisma; high expectations; personal attention to followers; and challenging followers with new ideas (Bass, 2002). But even this approach works against CEOs trying to build decentralised, self-organising cellular networks. Why? According to Marion and Uhl-Bien (2003), transformational/transactive leadership is still vision driven, top down, consensus and control oriented, with direct influence attempts by the leader. It focuses on follower 'buy-in' to the leader's vision of the future. More specifically, they argue that transformational leadership still holds to:

- top-down, leader controlled views of organisational processes
- hierarchical—and position-based formal leadership initiatives
- emphasis on followers carrying out the leader's vision
- stimulation of followers to align with the leader's vision
- direct influence efforts to assure that followers are following the leader's vision.

Though transformational leadership tries to emphasise follower alignment with the core vision, in reality it still relies on followers' compliance behavior.

Finally, building from Gibb (1954, 1958) and Brown (1989), Bryman (1996) picks up on distributed leadership to take us from trait, style, and contingency approaches to what he calls 'dispersed leadership'—a 'new leadership approach'. Hosking (1988) emphasises the network building functions of effective leadership and the cultivation of social influence. Katzenbach and Smith (1993) focus on a kind of leader who fosters the emergence of small teams. Kouzes and Posner (1993, p.156) say that good leaders 'turn their constituents into leaders' and liberate employees 'so that they can use their abilities to lead themselves and others' [Bryman, (1996), p.283]. Linstead and Grafton-Small (1992) view culture formation as 'dispersed' rather than flowing monolithically from the vision of a heroic leader. They have the right idea, but the 'how to do it' part is vague.

Gronn (2002) offers the best review of distributed leadership (but also see Bennett et al., 2003). It is "aggregated leadership . . . dispersed among some, many, or maybe all of the members" of an organization [Gronn, (2002), p.429]. He builds from Gibb's multiplicity or patterns of group functions' and a 'leadership complex' consisting of numerous roles (quoted on p.429). Gronn points to three essential ingredients:

1. collaborative modes of engagement
2. the intuitive understanding that develops as part of close working relations among colleagues
3. a variety of structural relations and institutionalised arrangements (p.429).

But, these can also be the ingredients of Janis's 'groupthink' (1972). Gronn's analysis is an after-the-fact description of leadership 'distribution' but his review offers no set of leader actions that would actually get a complex system to become more efficient, or change its nature so as to become more efficaciously adaptive in a changing highly-competitive business environment; and his review applies only to 'numerically small work groupings' (2002, p.447). Given this, distributed leadership, as currently described, is only one of several elements contributing to GE's success.

3 Why Jack Welch at GE?

Let's start with some evidence on performance:

- In great contrast to current CEOs, which Lucier et al. (2005) label 'temp workers', Welch was CEO for 20 years till he retired, i.e., 1981-2001.
- GE's revenues in 1980 were $25 billion; the year before Welch retired in 2001 they were $129.9 billion.
- GE's stock averaged a return of—21% per annum from the day he became CEO (Sirisha, 2002).
- Welch raised GE's market-capitalisation from $12 billion in 1981 (Hartman, 2003) to some $480 billion in 2001 (Sirisha, 2002).
- Welch supervised 993 acquisitions worth $13billion.
- He accomplished the above in a 100 year old, 'old-line' firm making mostly commodity-like products.
- Named Manager of the Century by Fortune Magazine in 1999.

They say a picture is worth a thousand words: in Figure 1, I use market capitalisation as the basis for comparing Jack Welch's accomplishments with others; as one can see, during the 20 years he was CEO at GE the stock went through five stock-splits and gained over 7,000% in increased value.

In what follows, I argue that Welch's leadership approach puts many elements of complexity theory into managerial practice—albeit something that neither he nor anyone else seems aware of. Since GE developed its 'boundaryless organisation' approach (Ashkenas et al., 1995), GE has moved to elaborate a system whereby 'best-practices' discovered in one section are quickly spread to other parts of what is now a vast 'related multidivisional' kind of firm (Williamson, 1975)—GE had 350 business units within 43 strategic business units [Slater, (2001), p.41]. GE accomplished this by developing rules along with fairly draconian incentives to make sure the flow of best-practice discoveries throughout the GE network occurred as fast as possible (Kerr, 2000). GE is a particularly important example since, with Welch as CEO, it has outperformed every major corporation around the globe in producing shareholder value (Byrne, 1998).

A preliminary analysis of the many actions by Welch, as recorded in Slater's (2001) book, his management by tension, creation of agent heterogeneity, use of various devices to create effective network functioning, and wide-ranging distributed leadership are strong characteristics of his leadership approach. My hypothesis is that Welch was effective because his approach was—albeit unknowingly and inadvertently—drawing strongly and consistently on basic theories and findings from complexity science.

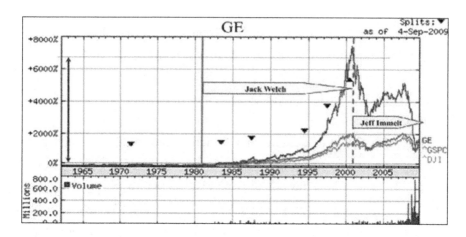

Figure 1 GE stock chart[2] (see online version for colours)

4 Complexity science as 'order-creation science'

'*New Science*' is Wheatley's (1992a) label for complexity science. To see how 'New Science' offers insight for organisational CEO-level leadership, I find it useful to divide complexity science into three phases. I define the first two here (I take up scalability—Phase 3—later on):

- *Adaptive tension:* Phase 1—the European School begins with the works of Prigogine (1955, 1997), Prigogine and Stengers (1984), Haken (1977), and then Cramer (1993) and Mainzer (1994), among many others. Their theory begins with the Benard (1901) process—an energy differential is set up between warmer and cooler surfaces of a container (measured as temperature, ΔT). In between the 1st and 2nd critical values ($Rc1$, $Rc2$), a region is created where the system undergoes a dramatic shift in the nature of fluid flow. For example, increasing the heat under water molecules in a vessel exposed to colder air above leads to geometric patterns of hotter and colder water—the chef's 'rolling boil' emerges; new order appears. The critical values define the 'melting zone' (Kauffman, 1993; Stauffer, 1987), within which new structures spontaneously emerge. Prigogine (1955) termed these 'dissipative structures' because they are pockets of new order—governed by the 1st Law of Thermodynamics (the conservation of energy law)—that speed up the dissipation of the imposed energy toward randomness and entropy according to the 2nd Law Swenson, 1989).

- *Emergence:* Phase 2—the American School—emphasises agent self-organisation absent outside influence. It consists largely of scholars associated with the Santa Fe Institute (Anderson et al., 1988; Cowan et al., 1994; Arthur et al., 1997). While Phase 1 focuses mostly on dramatic environmentally imposed tensions that cause phase transitions at Rc1,—the edge of order (instigated by what McKelvey, 2001, 2008, calls 'adaptive tension'), Phase 2 complexity scientists focus mostly on Rc2—the 'edge of chaos' (Lewin, 1999; Kauffman, 1993). Focusing mostly on living systems (Gell-Mann, 2002), Phase 2 emphasises the spontaneous coevolution of entities (i.e., the agents[3]) in a complex adaptive system. Heterogeneous agents restructure themselves continuously, leading to new forms of emergent order consisting of patterns of evolved agent attributes and hierarchical structures displaying both upward and downward causal influences. Bak (1996) extends this treatment in his discovery of 'self-organised criticality', a process in which 'tiny initiating events' (Holland, 2002) can lead to complexity cascades of avalanche proportions. The signature elements within the melting zone—between Rc1 and Rc2—are self-organisation, emergence and non-linearity. Kauffman's 'spontaneous order creation' in this zone begins when three elements are present:

1 heterogeneous agents
2 connections among them
3 motives to connect—such as mating, improved fitness, performance, learning, etc.

Remove any one element and nothing happens. According to Holland (2002) we recognise emergent phenomena as multiple level hierarchies bottom-up and top-down causal effects, and non-linearities.

Both phases are important to my argument. Phase transitions are often required to overcome the threshold-gate effects characteristic of most human agents, i.e., resistance to change. This requires the adaptive tension driver to rise above Rc1. Once an instigation event or tension occurs—what Holland (1995) calls the 'tag', broader coevolutionary dynamics may be set in motion. Neither R> Rc1 not tag-plus-coevolution seems both necessary and sufficient by itself, especially in social settings. This is why phase transition and coevolution are 'co-producers' (Churchman and Ackoff, 1950).

5 Twelve complexity-leadership A-Ds[4]

". . . Natural systems participate openly with their environment and complex structures emerge"

The foregoing quote by Wheatley (1992b, p.340), focusing on the connection between environment and emergent complexity—i.e., emergent new order—succinctly captures why Welch's CEO approach worked so well and connects so well with complexity science. I outline 12 A-Ds based on key concepts from basic complexity science that I have some evidence suggesting were at the centre of Jack Welch's management 'discipline' at GE. Each A-D stands as a complexity-based statement about how the basic themes of complexity science foster network and other developments in firms that, over some passage of time, eventually lead to vastly improved efficacious adaptation to complex and changing environments and performance in competitive conditions. I also take pains to show that each A-D reflects a Welch-style managerial focus that may be induced from his managerial activities at GE. Slater (2001) is the main source of GE data supporting my view that each is a Welch-instigated phenomenon.

194

I argue that, collectively, these A-Ds are necessary and sufficient to produce CEO effectiveness. They do so because they give rise to effective management in complex, changing environments. The effective installation of these A-Ds serves to make firms and CEOs more quickly and efficaciously adaptive. These actions are the means by which CEOs can enable and steer their firms in ways that do not destroy autonomy, agent heterogeneity, connectivity, incentives, and emergent self-organisation without inadvertently creating an organisational culture dominated by top-down control and incentivised to carry out the CEO's vision. In a real sense, these A-Ds represent complexity theory in practice. I argue that:

- many of these actions lie at the heart of Welch's success at GE
- these actions are more apt to characterise effective firms in the 21st century than ineffective ones
- these actions represent the four key ingredients required to create complex adaptive systems on cellular networks: tension, heterogeneous agents, connections, and positive feedback.

Put simply, nothing boils down what many people do not like about Welch as CEO as much as:

1. the tension underlying 'Be #1 or 2 . . . or else . . .' [Tichy and Sherman, (2005), p.114, somewhat paraphrased]
2. the divesting of units and—130,000 employees gave rise to the 'Neutron Jack' label.

The first points to the Phase 1 tension dynamics of complexity science and my first four A-Ds. The second is a rather negative signification of the dynamics comprising Phase 2—the remaining eight A-Ds-actions that produce change and novelty rather than Janis's 'groupthink' (1972). When Phases 1 and 2 are combined, we see that without tension 'phase-transition' quality changes do not occur and without heterogeneous human capital and social networking skills imposed tension produces negative rather than positive returns. Together they act as what Churchman and Ackoff (1950) called 'co-producers'.

5.1 A-Ds from Phase 1 of complexity science

I begin with the Phase 1 A-Ds. They stem from the European side of complexity science—Prigogine, Haken, Cramer, Mainzer, etc.,—who focus on the role of the 1st critical value, Ro, of imposing energy in causing phase transitions. Welch's 'Be #1 or 2 . . . or else . . .' is an Rc1-equivalent action that caused 'phase-transition-type' new developments here and there throughout GE. While my first two A-Ds are quite straightforward in meaning and implication, A-Ds 3 and 4 are more difficult and problematic to understand and implement. No doubt, the tension A-D is the most broadly recognised as signatory of Welch's management genius, but even so, the tension A-D would not have the same results without next three A-Ds, and, then, the first four would not gain much without the following eight.

1 Adaptive tensions[5]

Externally imposing and internally creating adaptive tension—see my earlier description of Phase 1 and the phase transition occurrences at Rc1—which activate agents and sets off the creation of new order in the form of complex adaptive systems (McKelvey, 2001, 2008). Tensions are not goals (point attractors), but they serve as energising devices pushing people over the Rn phase-transition threshold for CEOs to take advantage of. Adaptive tensions may stem from any selectionist context—from outside a firm, from any higher level (or even lower levels) within a firm, or from more specific domains such as technology, markets, costs, competitors, political changes, etc. Absent tension, nothing happens:

- Welch's 'Be #1 or 2 or else' . . . is the most obvious parallel here.
- Another phrase was 'face reality' [Slater, (2001), p.17]—i.e., the competitive context, which is where the important tensions come from. Welch put the 'face reality' at the top of his list.
- He very much possessed a 'survival of the fittest' mentality [Slater, (2001), p.49].
- He always emphasised 'broad objectives' [Slater, (2001), p.30], 'a few clear, general goals' [Slater, (2001), p.28]—no specifics.
- He followed Clausewitz saying, 'strategy was not a lengthy action plan. It was the evolution of a central idea through continually changing circumstances'. [6] [Slater, (2001), p.29]
- Operating margins went from 10% before Welch to over to 17.3% in 1999.

2 Draconian incentives

My discussion here is mostly patterned after network incentives developed at GE, under the leadership of Welch (Kerr, 2000). The sub-rules that GE focused on for incentivising agents are:

- Agents are incentivised to focus on adaptive tension—the 'Be #1 or 2 . . .'. Challenge and 'stretch' (Tichy and Sherman, 2005) were also used to bring on tension effects.
- Agents incentivised to get information out on the network in a form abstract enough for all users to try out (Kerr, 2000); when he was Head of the Crotonville training centre, Kerr says he would get panicked calls from employees asking him how to do this!
- Agents gaining success in one part of the network, or with one kind of human capital, are moved to other positions—given additional 'opportunities to fail' (Ken, 2000)—which is a way of building competence, diversity, and (inadvertently) weak ties.
- Agents incentivised to produce novelties, with the most critical (top priority) novelties expected at a consistent rate each year

(say, five 'most critical' novelties per year)—novelties created in response to the prevailing contextual tensions and rates of change in the external environment.

- Agents incentivised to build learning cultures; transform learning into action; get learning and action to spread across layers and silos [Slater, (2001), p.70-74].
- Agents incentivised to 'delayer . . . get rid of fat . . . remove the boundaries, listen . . .' etc. [Slater, (2001), pp.89-93].
- Agents are activated by the 'A, B, C rules'—people rated C are to be fired [Slater, (2001), pp.35-36]; a manager who cannot fire the Cs becomes one.
- Agents 'above' the cellular networks, such as CEOs, are incentivised to expect and review some specific number of 'most critical' novelties, and some novelties of lesser criticality without reservation—but note the 'nearly decomposable' rule in A-D #9.

3 Critical values

The edges of order and chaos (Rc1, Rc2), define the 'region of emergence' in complex adaptive systems (McKelvey, 2001, 2008). As Brown and Eisenhardt (1998) put it, below the edge of order bureaucratic behaviour prevails; above the edge of chaos, well, chaos prevails—there are so many degrees of freedom, so much variety, so many options, that selecting which forces to adapt to becomes problematic. Adaptive tensions cause phase transitions, (these are abrupt transitions to a new order), if the tension, T, is above the 1st critical value. Use of the 1st and 2nd critical values to define the region of emergence is critically important—below the 1st critical value, bureaucratic behaviour prevails; above the 2nd critical value, chaos prevails (Brown and Eisenhardt, 1997). Employee training and experience works to lower threshold gates (i.e., lowering resistance to change) so that adaptive tensions may take effect at lower values. Employees can also be trained so as to work in high-tension conditions without becoming dysfunctional because of chaotic conditions.

- For example, public utilities are notorious for having very high threshold gates before employees are apt to take innovative approaches. Worse, incentive systems do nothing to change this. In contrast, a reading of Slater (2001) on Welch's 'leadership secrets' shows that Welch tried to create a corporation with a flavour very much the opposite of a utility.

- Welch emphasised draconian incentives that lowered employees' threshold gates against networking, innovating, sharing, 'exceeding goals' [Slater (2001), p.131]; being a multibusiness enterprise was not an excuse for not spreading learning across boundaries—hence the book titled, The Boundaryless Organization (Ashkenas et al., 1995), which describes his efforts in this regard.

- The 1st critical value, which employees have to cross to reach the region of complexity, was lowered by the use of the incentives; the 2nd was raised by getting people more easily able to 'stretch' past normal levels of achievement to aim for higher levels, tougher goals, more difficult objectives without becoming dysfunctional (Tichy and Sherman, 2005).

- Welch said, ". . . people, excited by speed and inspired by 'Stretch' dreams, have an absolutely infinite capacity to improve everything" [Slater, (2001) p.133].

4 Attractor cages

Slater says, "Let's keep in mind that the managers of American businesses have been trained to do just that—manage. That means managing, controlling, supervising, [and] creating corporate structures that assure that things get done" (2001, p.21). This leads to top-down control, passive dependency, and child-like behaviour by employees (Argyris, 1957). Everything that traditional leadership theory teaches managers tilts them toward trying to incentivise employees to carry out the leader's vision (Marion and Uhl-Bien, 2001, 2003). In fact, Welch did it differently.

Welch gave subordinates opportunities to win or lose on their own. When some failed, he did not take over management; he just got rid of failing units and people. He used what complexity scientists call attractor cages' to do this. These cages define spaces within which unpredictable non-linear dynamics can be instigated to occur. For example, geology created the Galapagos Islands and Lake Victoria (the isolated cages) within which coevolution occurred—given the tension of finding food for survival on the islands and in the lake, a relatively few animals/fish (i.e., an attenuated gene pool) produced rapid genetic and ecological change.[7] The complexity phrase is 'strange attractor limit setting' plus the imposition of tension. How did Welch do this? There are four key elements:

1   *Limit setting:* for any particular 'direct report' subordinate, he created the cage by defining a few broad objectives, i.e., the business space (e.g., industry) within which this person needed to focus. Every once and a while the cage may need to be redefined, especially in changing times.

2   *Tension emphasis:* from his first ten-year focus on 'Be #1 or 2 in your industry . . .' to his second ten-year focus on Six Sigma achievement, Welch insisted on make—or-break achievement, coupled with draconian incentives. This is 'management by tension' as opposed to 'management by objectives'.

3   *Within-cage point attractors:* point attractors are goals or objectives that 'direct-report' subordinates decide are relevant targets for winning out over tensions imposed by the competitive context. Direct-reports set up the targets and then manage the negative feedback process to reward or punish subordinates who do or do not reach the target. The Welch 'challenge', so to speak, was for each direct-report to, then, set up his/her own

point attractors within the cage—i.e., specific goals, targets, etc., to be achieved within the specified time limit. With some 350 businesses within the GE complex, Welch could not just reach down and do this level of 'management' himself, as the quote from Slater, above, implies.

4   *Coevolution and scalability:* discussed as A-D #11.

By doing the above, CEOs can create 'cages' within which coevolution and new order can emerge and progress. Welch did not create the specific goals (point attractors) himself; this is what the direct-report subordinates in the attractor cage had to do. The idea of leaders enabling and steering complexity development—but not reaching down to do it themselves—is at the heart of the recent papers on complexity leadership by Marion and Uhl-Bien (2001, 2003) and Uhl-Bien et al. (2008). From Slater's book we see that:

- Welch defined attractor cages by emphasising 'a few clear, general goals' and 'broad objectives' [Slater, (2001), pp.28, 30].
- Welch said, "manage less . . . instil confidence . . . get out of the way . . . emphasise vision, not supervision" [Slater, (2001), p.22]; "managing less is managing better" [Slater, (2001), p.18].
- But like the strange attractor, there is a point where clarifications and corrections may need to be inserted. Thus, Welch pursued 'strategic audits' [Slater, (2001), p.45] and downsizing as ways of maintaining focus.
- Welch managed by imposing process-incentives, not content-directives.

5.2 A-Ds from Phase 2 of complexity science

The A-Ds from Phase 2 of complexity science mostly pertain to the development of employees' knowledge, skill, and networking capabilities coupled with positive-feedback aspects of evolution and change. These

A-Ds connect with the directive given by Collins in his book, *Good to Great* (2001, p.47): *'Get the right people on the bus'*. This becomes the task of building human capital (Becker, 1975) and social capital (Granovetter, 1973; Burt, 1992). These A-Ds fit with Welch's constant attempts to create a 'boundaryless organisation' (Ashkenas et al., 1995) and put people and their development first (Sirisha, 2002).

5 Heterogeneous agents

If all the agents have similar abilities, there is no advantage to networking (Holland, 1995). End of story. Relevant synonyms are 'diversity', unlike', 'novel', 'randomness'. In complexity science, agent heterogeneity is the opposite of Janis's `groupthink' (1972). We have some 3.8 billion years of mutation and crossover creating biological diversity to support this. Campbell (1974) called it 'blind variation', arguing that 'blind' variation was much more relevant for social innovation than 'rational' variations. Furthermore, Johnson (2000), LeBaron (2000), Allen (2001), and Page (2007) all show that novelty, innovation, and learning disappear as the attributes of agents collapse from heterogeneous to homogeneous. The definition of creativity favoured by psychologists— 'remote associates'—holds that creativity emerges when agents having different ideas or concepts interact and, consequently, are joined to produce something new (Mednick and Halpern, 1962).

- In the first ten years or so after Welch took over GE (his *'Neutron Jack'* era), he divested—130,000 of its 400,000 employees and acquired ~70,000 [Slater, (2001), p.99].
- This effort brought together employees with diverse experience and abilities (as compared to the long-term GE employees).
- This heterogeneity was brought in by acquisitions; consequently, it had more impact because it came in the form of the 993 newly acquired groups of people, each of which had more impact than lone individuals.

6 Build human capital

Human capital is the basis of agent heterogeneity. The idea of networked idiots does not offer much promise. The 'human capital' idea dates back to Becker's (1975) work on the subject. He argued that the economists' Cobb-Douglas production function needs a component to reflect the knowledge people hold, as well as capital and labour. This is especially true in today's knowledge economy. In some sense, the economic advantage of the USA, today, is much more a function of human capital, and its embodiment in physical and intangible capital, than financial capital or cheap labour. Zucker and Darby (1996) find that one genius appropriately networked is superior to larger networks comprised of less talented agents. Isolated geniuses are not any better than networked idiots!

The *'absorptive capacity'* literature (Cohen and Levinthal, 1990) suggests that if agents do not have some pre-existing level of knowledge relevant to understanding imposing 'variety' from the environment (Ashby, 1956), they will not be very good at collecting additional information pertaining to the imposing contextual adaptive tensions. Also, absorptive capacity is a positive feedback process—the more absorptive capacity an agent has the more new, technical information he/she absorbs; the more information absorbed, the higher his/her absorptive capacity.

- As he hired more diverse employees (heterogeneous agents), Welch also added to the human capital of GE. However, the employees were not chosen and placed randomly in the corporation (one way of bringing in heterogeneity). Instead, they arrived as employees of acquired businesses, meaning that their human capital was relevant and already integrated into some kind of already working network. The acquired businesses had the trust/cohesion/efficiency advantage of groupthink, but as a result also had more *heterogeneity clout.* GE under Welch was able to take advantage of the 'heterogeneity clout' without destroying the *groupthink trust/cohesion/efficiency*'—unlike most of M&A practices by most firms, which destroy both.

- Because of GE's ability to assimilate (they were successfully bringing in around three to five acquisitions per week (Kerr, 2000), the newly acquired human capital units retained their 'groupthink' effectiveness and yet had significant heterogeneity impact, thereby improving the overall productivity of GE.
- As Slater (2001, p.59) characterises, Welch used 'acquisitions to make the quantum leap'.

7 Weak tie flooding

Granovetter's (1973, 1982) classic research finding is that novelty and innovation happen more frequently in networks consisting of *'weak ties'* as opposed to *'strong ties'*.[8] The latter tend to produce groupthink (Janis, 1972). This weak-tie effect is reconfirmed by Burt's (1992) discovery of the entrepreneurial power of *'weak-tie bridges'*. And, of course, weak-tie effects go hand in hand with my 5th action-rule's emphasis on agent heterogeneity. Given an existing system, which tends toward strong-tie formations as agents get to know each other better and experience the build-up of what McKelvey (2003, 2010) terms *'entanglement ties'*—path dependencies resulting from ties building up over repeated interactions, with the effect that the behaviours of entangled-tie agents become increasingly similar and predictable (see also March, 1991). While modularisation speeds up adaptive response rates, modules (cells) are also prone to become strong-tie cliques. Put in terms of Burt's weak-tie bridging, weak-tie flooding is even more effective when bridging activities are included. The positive effects of weak-tie flooding appear in Uzzi's (2001, Guimera et al., 2005) study of the evolution of the Broadway music industry.

- Welch set the stage for weak-tie flooding by divesting units totalling—130,000 employees and then acquiring firms to bring back—70,000 [Slater, (2001), p.99-100].
- While acquired firms may enter with strong-tie networks within firms, they immediately have weak-tie potential across all the rest of the business units.
- Coupled with the physical proximity A-D, the flooding of GE with weak-tie effects was inevitable.
- I have already mentioned GE's emphasis of networking.

8 Moderate networking

Kauffman (1993), in an important book in the evolutionary biology literature, argues that some connections—not very many, actually—among agents improves system fitness. However, this fitness deteriorates as the number of connections among agents increases past an optimal level. He calls this effect *'complexity catastrophe'*, arguing that it thwarts Darwin's (1859) selectionist evolution-toward-improved-fitness theory. Using his NK[C] model, Kauffman also finds that the upper bound at which 'catastrophe' sets in is raised if agents within the system are connected to a moderate extent with agents outside the system (McKelvey, 1999). To this end, Barabasi and Bonabeau (2003) find that number of connections per node follows a power law [9], so it should be expected that one individual in a network will have many links and some will have almost none. In other words, it is not necessary that all agents have the same number of connections (Yuan and McKelvey, 2004). Moderate complexity is confirmed by the research of Rivkin (2000, 2001), among many others (Maguire et al., 2006; Levinthal and Posen, 2007; Ganco and Agarwal, 2009)[10]—parallel to Simon's (1962) 'nearly decomposable' systems, as I note below.

- Welch set in motion a number of network producing ideas—the 'work-out' process got employees to talk to each other and then to

205

the boss (Slater, 2001); the 'no hording of best practices' forced people to get their ideas into the GE network of idea circulation (Kerr, 2000).

- The yearly meetings in Boca Raton, Florida brought managers from all parts of GE together in ways that developed weak-ties across organisational units; the acquisitions brought new people in who were already in networks—stronger ties within acquired units; weak ties among units.
- At the same time, there was no sense of massive required networking that would bring on 'catastrophe'.
- Moving people who have succeeded in one job into another—that is, changing their job position and physical location is a way of creating new weak-ties, as GE has found out (Ken, 2000).

9 Modular design

How can corporations create 'cells' in cellular networks? Simon (1962) argued that systems (i.e., cellular networks) evolve toward fitness fastest when the cells (modules) are nearly, but not totally, disconnected from higher levels in biological or social system hierarchies—i.e., *'nearly decomposable'* into anarchy. Sanchez (1999; Sanchez and Mahoney, 1996) confirms this empirically in his extensive research on the effectiveness of modularly designed firms; also corroborated by Schilling (2000). Economists have long argued that one has to worry whether managers (or autonomous agents) always serve the best interests of shareholders. It is clear from the recent Enron, WorldCom, and investment bank investigations that CEOs and lower-level managers do not always put shareholder interests first. Even so, it is clear that the alternative—of strong top management control—is also antithetical to shareholders' best interests. CEOs have to aim at giving cellular networks much freedom and autonomy, but not total autonomy. I also dealt with this earlier in the 'attractor cages' section.

- Welch tried to get GE to think small, and 'act like a small company' [Slater, (2001), p.99].
- He did away with several layers of management. He 'unleashed empowered workers' [Slater, (2001), p.100]. Getting rid of layers of hierarchy, while at the same time focusing on worker empowerment and autonomy, is consistent with Simon's near decomposability. By doing this, Welch's emphasis was on adaptive speed.
- He held that small business units 'communicate better', 'move faster', and 'waste less' [Slater, (2001), pp.100-101], again fitting Simon's evolutionary advantage from near decomposability.
- Welch said: "We found that with fewer layers, we had wider spans of management. We weren't managing better. We were managing less, and that was better" (p.18).

10 Appropriate physical proximity

People who see each other all the time usually develop strong ties. People who never see each other tend not to interact. This is to say, networking is a function of physical adjacency. Of course, the internet, electronic mail, telephones, and so forth, overcome many limitations of physical adjacency, but many remain. Therefore, it is important to create physical 'mixing' events that bring heterogeneous agents into person-to-person contact. Combining these mixing events with increased awareness of newly appearing adaptive tensions meets some of the basic conditions of new order creation, as outlined in McKelvey (2001, 2008). CEOs can also create tags (tiny initiating events), which serve to set off coevolutionary dynamics. Job related 'new' mixing is also possible. GE used physical circumstances to foster appropriate internal complexity.

- The training facility at Crotonville was a key place for 'work-outs' (Tichy and Sherman, 2005). Whether at Crotonville or in a hotel, employees spent some three days away from GE in a physical location where they could first talk to each other and then, at the end, to their boss.

- Frequently, diverse members of a particular business were brought together—engineers, production, marketing, etc. [Slater, (2001), pp.117-122].
- Yearly meetings in Boca Raton were larger events where 500 managers from all 350 businesses of GE would congregate and attend sessions of various kinds [Slater, (2001), p.35]. Here, the physical setting was the key in making network development and weak-tie formation possible.
- The work-outs were about confronting the boss, while the Boca Raton meetings were platforms for Welch to repetitively re-emphasise the broad objectives to all the key players (i.e., keep defining/redefining the boundaries of the attractor cages)
- Underneath these overt agendas, the physical sites fostered making weak-tie connections and networking.

11a Coevolution

Coevolution is a fundamental dynamic in Phase 2 of complexity science. From biology, two key points are relevant:

1   Coevolution implies heterogeneous agents (genes), erosion of barriers so gene pools mix, and the interaction of species and habitat elements such that they constantly impose on each other to create adaptive tension.

Even so:

2   Coevolution is kept under control by damping mechanisms such as food stocks, climate, geology, diseases, and predator-prey relationships; organisms have no control over the rate at which they progress toward new order.

Evolution and ecology have long been part of organisation theory (Aldrich, 1979, 1999; McKelvey, 1982; Hannan and Freeman, 1989) with coevolution a more recent arrival (McKelvey, 1997; Lewin and Volberda, 1999). These treatments leave explicit managerial actions out of the mix. But, in organisations, as McKelvey discusses elsewhere (2002), coevolving systems are always liable to coevolve in unwanted directions, not coevolve fast enough in the right directions, start at a good rate and then suffer the effects of damping processes, etc. As a result, coevolution has to be explicitly managed.

- "Welch was convinced that GE's diversity and complexity could be turned into an asset by creating what he called 'a learning culture" [Slater, (2001), p70].

- "The boundaryless learning culture killed any view that assumed the GE Way was the only way, or even the best way" [Slater, (2001), p.'72].

- "That belief drove us to create a boundaryless company by de-layering and destroying organisational silos. Selflessly sharing good ideas, while endlessly searching for better ideas, became a natural act. We purged NIH—not invented here—from our system . . ."[Slater, (2001), p.'73].

- Breaking down boundaries and emphasising idea sharing surely set coevolution in motion at GE. Thus: "Our core competence is sharing best ideas across businesses Reward employees for knowledge sharing Hold idea sharing meetings on a regular basis" [Slater, (2001), pp. 78, 80].

11 b Scalability[11]

Tiny initiating events can spiral up (scale up) into large positive or negative outcomes (Holland, 1995, 2002; Newman, 2005; Andriani and McKelvey, 2009). Sam Walton's first store scaled up into Walmart. The Harvard student, Billy Gates, had an idea about personal computer file-management that scaled up into Microsoft. Oppositely, a variety of small localised traffic stoppages on the Union Pacific railroad after its merger with the Southern Pacific railroad, eventually accumulated to the point of shutting down the entire 30,000-mile railroad (Weick and Sutcliffe, 2001); similar build-ups of random tiny events eventually brought down Enron and Wall Street's Bear Sterns and Lehman Bros.

Good management fosters the positive scalability spirals; stops negative ones. Scalability requires heterogeneous agents, erosion of barriers so ideas mix, and the interaction of agents in and outside of firms such that they constantly impose on each other to create adaptive tension. Welch's management by tension, and then boundaryless organising coupled with coevolution, set scalability in motion. The best example is his switch from using 'Be #1 or 2 . . .' as an adaptive tension in the first ten years at GE (which forced managers to study and respond to their outside competitive context), to his strong emphasis on Six Sigma in the second ten years (which involved managers from top to bottom). Six Sigma is scalability in action (though inadvertently). Why? For Six Sigma to work it had to have strong top management support (Welch heavily incentivised top managers who made Six Sigma work), down through middle management and, then, down to basic operations where quality improvements were made in all basic production processes from GE capital to places where they manufactured things like parts for locomotives, jet engines, and MRI equipment.

- Six Sigma was applied to manufacturing and then to all service-related transactions as well [Sirisha, (2002), p.5].
- 40% of the bonuses for 7,000 top executives were based on Six Sigma performance: [Sirisha, (2002), p.5].
- Operating profit margins increased from 13.6% to 16.75 in 1999 [Sirisha, (2002),.5].
- Customer satisfaction was made top priority across all management levels [Sirisha, (2002), p.6].

- Six Sigma forced managerial attention from top to bottom on tiny events defined as three defects per million [Slater, (2001), p.155].
- These then translated into cost of poor quality, supplier quality, internal performance, and design activities [Slater, (2001), p.155].

12 *Coaching*

The OD literature (French and Bell, 1984) and researchers applying complexity theory to business both realise that coaching is needed to help many employees form network connections expeditiously (Goldstein, 1994; Kelly and Allison, 1999). One cannot assume that all relevant employees arrive with networking skills Given the possibility of both personal and task conflict, there is every reason to expect that coaches need to act as catalysts to help networking along.

- At GE professional 'facilitators' were used to make sure the work-outs worked (Slater, 2001).
- A compelling discussion of the coaching process is given in the Crotonville' and 'work-out' chapters (#s 11 and 16) in Tichy and Sherman (2005).

6 Why believe complexity science rather than what is in all the 'Welch' books?

From opera stars to athletes, people 'born with it' or who are instinctively good at it are often not good at telling others how to do it. In contrast, 'average' players like Tommy Lasorda (long-time coach of the Los Angeles Dodgers baseball team) often become genius coaches (because they have to study the game to get better at it). Jack Welch is an instinctively great manager, but I do not think he is very well clued in on the action specifics of how he got GE to be so remarkable. I do not think any of his books, or any other writings about his accomplishment, convey the right message. This explains why none of his protegees has replicated his amazing results in any other non-startup firm—they see results of what he did, but cannot replicate it. Bill Gates created an incredible Microsoft, which is its own story. But it is vastly different from a 100 year-old, old-line manufacturing company making mostly commodity-like products.

Recently, *Fortune Magazine* published an article titled, 'Get me a CEO from GE' (Kratz, 2005). The nature of this title suggests two things: other firms looked to GE to find their CEO and CEO-recruitments from GE were presumably good choices during the Welch era. Kratz mentions that 34 CEOs came from GE. In her story she mentions a number of CEOs who did or did not do well as CEO. She also crystallises these CEOs' perceptions of what they learned from Welch [Kratz, (2005), p.3]; if not the playbook, the key tools are:

- 'increase revenues and cut costs at the same time'
- Welch's 'one key device . . . was giving GE a simple roadmap and repeating it incessantly'
- 'I don't want you to call it a playbook . . . they're just tools'
- 'an absolute belief that great people build great companies'
- Matt Espe (CEO at IKON) boils this down to this: 'build a house that builds people'.

So, what kinds of shareholder value came from these 'tools' used by GE-trained CEOs? Of the various GE-trained CEOs mentioned by Kratz, only two of the 34 who left GE to become CEOs get star ratings. The first is Larry Bossidy while he was at AlliedSignal (which became Honeywell); his favourite term is 'execution'—but not the people! (Bossidy and Ram, 2002). During the nine years he was CEO the stock went up around 117%/year from start to finish (includes two stock splits). Below is the Yahoo stock chart. Still, while Bossidy was the best of those who left, his stock chart in no way looks as good as Welch's—under Welch GE stock went up—345%/year and with five stock splits!

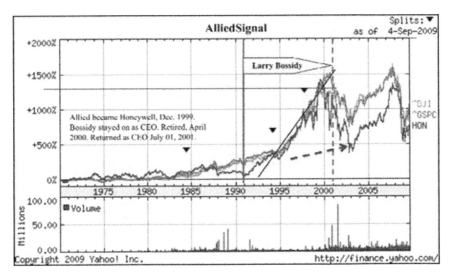

Figure 2 Larry Bossidy's performance at Allied Signal (became Honey-well in Dec. 1999)

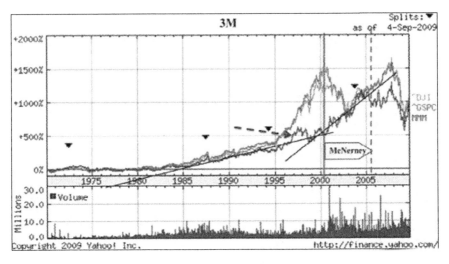

Figure 3 Jim McNerney's performance at 3M (see online version for colours)

The second best CEO from GE is Jim McNerney. During his five years at 3M we see nothing but strong positive gains in stock value; he clearly brought the laggard 3M stock to life; the change in rate of value increase is dramatic. He then left 3M to take over Boeing after the dismal performance of another GE-trained CEO, Harry Stonecipher (`cipher' is a pretty apt description of his performance). McNerney built on the stock jump at the end of Stonecipher's tenure and continued Boeing's dramatic stock rise—until it all came to a halt because of the liquidity crisis and crash of Wall St. in August 2007—I do not hold him accountable for the liquidity-caused decline. Another GE-trained CEO, Steve Bennett, brought a 500% stock improvement to Intuit. Of the 34 GE-trained CEOs only these three CEOs show untarnished positive stock gains for their firms—again, only three out of 34. But none as good as Welch.

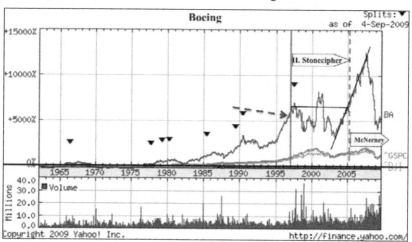

Figure 4 Jim McNerney's performance at Boeing (see online version for colours)

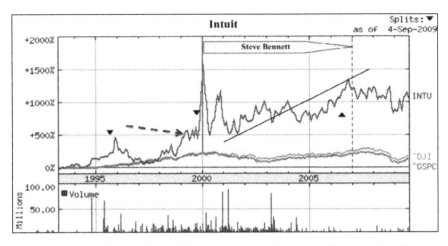

Figure 5 Steve Bennett's performance at Intuit (see online version for colours)

Tom Tiller was CEO of Polaris from 1998 to 2005. Its stock shows a strong positive rise up to 2005, but then collapses two years before the August 2007 liquidity crisis. A similar picture describes results from Randy Hogan at Pentair—strong positive showing but then a crash starting in 2005, a boom year. While John Trani at Stanley Works does not end a his stint with a crash, he shows only around a 100% increase in stock value in eight years—a modest performance indeed, given that the declines in Stanley Works stock were independent of the dot.com bust starting in 2001.

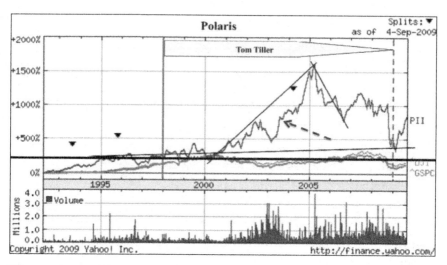

Figure 6 Tom Tiller's performance at Polaris (see online version for colours)

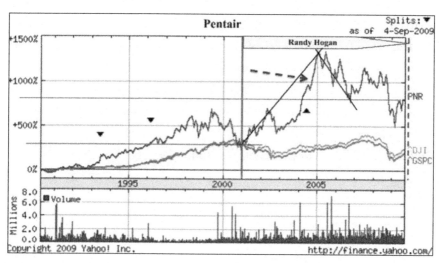

Figure 7 Randy Hogan's performance at Pentair (see online version for colours)

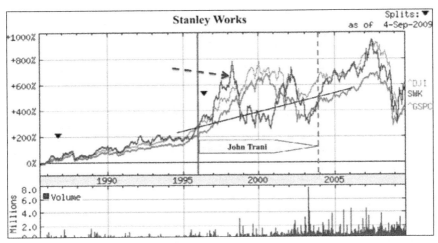

Figure 8 John Trani's performance at Stanley Works (see online version for colours)

On the decidedly negative side, no well-known GE-trained CEO matches Bob Nardelli, who ran The Home Depot into the ground over seven years. He stopped a rising stock dead in its tracks. Unless it is Jeff Immelt, who has been CEO of GE while its stock value has almost disappeared—see Figure 1. Almost as negative as Nardelli was the tenure of Kevin Sharer at Amgen. Like Nardelli, Glen Hiner and Gary Wendt rode down into oblivion with their stocks at Owens Coming and Conseco. Stanley Gault gets positive regards for his eleven years running Rubbermaid, but in fact the stock skyrocketed immediately after he left.

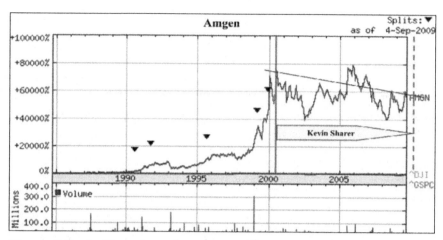

Figure 9 Kevin Sharer's performance at The Home Depot (see online version for colours

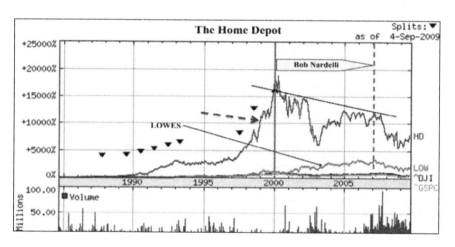

Figure 10 Bob Nardelli's performance at The Home Depot (see online version for colours)

Bottom line: Kratz (2005) points out that 17 of the 34 GE-trained CEOs performed worse than the S&P. Of the 17 who supposedly performed better, first, being better than the S&P is hardly noteworthy. Of all the CEOs she mentions, stock performance indicates that only Bossidy and McNerney show strong positive performances. But even they are nowhere near the outstanding results Welch accomplished. It is very clear from the record that none of the GE-trained CEOs came close to Welch's

218

performance over his 20 years heading up GE. Most lasted no more than half the time with nowhere near his level of accomplishment.

7 A-Ds used by non-GE-trained CEOs

The foregoing section focuses on GE managers who left to become CEOs, and as the record shows, only two, Bossidy and McNerney, have strong records. Evidence suggests that Jack Welch's methods mostly did not pass down to his subordinates at GE. My argument is that this is because he was unaware of—and no one else learned about—how he was inadvertently putting the 12 A-Ds of complexity leadership into practice. But what about evidence about the use of the A-Ds by people not connected with GE, but who have outstanding records as CEOs?

For the past two years I have had a variety of student teams focusing their term papers on analyses of famous CEOs associated with high-performing firms or well-known turnaround events. I challenged students to find out which of the A-Ds were used and whether all 12 were really necessary for stellar results. As one may see from Table 1, Google, Herb Kelleher at South West Airlines, Michael Dell at Dell, and Sandy Weill at Citigroup are/were using all or most of the A-Ds. Lou Gerstner used six of them when revitalising IBM. Vikram Pandit's precarious position of being 'about to be fired' at Citigroup over the past three years is due to his being the worst performer in the table, in terms of A-D use. It is interesting to see that Gerstner and Steve Jobs are high on most of the same A-Ds. One should know that when Jobs heads up Apple its stock goes up; when he is not CEO it stock flatlines.

Table 1 A-Ds used by non-GE-trained CEO

	Simple rules	Google	Pandit[1]	Yahoo	IBM*	SW	Jobs	Dell[1]	Weill[2]	Tata[3]	Immelt[4]
3	Weak-tie flooding	√		½	√	H	√	L→H	√	3	H
1	Heterogeneous agents	√	Should	½	√	L	√	L→H	√	4	H
6	Physical conditions	√		√	√	M	√	H	√	1	H
7	Adaptive tension	√			√	t	^	?→H	√+	4	M
9	Critical values	√		½	√	H		?→H	√	2	H
2	Human capital formation	√	Should		√	H	√	L→H	√	4	M
10	Attractor cages	√	Should			H	√	?→M	√+	4	
12	Coaching	√				H		?→H	√	2	H
8	Draconian incentives	#	Should			≠		?→H	√+		M
5	Modular design	√				+	½	L→H	√	1	
4	Moderate networking	√	Should			M	?	L→H	√	3	H−
11	Managing co-evolution	√				L?	¼	L→H		1	

Notes: ‡: comparisons done with the help of student researchers; Spring, 2008, 2009.
#: rewards for entrepreneurial results rather than 'Draconian' as in GE.
†: A-Ds the research Team thinks Vikram Pandit (current CEO of Citigroup) needs to focus on first – generally, all A-Ds appear to be missing at Citigroup.
½ Yahoo gets partial credit for these A-Ds.
*: A-Ds Lou Gerstner appears to have paid attention to when creating the company-saving turnaround at IBM.
t: tension in terms of income, margins, ROI, as opposed to Welch's market share.
≠ very strong 'Kelleher' culture; 90% of workers in 9 Unions – strong union culture.
+: people as 'modules'; Porter's complexity 'fit-locks'.
^ tension via Steve Jobs personality rather than tension by imposing 'stretch' objectives.
[1]: the arrow L→H indicates the style of management before Michael Dell returned to his firm and then the management style Dell is known for.
[2]: Sandy Weill is mostly responsible for creating Citigroup by merging Travelers Ins. with Citibank (after John Reed retired). Citigroup 'crashed' after Weill retired.
[3]: Tata Group now has major world-wide brands; resurrected/reconfigured by R. N. Tata in 1991: 4=full emphasis of the A-D; 3–3/4 emphasis; 2=half emphasis; 1=little emphasis of the A-D.
[4]: Jeff Immelt took over as CEO of GE after Welch retired; started in 2001, the time of the dot.com bust. GE stock has lost most of its value since then, even though Immelt is high on half of the A-Ds.

As one may see, the ordering of the A-Ds in the table is out of sequence. At the top, I have placed the A-D used most often. The least-often used A-D is at the bottom. This ranking is definitely not what I would recommend in terms of what to do first—but at least heterogeneous agents is 2nd and tension and critical values are 4th and 5th. It is interesting and important that weak-tie flooding is 1st, since that is what most quickly increases heterogeneity—so this is highly logical, very important and good to see. The attractor-cage concept is the most difficult for students to understand, which undoubtedly affects its use, and thus ranking. In working with Staff personnel at a world-famous DJI firm, I see that draconian incentives is a difficult management practice for many people to feel comfortable with which, then, lowers its ranking. Most worrisome, perhaps, is that managing coevolution (and scalability) is at the bottom. Getting top quality management practices to filter down, and good ideas to filter up appears to be outside the range of thinking of CEOs and firms of top quality.

One caveat, however: The student researchers only had access to 'outside the firm' books, articles, news reports, and other stories and commentaries attempting to describe what goes on inside these firms. These sources cannot be considered to be totally comprehensive in terms of offering useful insider information about all, and perhaps even any, of these A-Ds.

8 Conclusions

Leadership theory is still mostly stuck at the bottom of hierarchies (the 'supervisor level); it is mostly about how 'heroic or charismatic' superiors [Bennis, (2007), p.3], who have 'wisdom, intelligence, and creativity' [Sternberg, (2007), p.34] should 'lead' followers in a face-to-face context. While they say the foregoing are still appropriate, Marion and Uhl-Bien point out that leadership also involves ". . . creating the conditions that enable productive, but largely unspecified, future states" (2001, p.391, my italics). Brown and Gioia (2002) say that ". . . leadership is not solely a set of characteristics possessed by an individual, but an emergent property of a social system, in which 'leaders' and followers' share in the process of enacting leadership" [quote taken from Parry and Bryman, (2006), p.455, my italics].

Taking a fresh start, I try to learn from what Jack Welch actually did at GE:

1   to increase its stock value 1,000s of percentage points higher than the Dow Jones Stock Index
2   to stay in office for 20 years at a time when Lucier et al. (2005) refer to CEOs as 'temp workers'
3   produce some $480 billion in shareholder wealth
4   be identified as *'Manager of the Century'* by *Fortune Magazine.*

But this is not easy. From opera stars to athletes, people 'born with it or who are instinctively good at it are usually not good at telling others how to do it. Welch is an instinctively great manager, but I do not think

221

he is very well clued in on the action-specifics of why he did so well. This explains why none of his protegees has replicated his amazing results in any other non-startup firm—as the stock charts in this article indicate.

What did Welch actually do? I draw from complexity science to identify 12 A-Ds that I believe are the means by which Welch was able to enable and steer GE to produce incredible wealth in ways that did not destroy social and human capital, autonomy, agent heterogeneity, connectivity, incentives, complex adaptive systems dynamics, and emergent self-organisation—and all without inadvertently creating an organisational ambiance/culture dominated by top-down control and/or imposing a CEO-only vision. These A-Ds represent complexity theory put into practice. But, my stock-chart data show pretty clearly that most of the Welch protegees trained at GE—who left to become CEOs of other firms—did not do very well; they just did not get the right message about how and why Welch produced so much shareholder value. In contrast, I try to offer some evidence that other CEOs who have built well-performing firms or produced dramatic turnarounds did, in fact, use many of the A-Ds.

A key question remaining, however, is whether all 12 A-Ds are necessary. My logic says yes, but my student researchers did not find this to be true in their studies of outstanding CEOs/firms. My Table 1 shows that a number of CEOs of top-performing firms did not use all 12. If not all 12 are used, is there a critical subset that must be used? Gerstner appears to have used just six in his turnaround of IBM. But my student research teams may not have gotten access to all of the relevant data, given that they were using published materials and studying firms from outside in.

Second, there was clearly a tough side to Welch's leadership at GE. He was not called 'Neutron Jack' for nothing. Divesting 130,000 employees is not for the weak hearted. Labelling employees As, Bs, and Cs and then firing the Cs, and then firing the managers who cannot fire the Cs, is surely tough minded. The 'Be #1 or 2 . . .' rule is not for the weak hearted either. On it goes. In contrast, many introductions of complexity theory to practitioners have been on the soft side, like much of OD—translating self-organisation into a modern version of empowerment, using complexity sciences as a modern-day re-legitimisation of prosaic OD approaches (I will not say who). My A-Ds make it patently obvious that 'complexity in action' is very different from updated OD. Saying 'Be #1 or 2 . . .' is meaningless absent the threat of divestiture and losing one's job. Welch was tough and had a vision, but clearly avoided the Nardelli kind of top-down control that thwarts innovation, stops risk-taking, stops two-way communication, and builds strongtie defensive cliques rather than weak-tie networks. Put bluntly, Welch replaced old-style, top-down 'management by objectives' by 'management by tension'. This is complexity leadership at its best!

To bottom-line it: I define 12 the A-Ds that Jack Welch pursued incessantly, as corroborated by the various quotes and statements I draw from Slater's book, *Get Better or Get Beaten* (2001). These 12 A-Ds encapsulate four critical elements—tension, heterogeneous agents, connections, and scalability—that complexity scientists have found give rise to complex adaptive systems, of which GE is a good and very large example. Using stock-charts as data, I also show that only two of the 34 GE-trained CEOs were in anyway successful—and none anywhere nearly as successful in creating shareholder value as was Welch. Finally, I show that six or more of the A-Ds appear to figure importantly in the success of various well-known CEOs showing remarkable success, but who have no connection with GE. All said and done, this article:

1   outlines the principal elements of complexity leadership
2   shows that traditional leadership theory offers no explanation at all for Jack Welch's incredible success as the 20-year CEO of GE.

References

Aldrich, H.E. (1979) *Organizations and Environments,* Prentice Hall, Englewood Cliffs.

Aldrich, H.E. (1999) *Organizations Evolving,* Sage, Thousand Oaks.

Allen, P.M. (2001) 'A complex systems approach to learning, adaptive networks', *International Journal of Innovation Management,* Vol. 5, pp.149-180.

Anderson, P.W., Arrow, K.J. and Pines, D. (1988) 'The economy as an evolving complex system', *Proceedings of the Santa Fe Institute,* Vol. 5, Addison-Wesley, Reading.

Andriani, P. and McKelvey, B. (2007) 'Beyond Gaussian averages: redirecting organization science toward extreme events and power laws', *Journal of International Business Studies,* Vol. 38, pp.1212-1230.

Andriani, P. and McKelvey, B. (2009) 'From Gaussian to Paretian thinking: causes and implications of power laws in organizations', *Organization Science,* Vol. 20, No. 6, pp.1053-1071.

Argyris, C. (1957) *Personality and Organization,* Harper, New York.

Arthur, W.B., Durlauf, S.N. and Lane, D.A. (1997) 'The economy as an evolving complex system', *Proceedings of the Santa Fe Institute,* Vol. 27, Addison-Wesley, Reading.

Ashby, W.R. (1956) An *Introduction to Cybernetics,* Chapman and Hall, London.

Ashkenas, R., Ulrich, D., Jick, T. and Kerr, S. (1995) *The Boundaryless Organization,* Jossey-Bass, San Francisco.

Avolio, B.J., Kahai, S. and Dodge, G.E. (2001) 'E-leadership: implications for theory, research, and practice', *Leadership Quarterly,* Vol. 11, pp.615-618.

Bak, P. (1996) *How Nature Works,* Copernicus, New York.

Barabasi, A-L. and Bonabeau, E. (2003) 'Scale-free networks', *Scientific American,* Vol.288, pp.60-69.

Bass, B.M. (1985) *Leadership and Performance Beyond Expectations,* Free Press, New York.

Bass, B.M. (2002) 'Cognitive, social, and emotional intelligence of transformational leaders', in Riggio, R.E., Murphy, S.E. and Pirozzolo, F.J. (Eds.): *Multiple Intelligences and Leadership,* pp.105-118, Erlbaum, Mahwah.

Bass, B.M. and Avolio, B.J. (1994) *Improving Organizational Effectiveness through Transformational Leadership,* Sage, Thousand Oaks.

Becker, G.S. (1975) *Human Capital,* 2nd ed., University of Chicago Press, Chicago.

Benard, H. (1901) 'Les tourbillons cellulaires dans une nappe liquide transportant de la chaleur par convection en regime permanent', *Annales de Chimie et de Physique,* Vol. 23, pp.62-144.

Bennett, N., Wise, C., Woods, P. and Harvey, J.A. (2003) 'Distributed leadership: a review of the literature', National College for Leadership of Schools and Children's Services, Nottingham.

Bennis, W.G. (1996) 'Becoming a leader of leaders', in Gibson, R. (Ed.): *Rethinking the Future,* pp.148-162, Brealey, London.

Bennis, W.G. (2007) 'The challenges of leadership in the modern world', *American Psychologist,* Vol. 62, pp.2-5.

Bennis, W.G. and Biederman, P.W. (1996) *Organizing Genius: The Secrets of Creative Collaboration,* Addison-Wesley, Reading.

Bennis, W.G. and Nanus, B. (1985) *Leaders: Strategies for Taking Charge,* Harper and Row, New York.

Bennis, W.G. and O'Toole, J. (2000) 'Don't hire the wrong CEO', *Harvard Business Review,* Vol. 78, pp.170-176.

Bolden, R., Gosling, J., Marturano, A. and Dennison, P. (2003) 'A review of leadership theory and competency frameworks', Centre for Leadership Studies, University of Exeter, Exeter.

Bossidy, L. and Ram, C. (2002) *Execution: The Discipline of Getting Things Done,* Crown Business, New York.

Brown, M.E. and Gioia, D.A. (2002) 'Making things click: distributive leadership in an online division of an offline organization', *Leadership Quarterly,* Vol. 13, pp.297-419.

Brown, M.H. (1989) 'Organizing activity in the women's movement: an example of distributed leadership', in Klandermans, B. (Ed.): *International Social Movement Research,* Vol. 2, pp.225-240, JAI Press, Greenwich.

Brown, S.L. and Eisenhardt, K.M. (1997) 'The art of continuous change: linking complexity theory and time-paced evolution in relentlessly shifting organizations', *Administrative Science Quarterly,* Vol. 42, pp.1-34.

Brown, S.L. and Eisenhardt, K.M. (1998) *Competing on the Edge: Strategy as Structured Chaos,* Harvard Business School Press, Boston.

Bryman, A. (1996) 'Leadership in organizations', in Clegg, SR., Hardy, C. and Nord, W.R. (Eds.): *Handbook of Organizational Studies,* pp.276-292, Sage, London.

Burns, J.M. (1978) *Leadership,* Harper and Row, New York.

Burt, R.S. (1992) *Structural Holes: The Social Structure of Competition,* Harvard University Press, Cambridge.

Byrne, J.A. (1998) 'How Jack Welch runs GE', *Business Week,* June 8, pp.90-102.

Campbell, D.T. (1974) 'Unjustified variation and selective retention in scientific discovery', in Ayala, F.J. and Dobzhansky, T. (Eds.): *Studies in the Philosophy of Biology,* pp.139-161, Macmillan, London.

Chu, D., Strand, R. and Fjelland, R. (2003) 'Theories of complexity', *Complexity,* Vol. 8, No.3, pp.19-30.

Churchman, C.W. and Ackoff, R.L. (1950) 'Purposive behavior and cybernetics', *Social Forces,* Vol. 29, pp.32-39.

Cohen, W.M. and Levinthal, D.A. (1990) 'Absorptive capacity: a new perspective on learning and innovation', *Administrative Science Quarterly*, Vol. 35, pp.128-152.

Collins, J.C. (2001) *Good to Great: Why Some Companies Make the Leap . . . and Others Don't*, Harper-Collins Publishers, New York.

Cowan, GA., Pines, D. and Meltzer, D. (1994) 'Complexity: metaphors, models, and reality, *Proceedings of the Santa Fe Institute*, Vol. 19, Addison-Wesley, Reading.

Cramer, F. (1993) *Chaos and Order: The Complex Structure of Living Things* (D.L. Loewus, Trans.), VCH, New York.

Dansereau, F. and Yammarino, F.J. (1998a) *Leadership: Multiple-level Approaches: Classical and New Wave*, Vol. 1, JAI Press, Stamford.

Dansereau, F. and Yammarino, F.J. (1998b) *Leadership: Multiple-level Approaches: Contemporary and Alternative*, Vol. 2, JAI Press, Stamford.

Darwin, C. (1859) *On the Origin of Species*, John Murray, London.

Epstein, J.M. and Axtell, R. (1996) *Growing Artificial Societies: Social Science from the Bottom Up*, MIT Press, Cambridge.

Finkelstein, S. (2003) *Why Smart Executives Fail*, Portfolio/Penguin, New York.

French, W.L. and Bell, C.H. (1984) *Organization Development*, Prentice-Hall, Englewood Cliffs.

Ganco, M. and Agarwal, R. (2009) 'Performance differentials between diversifying entrants and entrepreneurial start-ups: a complexity approach', *Academy of Management Review*, Vol. 34, pp.228-252.

Gell-Mann, M. (2002) 'What is complexity?' in Curzio, A.Q. and Fortis, M. (Eds.): *Complexity and Industrial Clusters*, pp.13-24, Physica-Verlag, Heidelberg.

Gibb, C.A. (1954) 'Leadership', in Lindzey, G. (Ed.): *Handbook of Social Psychology*, Vol. 2, pp.877-917, Addison-Wesley, Reading.

Gibb, C.A. (1958) 'An interactional view of the emergence of leadership', *Australian Journal of Psychology*, Vol. 10, pp.101-110.

Goldstein, J. (1994) *The Unshackled Organization,* Productivity Press, Portland.

Granovetter, M. (1973) 'The strength of weak ties', *American Journal of Sociology,* Vol. 78, pp.1360-1380.

Granovetter, M. (1982) 'The strength of weak ties: a network theory revisited', in Marsden, P.V. and Lin, N. (Eds.): *Social Structures and Network Analysis,* pp.105-130, Sage, Beverly Hills.

Gronn, P. (2002) 'Distributed leadership as a unit of analysis', *Leadership Quarterly,* Vol. 13, pp.423-451.

Guimerd, R., Uzzi, B., Spiro, J. and Nunes Amaral, L.A. (2005) 'Team assembly mechanisms determine collaboration network structure and team performance', *Science,* Vol. 308, pp.697-702.

Haken, H. (1977) *Synergetics, An Introduction,* Springer-Verlag, Berlin.

Hannan, M.T. and Freeman, J. (1989) *Organizational Ecology,* Harvard University Press, Cambridge.

Hartman, A. (2003) 'The competitor: Jack Welch's burning platform', *Ruthless Execution,* FT Prentice Hall, Upper Saddle River.

Hazy, J., Goldstein, J.A. and Lichtenstein, B.B. (2007) *Complex Systems Leadership Theory,* ISCE Publishing, Mansfield.

Hogan, R., Curphy, G.J. and Hogan, J. (1994) 'What we know about leadership', *American Psychologist,* Vol. 49, pp.493-504.

Holland, J.H. (1995) *Hidden Order,* Addison-Wesley, Reading.

Holland, J.H. (2002) 'Complex adaptive systems and spontaneous emergence', in Curzio, A.Q. and Fortis, M. (Eds.): *Complexity and Industrial Clusters,* pp.24-34, Physica-Verlag, Heidelberg.

Hosking, D.M. (1988) 'Organizing, leadership and skilful process', *Journal of Management Studies,* Vol., 25, pp.147-166.

House, R.J. (1977) 'A 1976 theory of charismatic leadership', in Hunt, J.G. and Larson, L.L. (Eds.): *Leadership: The Cutting Edge,* pp.189-207, Southern Illinois University Press, Carbondale.

Janis, I.L. (1972) *Victims of Group Think,* Houghton Mifflin, Boston.

Johnson, N.L. (2000) 'Developmental insights into evolving systems: Roles of diversity, non-selection, self-organization, symbiosis', in Bedau, M.A., McCaskill, J.S., Packard, N.H. and Rasmussen, S. (Eds.): *Artificial Life VII*, pp.315-326, MIT Press, Cambridge.

Katzenbach, J.R. and Smith, D.K. (1993) *The Wisdom of Teams*, Harvard Business School Press, Boston.

Kauffman, S.A. (1993) *The Origins of Order*, Oxford University Press, New York.

Kelly, S. and Allison, M.A. (1999) *The Complexity Advantage*, McGraw-Hill, New York.

Kerr, S. (2000) 'The development and diffusion of knowledge at GE', paper presented at the *Organization Science Winter Conference*, February, Keystone, CO.

Klein, K.J. and House, R.J. (1998) 'On fire: charismatic leadership and levels of analysis', in Dansereau, F. and Yammarino, F.J. (Eds.): *Leadership: Multiple-level Approaches: Classical and New Wave*, Vol. 1, pp.3-21, JAI Press, Stamford.

Kotter, J.P. and Heskett, J.L. (1992) *Corporate Culture and Performance*, Free Press, New York.

Kouzes, J.M. and Posner, B.Z. (1993) *Credibility: How Leaders Gain and Lose It*, Jossey-Bass, San Francisco.

Kratz, E.F. (2005) 'Get me a CEO from GE!' *Fortune*, April 18, Vol. 151, No. 8, pp.147-152 available at http://money.cnn.com/magazines/fortune/fortune_archive/2005/04/18/8257015/index.htm (accessed on 14 Oct. 2009).

LeBaron, B. (2000) 'Empirical regularities from interacting long—and short-memory investors in an agent-based stock market', *IEEE Transaction on Evolutionary Computation*, Vol. 5, pp.442-455.

Levinthal, D. and Posen, H.E. (2007) 'Myopia of selection: does organizational adaptation limit the efficacy of population selection?', *Administrative Science Quarterly*, Vol. 52, pp.586-620.

Lewin, A.Y. and Volberda, H.W. (1999) 'Coevolution of strategy and new organizational forms', *Special Issue of Organization Science,* Vol. 10, No. 5.

Lewin, R. (1999) *Complexity: Life at the Edge of Chaos* 2nd ed., University of Chicago Press, Chicago.

Linstead, S. and Grafton-Small, R. (1992) 'On reading organizational culture', *Organization Studies,* Vol. 13, pp.331-355.

Lucier, C., Schuyt, R. and Spiegel, E. (2003) 'CEO succession 2002: deliver or depart', *Strategy Business,* Summer, Vol. 31, available at http://www.strategy-business.com (accessed on 14 Oct. 2009).

Lucier, C., Schuyt, R. and Tse, E. (2005) 'CEO succession 2004: the world's most prominent temp workers', *Strategy + Business,* Summer, Vol.39, available at http://www.strategy-business.com (accessed on 14 Oct. 2009).

Maguire, S., McKelvey, B., Mirabeau, L. and Oztas, N. (2006) 'Organizational complexity science', in Clegg, S., Hardy, C., Nord, W. and Lawrence, T. (Eds.): *Handbook of Organizational Studies* 2nd ed., pp.165-214, Sage, Thousand Oaks.

Mainzer, K. (1994) *Thinking in Complexity,* 5th ed. published in 2007, Springer-Verlag, New York.

March, J.G. (1991) 'Exploration and exploitation in organization learning', *Organization Science,* Vol. 2, pp.71-87.

Marion, R. and Uhl-Bien, M. (2001) 'Leadership in complex organizations', *Leadership Quarterly,* Vol. 12, pp.389-418.

Marion, R. and Uhl-Bien, M. (2003) 'Complexity theory and Al-qaeda: examining complex leadership', *Emergence: A Journal of Complexity Issues in Organizations and Management,* Vol. 5, pp.56-78.

McKelvey, B. (1982) *Organizational Systematics,* University of California Press, Berkeley.

McKelvey, B. (1997) 'Quasi-natural organization science', *Organization Science,* Vol. 8, pp.351-380.

McKelvey, B. (1999) 'Avoiding complexity catastrophe in coevolutionary pockets: strategies for rugged landscapes', *Organization Science, Vol.* 10, pp.294-321.

McKelvey, B. (2001) 'Energizing order-creating networks of distributed intelligence', *International Journal of Innovation Management, Vol.* 5, pp.181-212.

McKelvey, B. (2002) 'Managing coevolutionary dynamics: Some leverage points', paper presented at the *18th EGOS Conference*, 4-6 July, Barcelona, Spain.

McKelvey, B. (2003) 'Emergent order in firms: complexity science vs. the entanglement trap', in Mitleton-Kelly, E. (Ed.): *Complex Systems and Evolutionary Perspectives on Organizations*, pp.99-125, Elsevier Science, Amsterdam.

McKelvey, B. (2008) 'Emergent strategy via complexity leadership: using complexity science and adaptive tension to build distributed intelligence', in Uhl-Bien, M. and Marion, R. (Eds.): *Complexity and Leadership, Vol. I: Conceptual Foundations*, pp.225-268, Information Age Publishing, Charlotte.

McKelvey, B. (2010) 'Gen-Mann, Murray par bill McKelvey', in Olivier Germain (Ed.): *Les Grands Inspirateurs de la Theorie des Organisations*, Editions Management et Societe (EMS), Caen, Fr.

McKelvey, B., Xu, H., Vidgen, R. and Tivnan, B. (2009) 'Re-thinking Kauffman's NK fitness landscape: groupthink vs. weak-tie effects', Working paper, UCLA Anderson School of Management, Los Angeles, CA.

Mednick, S.A. and Halpern, S. (1962) 'Ease of concept attainment as a function of associative rank', *Journal of Experimental Psychology,* Vol. 64, pp.626-630.

Miles, R., Snow, C.C., Matthews, J.A. and Miles, G. (1999) 'Cellular-network organizations', in Halal, W.E. and Taylor, K.B. (Eds.): *21st Century Economics*, pp.155-173, St. Martin's Press, New York.

Nanus, B. (1992) *Visionary Leadership,* Jossey-Bass, San Francisco.

Newman, M.E.J. (2005) 'Power laws, Pareto distributions and Zipf's law', *Contemporary Physics,* Vol. 46, pp.323-351.

Page, S.E. (2007) *The Difference: How the Power of Diversity Creates Better Groups, Firms, Schools, and Societies,* Princeton University Press, Princeton.

Parry, K.W. and Bryman, A.(2006) 'Leadership in organizations', in Clegg, S.R., Hardy, C., Lawrence, T.B. and Nord, W.R. (Eds.): *Handbook of Organization Studies,* 2nd ed, pp.447-468, Sage, London.

Peters, T.J. and Waterman, R.H. (1982) *In Search of Excellence,* Harper and Row, New York.

Prigogine, I. (1955) *An Introduction to Thermodynamics of Irreversible Processes,* Thomas, Springfield.

Prigogine, I. (1997) *The End of Certainty,* Free Press, New York.

Prigogine, I. and Stengers, I. (1984) *Order out of Chaos,* Bantam, New York.

Rivkin, J.W. (2000) 'Imitation of complex strategies', *Management Science,* Vol. 46, pp.824-844.

Rivkin, J.W. (2001) 'Reproducing knowledge: replication without imitation at moderate complexity', *Organization Science,* Vol. 12, pp.274-293.

Rost, J.C. (1993) *Leadership for the Twenty-first Century,* Praeger, Westport.

Sanchez, R. (1999) 'Modularity and the management of knowledge assets', paper presented at the *College of Organization Science Conference, INFORMS Conference,* November, Philadelphia.

Sanchez, R. and Mahoney, J.T. (1996) 'Modularity, flexibility, and knowledge management in product and organization design', *Strategic Management Journal,* Vol. 17, pp.63-76.

Schein, E.H. (1992) *Organizational Culture and Leadership,* Jossey-Bass, San Francisco.

Schilling, M.A. (2000) 'Toward a general modular systems theory and its application to interfirm product modularity', *Academy of Management Review,* Vol. 25, pp.312-334.

Schroeder, M. (1991) *Fractals, Chaos, Power Laws,* Freeman, New York.

Simon, H.A. (1962) 'The architecture of complexity', *Proceedings of the American Philosophical Society,* Vol. 106, pp.467-482, (Reprinted and expanded in *Sciences of the Artificial* 3rd ed., 1996, MIT Press, Cambridge).

Sirisha, D. (2002) 'GE and Jack Welch', *ICMR Center for Management Research,* Case # LDEN/002, Hyderabad, India.

Slater, R. (2001) *Get Better or Get Beaten: 29 Leadership Secrets from GE's Jack Welch,* McGraw-Hill, New York.

Sorensen, J.B. (2002) 'The strength of corporate culture and the reliability of firm performance', *Administrative Science Quarterly,* Vol. 47, pp.70-91.

Stauffer, D. (1987) 'On forcing functions in Kauffman's random Boolean networks', *Journal of Statistical Physics,* Vol. 46, pp.789-794.

Sternberg, R.J. (2007) 'A systems model of leadership', *American Psychologist,* Vol. 62, pp.34-42.

Swenson, R. (1989) 'Emergent attractor and the law of maximum entropy production: foundations to a theory of general evolution', *Systems Research,* Vol. 6, pp.187-197.

The Economist (2001) 'Churning at the top', 17th-23rd March, pp.75-77.

Tichy, N.M. and Sherman, S. (2005) *Control your Destiny or Someone Else Will,* 2nd ed., HarperCollins, New York.

Uhl-Bien, M. and Marion, R. (2008) *Complexity Leadership,* Information Age Publishing, Charlotte.

Uhl-Bien, R., Marion, R., and McKelvey, B. (2008) 'Complexity leadership theory: shifting leadership from the industrial age to the knowledge era', *Leadership Quarterly,* Vol. 18, pp.298-318.

Uzzi, B. (2001) 'On the evolution of the Broadway music industry', paper presented at the *Organization Science Winter Conference,* February,

Keystone, CO. von Ghyczy, T von Oetinger, B. and Bassford, C. (2001) *Clausewitz on Strategy,* Wiley, New York.

Weick, K.E. and Sutcliffe, K.M. *(2001) Managing the Unexpected: Assuring High Performance in an Age of Complexity,* Jossey-Bass, San Francisco.

Wheatley, M.J. *(1992a) Leadership and the New Science,* Berrett-Koehler, San Francisco.

Wheatley, M.J. (1992b) 'Searching for order in an orderly world: a poetic for post-machine-age managers', *Journal of Management Inquiry, Vol.* 1, pp.337-342.

Williamson, O.E. *(1975) Markets and Hierarchies,* Free Press, New York.

Willmott, H. (1993) 'Strength is ignorance: slavery is freedom: managing culture in modern organizations', *Journal of Management Studies,* Vol. 30, pp.515-552.

Yuan, C. and McKelvey, B. (2004) 'Situated learning theory: adding rate and complexity effects via Kauffman's NK model', *Nonlinear Dynamics, Psychology, and Life Sciences,* Vol. 8, pp.65-101.

Zucker, L.G. and Darby, M.R. (1996) 'Star scientists and institutional transformation: patterns of invention and innovation in the formation of the biotechnology industry', *Proceedings of the National Academy of Sciences,* Vol. 93, 12, pp.709-712, 716.

Notes

1   A 'cell' is a team, department, strategic business unit or firm. A 'cellular network' has to be able to 'reorganise continually'; requires collaborative skills for making cross boundary linkages; requires 'entrepreneurship, self-organisation, and member ownership' [Miles et al., (1999), p.163].

2   Figures 1 through 10 are 'Reproduced with permission of Yahoo! Inc.©2009 Yahoo! Inc.YAHOO! and the YAHOO! logo are registered trademarks of Yahoo! Inc.' (quoted from an e-mail from Yahoo Permissions).

3   'Agent' is a term broadly used to refer to cells, organisms, species, conversation elements, people, employees, groups, firms, industries, and societies, among many other more specific definitions.

4   My original term was 'simple rules', which comes from computational modeling and Epstein and Axtell's book, *Growing Artificial Societies* (1996, p.6). Computational agents follow 'simple rules'. But Welch's complexity leadership actions require consistent application over time, and they are not really 'simple'. Various readers have suggested that 'action-disciplines' is more apt. Hence, 'complexity-leadership action-disciplines'.

5   A-Ds 1,2,3,4, and 5 are further elaborated in McKelvey (2008).

6   For background on Clausewitz, see von Ghyczy et al. (2001).

7   Darwin (1859) described what happened on the Galapagos Islands and Chu et al. (2003) do so about Lake Victoria.

8   Weak ties are typically defined as connecting 'once a year; strong ties are connections 'once a week'.

9   A power law is a Pareto distribution plotted on log X and Y-axes. A Pareto distribution is usually a rank frequency distribution with long tails; thus, Barabasi and Bonabeau find that most members of a network are loners and one social star is usually at the top, having many more network connections than any other node. Andriani and McKelvey (2009) list 101 studies of power-law rank/frequency social and organisational distributions.

10 For a recent critical review of the NK model applications to organisations, see McKelvey et al. (2009).

11 Scalability is part of the 3rd Tconophysics' phase of complexity science. It dates back to the fractals of non-linear dynamics and chaos theory (Schroeder, 1991), and then power law studies (see endnote no. 8) (Newman, 2005; Andriani and McKelvey, 2007) and most recently scale-free theory (Andriani and McKelvey, 2009).

Part III
Dynamics of Organizations

Chapter 7

Prologue
Jerry Harvey
Professor Emeritus
The George Washington University

The Abilene Paradox: The Management of Agreement

Jerry Harvey

Prologue:

Jerry Harvey[11]

Originally, I gave the "Abilene Paradox" paper as a speech, not having any idea of what I was doing. I included in my delivery the full effect of the dialogue that occurred during our family's "trip to Abilene." I think it was the word "sheeeit" that surprised the audience. I think it was a shock. At the end of the talk, I was surprised that the audience gave me a very gracious ovation and didn't run me out of town. Apparently what I was saying resonated with them, so I said to myself "Hey, this is a good idea". I decided to write it out. When I did begin writing, it didn't take long. I don't remember how long it took—maybe 8 to 10 hours.

I had several problems getting the paper published. I wrote the original copy as a short book. I sent it to the Editor of the Addison-Wesley OD Series for review and consideration for possible publication. I got a letter back saying, "Dear Professor Harvey"—although I knew the editor very well—"I have let my editorial board read your work as a possible book for the Addison-Wesley series, and the nicest thing they could say about it was it would make an adequate high school graduation thesis," and then he got nasty. As one might surmise, his response didn't enhance my friendship with the editor. I have always wanted to meet him again but haven't seen him since then.

However, the Abilene Paradox seems to have struck a chord in the management world. I don't really have the foggiest idea why. I usually don't have any idea what causes me to write something. I never sit down to accomplish a specific goal. But once they were published, the concepts put forth in the Abilene journey have appeared in virtually all walks of life. They have even had an impact on military organizations, maybe more than any other type of organization. I don't really know why, but I get

---

[11]   This prologue is a rendering of an interview with Jerry Harvey on June 6, 2013.

frequent examples from the military where they will say in meetings, "We are going to Abilene," and everybody knows what that means but me. Closer to home, I thought our faculty took frequent trips to Abilene. I couldn't sit in a faculty meeting without saying "we're on the road"— and incidentally, it spoke clearly to the faculty. I soon understood that the Abilene Paradox is about managing not conflict, but agreement— or coping with the fact that we agree with others. In the context of agreement, concepts such as action anxiety, real risk, lack of certainty, separation anxiety (anaclitic depression), and negative fantasies become explanations for the relationships between the group and the individual.

Exploring the dynamics of the Abilene Paradox has allowed me to learn that I am a part of many trips to Abilene; in fact, I drive the bus frequently. For example, Gordon Lippitt had a friend in films and mentioned the paper to Peter Jordan, President of CRM. I subsequently sent the paper to Peter, not knowing what, if anything, was going to be done with it. Pete called back and said he would like to do a film on it. I wrote back that I would want to edit it, and he said, "We don't allow anybody to edit our films". Thus, I had to decide whether to allow it to be filmed, unedited by me, without really knowing what it was, and that is what led to the movie—Gordon is to blame.

I had a lot of reaction from my faculty, both of delight and of fury, that I would write something so un-academic. Some of them also reacted especially to the movie with jealousy. I had been experiencing what I had written about, anxiety of separation and negative fantasies. Anaclitic depression is a form of depression that occurs when an individual is abandoned by others around him. It can happen at any age, at any time, and is very central to the causing the Abilene Paradox. It is the fear of being abandoned that leads us to Abilene.

The movie led to my getting an invitation to do a sitcom TV series, named the Abilene Paradox. When the person called me, I hung up on him, thinking it was one of the jealous faculty members or someone else making a joke. I got a call back immediately saying that I would have to agree to the sitcom. They already had the money—a bunch of backers were ready to support the effort. They wanted me to come to Hollywood to shoot 14 segments. They said the chances were 5% it would hit and 95% that it wouldn't-primarily because I was no actor. I said their argument was persuasive. After I hung up again, he called back and said this was no joke: they wanted me to come to Hollywood. I told him no. I had just had heart surgery and was down and out and physically didn't have the energy to do it. They didn't care whether I had the energy or not, as long as I was willing to give it a try. I didn't give it a try. I could have been a famous TV star.

I always wonder what would have happened had I given it a try. It is a negative fantasy. I now understand that I have had numerous negative fantasies. If lined up end to end, they would reach the moon. I think, however, there is always real risk in trying to get out of Abilene. You may piss people off in whatever you do or say, however, you choose to act, and you may not. I have never been able to decide for myself which will happen to me. I take enormous risk sometimes in my consulting, but I can't tell whether it is going to blow up in my face or whether I am going to succeed in doing something productive. That is always a puzzle to me.

On the positive side, not all of my colleagues were upset with my Abilene endeavors. Elliot Jaques was thrilled with the Abilene Paradox. He said he was able to understand why people responded so negatively to the idea of the requisite organization and that he had been on a trip to Abilene. I read all of his manuscripts after *A General Theory of Bureaucracy* (Jaques, 1976). In fact, the way I met Elliot is that I wrote and told him he was the worst writer that I had ever read and that I could help him write if he would come to me. Of course, I was as a junior faculty member at the George Washington University and he was a senior with a great reputation in the OD field. Elliot called and said he lived on Ridge Road in Alexandria and he would see me the next day. We talked about his writing; it was atrocious. I read everything he wrote from then on, and he never improved.

I loved Elliot Jaques. When he died, we had a memorial service for him in a pub. It was a wonderful service where people who had any disagreement with Elliot, any fight they couldn't win in other circumstances, could bring it up and try to wipe the slate clean. Elliot's wife agreed to this. It was scary for me. I had never done a memorial service before and didn't know what to do—so I thought I was caught up in a trip to Abilene. I didn't want to do it, but she and others wanted me to. Hell, I did it. So it wasn't a trip to Abilene after all. As it turned out, leading Elliot's service was a wonderful experience.

The concepts that make up the Abilene Paradox seem to have remained as plausible explanations of the dynamics of managing agreement. I really don't have any idea of where it is going to end up. I presume it will remain viable. I get all kinds of calls even now to present the idea to other people, like the students in the George Washington University Executive Leadership Program in Ashburn, Virginia. I can no longer do it, but I get those calls, and people are still delighted by the concept and I don't know why. I have given up trying to understand the delight.

References

Jaques, E. (1976). *A general theory of bureaucracy.* Farnham, UK: Gower.

The Abilene Paradox: The Management of Agreement[12]

Jerry Harvey

The July afternoon in Coleman, Texas (population 5,607) was particularly hot-104 degrees as measured by the Walgreen's Rexall Ex-Lax temperature gauge. In addition, the wind was blowing fine-grained West Texas topsoil through the house. But the afternoon was still tolerable—even potentially enjoyable. There was a fan going on the back porch; there was cold lemonade, and finally, there was entertainment. Dominoes. Perfect for the conditions. The game required little more physical exertion than an occasional mumbled comment. "Shuffle 'em," and an unhurried movement of the arm to place the spots in the appropriate perspective on the table. All in all, it had the makings of an agreement Sunday afternoon in Coleman—that is, it was until my father-in-law suddenly said, "Let's get in the car and go to Abilene and have dinner at the cafeteria."

I thought, "What, go to Abilene? Fifty-three miles? In this dust storm and heat? And in an unairconditioned 1958 Buick?"

But my wife chimed in with, "Sounds like a great idea. I'd like to go. How about you, Jerry?" Since my own preferences were obviously out of step with the rest I re-plied, "Sounds good to me," and added, "I just hope your mother wants to go."

"Of course I want to go," said my mother-in-law. "I haven't been to Abilene in a long time."

So into the car and off to Abilene we went. My predictions were fulfilled. The heat was brutal. We were coated with a fine layer of dust that was cemented with perspiration by the time we arrived. The food at the cafeteria provided first-rate testimonial material for antacid commercials.

---

[12]   Originally Published as: Harvey, J. (1988). "The Abilene paradox: The management of agreement." Organizational Dynamics **Summer**: 17-43.

Some four hours and 106 miles later we returned to Coleman, hot and exhausted. We sat in front of the fan for a long time in silence. Then, both to be sociable and to break the silence, I said, "It was a great trip, wasn't it?"

No one spoke. Finally my mother-in-law said, with some irritation, "Well, to tell the truth, I really didn't enjoy it much and would rather have stayed here. I just went along because the three of you were so enthusiastic about going. I wouldn't have gone if you all hadn't pressured me into it."

I couldn't believe it. "What do you mean 'you all'?" I said. "Don't put me in the 'you all' group. I was delighted to be doing what we were doing. I didn't want to go. I only went to satisfy the rest of you. You're the culprits."

My wife looked shocked. "Don't call me a culprit. You and Daddy and Mama were the ones who wanted to go. I just went along to be sociable and to keep you happy. I would have had to be crazy to want to go out in heat like that."

Her father entered the conversation abruptly. "Hell!" he said.

He proceeded to expand on what was already absolutely clear. "Listen, I never wanted to go to Abilene. I just thought you might be bored. You visit so seldom I wanted to be sure you enjoyed it. I would have preferred to play another game of dominoes and eat the leftovers in the icebox."

After the outburst of recrimination we all sat back in silence. Here we were, four reasonably sensible people who, of our own volition, had just taken a 106-mile trip across a godforsaken desert in a furnace-like temperature through a cloud-like dust storm to eat unpalatable food at a hole-in-the-wall cafeteria in Abilene, when none of us had really wanted to go. In fact, to be more accurate, we'd done just the opposite of what we wanted to do. The whole situation simply didn't make sense.

At least it didn't make sense at the time. But since that day in Coleman, I have observed, consulted with, and been a part of more than one organization that has been caught in the same situation. As a result, they have either taken a side-trip, or, occasionally, a terminal journey to Abilene, when Dallas or Houston or Tokyo was where they really wanted to go. And for most of those organizations, the negative consequences of such trips, measured in terms of both human misery and economic loss, have been much greater than for our little Abilene group.

This article is concerned with that paradox—the Abilene Paradox. Stated simply, it is as follows: Organizations frequently take actions in contradiction to what they really want to do and therefore defeat the very purposes they are trying to achieve. It also deals with a major corollary of the paradox, which is that *the inability to manage agreement is a major source of organization dysfunction.* Last, the article is designed to help members of organizations cope more effectively with the paradox's pernicious influence.

As a means of accomplishing the above, I shall: (1) describe the symptoms exhibited by organizations caught in the paradox; (2) describe, in summarized case-study examples, how they occur in a variety of organizations; (3) discuss the underlying causal dynamics; (4) indicate some of the implications of accepting this model for describing organizational behavior; (5) make recommendations for coping with the paradox; and, in conclusion, (6) relate the paradox to a broader existential issue.

SYMPTOMS OF THE PARADOX

The inability to manage agreement, not the inability to manage conflict, is the essential symptom that defines organizations caught in the web of the Abilene Paradox. That inability to manage agreement effectively is ex-pressed by six specific subsymptoms, all of which were present in our family Abilene group.

1. Organization members agree privately, as individuals, as to the nature of the situation or problem facing the organization. For

example, members of the Abilene group agreed that they were enjoying themselves sitting in front of the fan, sipping lemonade, and playing dominoes.

2. Organization members agree privately, as individuals, as to the steps that would be required to cope with the situation or problem they face. For members of the Abilene group "more of the same" was a solution that would have adequately satisfied their individual and collective desires.

3. Organization members fail to accurately communicate their desires and/or beliefs to one another. In fact, they do just the opposite and thereby lead one another into misperceiving the collective reality. Each member of the Abilene group, for example, communicated inaccurate data to other members of the organization. The data, in effect, said, "Yeah, it's a great idea. Let's go to Abilene," when in reality members of the organization individually and collectively preferred to stay in Coleman.

4. With such invalid and inaccurate information, organization members make collective decisions that lead them to take actions contrary to what they want to do, and thereby arrive at results that are counterproductive to the organization's intent and purposes. Thus, the Abilene group went to Abilene when it preferred to do something else.

5. As a result of taking actions that are counterproductive, organization members experience frustration, anger, irritation, and dissatisfaction with their organization. Consequently, they form subgroups with trusted acquaintances and blame other subgroups for the organization's dilemma. Frequently, they also blame authority figures and one another. Such phenomena were illustrated in the Abilene group by the "culprit" argument that occurred when we had returned to the comfort of the fan.

6. Finally, if organization members do not deal with the generic issue—the inability to manage agreement—the cycle repeats itself

with greater intensity. The Abilene group, for a variety of reasons, the most important of which was that it became conscious of the process, did not reach that point.

To repeat, the Abilene Paradox reflects a failure to manage agreement. In fact, it is my contention that the inability to cope with (manage) agreement, rather than the inability to cope with (manage) conflict, is the single most pressing issue of modern organizations.

OTHER TRIPS TO ABILENE

The Abilene Paradox is no respecter of individuals, organizations, or institutions. Following are descriptions of two other trips to Abilene that illustrate both the pervasiveness of the paradox and its underlying dynamics.

Case No. 1: The Boardroom.
The Ozyx Corporation is a relatively small industrial company that has embarked on a trip to Abilene. The president of Ozyx has hired a consultant to help dis-cover the reasons for the poor profit picture of the company in general and the low morale and productivity of the R&D division in particular. During the process of investigation, the consultant becomes interested in a research project in which the company has invested a sizable proportion of its R&D budget.

When asked about the project by the consultant in the privacy of their offices, the president, the vice-president for research, and the research manager each describes it as an idea that looked great on paper but will ultimately fail because of the unavailability of the technology required to make it work. Each of them also acknowledges that continued support of the project will create cash flow problems that will jeopardize the very existence of the total organization.

Furthermore, each individual indicates he has not told the others about his reservations. When asked why, the president says he can't reveal his "true" feelings because abandoning the project, which has been widely publicized, would make the company look bad in the press and, in addition, would probably cause his vice-president's ulcer to kick up or perhaps even cause him to quit, "because he has staked his professional reputation on the project's success."

Similarly, the vice-president for re-search says he can't let the president or the re-search manager know of his reservations be-cause the president is so committed to it that "I would probably get fired for insubordination if I questioned the project."

Finally, the research manager says he can't let the president or vice-president know of his doubts about the project because of their extreme commitment to the project's success.

All indicate that, in meetings with one another, they try to maintain an optimistic facade so the others won't worry unduly about the project. The research director, in particular, admits to writing ambiguous progress reports so the president and the vice-president can "interpret them to suit themselves." In fact, he says he tends to slant them to the "positive" side, "given how com-mitted the brass are."

The scent of the Abilene trail wafts from a paneled conference room where the project research budget is being considered for the following fiscal year. In the meeting it-self, praises are heaped on the questionable project and a unanimous decision is made to continue it for yet another year. Symbolically, the organization has boarded a bus to Abilene.

In fact, although the real issue of agreement was confronted approximately eight months after the bus departed, it was nearly too late. The organization failed to meet a payroll and underwent a two-year period of personnel cutbacks, retrenchments, and austerity. Morale suffered, the most competent technical personnel resigned, and the organization's prestige in the industry declined.

Case No, 2: The Watergate

Apart from the grave question of who did what, Watergate presents America with the profound puzzle of why. What is it that led such a wide assortment of men, many of them high public officials, possibly including the President himself, either to instigate or to go along with and later try to hide a pattern of behavior that by now appears not only reprehensible, but stupid? (The Washington Star and Daily News, editorial, May 27, 1973.)

One possible answer to the editorial writer's question can be found by probing into the dynamics of the Abilene Paradox. I shall let the reader reach his own conclusions, though, on the basis of the following excerpts from testimony before the Senate investigating committee on "The Watergate Affair."

In one exchange, Senator Howard Baker asked Herbert Porter, then a member of the White House staff, why he (Porter) found himself "in charge of or deeply involved in a dirty tricks operation of the campaign." In response, Porter indicated that he had had qualms about what he was doing, but that he ". . . was not one to stand up in a meeting and say that this should be stopped I kind of drifted along." And when asked by Baker why he had "drifted along," Porter replied, "In all honesty, because of the fear of the group pressure that would ensue, of not being a team player," and ". . . I felt a deep sense of loyalty to him [the President] or was appealed to on that basis." *(The Washington Post, June 8, 1973, p. 20.)*

Jeb Magruder gave a similar response to a question posed by committee counsel Dash. Specifically, when asked about his, Mr. Dean's, and Mr. Mitchell's reactions to Mr. Liddy's proposal, which included bugging the Watergate, Mr. Magruder replied, "I think all three of us were appalled. The scope and size of the project were something that at least in my mind were not envisioned. I do not think it was in Mr. Mitchell's mind or Mr. Dean's, although I can't comment on their states of mind at that time."

Mr. Mitchell, in an understated way, which was his way of dealing with difficult problems like this, indicated that this was not an "acceptable project." *(The Washington Post,* June 15, 1973, p. A14.)

Later in his testimony Mr. Magruder said, ". . . I think I can honestly say that no one was particularly overwhelmed with the project. But I think we felt that this information could be useful, and Mr. Mitchell agreed to approve the project, and I then notified the parties of Mr. Mitchell's approval." *(The Washington Post,* June 15, 1973, p. A14.)

Although I obviously was not privy to the private conversations of the principal characters, the data seem to reflect the essential elements of the Abilene Paradox. First, they indicate agreement. Evidently, Mitchell, Porter, Dean, and Magruder agreed that the plan was inappropriate. ("I think I can honestly say that no one was particularly overwhelmed with the project.") Second, the data indicate that the principal figures then proceeded to implement the plan in contra-diction to their shared agreement. Third, the data surrounding the case clearly indicate that the plan multiplied the organization's problems rather than solved them. And finally, the organization broke into subgroups with the various principals, such as the President, Mitchell, Porter, Dean, and Magruder, blaming one another for the dilemma in which they found themselves, and internecine warfare ensued.

In summary, it is possible that be-cause of the inability of White House staff members to cope with the fact that they agreed, the organization took a trip to Abilene.

ANALYZING THE PARADOX

The Abilene Paradox can be stated succinctly as follows: Organizations frequently take actions in contradiction to the data they have for dealing with problems and, as a result, compound their problems rather than solve them. Like all paradoxes, the Abilene Paradox deals with absurdity. On the surface, it makes little sense for organizations, whether they are couples or companies, bureaucracies or governments, to take actions that are diametrically opposed to the data they possess for solving crucial organizational problems. Such actions are particularly absurd since they tend to compound the very problems they are designed to solve and thereby defeat the purposes the organization is trying to achieve. However, as Robert Rapaport and others have so cogently expressed it, paradoxes are generally paradoxes only because they are based on a logic or rationale different from what we understand or expect.

Discovering that different logic not only destroys the paradoxical quality but also offers alternative ways for coping with similar situations. Therefore, part of the dilemma facing an Abilene-bound organization may be the lack of a map—a theory or model—that provides rationality to the paradox. The purpose of the following discussion is to pro-vide such a map.

The map will be developed by examining the underlying psychological themes of the profit-making organization and the bureaucracy and it will include the following landmarks: (1) Action Anxiety; (2) Negative Fantasies; (3) Real Risk; (4) Separation Anxiety; and (5) the Psychological Reversal of Risk and Certainty. I hope that the discussion of such landmarks will provide harried organization travelers with a new map that will assist them in arriving at where they really want to go and, in addition, will help them in assessing the risks that are an inevitable part of the journey.

ACTION ANXIETY

Action anxiety provides the first landmark for locating roadways that bypass Abilene. The concept of action anxiety says that the reasons organization members take actions in contradiction to their understanding of the organization's problems lies in the intense anxiety that is created as they think about acting in accordance with what they believe needs to be done. As a result, they opt to endure the professional and economic degradation of pursuing an unworkable research project or the consequences of participating in an illegal activity rather than act in a manner congruent with their beliefs. It is not that organization members do not know what needs to be done—they do know. For example, the various principals in the research organization cited *knew* they were working on a re-search project that had no real possibility of succeeding. And the central figures of the Watergate episode apparently *knew* that, for a variety of reasons, the plan to bug the Watergate did not make sense.

Such action anxiety experienced by the various protagonists may not make sense, but the dilemma is not a new one. In fact, it is very similar to the anxiety experienced by Hamlet, who expressed it most eloquently in the opening lines of his famous soliloquy:

To be or not to be; that is the question:
Whether 'tis nobler in the mind to suffer
The slings and arrows of outrageous fortune
Or to take arms against a sea of troubles
And by opposing, end them? . . .
(Hamlet, Act III, Scene II)

It is easy to translate Hamlet's anxious lament into that of the research manager of our R&D organization as he contemplates his report to the meeting of the budget committee. It might go something like this:

To maintain my sense of integrity and self-worth or compromise it, that is the question. Whether 'tis nobler in the mind to suffer the ignominy that comes from managing a nonsensical research project, or the fear and anxiety that come from making a report the president and V.P. may not like to hear.

So, the anguish, procrastination, and counterproductive behavior of the re-search manager or members of the White House staff are not much different from those of Hamlet; all might ask with equal justification Hamlet's subsequent searching question of what it is that

251

makes us rather bear those ills we have than fly to others we know not of.
(Hamlet, Act III, Scene II)

In short, like the various Abilene protagonists, we are faced with a deeper question: Why does action anxiety occur?

NEGATIVE FANTASIES

Part of the answer to that question may be found in the negative fantasies organization members have about acting in congruence with what they believe should be done. Ham-let experienced such fantasies.

Specifically, Hamlet's fantasies of the alternatives to the current evils were more evils, and he didn't entertain the possibility that any action he might take could lead to an improvement in the situation. Hamlet's was not an unusual case, though. In fact, the "Hamlet syndrome" clearly occurred in both organizations previously described. All of the organization protagonists had negative fantasies about what would happen if they acted in accordance with what they believed needed to be done.

The various managers in the R&D organization foresaw loss of face, prestige, position, and even health as the outcome of confronting the issues about which they believed, incorrectly, that they disagreed. Similarly, members of the White House staff feared being made scapegoats, branded as disloyal, or ostracized as non-team players if they acted in accordance with their under-standing of reality.

To sum up, action anxiety is sup-ported by the negative fantasies that organization members have about what will happen as a consequence of their acting in accordance with their understanding of what is sensible. The negative fantasies, in turn, serve an important function for the persons who have them. Specifically, they provide the individual with an excuse that releases him psychologically, both in his own eyes and frequently in the eyes of others, from the responsibility of having to act to solve organization problems.

It is not sufficient, though, to stop with the explanation of negative fantasies as the basis for the inability of organizations to cope with agreement. We must look deeper and ask still other questions: What is the source of the negative fantasies? Why do they occur?

REAL RISK

Risk is a reality of life, a condition of existence. John Kennedy articulated it in another way when he said at a news conference, "Life is unfair." By that I believe he meant we do not know, nor can we predict or control with certainty, either the events that impinge upon us or the outcomes of actions we undertake in response to those events.

Consequently, in the business environment, the research manager might find that confronting the president and the vice-president with the fact that the project was a "turkey" might result in his being fired. And Mr. Porter's saying that an illegal plan of surveillance should not be carried out could have caused his ostracism as a non-team player. There are too many cases when confrontation of this sort has resulted in such consequences. The real question, though, is not, Are such fantasized consequences possible? but, Are such fantasized consequences likely?

Thus real risk is an existential condition, and all action do have consequences that, to paraphrase Hamlet, may be worse than the evils of the present. As a result of their unwillingness to accept existential risk as one of life's givens, however, people may opt to take their organizations to Abilene rather than run the risk, no matter how small, of ending up somewhere worse.

Again, though, one must ask, What is the real risk that underlies the decision to opt for Abilene? What is at the core of the paradox?

FEAR OF SEPARATION

One is tempted to say that the core of the paradox lies in the individual's fear of the un-known. Actually, we do not fear what is un-known, but we are afraid of things we do frightens us into such apparently inexplicable organizational behavior?

Separation, alienation, and loneliness are things we do know about—and fear. Both research and experience indicate that ostracism is one of the most powerful punishments that can be devised. Solitary confinement does not draw its coercive strength from physical deprivation. The evidence is over-whelming that we have a fundamental need to be connected, engaged, and related and a reciprocal need not to be separated or alone. Everyone of us, though, has experienced aloneness. From the time the umbilical cord was cut, we have experienced the real anguish of separation—broken friendships, divorces, deaths, and exclusions. C. P. Snow vividly described the tragic interplay between loneliness and connection:

"Each of us is alone; sometimes we escape from our solitariness, through love and affection or perhaps creative moments, but these triumphs of life are pools of light we make for ourselves while the edge of the road is black. Each of us dies alone."

That fear of taking risks that may result in our separation from others is at the core of the paradox. It finds expression in ways of which we may be unaware, and it is ultimately the cause of the self-defeating, collective deception that leads to self-destructive decisions within organizations.

Concretely, such fear of separation leads research committees to fund projects that none of its members want and, perhaps, White House staff members to engage in illegal activities that they don't really support.

THE PSYCHOLOGICAL REVERSAL OF RISK AND CERTAINTY

One piece of the map is still missing. It relates to the peculiar reversal that occurs in our thought processes as we try to cope with the Abilene Paradox. For example, we frequently fail to take action in an organizational setting because we fear that the actions we take may result in our separation from others, or, in the language of Mr. Porter, we are afraid of being tabbed as "disloyal" or are afraid of being ostracized as "non-team players." But therein lies a paradox within a paradox, because our very unwillingness to take such risks virtually ensures the separation and aloneness we so fear. In effect, we reverse "real existential risk" and "fantasied risk" and by doing so trans-form what is a probability statement into what, for all practical purposes, becomes a certainty.

Take the R&D organization de-scribed earlier. When the project fails, some people will get fired, demoted, or sentenced to the purgatory of a make-work job in an out-of-the-way office. For those who remain, the atmosphere of blame, distrust, suspicion, and backbiting that accompanies such failure will serve only to further alienate and separate those who remain.

The Watergate situation is similar. The principals evidently feared being ostracized as disloyal non-team players. When the illegality of the act surfaced, however, it was nearly inevitable that blaming, self-protective actions, and scapegoating would result in the very emotional separation from both the President and one another that the principals feared. Thus, by reversing real and fantasied risk, they had taken effective action to ensure the outcome they least desired.

One final question remains: Why do we make this peculiar reversal? I support the general thesis of Alvin Toffler and Philip Slater, who contend that our cultural emphasis on technology, competition, individualism, temporariness, and mobility has resulted in a population that has frequently experienced the terror of loneliness and seldom the satisfaction of engagement. Consequently, though we have learned of the reality of separation, we have not had the opportunity to learn the reciprocal skills of connection, with the result that, like the ancient dinosaurs, we are breeding organizations with self-destructive decision-making proclivities.

A POSSIBLE ABILENE BYPASS

Existential risk is inherent in living, so it is impossible to provide a map that meets the no-risk criterion, but it may be possible to describe the route in terms that make the landmarks understandable and that will clarify the risks involved. In order to do that, however, some commonly used terms such as victim, victimizer, collusion, responsibility, conflict, conformity, courage, confrontation, reality, and knowledge have to be redefined. In addition, we need to explore the relevance of the redefined concepts for bypassing or getting out of Abilene.

• *Victim and victimizer.* Blaming and fault-finding behavior is one of the basic symptoms of organizations that have found their way to Abilene, and the target of blame generally doesn't include the one who criticizes. Stated in different terms, executives begin to assign one another to roles of victims and victimizers. Ironic as it may seem, however, this assignment of roles is both irrelevant and dysfunctional, because once a business or a government fails to manage its agreement and arrives in Abilene, all its members are victims. Thus, arguments and accusations that identify victims and victimizers at best become symptoms of the paradox, and, at worst, drain energy from the problem-solving efforts required to redirect the organization along the route it really wants to take.

• *Collusion.* A basic implication of the Abilene Paradox is that human problems of organization are reciprocal in nature. As Robert Tannenbaum has pointed out, you can't have an autocratic boss unless subordinates are willing to collude with his autocracy, and you can't have obsequious subordinates unless the boss is willing to collude with their obsequiousness.

Thus, in plain terms, each person in a self-defeating, Abilene-bound organization *colludes* with others, including peers, superiors, and subordinates, sometimes consciously and sometimes subconsciously, to create the dilemma in which the organization finds itself. To adopt a cliché of modern organization, it takes a real team effort to go to Abilene." In that sense each person, in his own collusive manner, shares responsibility

256

for the trip, so searching for a locus of blame outside oneself serves no useful purpose for either the organization or the individual. It neither helps the organization handle its dilemma of unrecognized agreement nor does it provide psychological relief for the individual, be-cause focusing on conflict when agreement is the issue is devoid of reality. In fact, it does just the opposite, for it causes the organization to focus on managing conflict when it should be focusing on managing agreement.

• *Responsibility for problem-solving action.* A second question is, Who is responsible for getting us out of this place? To that question is frequently appended a third one, generally rhetorical in nature, with "should" overtones, such as, Isn't it the boss (or the ranking government official) who is responsible for doing something about the situation?

The answer to that question is no. The key to understanding the functionality of the no answer is the knowledge that, when the dynamics of the paradox are in operation, the authority figure—and others—are in unknowing agreement with one another concerning the organization's problems and the steps necessary to solve them. Consequently, the power to destroy the paradox's pernicious influence comes from con-fronting and speaking to the underlying reality of the situation, and not from one's hierarchical position within the organization. Therefore, any organization member who chooses to risk confronting that reality possesses the necessary leverage to release the organization from the paradox's grip.

In one situation, it may be a re-search director's saying, "I don't think this project can succeed." In another, it may be Jeb Magruder's response to this question of Senator Baker:

If you were concerned because the action was known to you to be illegal, because you thought it improper or unethical, you thought the prospects for success were very meager, and you doubted the reliability of Mr. Liddy, what on earth would it have taken to decide against the plan?

Magruder's reply was brief and to the point:

Not very much, sir. I am sure that if I had fought vigorously against it, I think any of us could have had the plan cancelled. (Time, June 25, 1973, p. 12.)

• *Reality, knowledge, confrontation.* Accepting the paradox as a model describing certain kinds of organizational dilemmas also requires rethinking the nature of reality and knowledge, as they are generally described in organizations. In brief, the underlying dynamics of the paradox clearly indicate that organization members generally know more about issues confronting the organization than they don't know. The various principals attending the research budget meeting, for example, knew the research project was doomed to failure. And Jeb Magruder spoke as a true Abilener when he said, "We knew it was illegal, probably, inappropriate." *(The Washington Post, June 15, 1973, p. A16.)*

Given this concept of reality and its relationship to knowledge, confrontation be-comes the process of facing issues squarely, openly, and directly in an effort to discover whether the nature of the underlying collective reality is agreement or conflict. Accepting such a definition of confrontation has an important implication for change agents interested in making organizations more effective. That is, organization change and effectiveness may be facilitated as much by confronting the organization with what it knows and agrees upon as by confronting it with what it doesn't know or disagrees about.

REAL CONFLICT AND PHONY CONFLICT

Conflict is a part of any organization. Couples, R&D divisions, and White House staffs all engage in it. However, analysis of the Abilene Paradox opens up the possibility of two kinds of conflict—real and phony. On the surface, they look alike. But, like headaches, they have different causes and therefore re-quire different treatment.

258

Real conflict occurs when people have real differences. ("My reading of the re-search printouts says that we can make the project profitable." "I come to the opposite conclusion.") ("I suggest we 'bug' the Water-gate." "I'm not in favor of it.")

Phony conflict, on the other hand, occurs when people agree on the actions they want to take, and then do the opposite. The resulting anger, frustration, and blaming behavior generally termed "conflict" are not based on real differences. Rather, they stem from the protective reactions that occur when a decision that no one believed in or was com-mitted to in the first place goes sour. In fact, as a paradox within a paradox, such conflict is symptomatic of agreement!

GROUP TYRANNY AND CONFORMITY

Understanding the dynamics of the Abilene Paradox also requires a "reorientation" in thinking about concepts such as "group tyranny"— the loss of the individual's distinctive-ness in a group, and the impact of conformity pressures on individual behavior in organizations. Group tyranny and its result, individual conformity, generally refer to the coercive effect of group pressures on individual behavior. Sometimes referred to as Group-think, it has been damned as the cause for everything from the lack of creativity in organizations ('A camel is a horse designed by a committee") to antisocial behavior in juveniles ("My Johnny is a good boy. He was just pressured into shoplifting by the kids he runs around with").

However, analysis of the dynamics underlying the Abilene Paradox opens up the possibility that individuals frequently perceive and feel as if they are experiencing the coercive organization conformity pressures when, in actuality, they are responding to the dynamics of mismanaged agreement. Conceptualizing, experiencing, and responding to such experiences as reflecting the tyrannical pressures of a group again serves as an important psychological use for the individual: As was previously said, it releases him from the responsibility of taking action and thus becomes a defense against action. Thus, much behavior within an organization that heretofore has been conceptualized as reflecting the tyranny of conformity pressures is really an expression of collective anxiety and therefore must be reconceptualized as a defense against acting.

A well-known example of such faulty conceptualization comes to mind. It involves the heroic sheriff in the classic Western movies who stands alone in the jailhouse door and singlehandedly protects a suspected (and usually innocent) horse thief or murderer from the irrational, tyrannical forces of group behavior—that is, an armed lynch mob. Generally, as a part of the ritual, he threatens to blow off the head of anyone who takes a step toward the door. Few ever take the challenge, and the reason is not the sheriff's six-shooter. What good would one pistol be against an armed mob of several hundred people who *really* want to hang somebody? Thus, the gun in fact serves as a face-saving measure for people who don't wish to participate in a hanging anyway. (We had to back off. The sheriff threatened to blow our heads off.")

The situation is one involving agreement management, for a careful investigator canvassing the crowd under conditions in which the anonymity of the interviewees' responses could be guaranteed would probably find: (1) that few of the individuals in the crowd really wanted to take part in the hanging; (2) that each person's participation came about because he perceived, falsely, that others wanted to do so; and (3) that each per-son was afraid that others in the crowd would ostracize or in some other way punish him if he did not go along.

DIAGNOSING THE PARADOX

Most individuals like quick solutions, "clean" solutions, "no risk" solutions to organization problems. Furthermore, they tend to prefer solutions based on mechanics and technology, rather than on attitudes of "being." Un-fortunately, the underlying reality of the paradox makes it impossible to provide either no-risk solutions or action technologies divorced from existential attitudes and realities. I do, however, have two sets of suggestions for dealing with these situations. One set of suggestions relates to diagnosing the situation, the other to confronting it.

When faced with the possibility that the paradox is operating, one must first make a diagnosis of the situation, and the key to diagnosis is an answer to the question, Is the organization involved in a conflict-management or an agreement-management situation? As an organization member, I have found it relatively easy to make a preliminary diagnosis as to whether an organization is on the way to Abilene or is involved in legitimate, substantive conflict by responding to the Diagnostic Survey shown in the accompanying figure. If the answer to the first question is "not characteristic," the organization is probably, not in Abilene or conflict. If the answer is "characteristic," the organization has a problem of either real or phony conflict, and the answers to the succeeding questions help to determine which it is.

In brief, for reasons that should be apparent from the theory discussed here, the more times "characteristic" is checked, the more likely the organization is on its way to Abilene. In practical terms, a process for managing agreement is called for.

ORGANIZATION DIAGNOSTIC SURVEY

Instructions: For each of the following statements please indicate whether it is or is not characteristic of your organization.

1. There is conflict in the organization.

2. Organization members feel frustrated, impotent, and unhappy when trying to deal with it. Many are looking for ways to escape. They may avoid meetings at which the conflict is discussed, they may be looking for other jobs, or they may spend as much time away from the office as possible by taking unneeded trips or vacation or sick leave.

3. Organization members place much of the blame for the dilemma on the boss or other groups. In "back room" conversations among friends the boss is termed incompetent, ineffective, "out of touch," or a candidate for early retirement. To his face, nothing is said, or at best, only oblique references are made concerning his role in the organization's problems. If the boss isn't blamed, some other group, division, or unit is seen as the cause of the trouble: "We would do fine if it were not for the damn fools in Division X."

4. Small subgroups of trusted friends and associates meet informally over coffee, lunch, and so on to discuss organizational problems. There is a lot of agreement among the members of these subgroups as to the cause of the troubles and the solutions that would be effective in solving them. Such conversations are frequently punctuated with statements beginning with, 'We should do . . .'

5. In meetings where those same people meet with members from other subgroups to discuss the problem they "soften their positions," state them in ambiguous language, or even reverse them to suit the apparent positions taken by others.

6. After such meetings, members complain to trusted associates that they really didn't say what they wanted to say, but also provide a list of convincing reasons why the comments, suggestions, and reactions they wanted to make would have been impossible. Trusted associates commiserate and say the same was true for them.

7. Attempts to solve the problem do not seem to work. In fact, such attempts seem to add to the problem or make it worse.

8. Outside the organization individuals seem to get along better, be happier, and operate more effectively than they do within it.

And finally, if the answer to the first question falls into the "characteristic" category and most of the other answers fall into the category "not characteristic," one may be relatively sure the organization is in a real conflict situation and some sort of conflict management intervention is in order.

COPING WITH THE PARADOX

Assuming a preliminary diagnosis leads one to believe he and/or his organization is on the way to Abilene, the individual may choose to actively confront the situation to determine directly whether the underlying reality is one of agreement or conflict. Although there are, perhaps, a number of ways to do it, I have found one way in particular to be effective—confrontation in a group setting. The basic approach involves gathering organization members who are key figures in the problem and its solution into a group setting. Working within the context of a group is important be-cause the dynamics of the Abilene Paradox involve collusion among group members; therefore, to try to solve the dilemma by working with individuals and small sub-groups would involve further collusion with the dynamics leading up to the paradox.

The first step in the meeting is for the individual who "calls" it (that is, the confronter) to own up to his position first and be open to the feedback he gets. The owning up process lets the others know that he is concerned lest the organization may be making a decision contrary to the desires of any of its members. A statement like this demonstrates the beginning of such an approach:

I want to talk with you about the research project. Although I have previously said things to the contrary, I frankly don't think it will work, and I am very anxious about it. I suspect others may feel the same, but I don't know. Anyway, I am concerned that I may end up misleading you and that we may end up misleading one another, and if we aren't careful, we may continue to work on a problem that none of us wants and that might even bankrupt us. That's why I need to know where the rest of you stand. I would appreciate any of your thoughts about the project. Do you think it can succeed?

What kinds of results can one expect if he decides to undertake the process of confrontation? I have found that the results can be divided into *two* categories, at the technical level and at the level of existential experience. Of the two, I have found that for the person who undertakes to initiate the process of confrontation, the existential experience takes precedence in his ultimate evaluation of the outcome of the action he takes.

• *The technical level.* If one is correct in diagnosing the presence of the paradox, I have found the solution to the technical problem may be almost absurdly quick and simple, nearly on the order of this:

"Do you mean that you and I and the rest of us have been dragging along with a re-search project that none of us has thought would work? It's crazy. I can't believe we would do it, but we did. Let's figure out how we can cancel it and get to doing something productive." In fact, the simplicity and quick-ness of the solution frequently don't seem possible to most of us, since we have been trained to believe that the solution to conflict requires a long, arduous process of debilitating problem solving.

Also, since existential risk is always present, it is possible that one's diagnosis is incorrect, and the process of confrontation lifts to the level of public examination real, substantive conflict, which may result in heated debate about technology, personalities, and/or administrative approaches. There is evidence that such debates, properly man-aged, can be the basis for creativity in organizational problem solving. There is also the possibility, however, that such debates can-not be managed, and substantiating the concept of existential risk, the person who initiates the risk may get fired or ostracized. But that again leads to the necessity of evaluating the results of such confrontation at the existential level.

• *Existential results.* Evaluating the outcome of confrontation from an existential framework is quite different from evaluating it from a set of technical criteria. How do I reach this conclusion? Simply from interviewing a variety of people who have chosen to confront the paradox and listening to their responses. In short, for them, psycho-logical success and failure apparently are divorced from what is traditionally accepted in organizations as criteria for success and failure.

For instance, some examples of success are described when people are asked, "What happened when you confronted the issue?" They may answer this way:

I was told we had enough boat rockers in the organization, and I got fired. It hurt at first, but in retrospect it was the greatest day of my life. I've got another job and I'm delighted. I'm a free man.

Another description of success might be this:

I said I don't think the research project can succeed and the others looked shocked and quickly agreed. The upshot of the whole deal is that I got a promotion and am now known as a "rising star." It was the high point of my career.

Similarly, those who fail to confront the paradox describe failure in terms divorced from technical results. For example, one may report:

I didn't say anything and we rocked along until the whole thing exploded and Joe got fired. There is still a lot of tension in the organization, and we are still in trouble, but I got a good performance review last time. I still feel lousy about the whole thing, though.

From a different viewpoint, an individual may describe his sense of failure in these words:

I knew I should have said something and I didn't. When the project failed, I was a convenient whipping boy. I got demoted; I still have a job, but my future here is definitely limited. In a way I deserve what I got, but it doesn't make it any easier to accept because of that.

Most important, the act of confrontation apparently provides intrinsic psychological satisfaction, regardless of the technological outcomes for those who attempt it.

The real meaning of that existential experience, and its relevance to a wide variety of organizations, may lie, therefore, not in the scientific analysis of decision making but in the plight of Sisyphus. That is something the reader will have to decide for himself.

THE ABILENE PARADOX AND THE MYTH OF SISYPHUS

In essence, this paper proposes that there is an underlying organizational reality that includes both agreement and disagreement, co-operation and conflict. However, the decision to confront the possibility of organization agreement is all too difficult and rare, and its opposite, the decision to accept the evils of the present, is all too common. Yet those two decisions may reflect the essence of both our human potential and our human imperfectability. Consequently, the choice to confront reality in the family, the church, the business, or the bureaucracy, though made only occasionally, may reflect those "peak experiences" that provide meaning to the valleys.

In many ways, they may reflect the experience of Sisyphus. As you may remember, Sisyphus was condemned by Pluto to a perpetuity of pushing a large stone to the top of a mountain, only to see it return to its original position when he released it. As Camus suggested in his revision of the myth, Sisyphus's task was absurd and totally devoid of meaning. For most of us, though, the lives we lead pushing papers or hubcaps are no less absurd, and in many ways we probably spend about as much time pushing rocks in our organizations as did Sisyphus.

Camus also points out, though, that on occasion as Sisyphus released his rock and watched it return to its resting place at the bottom of the hill, he was able to recognize the absurdity of his lot and, for brief periods of time, transcend it.

So it may be with confronting the Abilene Paradox. Confronting the absurd paradox of agreement may provide, through activity, what Sisyphus gained from his passive but conscious acceptance of his fate. Thus, through the process of active confrontation with reality, we may take respite from pushing our rocks on their endless journeys and, for brief moments, experience what C. P. Snow termed "the triumphs of life we make for ourselves" within those absurdities we call organizations.

SELECTED BIBLIOGRAPHY

Chris Argyris in *Intervention Theory and Method: A Behavioral Science View* (Addison-Wesley, 1970) gives an excellent description of the process of "owning up" and being "open," both of which are major skills required if one is to assist his organization in avoiding or leaving Abilene.

Albert Camus in *The Myth of Sisyphus and Other Essays* (Vintage Books, Random House, 1955) provides an existential viewpoint for coping with absurdity, of which the Abilene Paradox is a clear example.

Jerry B. Harvey and R. Albertson in "Neurotic Organizations: Symptoms, Causes and Treatment," Parts I and II, *Personnel Journal* (September and October 1971) provide a detailed ex-ample of a third-party intervention into an organization caught in a variety of agreement-management dilemmas.

Irving Janis in *Victims of Groupthink* (Houghton-Mifflin Co., 1972) offers an alternative viewpoint for understanding and dealing with many of the dilemmas described in "The Abilene Paradox." Specifically, many of the events that Janis describes as examples of conformity pressures (that is, group tyranny) I would conceptualize as mismanaged agreement.

267

In his *The Pursuit of Loneliness* (Beacon Press, 1970), Philip Slater contributes an in-depth description of the impact of the role of alienation, separation, and loneliness (a major contribution to the Abilene Paradox) in our culture.

Richard Walton in *Interpersonal Peace-making: Confrontation and Third Party Consultation* (Addison-Wesley, 1969) describes a variety of approaches for dealing with conflict when it is real, rather than phony.

Epilogue:

Jerry Harvey

THE PERIPATETIC PARADOX

Once the article was printed, it apparently "took off." In the years since it first appeared, for example, I have been inundated with cards, letters, and telephone calls from people who have described other "trips to Abilene," including couples who have gotten married when they wanted to remain single, couples who have gotten divorced when they wanted to stay married, parishioners who built church buildings none of them wanted, school systems that implemented curricula none of their stakeholders supported, and countries that went to war when their citizens wanted peace.

In a similar vein, I have frequently been thanked and occasionally castigated for facilitating marriages, divorces, promotions, demotions, good business decisions, lousy business decisions, family reconciliations, and family fights.

THE TRANSFORMING PARADOX

McGraw-Hill has seen fit to make a movie about the Paradox. Filmed in the style of *The Waltons,* with me as the narrator, the film has provided me with a number of great learning experiences, one of which occurred not long ago as I walked down the aisle of a plane bound for Dallas. As I passed a rather frumpy-appearing woman, she looked up and shouted for all to hear, "Are you the star of that movie, *The Abilene Paradox?*" Where that gorgeous femme fatale came from, I don't know, but as I modestly replied (in my suavest actor's voice), "Yes, Ma'am, I am," I thought to myself, "Robert Redford, eat your heart out."

Paradoxically, the Paradox has had its dark side, too. For example, a videotape of me (talking about the Paradox) has been reproduced and "bootlegged" literally all over the world without my permission or the permission of the organization that legitimately produced it. Consequently, every time a naïve (and sometimes not-so-naïve) person tells me, "Our organization showed the videotape of your Abilene speech at our training program and we really enjoyed it," my blood boils at the lack of ethics on the part of those who knowingly did (and do) it. I also bridle when I realize the amount of money I might have made had I known how to market it and control its distribution. Ultimately, though, I think my own sense of greed disturbs me the most because, deep down, I know I have been given a gift which is mine to share, not to hoard.

THE PARADOX AS PHANTOM

All this has occurred despite the fact that, to this day, I cannot prove scientifically that the Abilene Paradox actually occurs. For example, it is altogether possible that my in-laws really wanted to go on the original trip, but changed their stories once we arrived in Abilene and had such a lousy time. All I know for sure is that from the time the trip was first suggested I didn't want to go, and *I drove the Buick.* In that sense the problem, existentially, was mine.

So, given all that has occurred, would I change any of what I wrote? Not really. Oh, I might make a few cosmetic alterations, such as reinserting the interview with the lemmings; stressing the role which anaclitic depression plays in causing the separation anxiety central to trips to Abilene; and exploring in greater depth the ethical, moral, and spiritual aspects of the Paradox.

Still, in Heiddeger's terms, those are extensions of the same basic idea. Whether my expression of the idea is flawed or not, I accept it for what it is—my initial effort to do the best I could with *the* thought that the Good Lord—out of confusion, compassion, appreciation, administrative errors in the Idea Assignment Division, or other reasons beyond the limits of my human comprehension saw fit to offer me.

An Abilene Defense: Commentary One
Rosabeth Moss Kanter

Public agreement, private disagreement. "The Abilene Paradox" points out that this situation almost inevitably leads to people going along for the ride even when they know better. The result: trouble.

The Abilene Paradox has two parts. The first involves a person's inaccurate assumptions about what others think and believe. This sometimes takes the guise of what social scientists call "pluralistic ignorance= everybody in a group holds a similar opinion but, ignorant of the opinion of others, believes himself to be the only one feeling that way. The second part of the paradox involves a person's unwillingness to speak up about what she does think and believe. It is easier, more comfortable, or safer to keep quiet and be swept along by the current. Combine pluralistic ignorance with the path of least resistance and, before you know it, you're in Abilene.

Part one, then, is a problem of data. Part two is a problem of risk. The manager's tasks are to manage communication to allow the data to surface and to manage the organizational context to enhance power and reduce risk.

MANAGE COMMUNICATION

How can communication be managed in this way? Here are some guidelines:

Establish debates. Clearly, the first task for a manager is to set communication norms—and he or she has to go first. Participative management has become a cliché, but the idea of consulting others about possible decisions and genuinely pushing to hear the negatives still makes sense. One way to encourage other people to express what they really think is to frame every issue as a debate between alternatives—a matter of pros and cons. Instead of presenting issues as matters of concurrence— I'd like to do X, wouldn't your—they should be presented as matters for debate: "X has been proposed; let's examine the pros and cons." Instead of

271

considering only one choice, always seek alternative courses of action—"What else might we be doing with that money or that timer—and then evaluate the main choice against the alternatives. Doing this requires actively valuing the additional time that debate can take, but a "bias for action" without considering alternatives can indeed land an organization in Abilene.

Assign gadflies, devil's advocates, fact checkers, and second guessers. There are certain well-established roles whose very definition involves confrontation, contrariness, and argument. Making sure that there is always someone playing the role of questioner ("Is that conclusion accurate?") or prober ("C'mon now, you can't really believe that!") is a way to ensure that contrary opinions will begin to surface. If the role is formally assigned, some of the risk associated with speaking up is reduced, and everyone understands it's nothing personal. Making this into an assigned role also permits rotation, so that everyone gets to play devil's advocate from time to time. Gradually the questioning style will become part of the normal routine. Third parties such as consultants and facilitators often play this role. But think how effective it would be as part of the work group's own repertoire!

Encourage organizational graffiti. My colleague Barry Stein deserves credit for this idea, which he is implementing in a very large company with a tradition of bureaucracy and conformity. The problem: People were not yet ready for open communication about their concerns. What was needed was devices that would allow people to comment on their concerns regularly but anonymously. The solution was to use unattended computer terminals as a site for the corporate equivalent of "graffiti"—remarks of any kind about any issue. Although written surveys and consultant interviews often serve this function, the appeal of organizational graffiti is that it is spontaneous, ongoing, timely, free-form, open-ended, and—as people comment on each other's inputs—interactive.

MANAGE THE ORGANIZATIONAL CONTEXT

How can the organizational context be managed to enhance power and reduce risk? Here are a few ways.

Make confronters into heroes. Instead of shooting messengers, reward them. Of course, this is really hard. How many of us thank the bearers of bad news? How many whistle blowers on corporate misconduct have kept their jobs, let alone gotten tokens of appreciation? And what rewards go to people who stop the trip to Abilene—a passive result—as opposed to those who push action forward? But still, if managers learn to value the honest expression of concerns because doing so will prevent more trouble later, then there is hope. If the organization provides role models, if the prizewinners and recognition garnerers include people known for their outspokenness rather than for their conformity, then more people can be encouraged to speak up.

Develop a "culture of pride." This is one of the cornerstones of the successful, innovative companies I identified in *The Change Masters*. A culture of pride builds collective self-esteem through abundant praise and recognition. People are made visible; they are valued for their accomplishments. Standards of high performance are communicated over and over again. Thus when collective pride is high, individual self-esteem is also high. Self-identified winners feel more secure psychologically and find it easier to take risks. *Create empowering structures.* If people are informed and well-connected, they can more readily exercise independent judgment and speaking up is less risky. Organizational power comes from access to information, political support, and resources; powerlessness, in contrast, means not only a lack of access to, but also a dependence on, the boss to provide everything. Some of the structures that provide power include networks of peers who provide political backing and a forum for communication; sufficient employment security so that the job is not on the line every time the person speaks up; and affiliations with more than one work unit or reporting relationships with more than one boss, so that the person always has an alternative set of ties.

CHECKPOINTS AND MILESTONES

Surfacing data and empowering people are good ways to *help* prevent starting out for Abilene, but they do not always *guarantee* that organizations won't begin some troublesome trips anyway, without full discussion of the consequences. Sometimes that's because no one really understands the consequences yet, or feelings and opinions really are not that strong. The organization can find itself partway to Abilene before anyone knows they were headed there. This situation is increasingly common as decisions become more complex.

Even harder than preventing bad decisions from being implemented is turning them around halfway to their destination. So my final thought is this: All organizational trips should include some checkpoints to permit the travelers to pause, regroup, and consult the map one more time.

If you don't want to go to Abilene after all, it's never too late to take a road to somewhere else.

An Abilene Defense: Commentary Two
Arthur Elliott Carlisle

In educating his nephew Wormwood in the wiles of temptation, the old devil Screwtape talks of the discord that can be engendered by urging people to argue in favor of what they believe (often incorrectly) other people want to do; this in spite of their own desire to do exactly the opposite. The net result is, of course, that no one's wishes are fulfilled and attempts to develop mutually satisfying and successful joint ventures fail.

The participants become angered by their frustration and, in this particular case, a discussion on whether to have tea in the garden or in the house results in not having tea at all (C.S. Lewis, *The Screwtape Letters,* New York: The Macmillan Company, 1944, pp. 133 and 134). This oft-recurring theme provides the basis for many literary comedies of manners and, fortunately, Jerry Harvey made it operational for managers in the "Abilene Paradox."

The behaviors described by Professor Harvey are reenacted all too frequently in decision-making sessions where managers must jointly determine courses of action that are often of vital importance to their organizations. They are important symptoms—symptoms that cannot be ignored, because they demonstrate an inability to manage an organization in a truly professional manner. Indeed, they reflect deep-seated organizational problems that go far beyond questions of conflict or agreement. Effective management requires the setting of clear objectives—where possible by consensus, but occasionally by edict—after hearing *all* sides and positions.

CLIMATE OF FEAR: A FAILURE OF MANAGEMENT

A failure of management occurs when a climate exists in which organization members are unwilling to express conflicting opinions whether the boss is present or not. This reluctance results from the fear of being viewed by both peers and superiors as someone who is not a team player or as someone who does not support the boss's known pet projects. Furthermore, when being a "yes-(wo)man" is believed to be the best route to promotion, something is profoundly wrong. This sort of behavior at best results in reduced organizational effectiveness and at worst leads to organizational decline or even dissolution.

In Western industrialized countries management has entered a new era, one in which business organizations are facing substantially increased competition—not only from abroad, but also from domestic firms seeking new markets with fundamentally different products. For example, the invasion of the electronic calculator from outside the industry caught traditional manufacturers like Marchant and Friden with a line of outmoded products. There is every reason to believe this pattern will continue. Organizational survival now requires a level of expertise beyond what has been needed in the past, and this expertise is often available only at lower organizational levels.

To an ever-increasing extent, subordinates are better-trained in analytical and technical skills than are their superiors. Both domineering and charismatic leadership have become truly dangerous as a general modus operandi. An attitude at lower levels that "(s)he may not always be right, but (s)he's always the boss" or an all-consuming desire to be viewed as a team member at whatever cost can result in the loss of contributions by truly talented personnel who could improve organizational performance.

Avoiding the Abilene Paradox requires, first, recognition of its potential as a trap—recognition at the highest organizational levels, including the members of the board of directors. (Directors are often guilty of "Abilene" behavior.) The next phase involves *both* management training *and* organization development. Managers must be reminded of their responsibility to communicate and gain commitment to the attainment of multiple objectives. Organization development is essential for maintaining a climate in which the Abilene Paradox cannot flourish, let alone survive.

THE RIGHT KIND OF CLIMATE

Managers tend to pattern their leadership styles after those of their superiors; therefore, managers at the highest levels must make it clear, by their own example, that *all* the organization's managers are responsible for creating a healthy organizational climate. This climate is one in which:

- Members are not afraid to express their opinions and, when they feel it appropriate, to challenge those of others when they have the facts.
- The "Kill the messenger who brings the bad news" syndrome is no longer part of the organizational canon.
- Dissent, if backed up with data and analysis, does not brand the dissenter as a loner, a troublemaker, or someone who is not a team

player; instead, it is recognized as a *professional responsibility* and rewarded.

- Changing one's mind, particularly after new information or argument is presented, is not seen as a sign of weakness, but rather of strength and self-confidence.
- Attainment of realistic group and individual objectives, rather than pleasing the boss or being a good team member, is the basis for organizational reward and advancement.

An organization that is to avoid the destructive consequences of an Abilene Paradox requires one additional ingredient: Management training and organization development are not enough if the necessary raw materials are lacking. At managerial and technical levels, hiring and promotional practices must seek self-confident, sensitive (but *not* super-sensitive), non-risk-aversive men and women, competent enough to be readily hired else-where. Such individuals do not play Screwtape's "Let's have tea in the garden" game.

Chapter 8

Prologue

Mary Jo Hatch

The C. Coleman McGehee Scholars Research Professor Emerita of Banking and Commerce, University of Virginia

Dynamics of Organizational Culture

Mary Jo Hatch

Prologue:

Mary Jo Hatch

In my first year of doctoral studies at Stanford, I wrote a paper for Jim March's Ph.D. seminar called "The Dynamics of Organizational Culture." That paper anticipated the article reproduced here by 10 years, which is roughly the amount of time I have been told it takes after earning a Ph.D. to begin to theorize. In any event, this article emerged after a grueling decade-long struggle and even then only with the guidance of four extremely helpful and engaged reviewers from the *Academy of Management Review*.

To my thinking, the main contribution of this article came from explaining how organizational culture works and exposing and exploring its dynamic processes as defined from a point of view established *within them*. I called the model *dynamic*, not only to point out that culture is dynamic, but to show that *you* had to be dynamic along with its processes if you wanted to understand how culture works or manage effectively within it. At the time I had intended to go beyond questioning the static characteristics and attributes of a culture to investigate why and how culture changes and, along with that, to acknowledge both positivist and symbolic-interpretive perspectives. My mentor in this effort, Michael Owen Jones, led me to Herskovitz (1948) and other notable figures in cultural anthropology, who observed that culture changes more quickly in some areas than in others, leaving the impression that parts of it stay the same while other parts change. The term "cultural dynamics" came from the title of one of Herskovitz's books (Herskovitz, 1964).

Once "The Dynamics of Organizational Culture" was published, I sat back and waited for these important ideas to be recognized by my contemporaries, but apart from the Executive Leadership Program students I met at George Washington University, hardly anyone gave the article much attention. What is more, my students were forced to read it. Realizing that establishing the merit of these ideas was going to take patience and perseverance, I stubbornly kept writing about them. It was this stubbornness that gave me discipline, and it also informed the content of my scholarship for the rest of my career. Following from this article came not only more writing about the dynamics of organizational culture; I wrote about many other things in ways that evidence that first article.

For example, Hatch (2000) compared cultural dynamics to Weber's theory of the routinization of charisma and gave me a dynamic way to think about the role of leadership that only came to fruition when Majken Schultz and I wrote about corporate brand charisma and the role middle managers play in its activation and routinization (Hatch & Schultz, 2013). Theories of the dynamics of collective creativity with Michael Owen Jones (Hatch & Jones, 1997) and the dynamics of organizational identity (Hatch & Schultz, 2002) followed directly from the dynamic way of theorizing developed in "The Dynamics of Organizational Culture." Michael Owen Jones's influence surfaced again in Hatch (2004), when I collected all the dynamic ideas about culture I could find in the organizations literature and traced them backwards to ideas put forward in cultural anthropology and sociology years before they emerged in organization studies, though that was rarely acknowledged in the organizational literature. That article taught me the value of rereading the classics, a value that informs the writing and revising of my organization theory textbooks (Hatch, 2011; Hatch with Cunliffe, 2013).

Then there is my work on corporate branding with Majken Schultz. All our work on branding is underpinned by the dynamics of organizational identity that, at least for me, was anticipated by the dynamics of organizational culture. (There is a callout to identity in the main figure of the cultural dynamics article.) My effort to explain how the dynamics of culture and identity are related was the subject of Hatch (2010), in which I discovered parallels between my ways of theorizing and John Dewey's pragmatism. Connecting Dewey to culture led to my article on the pragmatics of branding (Hatch, 2012a). Earlier the theory of cultural dynamics similarly led me to hermeneutic theory. (I have always believed the cyclical way I drew the cultural dynamics model was an impoverished attempt to grapple with the hermeneutic circle that I was trying to represent.) This connection to hermeneutics eventually manifested in an article written with literary scholar James Rubin on the hermeneutics of branding (Hatch & Rubin, 2006).

As you can see by these reflections, writing "The Dynamics of Organizational Culture" proved generative of many other ideas as well as of my way of theorizing about organizational phenomena that is still in progress. Eventually I started describing what I had been doing all these years and how my way of theorizing incorporates a temporal perspective. This happened when my passion for painting led me to David Hockney, who discussed how painting incorporates time. Using his examples from his own and other people's art (found in Joyce, 1999), I produced an essay called "Doing Time in Organization Theory" (Hatch, 2003) that explains how dynamic theorizing reveals the ways in which the phenomena under investigation happen. Confronting time that way anticipated work I am doing currently with Majken Schultz on organizational historicizing, a construct that seems to be leading back to culture through inclusion of remembering and forgetting the past and how this affects what is done in the present and the future. Until recently culture lost much ground to institutional theory, but its greater ability to address how organizations and institutions change seems to be producing something of a comeback, which I commented on in Hatch (2012b) and Hatch and Zilber (2012).

Finally, I still think about Jim March's reaction to my student version of this article, and I also remember his oft-repeated critical challenge to "us" culture researchers: "When are you guys (i.e., interpretivists) ever going to get around to addressing the validity of your construct?" It has taken time to get there, but a paper I am thinking about now addresses Jim's challenge by offering criteria evident in art and design dissertations that I believe could be applied to the evaluation of interpretive research, for example demonstration of intuition and empathy (Hatch, 2013). Please stay tuned.

References

Hatch, M. J. (1993). The dynamics of organizational culture. *Academy of Management Review, 18,* 657-693.

Hatch, M. J. (2000). The cultural dynamics of organizing and change. In N. Ashkanasy, C. Wilderom, & M. Peterson (Eds.), *Handbook of organizational culture and climate* (pp. 245-260). Thousand Oaks, CA: Sage.

Hatch, M. J. (2003). Doing time in organization theory. *Organization Studies, 23,* 869-875.

Hatch, M. J. (2004). Dynamics in organizational culture. In M. S. Poole & A. Van de Ven (Eds.), *Handbook of organizational change and innovation* (pp. 190-211). Oxford, UK: Oxford University Press.

Hatch, M. J. (2010). Material and meaning in the dynamics of organizational culture and identity with implications for the leadership of organizational change. In N. Ashkanasy, C. Wilderom, & M. Peterson (Eds.), *The handbook of organizational culture and climate* (2nd ed., pp. 341-358). Thousand Oaks, CA: Sage.

Hatch, M. J. (2011). *Organizations: A very short introduction.* Oxford, UK: Oxford University Press.

Hatch, M. J. (2012a). The pragmatics of branding: An application of Dewey's theory of aesthetic expression. *European Journal of Marketing, 46,* 885-899.

Hatch, M. J. (2012b). Bringing culture back from institutional Siberia. *Journal of Management Inquiry, 21,* 84-87.

Hatch, M. J. (2013, April 17). How art and design dissertations will craft the future. Presented at the European Academy of Design Conference, Gothenburg, Sweden.

Hatch, M. J., & Jones, M. O. (1997). Photocopylore at work: Aesthetics, collective creativity and the social construction of organizations. *Studies in Cultures, Organizations and Society, 3,* 263-287.

Hatch, M. J., & Rubin, J. (2006). The hermeneutics of branding. *Journal of Brand Management, 14,* 40-59.

Hatch, M. J., & Schultz, M. S. (2002). The dynamics of organizational identity. *Human Relations, 55,* 989-1018.

Hatch, M. J., & Schultz, M. (2013). The dynamics of corporate brand charisma: Routinization and activation at Carlsberg IT. *Scandinavian Journal of Management, 29,* 147-162.

Hatch, M. J., & Zilber, T. (2012). Conversation at the border between organizational culture theory and institutional theory. *Journal of Management Inquiry, 21,* 94-97.

Hatch, M. J., with Cunliffe, A. (2013). *Organization theory: Modern, symbolic and postmodern perspectives* (3rd ed.). Oxford, UK: Oxford University Press.

Herskovits, M. J. (1948). *Man and his works.* New York, NY: Knopf.

Herskovits, M. J. (1964). *Cultural dynamics.* New York, NY: Knopf.

Joyce, P. (1999). *Hockney on art: Conversations with Paul Joyce.* Boston, MA: Little Brown.

Dynamics of Organizational Culture[13]

Mary Jo Hatch

Abstract. Schein's (1985) model of organizational culture as assumptions, values, and artifacts leaves gaps regarding the appreciation of organizational culture as symbols and processes. This article examines these gaps and suggests a new model that combines Schein's theory with ideas drawn from symbolic-interpretive perspectives. The new model, called cultural dynamics, articulates the processes of manifestation, realization, symbolization, and interpretation and provides a framework within which to discuss the dynamism of organizational cultures. Implications of the cultural dynamics model for collecting and analyzing culture data and for future theoretical development are presented.

The concept of culture has been central to anthropology and folklore studies for over a century. Practitioners of these disciplines have produced an enormous body of literature, and during the 1940s and 50s some of their research dealt directly with the customs and traditions of work organizations (e.g., Chapple,1941, 1943; Dalton, 1959; Messenger,1978;Roy, 1952, 1954, 1960; Whyte, 1948, 1951, 1961). This trend was paralleled in sociology by Jacques (1951), among others, who wrote about the culture of the factory. Although organizational culture studies began to appear around the early 1970s (Clark, 1972; Pettigrew, 1973; Trice, Belasco, & Alutto, 1969; Turner, 1973), it was not until the1980s that management scholars widely adopted the culture concept (Deal & Kennedy, 1982; Kilmann, Saxton, Serpa, & Associates, 1985; Ouchi, 1981; Pascale & Athos, 1981; Peters & Waterman, 1982; Sathe, 1985). In this regard, Schein (1981, 1983, 1984, 1985) was especially influential because he, more than the others (including anthropologists and folklorists), articulated a conceptual framework for analyzing and intervening in the culture of organizations.

---

[13]   Originally Published as: Hatch, M.J. (1993). "Dynamics of organizational culture." Academy of Management Review **18**(4).

Since the establishment of the organizational culture construct, some organizational researchers have applied ideas directly from Schein (Pedersen, 1991; Pedersen & Sorensen, 1989; Phillips, 1990; Schultz, In press), whereas others have challenged his approach. For example, subculture researchers have disputed Schein's assumption that organizational cultures are unitary (Barley, 1983; Borum & Pedersen, 1992; Gregory, 1983; Louis, 1983; Martin & Siehl, 1983; Riley, 1983; Van Maanen & Barley, 1985; Young, 1989). Other researchers, noting the apparent ambivalence and ambiguity found in culture, have contested the idea that the function of culture is to maintain social structure (Feldman, 1991; Martin, 1992; Meyerson, 1991a, 1991b; Meyerson & Martin, 1987). Still others, working under the broad label of symbolic-interpretive research, have pursued perspectives that Schein ignored. The symbolic-interpretivists generally follow traditions established by Berger and Luckmann (1966) or Schutz (1970), focusing on symbols and symbolic behavior in organizations and interpreting these phenomena in a variety of ways (e.g., Alvesson, 1987; Alvesson & Berg, 1992; Broms & Gahmberg, 1983; Czarniawska-Joerges, 1988, 1992; Eisenberg & Riley, 1988; Kreiner, 1989; Pettigrew, 1979; Putnam, 1983; Rosen, 1985; Smircich, 1983; Smircich & Morgan, 1983; Turner, 1986; Wilkins, 1978). However, in spite of all these approaches to understanding organizational culture (for an overview see compendiums edited by Frost, Moore, Louis, Lundberg, & Martin, 1985, 1991; Gagliardi, 1990; Jones, Moore, & Snyder, 1988; Pondy, Frost, Morgan, & Dandridge, 1983; Turner, 1990), Schein's formulation remains one of the only conceptual models ever offered.

Although arguments against conceptual models of organizational culture have been made on the grounds that they oversimplify complex phenomena, such models serve an important role in guiding empirical research and generating theory. I argue that Schein's model continues to have relevance, but it would be more useful if it were combined with ideas drawn from symbolic-interpretive perspectives. More important, I introduce dynamism into organizational culture theory by reformulating Schein's original model in processual terms. Four processes are examined: manifestation, realization, symbolization, and interpretation. These processes are defined and presented in a new model called cultural dynamics.

Two of the processes included in the cultural dynamics model are widely recognized and have appeared in theories of organization before: Realization is part of Weick's (1979) enactment theory, and interpretation is a focal concern of symbolic-interpretive research. I will review and extend these ideas to the cultural dynamics model. Manifestation and symbolization processes, however, are relative newcomers and are proposed here to further specify organizational cultural theory. In introducing and examining these processes, my intent is to engage in theory building and to invite additional exploration and interpretation with the potential to redirect empirical research in organizational culture studies.

SCHEIN'S MODEL OF ORGANIZATIONAL CULTURE

According to Schein, culture exists simultaneously on three levels: On the surface are artifacts, underneath artifacts lie values, and at the core are basic assumptions (Figure 1). Assumptions represent taken-for granted beliefs about reality and human nature. Values are social principles, philosophies, goals, and standards considered to have intrinsic worth. Artifacts are the visible, tangible, and audible results of activity grounded in values and assumptions. In Schein's (1985: 9) words culture is

[t]he pattern of basic assumptions that a given group has invented, discovered, or developed in learning to cope with its problems of external adaptation and internal integration, and that have worked well enough to be considered valid, and, therefore, to be taught to new members as the correct way to perceive, think, and feel in relation to these problems.

286

Schein claimed that basic assumptions hold the key to understanding (and changing) a culture. Recently he argued that assumptions are best examined using clinical techniques and recommended that a "motivated group of insiders" raise its own assumptions to consciousness with the aid of a clinically trained helper/consultant (Schein, 1987, 1991; see also Finney & Mitroff, 1986). However, researchers who want to pursue culture beyond this inner circle may find the clinical approach unworkable. Schein's model has value for nonclinical studies, but the underspecification of his theory hampers these applications. In particular, the usefulness of his model depends upon identifying the links among a culture's artifacts, values, and assumptions—links that Schein has not explained but that are the central topic of this article.

Although Schein has not discussed cultural dynamics in the terms used here, he has written about dynamics as group learning. He claimed that a founder's beliefs and values are taught to new members and, if validated by success (e.g., organizational survival instead of

FIGURE 1
Schein's (1985) Model

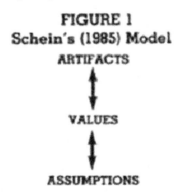

failure), undergo cognitive transformation into assumptions (Schein, 1983, 1985, 1991). Schein's view of dynamics differs from mine. I believe that underlying the process of leadership and socialization that Schein discusses, culture is constituted by local processes involving both change and stability. These processes need to be explained in the mundane terms of everyday organizational life.

The term cultural dynamics originated in cultural anthropology, where it refers to such issues as the origins and evolution of cultures, enculturation processes, and the problem of change versus stability (e.g., through diffusion, innovation, cultural conservatism, and resistance to change). Thus, in borrowing the term cultural dynamics, and extending Schein's arguments from origins, evolution, and enculturation to the dialectic of change and stability, I follow the lead of eminent cultural anthropologists such as Redfield (1941), Kroeber (1944), Malinowski (1945), and Herskovits (1948).

THE CULTURAL DYNAMICS OF ORGANIZATIONS

In developing the cultural dynamics perspective, I argue for two fundamental changes to Schein's model (Figure 1). First, symbols are introduced as a new element. The introduction of symbols permits the model to accommodate the influences of both Schein's theory and symbolic interpretive perspectives. Second, the elements of culture (assumptions, values, artifacts, and symbols) are made less central so that the relationships linking them become focal. This move initiates the shift from static to dynamic conceptions of culture, whereupon I reformulate Schein's theory in terms of dynamism by describing the relationships between cultural elements as processes (see Figure 2).

The advantage of a dynamic version of organizational culture theory lies in the new questions it poses. Schein's view focuses on what artifacts and values reveal about basic assumptions. In contrast, the dynamic perspective asks: How is culture constituted by assumptions, values, artifacts, symbols, and the processes that link them?

FIGURE 2
The Cultural Dynamics Model

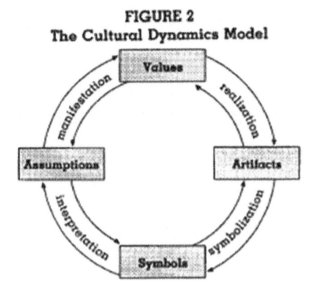

In regard to this example, Schein (1985:18) explained:

Whereas Schein explored how culture changes or can be changed, the dynamic view recognizes both stability and change as outcomes of the same processes (cf. Herskovits, 1948). Cultural dynamics does not undermine Schein's interests; it reaches beyond them toward a more complex, process-based understanding of organizational culture.

I identified the processes of the cultural dynamics model by considering how cultural elements are related, that is, by asking what happens inside the arrows of Figure 1. According to the new model, I propose that culture is constituted by manifestation, realization, symbolization, and interpretation processes. Although Schein (1985) used the terms manifest and realized (often interchangeably), he did not specify the definitions or the implications of manifestation and realization processes. A broader view led me to incorporate symbolic-interpretive approaches, which suggested the inclusion of symbols and the processes of symbolization and interpretation.

I should briefly explain the circularity of the cultural dynamics model (Figure 2). I could begin anywhere and move in either a clockwise or a counterclockwise direction. I will arbitrarily start with manifestation, considering both the clockwise and the counterclockwise modes of that process, and then proceed to realization, symbolization, and interpretation[14]. Such steps may lead to the conclusion that culture is the product of rather linear processes. This is not the case. The model in Figure 2 is much more dynamic: All of the processes co-occur in a continuous production and reproduction of culture in both its stable and changing forms and conditions. In other words, numerous instances of the cultural processes occur and recur more or less continuously throughout the cultural domain such that many different orders might be claimed, and I could even argue for simultaneity. Thus, none of the processes can stand on its own; each needs the perspective provided by discussion of the others to be fully transparent.

Manifestation Processes

Schein (1985) identified assumptions as the essence of culture, suggested that assumptions underlie values, and argued that humans infer their assumptions from known values. However, he did not address the active role of assumptions in constituting and reconstituting culture; consideration of the manifestation process provides this dynamic viewpoint. In general terms, manifestation refers to any process by which an essence reveals itself, usually via the senses, but also through

---

[14] Also, I have made two minor distinctions in terminology regarding the clockwise and counterclockwise modes, depending on whether these operate in the top or bottom half of the model. In the clockwise direction, top-half modes are called proactive, whereas bottom-half modes are called prospective; in the counterclockwise direction, top-half modes are called retroactive, whereas bottom-half modes are called retrospective. Discussion of this aspect of the model is deferred until the processes have been defined and illustrations have been given.

cognition and emotion. In terms of the cultural dynamics framework, manifestation permits cultural assumptions (the essence of culture in Schein's theory) to reveal themselves in the perceptions, cognitions, and emotions of organizational members. That is, manifestation contributes to the constitution of organizational culture by translating intangible assumptions into recognizable values. This constitution occurs through the advantage that manifestation gives to certain ways of seeing, feeling, and knowing within the organization. The cultural dynamics model suggests that manifestation occurs in two ways: through those processes that proactively influence values (the arrow from assumptions to values in Figure 2) and through those processes that influence assumptions via the retroactive effects of value recognition (the arrow from values to assumptions in Figure 2).

Proactive manifestation. What organizational members assume to be true shapes what they value. This shaping occurs through the processes of proactive manifestation through which assumptions provide expectations that influence perceptions, thoughts, and feelings about the world and the organization. These perceptions, thoughts, and feelings are then experienced as reflecting the world and the organization. Members recognize among these reflections aspects they both like and dislike, and on this basis they become conscious of their values (without necessarily being conscious of the basic assumptions on which their experiences and values are based).

Consider the assumption that humans are lazy. According to the cultural dynamics perspective, this assumption produces expectations of laziness, which lead to perceptions of lazy acts. These perceptions, in combination with other manifesting assumptions, color thoughts and feelings about these acts. For instance, in an organization that assumes that success depends upon sustained effort, laziness is likely to be considered in a negative light, and perceptions of laziness along with negative thoughts and feelings about it can easily develop into a value for controlling laziness. Meanwhile, the laziness assumption also works to inhibit expectations of industrious acts (because humans are lazy, why would they act in this way?), and perceptions, thoughts, and feelings about these acts will be constrained. This inhibition suppresses a value for autonomy (because giving lazy people autonomy will almost certainly lead to little or no effort being exerted), which further supports the value for control by eliminating a potentially competing force from the value set. That is, although autonomy would be compatible with an assumption that organizational success depends upon effort, the laziness assumption interferes with an effort/autonomy value set and supports an effort/control value set.

As Schein made clear, the core of culture is a set of assumptions. On this basis, I argue that multiple assumptions engage in manifestations simultaneously, and interactively, to reveal values. As illustrated in the example, there is not a one-to-one correspondence between particular assumptions and values, but rather assumptions are revealed in a holistic way. How then is their manifestation experienced by organizational members? Are values experienced one by one? Schein claimed that assumptions are taught to organizational members as "the correct way to perceive, think, and feel" (Schein, 1985: 9, emphasis added). This claim could imply that manifestation presents values in a more or less holistic fashion that partially reflects the gestalt of underlying assumptions.

Such a view is compatible with Schein's (1985: 15) reference to values as a "sense of what 'ought' to be, as distinct from what is." According to this definition, members who are under the influence of assumptions will notice and respond to some aspects of the organizational world more than other aspects. Their perceptions, thoughts, and feelings reveal a more or less holistic expectation, not of the organization as experienced, but of the organization "as it should be." It is important to note that "should be" can be understood either in the normative sense of "ought," or as general expectations. That is, values may be based in aspirations, or they may simply reveal what members assume is normal.

In either case, values are not experienced one by one; they are experienced as a gestalt.

In his discussion of self-fulfilling prophesies as substitutes for strategy, Weick (1987) helped to clarify the proactive manifestation process with the idea of presumptions of logic. He defined presumption of logic as "general expectations about the orderliness of what will occur" (1987: 225). Weick claimed that order is evoked within chaotic situations by presumptions of logic that will be assumed to have structured and defined the situation from the outset. In other words, order is imposed on chaos and then discovered within it. He argued:

> Most managerial situations contain gaps, discontinuities, loose ties among people and events, indeterminacies, and uncertainties. These are the gaps that managers have to bridge. It is the contention of this argument that managers first think their way across these gaps and then, having tied the elements together cognitively, actually tie them together when they act. (1987: 225)

Within cultural dynamics, the process of using general expectations to tie chaotic elements together prior to action is one aspect of the proactive manifestation process. The general expectations that make thinking across the gaps possible are grounded in cultural assumptions (e.g., about the nature of reality and the organization) and revealed as values (e.g., preferred ways of bridging the gaps). In the next step of Weick's argument, the expectations/values direct the action that actually ties the elements together, which, in the terminology of cultural dynamics, is the realization process (described in a following section).

Weick's focus is narrower than that of the cultural dynamics model. He referred only to managers rather than to all organizational members, discussed decision making but not routine behavior, treated chaotic but not mundane situations, and considered only cognition, ignoring perception and emotion. Nonetheless, his characterization captures an important aspect of proactive manifestation. Cultural assumptions are experienced as general expectations that provide possible responses to a situation, responses that reflect and embody cultural values. Proactive manifestation is the process that generates values and expectations that are capable of organizing action and experience. The values themselves are constituted by perceptions, cognitions, and emotions activated by cultural assumptions.

Retroactive manifestation. The retroactive mode of manifestation addresses the contribution of values to assumptions (see Figure 2). This contribution consists of two possibilities: values retroactively maintain or alter existing assumptions. In retroactive maintenance, values and assumptions are harmonious, and no further processing is necessary. In this case, the alignment of assumptions and values reaffirms basic assumptions as organizational members experience an "all's right with the world" confirmation of their culture. With respect to retroactive alteration of assumptions, Schein (1985) argued that assumptions can be altered by the introduction of new values (usually by top managers) and the experience of success attributed to them. If new values provide successful outcomes, Schein argued, then their maintenance over time will lead to their being taken for granted, at which point they become part of the culture's core assumptions. What Schein did not discuss is that, in order for this to happen, the new values must be at odds with existing assumptions at the start of the process; otherwise no change would occur, and retroactive manifestation would reaffirm existing assumptions.

In the cultural dynamics perspective, once a value emerges from basic assumptions, it has a retroactive effect of reaffirming and buttressing the assumptions from which it emerged. Of course, if a value enters the cultural domain by another means (e.g., importation from another culture), culture can absorb the new value via the same retroactive manifestation processes that would ordinarily reaffirm the culture's preexisting assumptions. Because assumptions are not phenomena about which

294

members are normally conscious, organizational members will find it difficult if not impossible to distinguish culturally based values from other values once the values have been recognized as (or mistaken for) values of the culture. The incorporation of new values will proceed as if they were being reaffirmed, but, instead, the presence of the new values among the old values will serve to realign the basic assumptions. However, if new values are not retroactively taken to be part of the culture, the manifestation process will ignore them.

One question remains. Because values are manifestations of cultural assumptions, where would values that are not culturally based come from? Possibilities include contact either with other cultures or with some force independent of the organizational culture, such as nonsocialized individuals producing random variation or innovation (Herskovits, 1948; Kroeber, 1944; Malinowski, 1945). In this case, the access point is not likely to be values, but artifacts (objects, ideas, or actions realized by others), which will be discussed in the following section on retroactive realization.

Studying manifestation processes. The study of manifestation processes calls for the study of how various expectations of "how it should be" come about in organizations. The proactive question that the manifestation process puts to culture data is to explain how certain values and expectations are carved from assumptions by activating perceptions, cognitions, and emotions. A related question is: What perceptions, thoughts, and feelings are constrained in the manifestation process? For instance, Weick (1987) suggested that strategy formulation is one organizational event in which manifestation processes and their associated expectations play a significant role. Strategy formulation processes could be studied using scenarios produced by strategists to reveal the perceptions, cognitions, and emotions that define values and expectations in this situation.

Other situations (especially those involving nonmanagerial employees) should be identified and examined from a process perspective, in order to bring researchers into contact with the full range of proactive manifestation processes and the expectations that they involve. The retroactive process explains how culturally manifested values reaffirm basic assumptions and how values originating outside the culture can realign basic assumptions. Studies that focus on interventions to manage organizational culture (e.g., Kunda, 1992) hold promise for revealing the retroactive manifestation processes.

To summarize, the manifestation process constitutes expectations of "how it should be" that can be specified as a list of cultural values. Expectations, specified as values or not, can then be taken up by realization processes to serve as cultural frameworks for organizational activity (see Figure 2). Proactive manifestation is an imaginative act in which an expectation of the situation and its potential is produced via cognitions, emotions, and perceptions grounded in cultural assumptions. Retroactive manifestation updates assumptions to align with values that are actively acknowledged within the culture, a process that feeds into retrospective interpretation, which is discussed in a following section.

Realization Processes

Schein (1985) pointed out that artifacts are the most tangible aspects of culture. Cultural dynamics claims that realization brings this tangibility about. In general terms, to realize something means to make it real (i.e., not pretended or merely imagined), to bring it into being. Williams (1983: 260) described it as an act of the imagination that serves as "the means and effect of bringing something vividly to life." In terms of the cultural dynamics model, proactive realization is responsible for the transformation of values into artifacts (e.g., rites, rituals, organizational stories, humor, and various physical objects), whereas retroactive realization has the potential to transform values and expectations by making them appear differently than they did prior to their proactive realization as artifacts. Thus, cultural realization is initially defined as the process of making values real by transforming expectations into social or material reality and by maintaining or altering existing values through the production of artifacts.

Proactive realization. Proactive realization is related to Weick's notion of enactment and to the concept of materialization of ideas discussed by Czarniawska-Joerges and Joerges (1990). In terms of enactment, Weick (1987: 225) claimed that "the lesson of self-fulfilling prophecies . . . is that strong beliefs that single out and intensify consistent action can bring events into existence." Similarly, Czarniawska-Joerges and Joerges (1990: 50-51) argued:

Not all ideas are put into action. Obviously, to be put into action an idea must be supplied by an image of action, a mental picture of possible action. Ideas that were unrealizable for centuries slowly acquire an action-image resulting from the changes in other ideas and in things (technology). But an image of action is not yet an action. How can it be materialized? Not by decision as an act of choice . . . . Rather, it is an act of will, prompted by positive expectations concerning the process itself . . . . its results, or both . . . . The cognitive process moves, then, prompted by an act of will, towards calibrating the "image of action" into something more like a "plan of action" (Miller, Galanter, & Pribram, 1960) and then into deeds. And this last element is the one that truly deserves to be called "materialization."

The materialization argument is restricted to cognition, whereas cultural dynamics considers perceptual and emotional processes as well. Furthermore, Czarniawska-Joerges and Joerges confined themselves to discussing ideas as images of action that are capable of materializing in deeds, whereas realization in the cultural dynamics model focuses on cultural expectations and values realized through action in artifacts. Nonetheless, the parallels between the arguments are clear.

Proactive realization occurs through activity that gives substance to expectations revealed by the manifestation process. That is, realization follows manifestation only if expectations and their associated values find their way into activity that has tangible outcomes. Many different activities can contribute to the realization of expectations; among them are the production of objects (e.g., company products, official reports, internal newsletters, buildings); engagement in organizational events (e.g., meetings, company picnics, award banquets, office parties); participation in discourse (e.g., formal speeches, informal conversation, joking); and importation of objects, events, and language artifacts via imitation or physical transportation of cultural objects or members of other cultures.

Although activity produces artifacts, behavior itself is not culture. As Schein (1991: 251) argued, in addition to cultural influences, "overt behavior is also influenced by local circumstances and immediate events." Not everything that happens in organizations can be explained by culture because other forces contribute to the same activities that are open to cultural influence. Thus, proactive realization is defined as the process wherein culturally influenced activity produces artifacts such that a given set of values or expectations receives some degree of representation in tangible forms (shown by the arrow from values to artifacts in Figure 2). The representation of the expectation in the artifact will always be imperfect as a result of noncultural influences on behavior in organizations (e.g., genetic, idiosyncratic). Therefore, activity and the artifacts an organization leaves behind are infused with cultural values but do not unequivocally indicate them. Thus, the realization process helps to explain the difficulty of analytically recovering values from a collection of artifacts.

To use the humans-are-lazy example again, an assumption that the organization is filled with laggards contributes to a value for control that enhances the likelihood that certain social and material forms will appear. For instance, time clocks, daily productivity reports, performance meetings, and visually accessible offices are acceptable ideas in a culture that values controlling laziness. Proactive realization is the process by which manifest expectations are made tangible in artifacts. From this point of view, artifacts are left in the wake of culturally influenced activity. Thus, time clocks might be installed, daily activity reports requested and filed, performance assessed, and visually accessible offices built, all as partial means of realizing the expectation of "how it should be" in an organization assumed to be filled with laggards. The time clocks, activity reports, meetings, and accessible offices are left behind to take their place amid a pool of previously realized objects, events, and discourses, the "survivals" of earlier realization processes (Herskovits, 1948; Jones, 1991; Tyler, 1958/1871).

Retroactive realization. The retroactive mode of realization addresses the post hoc contribution of artifacts to values and to expectations of "how things should be." Similar to manifestation, two distinct possibilities should be examined. In one case, artifacts realized from values and expectations maintain or reaffirm these values and expectations, whereas artifacts produced by another culture or by forces not aligned with cultural values could introduce artifacts that retroactively challenge values and expectations.

In the latter case, two more possibilities emerge. The artifacts are ignored or physically ejected (e.g., destroyed or removed) by members of the organization, or they are accepted and incorporated alongside culturally produced artifacts to reflect back on the values. If absorbed into the culture, such artifacts work retroactively to realign values as the culture adjusts to their presence. To the extent that values are realigned, assumptions may also be adjusted via retroactive manifestation processes.

Successful avant-garde works of art provide an extreme example of retroactive realization processes. At first, a new work of art that challenges accepted values is resisted or denied its place in the art world, but over time it comes to be seen in new ways that allow for its acceptance. Retroactive realization explains this as a process of value realignment with a novel artifact. The artifact, by challenging established values, fosters an alteration in the values of at least some viewers, whose appreciation diffuses until the work is accepted by a wider audience. Within business organizations, a similar effect can be observed surrounding the introduction of radical innovations, daring strategic plans, and visionary reorganizations. As with avant-garde art, these novel artifacts live or die by their ability to transform established values enough to permit their acceptance into the culture. What is essential to value realignment is that a critical mass of appreciation for a new artifact be built up so that diffusion takes hold within retroactive realization processes. Of course, grand-scale value realignment on the order of these examples is rare; retroactive realignment more typically involves less obvious readjustments. You should also remember that manifestation and realization processes do not operate in isolation; they are complemented by symbolization and interpretation processes, which are explained in following sections.

Studying realization processes. The study of realization processes calls for the study of how values and expectations are used and maintained or transformed in the course of constructing behavior that has tangible outcomes. Studies of the production, reproduction, and transformation of artifacts through the daily activities of organizations could be used to examine how values and expectations unfold. For instance, Barley (1986) used ethnographic observation in a study of the introduction of new medical diagnostic equipment in two hospital radiology departments. Following Giddens (1979), Barley examined how everyday activity produced and reproduced the institutions in which it occurred, as revealed by the introduction of new technology. Cultural dynamics suggests interpreting Barley's data as a case of cultural importation of an artifact and retroactive value adjustment based on activity surrounding the new object and the events the object occasioned. The importation itself might be analyzed as a proactive realization of cultural values.

Cultural dynamics focuses observational studies like Barley's on the artifacts of action as well as activities. For instance, proactive realization studies might focus on how values and expectations of "how it should be" penetrate rituals such as quarterly review meetings (e.g., via preparations, arrangements, and presentations made by participants). Retroactive realization could be studied by observing how language use forms a verbal-action field in which cultural expectations and values are maintained or transformed via contact with organizational artifacts such as greetings, forms of address, stories, and humor. The field of organizational folklore (Jones, 1988, 1991; Jones et al., 1988) is rich with examples of cultural artifacts used in ways that maintain values via retroactive realization. For example, see Arora's (1988) study of the uses of proverbial speech by a university committee. Studies of introductions of artifacts from other cultures should be particularly revealing of value transformations via retroactive realization. Cook and Yanow's (1993) report of a flute manufacturing company that adopted a competitor's innovation provides an example.

In summary, the cultural significance of an artifact is not set for all time at the moment of its production or importation. True, the artifact at this moment is infused with the assumptions and values that led to its proactive realization, but these are localized in the realization processes of the producing members. Other members, who participated in the production indirectly, if at all, when exposed to the product may accept, reject, or ignore it. In any case, the product itself becomes available to a much broader interpretive process than the one that formed the context of its inception.

Symbolization Processes

Those who follow Schein typically consider symbols to be part of the more comprehensive category of artifacts; thus, all symbols are artifacts. In contrast, many symbolic-interpretive researchers, such as Tompkins (1987), claim that every artifact has symbolic significance; therefore, all artifacts are symbols. Thus, from opposing theoretical points of departure both traditions draw the same conclusion—the distinction between artifacts and symbols is unnecessary. However, others have argued that not all artifacts are symbols (Morgan, Frost, & Pondy, 1983), and I claim that eliding the distinction between artifacts and symbols buries the process of symbolization and blurs the boundary between Schein's perspective and the perspective offered by the symbolic-interpretive approach.

Symbolic-interpretive researchers defined a symbol as anything that represents a conscious or an unconscious association with some wider, usually more abstract, concept or meaning (e.g., Chapple & Coon, 1942; Dandridge, Mitroff, & Joyce, 1980; Gioia, 1986; Morgan, Frost, & Pondy, 1983). Gioia (1986) offered a representative list of organizational symbols: the corporate logo, slogans, stories, actions and nonactions, visual images, and metaphors. Eisenberg and Riley (1988) added organization charts, corporate architecture, rites, and rituals. Because lists of artifacts offer identical items (e.g., Ott, 1989), it would appear that symbols and artifacts are indistinguishable, and, in the static sense of their physical forms, I would agree. However, when attention is turned to the dynamics of culture, the distinction is clarified. In the dynamic view, focus shifts from concern with physical forms to the ways in which these forms are produced and used by organizational members (Ortner, 1973). As Cohen (1985: 14) argued, symbols "do more than merely stand for or represent something else . . . they also allow those who employ them to supply part of their meaning."

Borrowing Barthes' (1972) example, a bouquet of roses is given, not only as a bundle of flowers, but also as an expression of appreciation. The objective form of the symbol (the flowers) has literal meaning associated with aspects such as its smell, color, texture, and arrangement. Beyond this objective form and its literal meaning lie, for example, subjective

302

and figurative associations that add to the bouquet's meaning. These may include past gift-giving experiences, a person's history with and appreciation for roses, the significance friends attach to the roses, and perhaps lines of verse or scenes remembered from a play. Schutz (1970: 108-109) described this added meaning as "a kind of aura surrounding the nucleus of the objective meaning."

Prospective symbolization. Ricoeur (1976) recommended comparing the full meaning of a symbol to its literal meaning and called the difference the surplus of meaning. The notion of surplus meaning helps explain symbolization. Once realized, an artifact is an objective form with literal meaning. Symbolization combines an artifact with meaning that reaches beyond or surrounds it. Symbolization is thus a prospective response that links an artifact's objective form and literal meaning to experiences that lie beyond the literal domain. Cassirer (1946: 8) argued that symbolization produces reality: "Symbolic forms are not imitations, but organs of reality, since it is solely by their agency that anything real becomes an object for intellectual apprehension, and as such is made visible to us." Brown (1977: 40) built on Cassirer's argument, stating that "symbolic forms give existence to what, for us [emphasis added], otherwise would not be." Tompkins (1987) made the same point.

The genesis of symbolic forms is overlooked by arguments such as Brown's and Tompkins's. The cultural dynamics model suggests that these forms arise first as artifacts, and through additional cultural processing they come to be recognized as symbolic forms by organizational members. The production of the forms that will carry symbolic meaning occurs in the realm of proactive manifestation and realization. The forms are made real by culturally influenced action, not by symbolism. Once realized, however, they become "object[s] for intellectual apprehension" via the process of symbolization (and interpretation, which is discussed in a following section). Nothing in Cassirer's argument, however, indicates that symbolic forms are equivalent to what is "real." It is a mistake to interpret Cassirer as arguing that there is no reality apart from symbolic forms; his argument is that the ability to intellectually apprehend reality is limited by a person's recognition of symbolic forms. The ability to apprehend reality in other ways, such as through physical contact (e.g., bruising your leg on a table or desk), is not limited to symbolic events.

From the cultural dynamics perspective, these ideas suggest that artifacts must be translated into symbols if they are to be apprehended as culturally significant objects, events, or discourses. Such apprehension bestows the status of recognized existence on certain forms within the culture with the implication that, although all artifacts can be symbolized, not all will be, at least not at all times and places, for all organizational members. Berg (1985: 285-286) explained Cassirer's notion of the "agency of symbolic forms," claiming that symbolization translates physical or objective reality into symbolic reality:

The symbolic field is not "reality" as it once appeared but the collective symbolization of that reality. The symbolic field is essentially the result of an attempt to interpret experiences in one reality using objects, properties, and symbols from another reality . . . . when we talk about the organization, we refer to a metaphor of human experience . . . . a complex symbolic construction with links to the physical or objective reality.

The previous discussion suggests that prospective symbolization involves a shift from the experience of things strictly in terms of their objective forms and literal meanings to an awareness of things as having objective form and both literal and surplus meaning. Thus, prospective symbolization might be defined as a sort of exploitation of artifacts by symbols via associations that project both the objects of symbolization and the symbolizers from the literal domain to a domain that includes surplus meaning as well as literal awareness. From within the symbolic field, organizational members then retrospectively (re)construct their artifacts as meaningful on the basis of their symbolic memory.

Retrospective symbolization. The retrospective mode of symbolization enhances awareness of the literal meaning of symbolized artifacts. The important point from a cultural dynamics perspective is that not all artifacts are given equal treatment within the symbolic field. The prospective symbolization process implies that some artifacts will acquire more significant associations across more organizational members than will other artifacts in a given moment and at a particular place. Thus, at each instant there is a state within the symbolic field that represents that moment's symbolic configuration of meaning relative to its cultural artifacts. The artifacts themselves remain as a field of potential symbolic material, but, on a moment-to-moment basis, only certain parts of the field are illuminated by the retrospective symbolization process.

The example of a corporate status symbol illustrates the symbolization process. A large desk is merely a piece of furniture within organizational cultures for which it has limited or no surplus meaning. When organizational members do not respond to the symbolic opportunity presented by such an artifact, the desk remains in the literal realm where it may be experienced as a surface on which to work, a place to store papers and supplies, or something on which to bruise a knee. In these circumstances, prospective symbolization does not take place, at least not in a culturally interesting way. When organizational members enter the symbolic realm, however, they engage surplus meaning through prospective symbolization. This can be observed in the responses members give to their own desk in relation to the desks of their superiors, subordinates, and co-workers. In these circumstances, the members' experiences of the desk as furniture are inscribed within their memories and awareness of the surplus meaning associated with the artifact. The artifact now embodies the symbol, and this gives rise to retrospective

305

symbolization in which the desk stands out among other artifacts by virtue of its enhanced symbolic significance.

In summary, prospective symbolization is the process by which cultural symbols are made from associations between the literal experience of artifacts and surplus meaning. This process is represented by the arrow from artifacts to symbols in Figure 2. Aspects of the literal meaning of the artifact (e.g., large desks offer more convenient work surfaces) may be made more acute by feedback from the retrospective symbolization process represented by the arrow from symbols to artifacts. Symbolization involves an extension of consciousness beyond the literal realm. It translates some artifacts into symbols and projects those who use an artifact as a symbol into the symbolic realm. In the symbolic realm, surplus meaning joins, and at times dominates, members' consciousness of objective forms and literal meanings, leading some symbolic-interpretive researchers to claim that the literal domain is not a part of culture (e.g., Tompkins, 1987). The cultural dynamics perspective recognizes both the literal and the symbolic domains.

Studying symbolization processes. The study of symbolization processes as conceived in the cultural dynamics framework calls for direct involvement. One method of achieving this involvement is exemplified by ethnographers who submerge themselves in the cultural experiences they want to study and draw on personal meaning derived from these experiences in creating their ethnographies. For example, Van Maanen's (1991) study of Disneyland draws heavily on the experiences he had while working there. His admission that "it may just be possible that I now derive as much a part of my identity from being fired from Disneyland as I gained from being employed there in the first place" (1991: 76) attests to his involvement in prospective symbolization within this culture. Cultural dynamics also asks for specification of the surplus meaning associated with various artifacts (Disneyland's assigned jobs, uniforms, etc.). This is precisely what Van Maanen gives us by referring to his participation in the Disneyland culture, thus employing retrospective symbolization.

A second possible approach to the study of symbolization requires the adaptation of aesthetic techniques to the study of organization (e.g., Bjorkegren, 1991; Strati, 1990, 1992; Van Maanen, 1988; Witkin, 1990). When researchers study symbolization processes, they must use methods that create or simulate first-order experiences, such as aesthetic techniques do (e.g., acting, writing, drawing, making photographs). For example, Witkin's evocative description of a meeting room at Unilever provides access to the aesthetic experience of this organizational space:

Behind the chairs, at one end of the table, there are two flip chart boards, white in colour and rectangular in shape. Their flat vertical planes rise above equally flat-looking metal frames. They are supported at their base by two pairs of tiny legs descending from two horizontal bars. The supports only serve to accentuate the flatness of the boards, a flatness which is echoed in the strong smooth white plane of the table and the white planes of the wall. (Witkin, 1990: 333)

Witkin's (1990: 333) interpretation that "it is as though the room has been purged of the appearance of volumes" practically leaps out of his prospective symbolization of the room and produces evidence of the retrospective mode of symbolization; however, the retrospective mode is admittedly difficult to distinguish from interpretation (which is discussed next) and is in need of further explication.

Self-reflective use of aesthetic methods could help to explicate the processes of symbolization and teach researchers to distinguish these processes from the processes of interpretation. Currently, researchers who focus on ethnography as a literary genre are making some headway in this direction (Clifford & Marcus, 1986; Geertz, 1988; Jeffcutt, 1991; Linstead, 1993). In this approach, ethnographers turn the interpretive gaze on themselves and their ethnographies. The self-reflective technique allows ethnographers to confront their assumptions, but it could also bring an awareness of self-as-author caught in the act of writing (i.e., making symbols). Although the practice of self-reflection can easily shade into self-interpretation, the technique suggests a developing possibility for studying retrospective symbolization.

To summarize, organizational members are symbol manipulators, creating as well as discovering meaning as they explore and produce a socially constructed reality to express their self-images and to contextualize their activity and identity. Symbolization refers to culturally contextualized meaning creation via the prospective use of objects, words, and actions. The objects, words, and actions are transformed (e.g., through communication) into symbols, the dynamic constellation of which constitutes the symbolic field of a culture. The symbolic field then retrospectively transfigures artifacts by imbuing them with the charms of surplus meaning.

Interpretation

Schutz (1970: 320) claimed that "the meaning of an experience is established, in retrospect, through interpretation." Cohen (1985: 17-18) added that "by their very nature symbols permit interpretation and provide scope for interpretive manoeuvre [sic] by those who use them." In other words, the meaning that interpretation establishes involves the literal and surplus meanings combined by prospective symbolization processes. Ricoeur (1976: 55) offers further assistance with this point:

Only for an interpretation are there two levels of significance . . . . Symbolic signification . . . . is so constituted that we can only attain the secondary signification by way of the primary signification, where this primary signification is the sole means of access to the surplus of meaning. The primary signification gives the secondary signification, in effect, as the meaning of a meaning.

This passage suggests that interpretation involves a second-order experience of symbolization. In other words, the meaning that is established by interpretation is derivative of the direct (first-order) association of literal and surplus meaning defined as the prospective symbolization process. However, this second-order experience is not simply a repetition of the first-order event, as Gioia (1986: 55) explained:

When an organizational event or action with symbolic possibility is experienced, it is related to existing knowledge to generate meaning. That is, as a current symbol becomes associated with symbolic networks, understanding occurs . . . . understanding can only occur if new information can in some way be related to what is already known.

Gioia (1986) located the "already known" in scripts and schemas held in memory, but his ideas translate easily into the terms of culture theory. If assumptions are organized, at least in part, as knowledge structures, then the content of the scripts and schemas that structure and retain knowledge should reveal cultural assumptions (Barley, 1986; Martin, Feldman, Hatch, & Setkin, 1983). Thus, from the culture perspective, assumptions provide the "already known" of interpretation processes.

This notion brings us back to Schutz's two assertions. First, Schutz claimed that interpretation is retrospective. This claim implies that interpretation involves a move from the "already known" of a culture's basic assumptions to current symbols (retrospective interpretation) Second, Schutz asserted that interpretation establishes meaning. This assertion implies that current symbols have a reciprocal influence on basic assumptions (prospective interpretation). This reciprocity has been the central theme of the hermeneutic school of interpretation theory, where it is called the hermeneutic circle.

According to Wilson (1987: 385), the hermeneutic circle "involves successive revisions of interpretations of social phenomena as each new level of understanding calls for revision of the basis on which that understanding is founded." He continued:

"We do not build up a pattern of society from descriptions of single actions . . . . but rather develop an account in a hermeneutic fashion, forming ideas about overall patterns on the basis of particular events and then using these same ideas to understand more clearly the particular events that gave rise to them. Of course, when we are already familiar with a society because we live in it, this interpretive process can be quite unselfconscious and implicit, but the basic interdependence between descriptions of singular events and understandings of the larger social order remains." (Wilson, 1987: 396)

The hermeneutic perspective suggests that interpretation moves us back and forth between the already known (basic assumptions) and the possibility of new understanding (inherent, but often dormant, in symbols). The possibility for revision of meaning exists throughout this cycle. Thus, there is potential for two results of interpretation: altered understanding of symbolic meaning via retrospective interpretation and revisions to cultural assumptions via prospective interpretation.

Interpretation involves countless engagements of the hermeneutic circle. Some of this interpretation reflects existing cultural assumptions, but some of it revises assumptions by establishing new meaning within the core. In the cultural dynamics view, interpretation reconstructs symbols and revises basic assumptions in terms of both current experience and preestablished cultural assumptions.

In summary, cultural dynamics suggests that interpretation contextualizes current symbolization experiences by evoking a broader cultural frame as a reference point for constructing an acceptable meaning. This is shown in Figure 2 as the arrow from assumptions to symbols. Meanwhile, cultural assumptions, momentarily exposed during the process of interpretation, are opened to the influence of new symbols. In this way, the moment of interpretation makes it possible (but not necessary) for culture to absorb newly symbolized content into its core. In Figure 2, this is represented by the arrow from symbols to assumptions. From the cultural dynamics perspective, the prospective mode of interpretation maintains or challenges basic assumptions, whereas the retrospective mode reconstructs the meaning of symbols via feedback from the same interpretive move (as explained by the hermeneutic circle). Of course, the prospective interpretation process then either meshes or collides with the retroactive manifestation process discussed previously, and the explanation has at last come full circle with respect to Figure 2.

Studying interpretation processes. The study of interpretation processes calls for investigating how symbols mold and are molded by existing ways of understanding. The results of interpretation processes have been investigated using a variety of established techniques such asethnographic interviews (Spradley, 1979), scripts (Barley, 1986; Martin etal., 1983), semiotics (Barley, 1983; Fiol, 1991), deconstruction (Calas & Smircich, 1991; Martin, 1990), and discourse analysis (Coulthard, 1977). At least two of these techniques—interviews and discourse analysis—can be used to reveal the interpretation process in action.

Botti and Pipan (1991) used ethnographic interviews to explore interpretations of the service concept in two public service organizations in Italy—a registry office and a hospital. They offer rich descriptions of their subjects' interpretations of the symbols of service. For example, one group of registry office personnel defined service in terms of users, but the users were generally interpreted as unfriendly or threatening. The cultural dynamics model would ask how the symbol of "the user" participates in constructing and reconstructing assumptions about everyday life within the registry office and vice versa. One possibility would be to present alternative symbols (e.g., a warm and friendly customer on a cold and rainy day) and ask registry officer personnel to interpret them. The purpose would be to discover how interviewees respond to new symbols in the course of their normal interpretive activities. Is this "a user" in their view, or something else?

Another approach to studying interpretation processes is presented by Donnellon, Gray, and Bougon (1986). These researchers performed discourse analysis using a videotape of a group of students who were conducting an organizational simulation exercise. The taped material showed the students responding to another group's action that had resulted in layoffs within their group. Semantic coding of the recorded discourse allowed the researchers to study shifts in the focal group members' interpretations and in their inclinations toward proposed actions. They found that group members used four interpretive mechanisms in coming to a collective decision to strike: metaphor, logical argument, affect modulation (e.g., nonverbal behavior, fast pace, emotionally charged language), and linguistic indirection (e.g., passive voice, use of imprecise terms). The work of Donnellon and her colleagues could frame studies of how these interpretive mechanisms mold and are molded by symbols and assumptions. Furthermore, if their method could be adapted to the demands of field settings, it might reveal the uses of these as well as other interpretive mechanisms in organizations.

Although the collision of prospective interpretation and retroactive manifestation processes will require further development, one avenue of exploration might be found in studies of spontaneous humor in a management team (Hatch, In press; Hatch & Ehrlich, In press). The findings reported in the first study (Hatch, In press) indicate that ironic remarks (formulated as spontaneous humor) reveal contradictions between organizational practices and symbolic interpretations. This study suggests that where retroactive manifestation and prospective interpretation do not mesh, culture is constructed and interpreted as contradictory.

Summary

The preceding discussion maps the theoretical domain of a dynamic model of organizational culture, called cultural dynamics.

Much work remains to be done to fully develop each of the four major processes defined by the model, and separate discussions of each process were aimed at directing future research toward this end. Within these discussions, a variety of promising methods was also reviewed as a first step toward developing a methodological repertoire for the empirical study of cultural dynamics (see Table 1 for a summary). Each method was presented in relation to empirical examples drawn from the organization studies literature (additional examples are recommended in Table 1 for those who wish to pursue these methods). [15]

Table 1. A Comparison of Changing a Loosely Coupled System (LCS) With a Tightly Coupled System (TCS)

Dimension for Comparison	Process for Changing an LCS	Process for Changing a TCS
Focus	Continuous	Episodic
Scale	Small	Large
Type of initiative	Improvisational	Planned
Consulting process	Accommodative	Constrained
Locus of change	Local	Cosmopolitan

Note. Weick (2001).

APPLYING THE CULTURAL DYNAMICS PERSPECTIVE

Two applications of the cultural dynamics model will be presented in this section. First, Schein's explanation of a theoretical example will be compared to an explanation developed within the cultural dynamics perspective. This will allow the cultural dynamics model to be assessed in relation to its departure point in Schein. Second, using case data presented in the organizational studies literature (Gioia & Chittipeddi, 1991), the ability of the cultural dynamics model to extend empirical analysis in

---

[15]   Most of the methods will require adaptation, and other appropriate methods will surely emerge from the continuing stream of research focusing on organizational processes. Furthermore, because the cultural dynamics perspective advocates attention to all four processes, workable combinations of these methods will need to be developed, perhaps through the use of traditional ethnography (which is built on multiple methods) as a prototype.

informative ways will be demonstrated. Both demonstrations are intended to show that the cultural dynamics model offers a greater appreciation of cultural complexity and dynamism than researchers have enjoyed in the past.

Demonstration #1: Schein (1985)

In the previous presentation of manifestation and realization processes, I used as a theoretical example the assumption that humans are lazy. Schein (1985: 18-19) offered a related example that begins with the assumption that humans are opportunistic:

> If we assume . . . . that other people will take advantage of us whenever they have an opportunity, we expect to be taken advantage of and then interpret the behavior of others in a way that coincides with those expectations. We observe people sitting idly at their desk and perceive them as loafing rather than thinking out an important problem; we perceive absence from work as shirking rather than doing work at home.

> When a solution to a problem works repeatedly, it comes to be taken for granted. What was once a hypothesis, supported by only a hunch or a value, comes gradually to be treated as a reality. We come to believe that nature really works this way . . . . What I am calling basic assumptions are congruent with what Argyris has identified as "theories-in-use," the implicit assumptions that actually guide behavior . . . . Basic assumptions, like theories-in-use, tend to be nonconfrontable and nondebatable Clearly, such unconscious assumptions can distort data.

The passage implies that assumptions are responsible for distorting perceptions and leading managers to false conclusions such as "hardworking employees are loafers." Thus, assumptions produce perceptions that conform to assumptions. This leaves open the question of the origin of assumptions. Schein argued that assumptions come about when top management proposes the solution to a problem:

If the solution works, and the group has a shared perception of that success, the value gradually starts a process of cognitive transformation into a belief and, ultimately, an assumption. If this transformation process occurs—and it will occur only if the proposed solution continues to work, thus implying that it is in some larger sense "correct" and must reflect an accurate picture of reality—group members will tend to forget that originally they were not sure and that the values were therefore debated and confronted. (Schein, 1985: 16)

In Schein's (1985) explanation there is only a one-way temporal chain of events. In his view, the possibility for change in assumptions is limited to "values that are susceptible of physical or social validation" and thereby "become transformed into assumptions." According to cultural dynamics, assumptions are open to change on "both ends" (shown in Figure 2 by the arrows from both values and symbols to assumptions). That is, change can occur through reaction to alien or novel values (the retroactive phase of the manifestation process), or it can occur through ongoing processes of interpretation in which each interpretive event occasions an opportunity for change in assumptions (the prospective phase of interpretation). This can be illustrated through a cultural dynamics explanation for Schein's example:

An assumption that people will take advantage of others proactively manifests the expectation of workers being prevented from doing so by management. This expectation influences managers to be on the lookout for cases of loafing and shirking, and they find such cases (proactive realization) even where they do not exist, such as the motionless but thinking employee or the absent employee working at home. Such employees may be regarded as idle loafers and shirkers (prospective symbolization). This labeling conforms to and reconstructs (within the hermeneutic circle of interpretation) the assumption that humans are lazy. If, however, employees are seen in other ways (e.g., as a result of employees' efforts to influence managers' perceptions), the managers' assumptions may be challenged via prospective interpretation or through the retrospective/retroactive chain ending in a retroactive realignment of values and assumptions. In the retrospective/ retroactive mode, the same interpretation process strengthens (or weakens) the meaning of the symbol of the loafer/shirker through comparisons with the "already known," which enhances (or buries) awareness of the artifact via retrospective symbolization. Renewed awareness of the artifact presents opportunities for retroactive adjustment of values that can reaffirm (or further challenge) the assumption that people will take advantage of their employers.

In the cultural dynamics explanation, organizational members cycle back and forth between proactive/prospective and retrospective/ retroactive influences. The difference between the two explanations illustrates the greater dynamism of the cultural dynamics model relative to Schein's theory, which is restricted to an evolutionary or a developmental view of change. Those ideas that Schein represents are also represented in the cultural dynamics perspective; however, the cultural dynamics view goes beyond Schein's model to examine the symbolic-interpretive processes constituting cultural assumptions. Thus, cultural dynamics does not invalidate Schein's theory; it articulates the theory and significantly extends the range and power of its explanation.

Demonstration #2: Gioia and Chittipeddi (1991)

Gioia and Chittipeddi's (1991) empirical study of strategic change was selected because it focuses on processes and employs ethnography, a methodology typical of much culture research. This makes the study ideal for illustrating how the cultural dynamics perspective can extend the analysis of ethnographic data.

316

Gioia and Chittipeddi (1991) used ethnography (along with some innovative methods not described here) to study the initiation of a strategic change effort at a large American university. The university had just hired a new president who introduced his vision of a "Top 10 public university" immediately upon taking up his post. The researchers were able to recover the techniques the president used to formulate his vision (campus visits, consultations, interviews with stakeholders, past experience as chancellor of another university) and to follow its introduction within a task force that the president appointed to carry his vision forward. During two years of participant observation, Gioia and Chittipeddi found that the president used vision and hypothetical scenarios to introduce, support, and encourage change through a process they label "sense giving."

Seen from the cultural dynamics perspective, Gioia and Chittipeddi's vision concept collapses expectations into symbols. In effect, these authors focus on the manifestation of an expectation (becoming a Top 10 public university) and on interpretation of the symbol they assume that the expectation became, without considering the process by which this transformation occurred. Thus, they ignore the domain represented by the right side of the cultural dynamics model. As a result, their approach underemphasizes artifacts, realization, and symbolization. This underemphasis leads to an unanalyzed connection between the president's vision and the actions of other members of the organization. If the case is analyzed from the cultural dynamics viewpoint, Gioia and Chittipeddi's analysis can be extended to offer some suggestions about what was probably going on, given the cultural dynamics model.

Gioia and Chittipeddi (1991: 445) wrote:

Perhaps the key occurrence in this case was the devising of an overarching symbolic vision, expressed in evocative images ("a Top-10 public university"). This vision provided an interpretative framework within which thinking and acting could be viewed in terms of their

317

consistency with the requirements for achieving such a vision. The president himself later said that this symbol "took on a life of its own" and became a more powerful guiding image than he ever would have imagined.

In this passage, the authors equate the president's vision with an interpretative framework, whereas the cultural dynamics model suggests that the vision plays two distinct roles. At least initially, it is used by the president as an expectation of "how it should be" in terms of his values and personal aspirations for the organization. Others use the president's vision as a symbol of his intentions and retrospectively interpret it in terms of their own assumptions and understandings of how it has ("always") been. Later, if the vision is adopted by other organizational members, it may alter assumptions and reorganize cultural understanding. As an expectation, the vision lies within an action framework rather than an interpretive framework. It is as a symbol that the vision contributes to interpretation.

Recognizing the dual role of the president's vision as expectation and symbol permits us to address how the vision "took on a life of its own." Cultural dynamics suggests that the president's vision was taken up through a complex of processes described by the right half of the cultural dynamics model as understood from the perspective of organizational members (especially the task force). Accordingly, when the president's actions were influenced by his expectation/vision, he created the possibility that the products of his action (e.g., artifacts such as decisions taken, people hired or fired) would be symbolized and interpreted by others in a way that would retrospectively portray aspects of his vision within their symbolization and interpretation processes. However, the model also indicates that it was the expectations of those others, whether they reflected the president's vision or not, that guided their actions via proactive realization processes.

This analysis can be taken a step further if the possible effects of the lower level members' use of negotiation and resistance to the president's vision are considered. Gioia and Chittipeddi observed that organizational members resisted, attempted to change, or ignored the president's influence attempts. The cultural dynamics model suggests that the product of these actions then became available as artifacts for prospective symbolization. For instance, the president could have used the symbols he made from these responses to form interpretations that altered (or reinforced) his assumptions, thus absorbing him within the culture along with his vision for change.

This application of the cultural dynamics model implies that, although the president was a major player in the initiation of strategic change, his influence depended heavily on the ways in which others symbolized and interpreted his efforts. The outcome of the president's influence ultimately rested on others' interpretations and the effect these interpretations had on cultural assumptions and expectations. In this light, it is worthwhile questioning whether the president was as central to the initiation effort, or the organizational culture, as he at first appeared to be. At least it seems clear that a "bottom-up" analysis of the strategic initiation effort is needed to complement Gioia and Chittipeddi's "top down" point of view.

Further evidence of the need to question the centrality of the president comes from the circumstances surrounding the initiation of strategic change. The decision-making body undoubtedly chose its candidate at least partly on the basis of their expectations for the university and its future president. The artifact of their selection decision (the new president) proactively realized something of their values and expectations. In the president's words: "I was told in no uncertain terms by the people who hired me that they wanted strong leadership, and that they wanted the university to move to another plane" (Gioia & Chittipeddi, 1991: 439). Thus, the unending circularity of the cultural dynamics model provides the stimulus to consider the cultural history of the situation. In this case, the model suggests that the hiring of the new president was a proactive realization that led to importing an artifact of another culture (the president) with the potential to be symbolized and interpreted in an influential way within the university.

In proposing the cultural dynamics perspective, I advocate a balance of interest in all of the cultural elements and the processes that link them, thus pushing for more complete and complex cultural analyses. In the case of Gioia and Chittipeddi's study, this meant complementing their rich description with attention to artifacts and to realization and symbolization processes. This attention brought additional aspects of the case into view and recognized more complexity in the data than was indicated by the strategy formulation framework. In the case of Schein's example, the cultural dynamics model extended the developmental view of change by acknowledging the fluctuations and indeterminacies that underlie both stability and change in organizational cultures. The analyses illustrate the value of the new perspective and suggest that there are data to support the cultural dynamics model. The Gioia and Chittipeddi demonstration also indicates the need for studies that consider bottom-up as well as top-down points of view. These illustrations are given to demonstrate the logic of the cultural dynamics model and to encourage other readings using this perspective.

DISCUSSION AND IMPLICATIONS

Some readers have criticized the cultural dynamics perspective on the grounds that the level of analysis is ambiguous. These readers want to know whether the processes described by the model occur within individuals or among them and whether the processes are cognitive or social in nature. In large measure, it is through culture that a person constructs the sense of individual and organizational identity and creates images that are taken for the self and the organization. Within the cultural dynamics framework I assume that individuals cannot be conceptualized apart from their cultures and that cognition cannot be separated from social processes. In other words, the processes of cultural dynamics are simultaneously cognitive and social (as well as perceptual, emotional, and in some cases aesthetic), and individuals and their interrelationships are not usefully distinguished within this frame (see also Berger & Luckmann, 1966, on the notion of intersubjectivity). Therefore, cultural dynamics cannot be described in the either/or terms presented by such questions.

In order to see these and other implications of the model more clearly, the following discussion explains cultural dynamics as a contribution to organization theory. First, the theoretical domain of the model and its implications for bridging (Gioia & Pitre, 1990) objectivist and subjectivist perspectives are presented. In this context, the distinction between activity and reflexivity that separates top—and bottom-half processes is discussed. This distinction will be combined with the distinction between objective and subjective theoretical orientations to form a two-by-two matrix for analyzing the theoretical domain of cultural dynamics. Finally, some concluding thoughts about the cultural dynamics model and its implications for further development of organizational culture theory are offered.

The Theoretical Domain of Cultural Dynamics

Cultural dynamics brings together in one model ideas that have traditionally been kept separate in organization theory. For instance, whereas Burrell and Morgan (1979) drew barriers between functional and symbolic theories, cultural dynamics presents opportunities to view and explain culture from both perspectives. I do not, however, attempt to integrate these separate theoretical domains; instead I connect, bridge, and associate them. The cultural dynamics model may be thought of as a collage of some of the most compelling ideas about organizational culture found in the literature.

As in a collage, I have placed bits of other works together in a new (frame) work in which arrangement forms a basis for new insight. I do not deny that objectivist and subjectivist theories rest on incommensurable assumptions (Gioia & Pitre, 1990). Instead, I accept both as theoretical views of reality, acknowledge their differences, juxtapose their contributions, and examine and draw implications from the result. Thus, cultural dynamics incorporates both objectivist (some things about culture can be reasonably discussed as if they exist independent of human observation) and subjectivist perspectives (some aspects of culture cannot be objectified and are better theorized in terms of subjective experience).

The matter of the objectivity or subjectivity of organizational culture itself is undecidable. This is because researchers work within a conceptual system that constructs the phenomena to which they then assume the conceptual system refers. Although theorists cannot escape this difficulty, it is still possible to regard the objective/subjective dialectic as a useful theoretical distinction. Its usefulness lies in the existence of different appreciations of organizational reality. For example, theories of environmental determinacy such as resource dependency theory (Pfeffer & Salancik, 1978) are evidence of objectivist appreciations of organizational reality, whereas social constructionist theories such as enactment theory (Weick, 1979) evidence subjectivist appreciations. Thus, even though researchers cannot know if there are different realities associated with the objective perspective and subjective experience, they can feel confident that these are two distinct ways of theorizing about reality (Burrell & Morgan, 1979; Gioia & Pitre, 1990). Furthermore, it has been the thesis of this article that both of these ways of theorizing have made significant contributions to the development of organizational culture theory, and it is the stated ambition of the cultural dynamics approach to explicitly acknowledge both views.

An implication of the distinction between objective and subjective theorizing is that the concepts of values and symbols lie on the border (Alvesson & Berg, 1992, also make this observation). That is, these concepts have the capacity to represent the qualities and characteristics of both domains, and, thus, values and symbols offer transformation/ translation points between these "two worlds." This idea further implies that the concepts of values and symbols provide the means by which subjectivist and objectivist orientations can be made to communicate and coexist. Symbols and values invoke objectivist theorizing because of their relationship to artifacts experienced as external, and they invoke subjective theorizing by referring to basic assumptions that have no direct external referent. The cultural dynamics perspective attempts to move the discussion beyond the limiting assumptions of these two theoretical orientations by suggesting that culture can be represented equally well (or equally poorly) within either perspective, but that bridging them creates a more satisfying picture than either offers on its own.

In terms of the cultural dynamics model, I place cultural assumptions in the regions of experience that have been most adequately theorized from the subjectivist position (see Figure 3). Artifacts, conceived as externalized aspects of culture, have been better theorized using the objectivist perspective. The processes constituting assumptions and artifacts are also explained with reference to these different theoretical domains. Assumptions, constituted via prospective interpretation and retroactive manifestation, are theoretically aligned with a subjectivist orientation. Artifacts, constituted by proactive realization and retrospective symbolization, are theoretically aligned with an objectivist orientation.

This argument raises the additional question of why researchers should distinguish either between prospective interpretation and retroactive manifestation processes or between proactive realization and retrospective symbolization. I argue that theorizing about interpretation and symbolization is built around a discourse of reflexivity, whereas theorizing about manifestation and realization is couched in the discourse of activity. Values and symbols can be similarly distinguished; values are associated with an action frame, and symbols generally invoke reflexive discourse. Both of these discourses add depth to the understanding of organizational culture, and I offer the cultural dynamics model, which makes use of this distinction, as evidence of this claim.

323

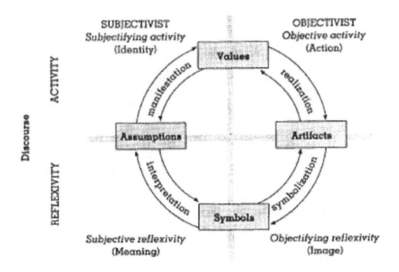

FIGURE 3
The Domain of Cultural Dynamics Showing Objectivist and Subjectivist Theoretical Orientations Subdivided by the Discourses of Activity and Reflexivity

To summarize these ideas, Figure 3 shows the domain of the cultural dynamics model segmented into objectivist and subjectivist theoretical orientations, subdivided by discourses of activity and reflexivity. As the figure suggests, I believe that prospective interpretation is a form of subjective reflexivity, whereas retroactive manifestation is a kind of subjectifying activity, in other words, activity that creates identity (i.e., a sense of self and organization as coherent entities). Thus, cultural dynamics complements the more well-known cultural processes of interpretation through an appreciation for retroactive manifestation that occurs via the subjectifying aspects of identity formation, cultural self-maintenance, and adjustment. Similarly, the more well-known process of proactive realization of artifacts via objective action is complemented by an appreciation for retrospective symbolization processes that objectify reflexive understanding by associating artifacts with the images formed by projecting symbolic content onto them and taking this projected content for reality.

324

In this way, the cultural dynamics model offers a definition of culture as constituted by continuous cycles of action and meaning-making shadowed by cycles of image and identity formation. This model introduces a more dynamic sense of culture than has heretofore been considered, and it helps to explain my previous refusal to distinguish individuals from their cultures. Further development of the model to more adequately address and incorporate the concepts of image and identity is needed.

The Dynamism of Cultural Dynamics

Although the development of the cultural dynamics model pushes organizational culture theory into new territory, especially with respect to achieving a new level of complexity, I am not satisfied that a truly dynamic view of culture has yet been offered. This is because the separate treatments by which the processes of culture were developed ultimately interfere with the holistic appreciation of the dynamism of the total model. For a more truly dynamic view, consider the relationships among manifestation, realization, symbolization, and interpretation processes.

Dynamism can be approximated if the connections among the processes of the cultural dynamics model are made focal. Thus, Figure 2 is seen, not as four separate processes, each with forward and backward modes of operation, but as two wheels of interconnected processes, one moving forward and the other backward with reference to the standard concept of time. Picture the forward (pro) processes forming one wheel within which a second wheel of backward (retro) processes turns. A truly dynamic appreciation of culture is found in the counteraction of the two wheels.

This image of culture suggests some directions for future theory building using the cultural dynamics approach. I believe that the forward turning wheel constructs the physical world insofar as culture rather than nature influences realization. I conceptualize this wheel in terms of its creative potential as a producer of human geographies, including the artifact level of organizational cultures. Similarly, I suggest that retrospective/retroactive processes produce the historical context from which organizational members draw the meaning that imbues their lives and their geographies with significance. Furthermore, the wheels are not really separate. Their counteraction implies that each process refers to the others; in effect, they form one wheel that simultaneously spins both ways.

To build organizational culture theory in the direction of this more dynamic image will require another dramatic shift similar in magnitude to the shift from elements (assumptions, values, artifacts, symbols) to cultural processes (manifestation, realization, symbolization, interpretation) proposed in this article. Based on the implications discussed previously, I suggest that the new goal be an explanation of organizational culture as the dynamic construction and reconstruction of cultural geography and history as contexts for taking action, making meaning, constructing images, and forming identities (Figure 3). At present, cultural dynamics only points in this direction.

CONCLUSION

Schein's (1985) model of organizational culture as assumptions, values, and artifacts leaves gaps regarding the appreciation of organizational culture as symbols and processes. This article has attempted to fill in these gaps and to suggest a dynamic model of this important organizational phenomenon. The proposed cultural dynamics perspective reformulates Schein's model by making a place for symbols alongside assumptions, values, and artifacts; by articulating the arrows linking assumptions, values, and artifacts; and by defining these links as processes having both forward (proactive/prospective) and backward (retrospective/retroactive) temporal modes of operation. It was further suggested that the proactive/retroactive modes represent the role of activity in culture, whereas the prospective and retrospective modes represent the possibility of reflexivity and cultural consciousness.

Because it represents culture as a wheel, the cultural dynamics model can be entered at any point on Figure 2—at least in principle. In practice, the point of entry for a particular analysis will be determined by the research question and the method of study. Nonetheless, the cultural dynamics model is intended for use in its entirety, and an analytical framework for doing this was offered via two demonstrations. The framework and suggested methods were proposed as starting points for researchers wishing to pioneer the cultural dynamics approach using empirical studies. Future directions were also suggested for theorists wishing to contribute to further theoretical development of the model.

Note: I want to thank Rudy Alvarez, Finn Borum, Neil Brady, Soren Christensen, Pasquale Gagliardi, Jai Ghorpade, Denny Gioia, Dick Goodman, Michael Owen Jones, Kristian Kreiner, Scott Lever, Joanne Martin, Jan Molin, Jesper Standgaard Pedersen, Steen Scheuer, Majken Schultz, Ann Westenholz, Dvora Yanow, and members of the UCLA CIBER Cross-Cultural Colloquium for their encouragement, help, and insightful comments. I also want to acknowledge Ed Schein for the initial inspiration of this work and for his kind words of encouragement along the way. An earlier version of this paper was presented at the annual meeting of the Academy of Management, Miami, Florida, 1991.

References

Alvesson, M. 1987. Organizations, culture, and ideology. *International Studies of Management and Organization.* 13(3):4-18.

Alvesson, M., & Berg, P. 0.1992. *Corporate culture and organizational symbolism.* Berlin: Walter de Gruyter.

Arora, S. L.1988. No tickee, no shirtee: Proverbial speech and leadership in academe. In M. 0. Jones, M. D. Moore, & R. C. Snyder (Eds.), *Inside organizations: Understanding the human dimension:* 179-189. Newbury Park, CA: Sage.

Barley, S. R.1983. Semiotics and the study of occupational and organizational cultures. *Administrative Science Quarterly.* 28: 393-413.

Barley, S. R. 1986. Technology as an association for structuring: Evidence from observations of CT scanners and the social order of radiology departments. *Administrative Science Quarterly,* 31: 78-108.

Barthes, R.1972. *Mythologies* (A. Lavers, Trans.). New York: Hill & Wang.

Berg, P. 0.1985. Organizational change as a symbolic transformation process. In P. Frost, L. Moore, M. Louis, C. Lundberg, & J. Martin (Eds.), *Organizational culture:* 281-299. Beverly Hills, CA: Sage.

Berger, P. L., & Luckmann, T. 1966. *The social construction of reality: A treatise in the sociology of knowledge.* Garden City, NY: Doubleday.

Bjorkegren, D. 1991. *Postmodernism, its enemies* and defenders. Paper presented at the 8th International SCOS Conference (The Valhalla Conference), Copenhagen, Denmark.

Borum, F., & Pedersen, J. S. 1990. Understanding the IT people, the subcultures, and the implications for management of technology. In F. Borum, A. L. Friedman, M. Monsted, J. S. Pederson, & M. Risberg (Eds.), *Social dynamics of the IT field: The case of Denmark:* 105-120. Berlin: Walter de Gruyter.

Botti, H., & Pipan, T. 1991. *Civil servant, service idea?* Paper presented to the 8th International COS Conference (The Valhalla Conference), Copenhagen, Denmark.

Broms, H., & Gahmberg, H. 1983. Communication to self in organizations and cultures. *Administrative Science Quarterly,* 28: 482-495.

Brown, R. H. 1977. *A poetic for sociology.* Chicago: University of Chicago Press.

Burrell, G., & Morgan, G. 1979. *Sociological paradigms and organizational analysis: Elements of the sociology of corporate life.* London: Heinemann.

Calas, M. B., & Smircich, L.1991. Voicing seduction to silence leadership. *Organization Studies,* 12: 567-602.

Cassirer, E.1946. *Language and myth.* New York: Harper & Row.

Chapple, E. D. 1941. Organization problems in industry. Applied Anthropology, 1(1): 2-9.

Chapple, E. D.1943. Anthropological engineering: Its use to administrators. *Applied Anthropology,* 2(2): 23-32.

Chapple, E. G., & Coon, C. S.1942. *Principles of anthropology.* New York: Holt.

Clark, B. R.1972. The organizational saga in higher education. *Administrative* Science *Quarterly, 17:*178-183.

Clifford, J., & Marcus, G. E.1986. *Writing culture: The poetics and politics of ethnography.* Berkeley: University of California Press.

Cohen, A. P. 1985. *The symbolic construction of community.* London: Tavistock Publications & Ellis Horwood Ltd.

Cook, S. D. N., & Yanow, D. In press. Culture and organizational learning. *Journal of Management Inquiry.*

Coulthard, M.1977. *An introduction to discourse analysis.* London: Longman.

Czarniawska-Joerges, B.1988. *Ideological control in nonideological organizations.* New York: Praeger.

Czarniawska-Joerges, B.1992. *Exploring complex organizations: A cultural perspective.* Newbury Park, CA: Sage.

Czarniawska-Joerges, B., & Joerges, B. 1990. Organizational change as materialization of ideas. *The study of power and democracy in Sweden* (Report No. 37, English Series). Stockholm: Stockholm School of Economics, The Economic Research Institute.

Dalton, M. 1959. *Men who manage.* New York: Wiley.

Dandridge, T. C., Mitroff, I., & Joyce, W. F. 1980. Organizational symbolism: A topic to expand organizational analysis. *Academy of Management Review,* 5: 77-82.

Deal, T. E. & Kennedy, A. A. 1982. *Corporate cultures: The rites and rituals of corporate life.* Reading, MA: Addison-Wesley.

Donnellon, A., Gray, B., & Bougon, M. G. 1986. Communication, meaning, and organized action. *Administrative Science Quarterly,* 31: 43-55.

Eisenberg, E. M., & Riley, P. 1988. Organizational symbols and sense-making. In G. M. Goldhaber & G. A. Barnett (Eds.), *Handbook of organizational* communication: 131-150. Norwood, NJ: Ablex.

Feldman, M. 1991. The meanings of ambiguity: Learning from stories and metaphors. In P. Frost, L. Moore, M. Louis, C. Lundberg, & J. Martin (Eds.), *Reframing organizational culture:* 145-156. Newbury Park, CA: Sage.

Finney, M., & Mitroff, I.1986. Strategic planning failures: The organization as its own worst enemy. In H. P. Sims (Ed.), *The thinking organization:* 317-335. San Francisco: Jossey-Bass.

Fiol, M. C. 1991. Seeing the empty spaces: Towards a more complex understanding of the meaning of power in organizations. *Organization Studies.* 12: 547-566.

Frost, P., Moore, L., Louis, M., Lundberg, C., & Martin, J. (Eds.). 1985. *Organizational culture.* Beverly Hills, CA: Sage.

Frost, P., Moore, L., Louis, M., Lundberg, C., & Martin, J. (Eds.).1991. *Reframing organizational culture.* Newbury Park, CA: Sage.

Gagliardi, P. (Ed.).1990. *Symbols and artifacts: Views of the corporate landscape.* Berlin: Walter de Gruyter.

Geertz, C. 1988. *Works and lives: The anthropologist as author.* Stanford, CA: Stanford University Press.

Giddens, A. 1979. *Central problems in social theory.* Berkeley: University of California Press.

Gioia, D. A. 1986. Symbols, scripts, and sensemaking. In H. P. Sims (Ed.), *The thinking organization:* 49-74. San Francisco: Jossey-Bass.

Gioia, D. A.1992. Pinto fires and personal ethics: A script analysis of missed opportunities. *Journal* of *Business Ethics, 11:* 43-53.

Gioia, D. A., & Chittipeddi, K.1991. Sensemaking and sensegiving in strategic change initiation. *Strategic Management Journal.* 12: 433-448.

Gioia, D. A., & Pitre, E.1990. Multiparadigm perspectives on theory building. Academy of *Management Review,* 15: 584-602.

Gioia, D. A., Thomas, J. B., Clark, S. M., & Chittipeddi, K. In press. Symbolism and strategic change in academia: The dynamics of sensemaking and influence. *Organization Science.*

Gregory, K. 1983. Native view paradigms: Multiple cultures and culture conflicts in organizations. *Administrative Science Quarterly.* 28: 359-376.

Hatch, M. J. In press. Ironic humor and the social construction of contradiction in a management team. *Academy of Management. Best Paper Proceedings.*

Hatch, M. J., & Ehrlich, S. B. In press. Where there is smoke: Spontaneous humor as an indicator of paradox and ambiguity in organizations. *Organization Studies.*

Herskovits, M. J. 1948. *Man and his works: The science of cultural anthropology.* New York: Knopf.

Honigmann, J. J. 1967. *Personality in culture.* New York: Harper & Row.

Jacques, E. 1951. *The changing culture of a factory.* London: Tavistock Institute.

Jeffcutt, P. 1991. *Styles of representation in organizational analysis: Heroism, happy endings and the carnivalesque in the organizational symbolism literature.* Paper presented at the 8th International SCOS Conference (The Valhalla Conference), Copenhagen, Denmark.

Jones, M. 0.1988. *How does folklore fit in?* Paper presented at the annual meeting of the Academy of Management, Anaheim, CA.

Jones, M. 0.1991. What if stories don't tally with the culture? *Journal of Organizational Change Management,* 4(3): 27-34.

Jones, M. 0, Moore, M. D., & Snyder, R. C.1988. *Inside organizations: Understanding the human dimension.* Newbury Park, CA: Sage.

Kilmann, R. H., Saxton, M. J., Serpa, R., & Associates (Eds.).1985. *Gaining control of the corporate culture.* San Francisco: Jossey-Bass.

Kniffen, F. B. 1976. American cultural geography and folklife. In D. Yoder (Ed.), *American folklife:* 51-70. Austin: University of Texas Press.

Kreiner, K. 1989. Culture and meaning: Making sense of conflicting realities in the workplace. *International Studies of Management and Organization,* 19(3): 64-81.

Kroeber, A. L.1944. *Configurations of culture growth.* Berkeley: University of California Press.

Kunda, G. 1992. *Engineering culture: Control and commitment in a high-tech corporation.* Philadelphia: Temple University Press.

Linstead, S. A. 1993. From postmodern anthropology to deconstructive ethnography. *Human Relations,* 46(1): 97-119.

Louis, M. R. 1983. Organizations as culture bearing milieux. In L. R. Pondy, P. J. Frost, G. Morgan, & T. C. Dandridge (Eds.), *Organizational symbolism:* 39-54. Greenwich, CT: JAI Press.

Malinowski, B.1945. *The dynamics of cultural change.* New Haven, CT: Yale University Press.

Martin, J.1990. Deconstructing organizational taboos: The suppression of gender conflict in organizations. *Organization* Science, 1: 339-359.

Martin, J.1992. *Cultures in organizations: Three perspectives.* New York: Oxford University Press.

Martin, J., Feldman, M. S., Hatch, M. J., & Sitkin, S. B. 1983. The uniqueness paradox in organizational stories. *Administrative Science Quarterly,* 28: 438-453.

Martin, J., & Siehl, C. 1983. Organizational culture and counterculture: An uneasy symbiosis. *Organizational Dynamics,* 12(2): 52-64.

Messenger, B.1978. *Picking* up *the linen threads: A study in industrial folklore.* Austin: University of Texas Press.

Meyerson, D. 1991a. "Normal" ambiguity? In P. Frost, L. Moore, M. Louis, C. Lundberg, & J. Martin (Eds.), *Reframing organizational culture:* 31-144. Newbury Park, CA: Sage.

Meyerson, D. 1991b. Acknowledging and uncovering ambiguities in cultures. In P. Frost, L. Moore, M. Louis, C. Lundberg, & J. Martin (Eds.), *Reframing organizational culture:* 254-270. Newbury Park, CA: Sage.

Meyerson, D., & Martin, J.1987. Cultural change: An integration of three different views. *Journal of Management Studies,* 24: 623-647.

Morgan, G. 1986. *Images of organization.* Beverly Hills, CA: Sage.

Morgan, G., Frost, P. J., & Pondy, L. R. 1983. Organizational symbolism. In L. R. Pondy, P. J. Frost, G. Morgan, & T. C. Dandridge (Eds.), *Organizational symbolism:* 3-35. Greenwich, CT: JAI Press.

Ortner, S. B. 1973. On key symbols. *American Anthropologist,* 75: 1338-1346.

Ott, J. S. 1989. *The organizational culture perspective.* Pacific Grove, CA: Brooks/Cole.

Ouchi, W. G. 1981. *Theory Z: How American business can meet the Japanese challenge.* New York: Avon.

Pascale, R. T., & Athos, A. G. 1981. *The art of Japanese management: Applications for American executives.* New York: Warner Books.

Pedersen, J. S. 1991. Continuity *and change: Central perspectives on organizational change and transformation in information technology firms.* (Ph.D. Series 2.91 Samfundslitteratur). Copenhagen, Denmark: Copenhagen Business School, Institute of Organization and Industrial Sociology.

Pedersen, J. S., & Sorensen, J. S.1989. *Organizational culture in theory and practice.* Alder-shot, England: Avebury & Gower.

Peters, T. J., & Waterman, R. H., Jr.1982. *In search of excellence: Lessons from America's best-run companies.* New York: Harper & Row.

Pettigrew, A.1973. *The politics of organizational decision-making.* London: Tavistock.

Pettigrew, A.1979. On studying organizational cultures. *Administrative Science Quarterly.* 24:570-581.

Pfeffer, J., & Salancik, G.1978. *The external control of organizations.*

Phillips, M. E.1990. *Industry as a cultural grouping.* Unpublished doctoral dissertation, University of California, Los Angeles.

Pondy, L. R., Frost, P. J., Morgan, G., & Dandridge, T. C. (Eds.).1983. *Organizational symbolism.* Greenwich, CT: JAI Press.

Putnam, L. L.1983. The interpretative perspective: An alternative to functionalism. In L. L. Putnam & M. E. Pacanowsky (Eds.), *Communication and organizations:* 31-54. Newbury Park, CA: Sage.

Redfield, R.1941. *The folk culture of the Yucatan.* Chicago: University of Chicago Press.

Ricoeur, P.1976. *Interpretation theory: Discourse and the surplus of meaning.* Fort Worth: Texas Christian University Press.

Riley, P.1983. A structurationist account of political cultures. *Administrative* Science *Quarterly,* 28: 414-437.

Rosen, M. 1985. Breakfast at Spiro's: Dramaturgy and dominance. *Journal of Management.*11: 31-48.

Roy, D.1952. Quota restriction and gold bricking in a machine shop. *American Journal of Sociology.* 57: 427-442.

Roy. D.1954. Efficiency in the *fix:* Informal intergroup relations in a piece-work machine shop, *American Journal of Sociology,* 60: 255-266.

Roy, D.1960. "Banana Time": Job satisfaction and informal interaction. *Human Organization,* 18(2): 158-168.

Sapir, E.1934. The emergence of the concept of personality in a study of cultures. *Journal of Social Psychology.* 5: 408-415.

Sathe, V. J.1985. *Culture and related* corporate *realities.* Homewood, IL: Irwin.

Schein, E. H.1981. Does Japanese management style have a message for American managers? *Sloan Management Review,* 23(1): 55-68.

Schein, E. H. 1983. The role of the founder in creating organizational culture. *Organizational Dynamics,* 12(1): 13-28.

Schein, E. H.1984. Coming to a new awareness of organizational culture. *Sloan Management Review.* 25(2): 3-16.

Schein, E. H.1985. *Organizational culture and leadership.* San Francisco: Jossey-Bass.

Schein, E. H.1987. *The clinical perspective in fieldwork.* Newbury Park, CA: Sage.

Schein, E. H. 1991. What is culture? In P. Frost, L. Moore, M. Louis, C. Lundberg, & J. Martin (Eds.), *Reframing organizational culture:* 243-253. Newbury Park, CA: Sage.

Schultz, M. In press. *Doing cultural analysis in organizations: Diagnosis and understanding.* Copenhagen, Denmark: Copenhagen Business Press.

Schutz, A.1970. On *phenomenology and social relations: Selected writing.* Chicago: University of Chicago Press.

Smircich, L.1983. Concepts of culture and organizational analysis. *Administrative* Science Quarterly, 28: 339-358.

Smircich, L., & Morgan, G.1983. Leadership: The management of meaning. *Journal of Applied Behavioral Science,* 18: 257-273.

Spradley, J. P.1979. *The ethnographic interview.* New York: Holt, Rinehart & Winston.

Strati, A.1990. Aesthetics and organizational skill. In B. A. Turner (Ed.), *Organizational symbolism:* 208-222. Berlin: Walter de Gruyter.

Strati, A.1992. Aesthetic understanding of organizational life. *Academy of Management Review,* 17: 568-581.

Tompkins, P. K. 1987. Translating organizational theory: Symbolism over substance. In F. M. Jablin, L. L. Putnam, K. H. Roberts, & L. W. Porter (Eds.), *Handbook of organizational communication: An interdisciplinary perspective:* 70-96. Beverly Hills, CA: Sage.

Trice, H. M., Belasco, J., & Alutto, J. A. 1969. The role of ceremonials in organizational behavior. *Industrial and Labor Relations Review,* 23(October): 40-51.

Turner, B. A.1973. *Exploring the industrial subculture.* London: Macmillan.

Turner, B. A.1986. Sociological aspects of organizational symbolism. *Organizational Studies,* 7: 101-115.

Turner, B. A. (Ed.).1990. *Organizational symbolism.* Berlin: Walter de Gruyter.

Tyler, E. B.1958/1871. *Primitive culture.* New York: Harper & Row.

Van Maanen, J.1988. *Tales of the field: On writing ethnography.* Chicago: University of Chicago Press.

Van Maanen, J. 1991. The smile factory: Work at Disneyland. In P. Frost, L. Moore, M. Louis, C. Lundberg, & J. Martin (Eds.), *Reframing organizational culture:* 58-76. Newbury Park, CA: Sage.

Van Maanen, J., & Barley, S. R. 1985. Cultural organization: Fragments of a theory. In P. Frost, L. Moore, M. Louis, C. Lundberg, & J. Martin (Eds.), *Organizational culture:* 31-54. Beverley Hills, CA: Sage.

Weick, K. E.1979. *The social psychology of organizing* (2nd ed.). Reading, MA: Addison-Wesley.

Weick, K. E. 1987. Substitutes for strategy. In D. J. Teece (Ed.), *The competitive challenge: Strategies for industrial innovation and renewal:* 221-233. Cambridge, MA: Ballinger.

Whyte, W. F. 1948. *Human relations in the restaurant industry.* New York: McGraw-Hill.

Whyte, W. F. 1951. *Pattern for industrial peace.* New York: Harper & Brothers. Whyte, W. F. 1961. *Men at work.* Homewood, IL: Dorsey Press.

Wilkins, A. 1978. *Organizational stories as an expression of management philosophy: Implications for social control in organizations.* Unpublished doctoral dissertation, Stanford University.

Williams, R. 1983. *Keywords: A vocabulary of culture and society.* London: Flamingo.

Wilson, T. P. 1987. Sociology and the mathematical method. In A. Giddens & J. Turner (Eds.), *Social theory today:* 383-404. Stanford CA: Stanford University Press.

Witkin, R. W. 1990. The aesthetic imperative of a rational-technical machinery: A study in organizational control through the design of artifacts. In P. Gagliardi (Ed.), *Symbols and artifacts: Views of the corporate landscape:* 325-338. Berlin: Walter de Gruyter.

Witkin, R. W., & Poupart, R. 1985. Running a commentary on imaginatively re-lived events: A method for obtaining qualitatively rich data. In A. Strati (Ed.), *The symbolics of skill.* Trento, Italy: University of Trento, Dipartimento di Politica Sociale.

Young, E. 1989. On the naming of the rose: Interest and multiple meanings as elements of organizational culture. *Organization Studies,* 10: 187-206.

Mary Jo Hatch received her Ph.D. in Organizational Behavior from Stanford University. She is an associate professor in the Department of Management at the College of Business Administration, San Diego State University, and was a visiting associate professor at the Copenhagen Business School in Denmark, when this paper was written. Her current research examines narrative and rhetoric in organization theory and explores links among organizational humor, paradox, and contradiction.

Chapter 9

Prologue

Sidney G. Winter

Professor Emeritus of Management and Technological Change
University of Pennsylvania, The Wharton School.

Capabilities: Structure, Agency, and Evolution

Michael G. Jacobides and Sidney G. Winter

Prologue:

Sidney G. Winter

I have greatly enjoyed the sessions that I have had with the students of the Executive Leadership Program (ELP), which have taken place over a span of time that amounts to at least half of the life of the program. Several factors have contributed to the enjoyment. First, the students are smart, interested, and lively. They also have significant work experience and are quite diverse both in the character of that experience and otherwise. Then there is the fact that, at least on my understanding, an invitation to teach for a day in the George Washington University ELP anticipates and legitimizes a sustained focus on "the way I see it . . . ." Of course, the focus is "sustained" only within the confines of part of a single day—but that chunk of time is still substantial relative to a typical lecture or class session. It is enough time to cover the fundamentals of a theoretical framework and then to sketch, at least, some of its applications. Such an opportunity to lay out the case for a theoretical approach is particularly appealing to a scholar who, like me, is at odds on key questions with mainstream theoretical thinking in the discipline in which he was trained.

There are some important interactions among the considerations just evoked, and these operate to enhance the appeal of the opportunity even more. Since the individuals in the ELP audience elected to become doctoral students, a reasonable degree of receptivity to social science theorizing can be presumed (and in my experience is emphatically confirmed). These are not people whose limited horizons are suggested by the phrase, "It's just a theory." Yet, relative to many students who have taken a shorter path to doctoral studies, they have greater concern with the real-world relevance of the theoretical ideas they encounter. As a group they are partially immunized against theoretical indoctrination by virtue of the wealth and diversity of their experience; interest in theory is thus qualified by informed skepticism. From my point of view, this all added up to a significant opportunity—an opportunity to spread the word about evolutionary economics to an audience that is potentially receptive and also potentially influential.

The paper that follows evokes many of the same themes that I have addressed with ELP students over the years. It illustrates the evolutionary approach to economics in its application to recently controversial areas of both theory and policy. My coauthor is Professor Michael G. Jacobides of the London Business School, who did his dissertation under my supervision at The Wharton School. I trust it is not inappropriate to nominate a paper with this sort of coauthorship for this volume; by doing so I mean to testify to the importance and shared rewards of doctoral education, for both professors and students.

The paper's discussion of the financial crisis of 2008 (section 5) draws on Michael's dissertation research on the U.S. mortgage banking industry; his prize-winning article on that subject is Jacobides (2005) in the references of the paper that follows. The evolutionary transformation of mortgage banking illustrates broader issues of the determination of vertical structure, which are intensively reviewed in section 3 of the paper.[16] This discussion also draws on Michael's research and on our prior joint work on the question, published as Jacobides and Winter (2005).

The paper provides quite a wealth of examples of theoretical and empirical issues that are seen quite differently by economists from two theoretical camps, evolutionary and mainstream. Each of these issues could serve as the main focus for a substantial discussion of contrasts between evolutionary economics and mainstream economic thinking today. This aspect—the element of incitement to "paradigm war" with

---

[16] The term "vertical structure" refers to the organizational aspect of the division of labor among activities in a value chain, i.e., the sequence of activities leading to a product, such as raw material production, component manufacturing, assembly, and distribution. The phrases "make or buy" and "boundaries of the firm" point to similar territory from different angles.

the economics mainstream—is mostly hidden beneath the surface of the paper, though it is certainly visible in the discussion of rational choice theorizing in sections 4.1 and 6.2. Since the important distinction between "rational choice" and a realistic view of "agency" is explicitly addressed in the paper, I leave it aside here.

Among other issues addressed that are among the battlegrounds of the larger war, I mention (i) the contrast between the "organizational capabilities" view of production and the "recipe theory" view expressed in mainstream neoclassical "production theory"; (ii) the contrast between the "heterogeneous firms" view, which sees differences among firms attempting similar things as central to the evolutionary process, and the neoclassical "representative firm" view, which sees such differences as a theoretical nuisance, or, at best, an empirical puzzle; and (iii) the contrast between emphasis on the time-embeddedness of economic action, manifested in the influence that ongoing technological, organizational, and institutional change has on individual actors, vs. the apparent neoclassical ambition to locate timeless, context-free economic truths that are akin to those of Newtonian physics, with self-interested incentives perhaps playing the role of "force."

My experience tells me that the ELP doctoral students are open to the idea that these sorts of theoretical issues are actually quite important in understanding how the world works, and understanding those workings is a key step toward making it work better.

Capabilities: Structure, Agency, and Evolution[17]

Michael G. Jacobides and Sidney G. Winter

Abstract. This paper examines conceptual issues and reviews empirical results bearing on the relationship between research approaches emphasizing organizational capabilities and those based in transaction cost economics (TCE)—or in organizational economics more generally. Following a review of conceptual fundamentals—what capability is and why organizations differ in capability—it assesses recent progress toward an integration of the capabilities and transaction cost approaches, primarily in the context of the analysis of vertical structure and related phenomena. This review suggests that progress has been substantial and that the key elements of a promising dynamic synthesis have been identified. The paper then considers issues that call for attention if further progress is to be achieved. The first of these is the role of agency, which must be seen in expansive terms (relative to standard economic rationality) if its evolutionary significance is to be fully appreciated. The second is the role of structure, or more specifically, industry architecture, which affects capability development by way of its effect on the feedback that firms receive. After drawing on the recent financial crisis for an illustration of these ideas, this paper considers the rise of interest in business models as a useful field of application, and it concludes with a discussion of the role of organizational economics (beyond TCE). We argue that, whatever the theoretical perspective at the level of the firm, analyses must reach beyond that level to grasp the important causal forces affecting capability development, firm boundaries, and structural features more generally.

Key words: organizational economics; behavioral economics; economics; organization; transaction costs; firm heterogeneity; rational choice; vertical integration; evolution; industry architecture

---

[17] Originally Published as: Jacobides, M.G. and S.G. Winter (2012). "Capabilities: Structure, agency, and evolution." Organization Science 23(5): 1365-1381.

1. Capabilities and Economics: From Trade to Integration?

One of the most important developments in the field of management during the last 15 years has been the increased attention paid to the concept of organizational capability—denoting the firm-specific and time—and space-contingent ability to perform a particular productive activity. During the 1990s, the importance of the differences between firms was rearticulated and reemphasized (Nelson 1991). Two decades later we have come to take the heterogeneity of organizations and their capabilities as given—at least within the field of management (Helfat 2003), as opposed to economics. As our understanding of heterogeneity, firm-specific capabilities, and the evolution of the latter grew, links emerged with work in organizational and, in particular, institutional economics. The last decade in particular has seen a substantial growth in research that develops and refines work in transaction cost economics (TCE), using it to explain empirically important phenomena such a cycles of integration and disintegration, the strategic choice of some firms to adopt permeable boundaries, and the struggles to define the boundaries and institutional setup of sectors—from agriculture to movies and financial services. Research has also sharpened our view of the process through which capabilities are shaped and developed.

We have moved well beyond the view that TCE and capability theories are rivals for the same explanatory ground. Not only has the complementarity of the two approaches been recognized and substantiated empirically, but now it also appears that the key elements of a dynamic synthesis are in hand. In this synthesis, capabilities and structures (firm boundaries, the division of labor) coevolve according to an intelligible economic logic. Yet it is a logic that may not be completely understandable within the framework of standard economic theory.

The quest for "integration" proposed in the call for this special issue might suggest on the one hand a demand to build bridges and resolve conceptual discords, or on the other, the need to address the phenomena more effectively and comprehensively. Although the former cause is not unworthy, it is the latter we espouse. Accordingly, we suggest that proposals for integration should be explicated and defended in terms of how they will improve or extend the reach of causal explanation.

The term "organizational economics" embraces at least two quite disparate lines of inquiry: TCE in the Coase-Williamson tradition and the various applications of "rational-actor" theorizing at the organizational level. Because the former is much more fully developed in terms of complementary empirical work, and its relationship to the capabilities approach is much better defined, TCE is our primary focus here. However, we do discuss the problems and opportunities of the rational-actor approach later in the paper.

This paper offers both a selective literature review/evaluation and theory development, illustrated by examples. We start with an overview of the elementary building blocks: the empirics and concepts of capabilities—the origins of heterogeneity, the evolution of capabilities, and the nature of the comparative institutional approach in TCE—and then assess progress to date in integrating the capabilities view with TCE. We then offer a framework to help understand capabilities and their context. First, we argue that the shaping role of agency must be understood to extend well beyond the theoretical confines of maximization and rationality. Our view is that economics-based analyses often misspecify and underestimate not only inertial properties but also the agency-related forces of change in an economic system. Second, we explain how structure both shapes and is further shaped by the capabilities of actors in an economic system. Our focus is on how structure determines the feedback that will drive the system's dynamics. Thus, we highlight the role of context and higher-level causal forces that cannot be understood simply by looking at the level of individual agents. Next, we provide an illustration of our conceptual framework, taking as an example the recent financial crisis. We conclude with a discussion of future research directions and assess the promise of organizational economics research, outside TCE, for our understanding of capabilities.

344

2. Capabilities, Heterogeneity, and Comparative Approach of TCE

2.1 The Notion of Capability

Although organizational capabilities have been the focus of a surge of attention in the literatures of management and organization studies over the past decade or two, the concept has a long history. In the economics literature, Richardson (1972) may have been the first to employ it in relation to the study of firm behavior, and very much in its present sense. In an essay that anticipated later work on interfirm alliances, networks and supply chains, as well as capabilities, he pointed out a key limitation of the production function construct used in standard economics: "It abstracts totally from the roles of organisation, knowledge, experience and skills, and thereby makes it the more difficult to bring these back into the theoretical foreground in the way needed to construct a theory of industrial organisation" (Richardson 1972, p. 888). He went on to label the effect of knowledge, experience, and skills with the term "capabilities," and he then developed the implications of "the fact that organizations tend to specialize in activities for which their capabilities offer some comparative advantage" (p.888).[1] Coincidentally, it was also in 1972 that Nelson and Winter gained National Science Foundation support for their research proposal, and the first published manifestation of their collaboration appeared the following year under the title "Toward an evolutionary theory of economic capabilities" (Nelson and Winter 1973).

There is a strong unifying thread in the long history of "capabilities" as a term—the emphasis on what an organization can actually do and the importance of the distinction between that issue and concepts such as "intentions," "incentives," "motivations," and variations of "having the recipe" (production function). As Richardson suggested, economics has long manifested a weak grip on the distinction between capability and these other concepts. This weakness, noted by Penrose (1959),[2] is critical in discussions relating to imitation, learning, diffusion of innovations, replication, intellectual property, and other rubrics under the broad heading of "knowledge transfer." In a way, this persistent weakness is surprising: what separates a recipe or an intention from a capability is, in a broad sense investment—and economists have done a lot of thinking about investment. Standard price theory offers the distinction between the short run and the long run, with the former (a) established by prior investments in plant and equipment and (b) powerfully shaping subsequent decisions about output level and product mix. It might seem that it is not such a long step to recognize that various investments in organizational learning are also needed for the firm to establish capabilities, and in a variety of ways, these investments further strengthen the shaping power of "short-run" circumstances.

Taking that step does, however, open the door to a lot of significant complications. To take even the conventional short run of the textbooks seriously is to recognize how profoundly the course of the economy is shaped by the hand of the past—that is, by mechanisms of path dependence. For example, the economic context of any particular time t is strongly shaped by sunk investments already in place at that time—including many that might no longer be profitable ex ante (see Sutton 1991). Of course, profitability calculations for new investments contemplated at t are also affected by the context at t; for example, an overhang of inefficient capacity in an industry may produce prices that are low enough to prompt a deferral of investment in new, efficient capacity. Thus it is hard to justify, in realistic economic terms, the argument that firms ultimately make an unconstrained "long-run" choice from a menu of options (or technologies) available to all. Present position should be presumed to drive the forward-looking calculus.

From an evolutionary perspective, the rolling determination of the future out of the past seems like an obvious fact that should be taken for granted. But that is not the style of mainstream economics, which has always been accommodating toward fully static analysis, and today, remains determinedly ahistorical. In the final section of the paper, we briefly address the implications of this for the relationship between organizational economics and capability theorizing.

2.2 Origins of Heterogeneity

Richardson's observation that capability differences underlie the division of labor among firms raises the question of why such heterogeneity exists. Although the fact of heterogeneity is both acknowledged and influential in management research, it is too early to "declare victory" with respect to causal understanding of its origins, mechanisms, and implications. And in the economic literature, some continue to see heterogeneity as a puzzle, apparently believing that ways of doing things should be identical in different firms, or at least equally effective. A departure from this presumed default case is considered to require some justification, such as the fact that the superior methods were only recently invented and are shielded from prompt imitation by secrecy or effective intellectual property protection—or, as suggested in the call for this special issue, are due to transactional conditions.

Certainly, these "exceptions" refer to causal mechanisms that are operative in the world. More fundamentally, though, one could turn the premise on its head: mechanisms that are intrinsic to the capability creation process itself are quite sufficient to explain heterogeneity; more specific reasons are not required. Thus, the popularity of the notion that heterogeneity is a puzzle is itself a puzzle. Why would anybody think that?

From the abundant evidence available at the personal level as well as in academic research, the prevalence of dispersion and diversity would seem to be the rule. Are all the drivers on the road at the same skill level? Do you often find that the worst exam paper and the best deserve the same grade? The sophisticates will complain about the absence of reference to statistical control in these simple questions. Point taken—but after we diligently control for the proverbial "everything in sight," what then is the picture? The answer, in our experience, is that convincing t-ratios are often seen, but a truly impressive R-squared with cross-sectional data is rare—so rare as to be automatically suspect, in fact. Common practices in empirical management research provide indirect evidence of substantial heterogeneity. Firm fixed effects and a lagged dependent variable on the right-hand side are commonplace specifications and often contribute the bulk of the explanatory power—but usually, the focus is on the far less potent operations of other "independent" variables. In short, there is generally a lot of variation at the micro level that is actor-specific, and that is difficult to explain statistically or to understand. Should we expect the case of organizational capabilities to be different?

In the case of capabilities, a good deal of thought theory, and modeling effort has gone into addressing the question of where the microlevel variation might be coming from. A fundamental point for capabilities (and more widely applicable too) is that when different actors confront "the same problem," their specific situations, available resources, and self-perceived competencies guide their initial steps toward solutions. In a sufficiently simple problem domain, with easy reconsideration available and a sufficiently sharp definition of "solution" agreed, divergent initial steps might not matter very much; all searchers might still arrive at the same destination. But such simple capability building probably does not deserve the name. In more complex cases, where "steps" involve costly and partially irreversible commitments, where initial steps in different directions open quite different vistas to view, where success is a matter of more or less and sooner or later, where local optima offer tempting stopping points—in such cases, initial divergences do not go away. Instead, they tend to become amplified and entrenched. They are sustained by a variety of mechanisms, both rational and behavioral. In particular, there tends to be a decline over time in objective possibilities for improvement via the transfer of methods among different units or organizations, as highly interactive systems are developed to a higher and higher state of tight coupling, with more and more carefully crafted interfaces linking formerly discrete, modular elements.

The general argument offered above is supported by contributions in several different literatures. As Nelson (1991, p. 66) noted, detailed studies of technical advances repeatedly illustrate the theme of different capabilities emerging from "differences in perception about the feasible paths," and such differences of view should certainly be expected under conditions of uncertainty. As Nelson further noted, "It is virtually inevitable that firms will choose somewhat different strategies. These, in turn, will lead to firms having different structures and different core capabilities, including their R&D capabilities" (1991, p. 69). The credibility of this logic, and the evidentiary value of the examples, has been substantially enhanced by the development of the family of models portraying the organizational quest for superior effectiveness as a search process on a "rugged landscape" (Levinthal 1997, Winter et al. 2007). These models provide much insight into how complexity, path dependence, and variety in initial conditions can generate populations of actors who find diverse answers to the same problem—with concomitant diversity in payoffs achieved within the limits that selection pressures allow. The models are of course "too simple," but considerable progress has been made toward illuminating more complex and more specifically organizational situations.

Empirical evidence on heterogeneity in skill and capability appears to be overwhelming. Virtually every study that has looked into the matter has found substantial heterogeneity, often to the bafflement of the authors, who have generally failed to explain away the variance and note that even "seemingly similar enterprises" exhibit substantial and persistent performance differentials (Gibbons et al. 2012). Substantial performance differences have also been documented within firms when comparing different plants (Chew et al. 1990). Econometric evidence on the distribution of efficiency of firms in different national contexts also confirms that there is a very substantial and nontransitory performance differential (see Bloom and Van Reenen 2010 for a summary and references to a substantial body of relevant work; see also Disney et al.

2003, Gibbons et al. 2012). Case study evidence is entirely consistent with such views of pervasive heterogeneity (Clark and Fujimoto 1991,Garvin 1988).

2.3 Imitation (and Competition) as Homogenization

Given that there is little doubt about the existence of mechanisms that promote diversity as capabilities are initially created and improved, the explanation for the puzzling attachment to the "default case" may reside in a belief that there are homogenizing forces sufficiently powerful to undo the initial diversity-evidence to the contrary notwithstanding. An important factor may be the pervasive tendency to overestimate the effectiveness of imitation as a mechanism of knowledge transfer. (Following our practice elsewhere, "imitation" here refers to a knowledge transfer situation in which the source is not actively cooperating or assisting in the transfer.) Among economists, this tendency may be partly attributable to the influence of Kenneth Arrow, who stated in a classic paper that "[h]owever, no amount of legal protection can make a thoroughly appropriable commodity of something so intangible as information" (1962, p. 615). In the strategy literature, a prominent example of this line of thinking is Porter's statement that "as rivals imitate one another's improvements strategies converge and competition becomes a series of races down identical paths that no one can win. Competition based on operational effectiveness alone is mutually destructive" (Porter 1996, p. 64).

From Arrow we received a partial truth, for there certainly is a domain of information where his eloquent statement is relevant. In particular, there is symbolically recorded information of a highly modular nature (i.e., with relatively context-free validity and value) where the language of the symbolic record is known to the imitator. A valuable reaction path for a chemical process, recorded in chemical notation, would be a strategically significant example. However, the domain of "operations" to which Porter is, according to most reports, not like

350

that at all. Rather, it is a domain fairly riddled with factors that sustain differences in the face of determined imitation efforts—tacitness, technical and social complexity, complementarities, and interactions within the full organizational system; contextual factors that may be unrecognized even by the participants; constructive motivational forces grounded in organizational culture; and local organizational jargons that can leave the untutored listener quite clueless about what is going on.

In assessing the homogenizing force of imitation, it is important to remember that its significance often depends critically on quantitative aspects of precision and comprehensiveness, as well as on the costs of achieving them. It is undoubtedly true, as Arrow and Porter suggested, that there is inevitably a great deal of leakage of information about the workings of almost any capability; in some cases the leakages support the creation of something broadly analogous to the capability that is observed. In highly competitive contexts, however, "close" is not good enough, and "perfect and complete" may require too big an investment in the imitation effort. The basic mechanisms generating heterogeneity then remain operative with respect to the details not captured—and, importantly, also where the capability creation effort is aimed at a new context rather than at producing a head-to-head competitor for the original.

Heterogeneity, expressed in differences in capabilities, provides a setting for competition and evolutionary selection. The second mechanism of heterogeneity reduction comes through the relative decline (or market exit) of those with lesser capabilities and the commensurate entry and growth of more capable players, leading to a convergence in the efficiency levels of capabilities in use, even if capabilities themselves do not converge. Yet this evolutionary process is imperfect and time-consuming: selection operates imperfectly, the signals from the environment (in terms of "what works" and "what does not") are noisy, and there is a substantial "credit assignment" problem (Denrell et al. 2004). Feedback is often not immediately forthcoming, and even when it comes, agency problems within organizations or between organizations and their shareholders mute its impact. So there are abundant theoretical grounds to expect the sorts of persistent differences in performance that the empirical evidence reveals (Bloom and Van Reenen 2010).

2.4 The Comparative Institutional Approach of TCE

Having reviewed the conceptual building blocks of capabilities and heterogeneity, we now turn to TCE, as this is the area of organizational economics that has most actively engaged with capabilities and heterogeneity to date.

TCE's primary emphasis has been on understanding comparative institutional structure and questions of vertical scope—in particular, the question of whether firms should integrate or not. In so doing, TCE has led to a healthy and vigorous debate on the relative merits and shortcomings of different governance mechanisms. In narrowing down and operationalizing its research programme, TCE—and work that emanates from it—has made some important methodological choices. First, it has focused on comparative institutional analysis, looking at the choice between competing ways to organize and coordinate economic activities—each "node" of these activities being taken as given. Second, it has focused on the microanalytics of transactions, i.e., why firms make specific governance choices at the transaction level of analysis, one transaction at a time, ceteris paribus. This reliance on "ceteris paribus" presents an important issue to which we will return. It suggests that causal explanation derives fully from transaction attributes, as opposed to either the context that shapes transactional choices and menus or the organizational factors that drive the skills and competencies of a firm as both a productive and a transactional entity.

With the establishment of heterogeneity as an important empirical fact, work in the TCE tradition has acknowledged and incorporated interfirm differences while maintaining its analytical stance. As Williamson noted in 1999 (p. 1103), "[T]he traditional TCE query 'What is the best generic mode (market, hybrid, firm) to organize X?' [should]

be replaced by the question 'How should firm A—which has pre-existing strengths and weaknesses (core competences and disabilities)—organize X?'" In a similar spirit, Madhok (2002) argued that an individual firm's choice must depend not only on the characteristics of the transactional conditions but also on its strategic objectives, the attributes of its own capabilities, and the governance context it has created. This proposal, adumbrated also in Argyres (1996), Argyres and Liebeskind (1999), and Leiblein and Miller (2003), among others, preserved the fundamental orientation toward the ceteris paribus choice, the emphasis on the microanalytic choice at the level of an individual organization, and the interest in comparative statics, even as it acknowledged the role of preexisting heterogeneity and path dependence in governance choice. Such a methodological stance, as valuable as it is in helping us understand the context for firms' calculus with respect to scope, does not address the causal structure of the system as a whole.

3. Synthesis and Dynamic Integration: Progress to Date

It is true that the literatures on capabilities and organizational economics (TCE in particular) developed in substantial isolation from each other for an extended period. At best, capabilities-based arguments were seen as possibly contributing in an additive fashion to those of institutional economists. Yet change has been in the works for more than a decade. Indeed, we remarked on this positive development in an earlier paper (Jacobides and Winter 2005) and sought to extend that progress further by proposing "a theoretical framework that explains how capabilities co-evolve with transaction costs to set the menu of choices that firms face in an industry" (2005, p. 396). A number of more recent contributions have further explored the dynamic aspects of the interactions between capabilities and transactional considerations, and in that sense, they have approached those interactions in a manner broadly consistent with our "coevolutionary" framework. Here, we highlight the key elements of the framework before turning to a review of some of the empirics.[3]

Following the path of much evolutionary reasoning, we sketch the logical elements under two major headings. First, there are the considerations that are largely "given" in the short run and which jointly determine the conditions of "temporary equilibrium" in the system under consideration.[4] For the purposes of our earlier paper, which focused on the evolution of vertical scope, the system was an industry in which firm capabilities are heterogeneous across vertical segments. As is illustrated by some of the examples below, broader systems are subject to analysis with much the same approach. The distributions of capabilities and transacting practices, among firms that are heterogeneous in those respects, are among the short-run "givens." The division of labor and the division of profits are among the key outcomes of the system in the short run. (We insist that these are indeed system outcomes whose causal logic cannot be adequately illuminated by a single-actor, ceteris paribus approach.)

The second major heading embraces the causal mechanisms that are, on the one hand, shaped by the context of short-run outcomes, and, on the other, determinative of the new and different short run that will follow. Selection forces reshape the distributions of capabilities and transacting methods, as the differential financial rewards of short-term operations shape both the feasibility and desired directions of firm-level investment decisions. Those rewards also condition revised perceptions of what works and where opportunity lies, affecting not only the participants previously active in the system but also a variety of others—for example, potential entrants.

Less straightforward causal mechanisms are, however, at the heart of the process of long-run change, which we consider here more explicitly. These can be succinctly described as involving the complementary and powerful effects of *agency* and *structured feedback*, taking both terms in a broad sense. Agency, in a broad sense, means more than a careful, rational patrol of the boundaries of established opportunity sets: it involves the active quest for opportunities to break through those limits, by changing both technology and organization (or transaction governance). We use the term "structured feedback" to reference the set of diverse mechanisms by which the path of actual experience, distributed over the circumstances and activities of the actors, guides the course of agency. These mechanisms include those of problem instantiation and recognition and the incentivizing of a variety of modes of search for problem solutions, as well as the more direct influences of experiential learning.[5] What agents find "rewarding," and what they will pursue, depends on what the system around them rewards. In the domain of technological evolution, such mechanisms were well expounded by Rosenberg (1969). For example, agents seeking gains focus on what they see as the "bottlenecks" in the overall process, improving some areas and turning others into new "problems"—bottlenecks to be solved.

In short, the actor-level allocations of problem-solving effort are endogenous in the evolution of the system.[6] This approach stands in contrast to research that portrays capability development as an abstract quest for "efficiency." We note that significant progress has been made in understanding these systemic forces to which we called attention, both at the level of the firm and at the level of the sector.

At the level of the firm, analyses offered in recent years have departed increasingly from the additive consideration of capabilities and transactional features that drive scope. First, more explicit acknowledgment has been made of the context-constrained choices firms face—i.e., the fact that they must choose from a realistic menu of what their transactional partners (with given capabilities) can offer (Ciarli et al. 2008, Jacobides 2008, Malerba et al. 2008). Second, research has shifted away from the empirical testing of one or more theories and toward narrower empirical puzzles such as the use of tapered integration and mixed procurement (Harrigan 1985, Parmigiani 2007).

The analysis of these puzzles has offered further ground for interaction between transactional and capabilities-based explanations. Bradach (1997) provides a fascinating analysis of franchise chains that are partly owned and partly franchised. Investigating why this might be the case, he finds that this structure creates benefits through a ratcheting process (between owned and franchised units) and through a "two-way learning system." Jacobides and Billinger (2006) extend the intuition by suggesting that boundary choices at the level of a firm must be viewed in systemic terms: looking at one boundary choice at a time is not sufficient to explain the logic with which boundaries are set. Rather, one needs to actively consider how the architecture of boundary choices (which the authors term "vertical architecture") shapes capabilities—and drives incentives within an organization. Looking at a major textile firm, they suggest that firms choose their scope not only on the margin, as a response to a cost-benefit calculus (where the capability part of the calculus is the result of past choices of scope) but also on the basis of the dynamic benefits that this choice confers. Firms can retain the option to outsource as a means of instilling some comparability and discipline and keep the epidermis of the organization "permeable," i.e., partly open. The analysis by Santos et al. (2006) of the footwear sector in Portugal presents similar findings, which are also corroborated by the quantitative study of Reitzig and Puranam (2009).

At the level of the sector, researchers have long been interested in the shaping influence that historical context of an industry's evolution exerts on the scope choices of firms by way of the menus of capabilities and transacting practices that are available. Early research by Silver (1984), reprised and amplified by Langlois (1988, 1992) and Langlois and Robertson (1989, 1995) considered how the early conditions of an industry often set the stage for historical trends toward a less integrated structure. The research establishes, for instance, that new sectors or technologies often start off being more integrated in key respects because the notionally available alternative of "the market" simply does not exist in the relevant sense—i.e., a well-developed, cospecialized market with established contracting practices in which suitably capable firms compete to deliver a required input. Jacobides (2005), studying the unbundling of mortgage banking in the United States, considered how the disintegrated structure emerged in a series of steps, mediated by the agency of firms attempting to reshape their transactional environments in the hope of reaping benefits by doing so. The research showed how firms with different knowledge bases, diverse skills, and uneven growth rates invested in the reduction of transaction costs and benefitted from the resulting alteration of the institutional structure of the sector.[7]

Not only has it been shown that capabilities and heterogeneity drive scope and even the transactional environment, but there is also evidence supporting feedback in the opposite causal direction. Scope and transaction governance considerations drive capabilities at the sector level. Cacciatori and Jacobides (2005), looking at the evolution of the construction sector in the United Kingdom, suggested that vertical scope shaped the process of knowledge accumulation. Further evidence is found by DiBiaggio (2007) for semiconductor firms, linking scope to innovation capabilities, and by Baldwin et al. (2006), who analyze the evolution of kayak designs. Fixson and Park (2008) provide compelling evidence on Shishanto and the bicycle industry, adding a strategic dimension in the shift from disintegration to reintegration, combining the dynamics of capabilities, transactions, and market dominance.

Just as the novelty of the capabilities involved tend to compel integration in the early years of a sector, the exogenous appearance of new types of capabilities can push a mature sector toward reintegration, as evidenced in automobiles (Langlois and Robertson 1995) or Swiss watches after the appearance of the quartz movement technology (Jacobides and Winter 2005). Alternatively, "systems integrators" may emerge to fill these capability gaps, creating a new institutional layout for the sector (Prencipe et al. 2003).

357

The scope of inquiry into sectoral organization has now extended far beyond the traditional concern with governance arrangements at a single vertical interface. A recent stream of literature under the banner of industry architectures (IAs) (Jacobides et al. 2006, Brusoni et al. 2009) considers not just issues of vertical scope but the broader questions of how firms pursue profit by trying to reshape the institutional rules and roles in their sector. Quinn and Murray (2009) provide an analysis of the change of food wholesale and retail practices in Ireland and the United Kingdom, showing how communities collaborated and competed to change the institutionally mandated arrangements between different parts of the value chain, with substantial implications for profit distribution. Ferraro and Gurses (2009) document how MCA and Lew Wasserman redefined the IA of the movie and TV sector (by introducing new ways in which studios connected to actors, for example) to benefit Wasserman's firm and to exploit its capabilities. Tee and Gawer (2009) show how differences in IAs in Europe and Japan hindered the adoption of DOCOMO's i-mode. Depeyre and Dumez (2009) consider how the state can shape both the IAs and capabilities. Looking at the U.S. defense industry, they consider how changes in procurement methods by the Pentagon changed the trajectory of U.S. firms that were trying to further shape their environment.

Linking IAs with their ultimate impact, value appropriation, Dedrick et al. (2010) compare the value capture of notebook PCs and Apple iPods in global value chains, and Pisano and Teece (2007) prescriptively consider how firms can leverage IA to benefit from innovation. Adner and Kapoor (2010) consider how the structure within the photolithography value-adding chain affects the ability of firms to benefit from technological innovation, and Tae and Jacobides (2011) consider how the structure of the IA in computing and in cars drove the patterns of profit distribution within these sectors, broadly defined. These studies taken together show how capability differences interact with IA (and the associated transactional environment) to shape both "who does what" and "who takes what" and how firms actively try to manipulate IA to improve their fortunes. The Cowhey et al. (2009) discussion of how firms in the information technology sector spent time and effort to ensure that the global regulatory and technological regime benefits them is a case in point. Firms' efforts to shape IA by lobbying (Shell 2004) or norm setting (Lee 2009) seem to be a pervasive feature of IA evolution.

These two emerging strands, which provide a first cut at integrating capabilities and transactional/institutional analyses at the level of a sector or a firm, have begun converging, opening promising paths of research. Santos and Eisenhardt (2009) have recently shown how entrepreneurs shape the nature of the markets they are engaged in so that they can leverage their own capabilities. Velkar (2009), Pisano and Teece (2007), and Wigand et al. (2005) consider how the interplay of firm—specific interests and IA shapes the creation of industry-wide standards. Summing up, substantial progress has been made in the effort to understand the dynamic interplay of capabilities and transaction costs and the resulting incentives; a number of cases have been examined carefully, and some specific causal arguments have been put forth—but not thoroughly tested. Wider vistas of institutional change involving the institutions of governance beyond the level of the transaction have been pointed out and partially explored. Much remains to be done, and interesting challenges lie ahead. Before turning to these challenges, we broaden the perspective and examine some major issues uncovered by the research thus far.

4. Implications and Theoretical Interpretations

An important benefit of the work from the last 10 years is that it has highlighted the theoretical issues that are central in attempting to address the traditional questions of economic organization from a capabilities—based or evolutionary perspective. The issues thus highlighted are not, for the most part, new ones. But it is clear that, in the past, evolutionary thinking found much more application in thinking about technological change than in thinking about organizational or institutional change (a fact that has its own evolutionary explanation). Thus, for example, some of the historical patterns in the progress of particular technologies were noted and their sources explored from an early stage (Dosi 1982; Nelson and Winter 1977, 1982). On the other hand, the important topic of industry evolution was long neglected, and even less has been said about the evolution of firm boundaries or contracting practices until quite recently.

Familiar truths may require adjusted statement for a novel context. The economics of organization "problem" is sufficiently different from the technological change "problem" to demand at least some adjustments of the explanatory structure, as well as some engagement with relatively unfamiliar issues. But economic organization does evolve, and it is not fundamentally more promising to imagine that it can be adequately addressed from a static viewpoint than it would be to imagine the same thing about technology. In this section, we consider some of the issues that particularly demand attention in light of the recent engagement with the problems of economic organization and the empirical findings summarized previously.

4.1 Rethinking Incentives: Agency vs. Rationality

Whether the focus is on technological change or organizational change, an evolutionary account gives incentives an important role. Yet these incentives—put more broadly, "agency"—appear to differ in nature from those highlighted by the analysis of profit-maximizing rational actors. This calls into question the identification of "rationality" with purposeful economic activity, and it suggests that this may in fact obscure an important part of the role of incentives.

The point is well illustrated in the examples noted above. In them, economic actors are seen as attempting to reshape the selection environment to their advantage. The typical result is failure, which offers encouragement to the more passive actors, who regarded such efforts as obviously foolhardy from the outset. The occasional successes, however, not only establish the foundation of great private fortunes but become the sources of profound systemic transformations—just as Schumpeter said (1934). Consider the previously cited example of Lew Wasserman and MCA (Ferraro and Gurses 2009) or, for that matter, Bill Gates and Microsoft.

An important theoretical question posed by such examples is whether they are usefully thought of as manifestations of economic rationality. They certainly do involve "agency" or "intentionality." The protagonists certainly draw on the energy of pecuniary motivation, otherwise known as profit seeking. Although these attributes would suffice for many people to establish the affirmative answer on economic rationality, there is a need for caution here. The formal rationality that is expounded in textbooks and explored in the research efforts of many disciplines is essentially a story about getting the right answer to a given, sharply defined problem. In contexts where the actor's specific objectives might be unknown (e.g., attitudes toward risk might be unknown, even if the profit-seeking motive can safely be assumed), it basically becomes a story about the internal consistency of the different answers to a hypothetical set of related problems. This very influential understanding of rationality is enshrined in the large literature of axiomatic utility theory founded by von Neumann and Morgenstern (1944). In this view, if you discard consistency—meaning, fundamentally, the transitivity relation on preferences—you throw away rationality itself, as it is defined in economics and other fields devoted to the practice of rational-actor theorizing.

If "consistency" captures the central aspect of entrepreneurship, then there is a reasonable foundation for an attempt to explicate organizational change by reference to familiar theories of economic rationality. If, however, the phenomena substantially transcend mere consistency, then there is need for a broader understanding of agency than the standard account of rationality allows. Likewise, descriptive analysis based on the use of maximization and optimal rules (themselves open to interpretation as a peculiar heuristic or routine, as noted by Nelson and Winter 1982, pp. 126-128) may need to be discarded in favor of the more plausible satisficing heuristic, which does not necessarily yield similar results. To reemphasize, there is no need to discard the idea that many of these entrepreneurs are out to make money, and they go about it quite deliberately. That proposition is not in dispute (for what it is, a powerful generalization that admits occasional exceptions), and thus it is not a basis for discriminating between a behavioral/evolutionary view of economic actors and the standard economic view based on rational choice. It is the differing levels of commitment to consistency (and the associated commitment to the use of optimization techniques within the bounds of a given, narrowly defined problem) that are the proper basis for that discrimination.

We argue that agency, in this broader sense, includes profit-seeking behavior that goes beyond what economics (or TCE) allows for. Its consequences include the creation of novelty, and it thus becomes a powerful shaping force for cumulative change, not just for the requirements of temporary equilibrium. Whereas economists have long claimed a distinctive competence in understanding how the self-interests of dispersed parties combine to yield economic order, the increasing formalization of theorizing has meant that the relatively complex aspects of political economy, institutional economics, and history have increasingly fallen out of the cognitive frame of the mainstream of the profession (as has been remarked by a great many observers before us). Incentives have been formalized but also narrowed in a way that excludes important strategic aspects visible to real actors. Agents are often seen as maximizing on one dimension—for example, as trying to maximize profit within given, established constraints of their maximization problem.

As with any formalization, some of the conceptual richness and complexity of the decision environment is pushed out of sight to ensure an elegant and tractable analytical structure. TCE improved the state of affairs by pointing out that if agents are truly selfish, they might also be expected to take opportunistic advantage of (inevitable) imperfections in contracts, implying a need for a variety of institutional mechanisms to govern their relationships. We would argue (as Smith, Keynes, Marshall, and, indeed, the majority of economists before Samuelson would) that agents also try to change the nature of the optimization problem—or, more plainly put, the nature of the choice setup. This is, of course, exactly the stance of creative engineers toward existing technology, and hardly anyone now affirms the adequacy of standard economic rationality for analysis in that domain.

The problem with formal rationality is that it ignores some very powerful incentives that operate in firms and sectors. Agents, drawing on their capabilities, try to change the environment to their advantage in a variety of ways. In so doing, they are affected by frames, cognitive bounds, and the way they perceive their environment; innovations involve changes in the way things are seen and perceived much as they depend on new "engineering" data. In the domain of organization, as in technology, it is innovation that we need to understand if we are to explain how we came to be where we are and where we are likely to go next. The sources of innovation have been much studied, and of course, the evidence supports the relevance of incentives and agency. It also supports, however, the importance of creativity, diverse sources of inspiration, "thinking outside the box," and, last but not least, serendipity (Denrell et al. 2003), a mode of discovery that demands motivation but actively resists the ex ante specification of alternatives. To understand the role of agency in the evolution of the system, it is important to make more room for these aspects and focus less on the problem of consistent choice among given and well-defined alternatives. The ability to imagine or design different ways of doing things is logically antecedent to the problem of choosing well among them, once they are well specified.

4.2 Structure, Feedback, and Evolution

An important element shaping the nature of choices is structure— whether at the level of the individual, the organization, or the sector. As we have shown, the work carried out during this last decade has highlighted the merit of incorporating structure explicitly in the analysis of capabilities and evolutionary dynamics. Structure shapes the nature of the alternatives pursued by individuals. Within organizations, structure shapes the perceptions, frames, and expectations of what actors need to achieve. Whether these are administrative goals in a state bureaucracy, key performance indicators in a business department of a large corporate structure, or objectives in an entrepreneurial venture, structures (the administrative divisions and other durable aspects of "command and control") have an important role in defining what the different subunits of an organization undertake. Individuals do not respond to "problems" in the abstract; they respond in a manner consistent with the specific roles that are implied or explicated to them, depending on their position within a structure. They may well know that their roles engage only part of the organization's overall objectives, but structure shapes both their framing of a problem and their incentives (Cyert and March 1963). As Dewey (1933) pointed out, people choose on the basis of the alternatives and criteria that are put to them, and structure within an organization plays a powerful role in shaping both.

Similar remarks apply at a higher level, to the division of labor between different types of industry participants. Structure shapes feedback and thereby guides the process of capability development. This shaping effect arises from mechanisms known since Adam Smith's famous 1776 discussion on the division of labor. As we have argued above, these include all the mechanisms of structured feedback, including the identification of problems that are worth solving and the establishment of incentives for solving them. The signals provided by the environment regarding the effectiveness of established and contemplated courses of action shape the types of activities an organization will undertake, and thus they shape the process of capability development.

Feedback sets the context for the forces of agency, engaged in the attempt to reshape the very structure that generated the feedback signals. Whereas structures evolve largely according to their own dynamic laws, and sometimes in unexpected ways, they also provide an entry point for deliberate change efforts. By changing structures (whether within organizations or in sectors through regulation, standards, and industry-wide rules or by even higher-level institutional innovations), behaviors can be modified and the evolution of capabilities redirected. Inquiry into this possibility should address both the cognitive elements inherent in the framing of any structural initiative or strategic choice and the role of feedback in shaping the subsequent evolution at both firm and industry levels. This constitutes an important agenda for future research.

4.3 Understanding Capabilities

In sum, there are building blocks in place for a coherent and compelling approach to understanding capabilities and their evolution. The approach draws heavily on the insights accumulated in the economics discipline and particularly in TCE research—but it makes no direct use of the quasi-normative, actor-level apparatus of rational choice theory. Also, although it focuses on purposeful economic activity, it considers the broader role of agency, including changes to the context, as opposed to the narrower, consistency-based formalizations of economic rationality.

The first challenge is to understand why capabilities differ between (and even within) firms and what mechanisms may exert a (often limited) pressure toward homogeneity through learning, imitation, and competition. The second required focus is on the structure within which capabilities evolve and the feedback mechanisms that operate both at the level of the organization (helping to select the practices that organizations accept and reward) and at the level of the sector (because the division of labor affects the feedback mechanisms that shape action). It also affects the cognitive bounds that shape evolution via the perception of innovative opportunity, as was observed by Simon (1962) and partly discussed by Cyert and March (1963).[8]

The institutional rules and structures, including the property rights arrangements and regulatory systems in place at any point in time, are parts of the overall structure that affect both the operation of feedback and the direction of the evolution of capabilities. These structural aspects are important because they are significant parameters in the organizational and industry environment, yet they are also endogenous features in the long-run process of industry evolution. That is, firms also shape and change institutional structures, including the specific forms of property rights.

Thus, to understand the evolution of capabilities, it is necessary first to understand the basic economics of the system and the forces that shape agency. Structure, either at the level of the firm or at the level of the sector (or industry architecture), is important in part because it shapes the direction of effort (through incentives and informational flows) and because it focuses attention (acting as a basis for cognitive framing).

By acknowledging the role of context at each stage of the evolutionary process, this approach offers a deeper and stronger causal grounding that cannot be accessed if we examine only one agent or one transaction at a time. This does not mean we should not pay close attention to the mechanics of choice (or, more importantly, to the mechanics of action) at the individual level—these are prime considerations. But it is the context that shapes them, and oftentimes in subtle ways—hence our emphasis on attending to the role of context.

5. Grounding in Practice: The Etiology of the Financial Crisis as a Conceptual Laboratory

In considering directions of possible theoretical advance, it is important to seek integration of achieved insights, as premised in this special issue. It is also important not to become trapped in a straitjacket of analytical convenience, as we have argued above. It is quintessentially important, however, to confront phenomena of interest not only to scholars but also to managers and policy makers. The usefulness of a proposed approach should be assessed in a realistic context. Here, we take the near-meltdown of the financial services sector in 2008 as an example and briefly describe how this episode both illustrates and illuminates the mechanisms discussed above.

The crisis affords considerable insight into the process of coevolution of capabilities, boundaries, and scope that changed the architecture of the financial services sector, ultimately creating critical vulnerabilities. As we discuss at length elsewhere (Jacobides and Winter 2009), what changed in the sector was the division of labor. It changed through the interplay of the mechanisms discussed above, including the interaction of feedback mechanisms with firm-level agency.

At the center of the structural origins of the crisis in the United States is mortgage banking, which was transformed from the 1970s onwards, and especially in the last decade, by the institution of a series of new markets along the previously integrated value chain. The first such market broke up the traditional mortgage banking value chain, separating the creation and servicing of a mortgage loan from providing the capital and holding the claim to that loan. The new secondary market for mortgage loans was facilitated by government policy in the interest of improving finance for housing. Its creation had far-reaching ramifications, beginning with encouraging the growth of mortgage banks-non-depository financial institutions that specialized in the creation of mortgage loans. Subsequent developments included the growth of the specialized loan marketing function (mortgage brokers) and specialized loan-servicing organizations. Existing organizational capabilities were modified, and new ones were created. These changes were largely responses, created by firm-level agency, to the opportunities offered in the emerging context, but they reshaped that context by fundamentally altering the prevailing incentives all along the chain. Ultimately—and with crucial amplification by several other causal factors—the changed incentives left "no one in charge" of protecting the quality of mortgage loans and, through that, the interests of the ultimate investors and, through that, the interests of the public at large.

Securitization, then, not only led to a new set of markets but also framed different ways in which particular types of (new) industry praticipants could monetize the benefits from a loan. Along with the new division of labor came a new set of rules, as well as a new selection mechanism and new pragmatic definitions of what it meant to be "competent" in the various segments. The evolution of the system, constrained and modulated at every stage by existing routines and interaction patterns, was guided by locally intentional innovations. These served the perceived purposes of participant firms and their employees. New ideas were embodied in new capabilities, and if they passed the "local tests" of what made more sense (or more money in the short term), they spread, through selection and imitation. These innovations led to further modifications of contractual arrangements as firms attended to changing the conditions around them. As they did so, the sources of gain and benefit, and, ultimately, the feedback mechanism, changed. Loan originators, for instance, established a means to benefit from selling a loan to a warehousing bank, obtaining closing fees up front, receiving a (somewhat risk-adjusted) payment, and further reducing their engagement with loan quality.

Also, consistent with our emphasis on context, these arrangements were shaped in particular conditions of demand and a particular macroeconomic environment. The viability of the arrangements would only be put into question if specific feedback made a change necessary. Regardless of the views of industry participants with greater or lesser appreciation of the viability of these arrangements, innovations that were deemed to have a "positive" outcome (in terms of generating cash flow and generating revenues for the employees putting them together) became more prevalent. Even if participants strongly suspected that the loans would not ultimately perform, their behavior was overwhelmingly shaped by the actual feedback at hand (principally, measured growth of revenue and profit achieved through origination of loans and derived securities). As Chuck Prince, CEO of Citibank, famously said in 2007, "When the music stops, in terms of liquidity, things will be complicated. But as long as the music is playing, you've got to get up and dance. We're still dancing" (Nakamoto and Wighton 2007).

The analysis above illustrates our second major point: that structure shapes feedback, and it is feedback, not foresight, that drives the evolution of a system. It also illustrates our third major contention: that a change in structure, through a change in the feedback mechanism and the selection process, can shape collective outcomes. The changes in the institutional structure led to a change in the nature and operation of feedback and the shared sense of what was more efficient; they did so by shaping incentives and honing cognition. What was painfully illustrated in 2008 was that endogenous changes in the structure and operation of complex sectors such as financial services can go through socially destructive periods, especially in contexts where success and failure do not become apparent immediately (loans will not show signs of stress, on average, before the cycle begins to turn). And this can happen even when some industry participants might understand how the system misdirects effort and attention.

The type of analysis sketched here is particularly important because it provides a complement to existing economic analysis—whether that taught in business schools or discussed between economic analysts and academics. It provides a broader view of agency, considers both the emergence and evolution of heterogeneity and capability, and looks at how capabilities, at the level of institutions and, ultimately, industries, evolve and are selected. In doing so, it offers a glimpse of the systemic logic that has led to the biggest economic crisis in 80 years. The problem with "microfoundational" agent-based analyses, as well as "ceteris paribus" comparative institutional analyses, is that they would miss precisely this point—i.e., they would not be able to capture the causal dynamics that operate at the level of the larger system. Sure enough, we could establish the factors that, on the margin, would make a bank in 2002 or 2007 make and hold, or originate and distribute, a mortgage loan, and we might consider the level of competence of an individual bank as a correlate of its past decisions about scope. Yet this would not yield much understanding of why the system evolved this way or what drove these dynamics. Neither would it help us see how a prevailing structure might lead, through the existing feedback mechanisms, to a better or worse individual and collective future.

Summing up, the explanatory challenge of the crisis reminds us that useful research cannot be guided purely by the quest for elegance or by reliance on a narrow range of "approved" approaches to describing the nature and motivations of economic actors. We would even argue that research that bridges previously unconnected bodies of knowledge is not necessarily appealing per se. Rather, integration becomes interesting when it advances understanding of a new or different causal mechanism and when it is attractive at the phenomenological level—i.e., when it lets us consider important phenomena that have eluded analysis to date. Such a phenomenological orientation is particularly relevant, or even (in our view) *mandatory*, given the current volatile environment.

6. Looking Ahead

In our literature review (see §3), we provided references to an impressive body of research that has addressed the dynamic interactions of capability and transactional considerations in the determination of significant features of economic organization. Our discussion has mostly emphasized that a lot has been done. Here, we emphasize that a great deal more could and should be done. Our claims of evidence for our proposed causal mechanisms carry a significant taint of "proof by selected example." Although large-sample statistical evidence of a relevant kind is intrinsically hard to come by in such a complex arena, research of that character would certainly be welcome. However, careful study of a larger class of examples would also be welcome. Expansion of the set of examples very commonly turns up distinctions among cases that are of theoretical significance. Occasionally, apparent anomalies show up that directly challenge the theoretical underpinnings—and it is the ability to cope with such challenges that is the fundamental test of a theoretical view. We propose, therefore, that any of the studies we have previously discussed is a viable model for research that would be new and interesting if carefully executed in a novel empirical arena—and interesting for its potential theoretical significance as well as for any qualified support it might provide for existing theoretical views.

That said, the most promising segment of the research frontier features, in our view, the questions of interaction between relatively large-scale structural phenomena and agency at the level of individual actors. What are firms doing in an effort to produce advantageous change in the institutional rules that control their positions in the system? There are numerous dimensions to activity of that kind, including the introduction of new contractual forms, new ways of governing supplier relations, participation in standard-setting activities, and lobbying before regulatory and legislative bodies. Although such questions have been explored in the existing research literature, there are relatively few examples that pursue them at the levels of both individual actors and institutional arrangements with due attention to the interlevel causal linkage. There is also a need to supplement the perspectives from economics and management, on the one hand, with those provided by other social sciences and law, on the other. For example, the phrases "regulatory capture" and "organizational fields" suggest important perspectives on some of the same phenomena that we would place under the heading "industry architecture."

6.1 New Business Models as Structural Innovations

Recent research interest in "business models" suggests another promising path into the interesting terrain of structure and agency. Over the last few years, several accounts of business models have come to the fore (Zott and Amit 2007, Zott et al. 2012). Motivated by the ever—expanding discussions in the practitioner world, academics have tried to make sense of the pervasive interest in business models as well as the fact that these models do not seem to sit comfortably with mainstream research in management. As Baden-Fuller and Morgan (2010, p. 159) observe, "The real world of firms is made up of very many enterprises that behave and are organized in very different, individualistic ways. In contrast, theories of firm behaviour tend to be very general. Business models operate at an intermediate level between these two poles." Thus, the interest in business models arises in part from the fact that standard theory does not illuminate the role of the structure of business activity— its industry architecture, in our parlance.

Our theory review indicates that there is an emerging body of research that can usefully inform the growing business model discussions. For instance, whereas we concur with McGrath (2010) that firms can choose their "units of business," i.e., "the good or service that appears on the invoice," we also contend that these choices are not entirely "free," as they are made within the context of an architecture. The MCA/ Wasserman case (Ferraro and Gurses 2009) and food retailing (Quinn and Murray 2009) are cases in point. Analyzing the coevolution of firm strategy and the institutional environment, as we advocate, can provide an analytically useful contrast between the industry-wide environment where firms operate, with its slowly evolving conventions and architecture, and the firm-specific choices embodied in the business model (see Teece 2010, p. 173). Research that complemented individual-level modeling with analysis of structure at the level of a sector could provide a better sense of both the drivers and the dynamics of the changing rules, those constraints that business models must satisfy.[9] This would also allow business model research to become more "socialized," less focused on the heroic depictions of successful firms, and more attuned to the dynamics of coevolution between individual business models and the industry context that supports or rejects them.

As we consider the potential success and "sustainable advantage" of a business model, issues of capabilities and heterogeneity come sharply into the picture. Business models, in principle, are imitable; once established (usually through the efforts, ingenuity, and constant prodding of the entrepreneur or firm that came up with them), they can be emulated, with no such setup costs, by others. Hence it is quite plausible that a business model innovation might change the dynamics of a sector dramatically yet fail to reward the innovator. As usual, durable success depends on having something distinctive, be it an element of superior skill or knowledge or simply an ability to implement (or even finance) the business model. It also depends on the ability to fend off future efforts to change the structure yet again, a point that seems to be underemphasized in the business model literature. As we emphasized early in our paper, it is important to distinguish the "idea" from its manifestation in concrete capabilities and consider what it is that intervenes between the (potentially imitable) idea and the actual venture and offers the prospect of sustained success.

In all, we argue that a more detailed consideration of the context of business models could contribute positively not only to the business models discussion itself but also to understanding the origin and evolution of capabilities. This view of business models gives rise to a number of potential questions that research can address, expanding our understanding not only of theory but also of the real world. A particularly significant question is this: What exactly constrains the existing menu of business models? Moreover, are the difficulties of business model innovation primarily related to shortcomings of the original creative insight, to the acceptance of new business models within a sector, or to the challenges of implementation—the long distance between the idea and its successful implementation? To address such questions, we will once again need to take heterogeneity seriously and consider how it relates both to business model success and to the ability of the innovators to defend their newly found turf.

6.2 Organizational Economics (Outside TCE) and Capabilities Research

In this paper, we have addressed some basic issues raised by the proposal for stronger integration of organizational economics and organizational capabilities. As we noted at the start, the term "organizational economics" is used in this proposal to cover two quite disparate lines of inquiry: transaction cost economics and the use of rational-actor theorizing to illuminate the workings of organizations. Regarding the former, our stance is not only that integration is possible but also that the enterprise is already well advanced. Certainly, much remains to be sorted out, and the most important applications no doubt lie ahead, but it is already possible to see "how the story goes" and to recognize its promise. There are several reasons for the relative ease of integration of these two lines of thinking; certainly, an important one is that both schools consider detailed microlevel accounts of particular cases as a type of evidence that is worthy of respect.

Regarding the possibility of integration with organizational economics in the narrower, rational-actor sense, our appraisal is less sanguine. The issues that we have highlighted in the capabilities context are fundamental, long-familiar, and pervasive in domains where the economics discipline faces the challenge of understanding the dynamics of complex social arrangements. The problem is posed by the analytical tractability barrier that blocks the application of the rational choice tools entirely, forces abandonment of the quest for explanation above the individual-actor level (as we have stressed), or yields "solutions" involving ever-increasing departures from phenomenological realism. Whatever one thinks about "realism" as an issue of scientific methodology, it is quite clear that effective communication with other social scientists, managers, and policy makers is impeded by a thorough-going commitment to rational—choice formalisms. Among the lessons of the financial crisis is the point that the rare instances of practical use of such methods (here, the modeling of securities markets) do not necessarily yield durable success, if higher-level managers do not understand them.

In an article that provoked much controversy, Paul Krugman attributed the failure of economists to predict the crisis to the fact that they "mistook beauty, clad in impressive-looking mathematics, for truth" (Krugman 2009b, p. 37). He subsequently commented that "the temptation is always to keep on applying these extreme (neoclassical) simplifications, even where the evidence clearly shows that they're wrong. What economists have to do is learn to resist that temptation. But doing so will, inevitably, lead to a much messier, less pretty view" (Krugman 2009a). This again presents many of the same basic issues set forth in our capabilities discussion and undoubtedly reflects the same difficulties arising from the analytical tractability barrier.

Given increasing recognition of the subtlety of the problems faced by individual actors, and the increasing sophistication of the analytical tools used to explore those problems, there is an increasing challenge for theoretical research that seeks to relate the behavior of individual actors to causal forces operating at higher levels of analysis. In textbook economics, analysis of the optimizing behavior of firms and consumers is followed by discussion of market clearing—the endogenous determination of the prices that are the parameters of the environment for individual actors. Much valuable insight, both descriptive and normative, was obtained via that type of analysis, in both partial and general equilibrium settings. It is hard to find its counterpart in organizational economics, and full recognition of the importance of the issue is not commonplace. Undoubtedly, this is because the theoretical problem is itself hard, especially in its dynamic version, and it will remain so.

The "good old days" of easy aggregation from the actor level to the market, industry, or economy level are clearly behind us. The question of the origins of heterogeneity is a basic one. Models of the quasi-normative kind characterizing a "right answer" to some organizational problem in some stylized environment—rarely provide a plausible point of entry for the variety in initial conditions that, almost certainly, is fundamental to the observed heterogeneity. That actor-level heterogeneity is, in turn, fundamental to the patterns observed at higher levels. Neither do such models make it easy to allow for the complex ways in which those initial differences become elaborated over time. They frequently do not even attempt the ever-lengthening stride to the next stepping stone of traditional economic analysis, where the concern is with how the individual actors relate to each other in the competitive context of a market, an industry, or a whole economy—and whether that works out, on the whole, for good or ill.

Emphatically, we do not want to be understood as denying the past contributions of basic economic analysis to the understanding of capabilities or the continuing and future prospects for valuable work of that kind. Such "basic" analysis has commonly involved rational— actor theorizing, and more so in recent decades than in the past. We note that team theory (Marschak and Radner 1972) and its more recent revivals (e.g., Bolton and Dewatripont 1994) have important affinities with a capability-based view in that they consider different ways in which agents might be able to connect and organize to carry out some collective task, sometimes assuming away incentive issues to focus on coordination. These and other models of organizational structure consider how different configurations of actors that take several different attributes (hierarchy, polyarchy, etc.) lead to particular sets of outcomes (Garicano 2000, Christensen and Knudsen 2010). So, in essence, the differences between these configurations (and not just in the fact that they belong to one organization) drive performance differentials, and in that context, capability differences are at least partly explained by the structure in which agents are embedded. The interpretation of that structure as one of many possible equilibria for a game among organizational participants is also congenial and instructive (Gibbons 2006), linking game-theoretic equilibrium selection with incentives, performance differentials, and heterogeneity.

Many further examples along this line could be provided. In the future as in the past, analytical parables about highly stylized situations will be a powerful source of heuristic insights into more complex situations.[10] Incorporation of such insights in understanding of capabilities will be feasible and valuable, as it has been in the past. True integration is another matter, and it is a long way off. Parables will not suffice to engage the actual complexity of the phenomena, and analysis that does so will inevitably—as Krugman (2009a) suggested in the case of macroeconomics—provide a "much messier, less pretty view".

In this paper, we have argued the importance of the multiple causal forces operating above the actor level as well as the reciprocal causation between the agency of individual actors and the structure of the larger systems in which they operate. Useful insights into these important issues can likely be derived by many different methods. We have our views regarding which methods are likely to prove most effective in addressing these issues, but our strongest affirmations relate to the proposition that the higher-level forces are real and important. If our collective game is about understanding the real world, it is imperative that we keep those forces in view. In this paper, we have provided some concrete suggestions on how to build a research program that incorporates and investigates these forces and goes beyond the admonition to consider dynamics and interactions. We have also argued that, as we engage in this program, a phenomenological orientation is crucial to ensure that we have impact as a field on strategy and policy alike.

Summing up, there is already a substantial amount of work that has developed around the intersection of capabilities and economics, both in terms of TCE and in terms of the use of formal models of rational economic action. The field has progressed substantially toward a dynamically integrated view, especially in the case of the insights of TCE. There appear to be even greater promise looking forward—especially if one considers the potential fields of application of this research and its ability to assist decision makers in firms and policy positions alike.

Acknowledgments

The authors thank participants in the Bergen conference and the DRUID London and the Rome SMS meetings for comments and suggestions. M. G. Jacobides acknowledges the Research and Material

Development Fund of the London Business School, and S. G. Winter thanks the Mack Center of the Wharton school for financial assistance.

Endnotes

1. Richardson put forward Coase's classic "Why firms?" question (Coase 1937) in his own way and referenced Coase, but he said that he took a different view. The reference to Coase seems pro forma. Nelson and Winter were evidently unaware of Richardson, whose concerns were close to theirs.

2. See Penrose's discussion (1959, pp. 47-48, 53 emphasizing the role of experience as a limit to the efficient growth of the firm and, in effect, the importance of the tacit knowledge element in experience: "[E]xperience itself can never be transmitted; it produces a change—frequently a subtle change—in individuals and cannot be separated from them." We would extend the statement by saying that the change is not only in individuals but also in groups and their routine interactions. See Kor and Mahoney (2004) for a discussion.

3. For a contrasting assessment of the amount of recent progress, see Argyres and Zenger (2012).

4. Of course, we do not posit that the system is ever really in "equilibrium," however that might be defined. The point is that some causal mechanisms are faster than others, and it is a helpful analytical strategy to recognize that the faster-moving mechanisms deliver results that then define a context shaping the operation of the slower-moving ones.

5. Some agents also try to change the menu of options by reaching well beyond the guidance of experience, creating imagined futures that they try to bring to fruition. Yet even these are but a small subset of the imaginable conditions and permutations, and structure plays an important selective role in this process of "menu evolution."

6. In our earlier paper on vertical scope, the message of the previous paragraph was implicit in our identification of four key mechanisms: (1) selection amplifies the impact of capabilities on scope, through competition and imitation; (2) endogenous reductions in transaction costs arise from actors' efforts to realize the latent gains from such reductions; (3) changes in scope affect the capability development process (structured feedback); and (4) capability development affects the roster of participants, including entrants from new sectors (Jacobides and Winter 2005, pp. 399-406). In addition to spelling out the general mechanisms in some detail, we illustrated their working in accounts of the evolution of two sectors, the U.S. mortgage banking and the Swiss watch industries.

7. Baldwin (2008) provides a detailed and careful conceptual analysis of the process and conditions under which transactions emerge in the first place. This substantially advances the discussion of "mundane transaction costs" (Langlois 1992, 2006) that concerns itself with similar dynamics.

8. More recent research linking structure and the division of labor with cognition includes Kaplan (2008), Kaplan and Tripsas (2008), Trispas and Gavetti (2000), and Trispas (2009). Gavetti (2012) suggests a prominent role for cognitive considerations in strategy analysis.

9. See Johnson and Suskewicz (2009) for an interesting illustration on the role of industry-wide dynamics on fossil fuel and the need to take a systemic view of business models at the level of industry.

10. Such parables can be constructed under a variety of rules, including those of rational choice modeling but also, for example, NK modeling of the kind pioneered by Levinthal (1997).

References

Adner, R., R. Kapoor. 2010. Value creation in innovation ecosystems: How the structure of technological interdependence affects firm performance in new technology generations. Strategic Management J. 31(3) 306-333.

Argyres, N. 1996. Evidence on the role of firm capabilities in vertical integration decisions. Strategic Management J. 17(2) 129-150.

Argyres, N. S., J. P. Liebeskind. 1999. Contractual commitments, bargaining power, and governance inseparability: Incorporating history into transaction cost theory. Acad. Management Rev. 24(1) 49-63.

Argyres, N., T. R. Zenger. 2012. Capabilities, transaction costs, and firm boundaries: An integrative theory. Organ. Sci., ePub ahead of print July 30, http://dx.doi.org/10.1287/orsc.1110.0736.

Arrow, K. J. 1962. Economic welfare and the allocation of resources for invention. R. R. Nelson, ed. The Rate and Direction of Inventive Activity. Princeton University Press, Princeton, NJ, 609-625.

Baden-Fuller, C., M. S. Morgan. 2010. Business models as models. Long Range Planning 43(2-3) 156-171.

Baldwin, C. Y. 2008. Where do transactions come from? Modularity, transactions, and the boundaries of firms. Indust. Corporate Change 17(1) 155-195.

Baldwin, C. Y., C. Hienerth, E. von Hippel. 2006. How user innovations become commercial products: A theoretical investigation and case study. Res. Policy 35(9) 1291-1313.

Bloom, N., J. Van Reenen. 2010. Why do management practices differ across firms and countries? J. Econom. Perspect. 24(1) 203-224.

Bolton, P., M. Dewatripont. 1994. The firm as a communication network. Quart. J. Econom. 109(4) 809-839.

Bradach, J. L. 1997. Using the plural form in the management of restaurant chains. Admin. Sci. Quart. 42(2) 276-303.

Brusoni, S., M. G. Jacobides, A. Prencipe. 2009. Strategic dynamics in industry architectures and the challenges of knowledge integration. Eur. Management Rev. 6(4) 209-216.

Cacciatori, E., M. G. Jacobides. 2005. The dynamic limits of specialization: Vertical integration reconsidered. Organ. Stud. 26(12)1851-1883.

Chew, W., T. Bresnahan, K. B. Clark. 1990. Measurement, Coordination, and Learning in a Multiplant Network. Harvard Business School Press, Boston.

Christensen, M., T. Knudsen. 2010. The design of decision-making organizations. Management Sci. 56(1) 71-89.

Ciarli, T., R. Leoncini, S. Montresor, M. Valente. 2008. Technological change and the vertical organization of industries. J. Evolutionary Econom. 18(3/4) 367-387.

Clark, K. B., T. Fujimoto. 1991. Product Development Performance, Strategy, Organization, and Management in the World. Harvard Business School Press, Boston.

Coase, R. H. 1937. The nature of the firm. Economica 4(16) 386-405.

Cowhey, P. F., J. D. Aronson, J. Richards. 2009. Shaping the architecture of the U.S. information and communication technology architecture: A political economic analysis. Rev. Policy Res. 26(1-2) 105-125.

Cyert, R. M., J. G. March. 1963. A Behavioral Theory of the Firm. Prentice-Hall, Englewood Cliffs, NJ.

Dedrick, J., K. L. Kraemer, G. Linden. 2010. Who profits from innovation in global value chains? A study of the iPod and notebook PCs. Indust. Corporate Change 19(1) 81-116.

Denrell, J., C. Fang, D. A. Levinthal. 2004. From T-mazes to labyrinths: Learning from model based feedback. Management Sci. 50(10) 1366-1378.

Denrell, J., C. Fang, S. G. Winter. 2003. The economics of strategic opportunity. Strategic Management J. 24(10) 977-990.

Depeyre, C., H. Dumez. 2009. A management perspective on market dynamics: Stabilizing and destabilizing strategies in the US defense industry. Eur. Management J. 27(2) 90-99.

Dewey, J. 1933. How We Think: A Restatement of the Relation of Reflective Thinking to the Educative Process. Heath, Lexington, Boston.

Dibiaggio, L. 2007. Design complexity, vertical disintegration and knowledge organization in the semiconductor industry. Indust. Corporate Change 16(2) 239-267.

Disney, R., J. Haskel, Y. Heden. 2003. Restructuring and productivity growth in UK manufacturing. Econom. J. 113(489) 666-694.

Dosi, G. 1982. Technological paradigms and technological trajectories: A suggested interpretation of the determinants and directions of technical change. Res. Policy 11(3) 147-162.

Ferraro, F., K. Gurses. 2009. Building architectural advantage in the US motion picture industry: Lew Wasserman and the Music Corporation of America. Eur. Management Rev. 6(4) 233-249.

Fixson, S. K., J. K. Park. 2008. The power of integrality: Linkages between product architecture, innovation, and industry structure. Res Policy 37(8) 1296-1316.

Garicano, L. 2000. Hierarchies and the organization of knowledge in production. J. Political Econom. 108(5) 874-904.

Garvin, D. A. 1988. Managing Quality. Free Press, New York.

Gavetti, G. 2012. Toward a behavioral theory of strategy. Organ. Sci. 23(1) 267-285.

Gibbons, R. 2006. What the folk theorem doesn't tell us. Indust. Corporate Change 15(2) 381-386.

Gibbons, R., R. Henderson, N. P. Repenning, J. Sterman. 2012. What do managers do? Suggestive evidence and potential theories about building relationships. R. Gibbons, J. Roberts, eds. Handbook of Organizational Economics. Princeton University Press, Princeton, NJ. Forthcoming.

Harrigan, K. R. 1985. Vertical integration and corporate strategy. Acad. Management J. 28(2) 397-425.

Helfat, C. E. ed. 2003. The SMS Blackwell Handbook of Organizational Capabilities: Emergence, Development and Change. Blackwell, Oxford, UK.

Jacobides, M. G. 2005. Industry change through vertical disintegration: How and why markets emerged in mortgage banking. Acad. Management J. 48(3) 465-498.

Jacobides, M. G. 2008. How capability differences, transaction costs, and learning curves interact to shape vertical scope. Organ. Sci. 19(2) 306-326.

Jacobides, M. G., S. Billinger. 2006. Designing the boundaries of the firm: From "make, buy, or ally" to the dynamic benefits of vertical architecture. Organ. Sci. 17(2) 249-261.

Jacobides, M. G., S. G. Winter. 2005. The co-evolution of capabilities and transaction costs: Explaining the institutional structure of production. Strategic Management J. 26(5) 395-413.

Jacobides, M. G., S. G. Winter. 2009. Survival of the reckless: Feedback, foresight and the evolutionary roots of the financial crisis. Working paper, London Business School, London.

Jacobides, M. G., T. Knudsen, M. Augier. 2006. Benefiting from innovation: Value creation, value appropriation and the role of industry architectures. Res. Policy 35(8) 1200-1221.

Johnson, M. W., J. Suskewicz. 2009. How to jump-start the clean economy. Harvard Bus. Rev. 87(11) 52-60.

Kaplan, S. 2008. Cognition, capabilities, and incentives: Assessing firm response to the fiber-optic revolution. Acad. Management J. 51(4) 672-695.

Kaplan, S., M. Tripsas. 2008. Thinking about technology: Applying a cognitive lens to technical change. Res. Policy 37(5) 790-805.

Kor, Y. Y., J. T. Mahoney. 2004. Edith Penrose's (1959) contributions to the resource-based view of strategic management. J. Management Stud. 41(1) 183-191.

Krugman, P. 2009a. A few notes on my magazine article. The Conscience of a Liberal (blog), September 5, http://krugman.blogs.nytimes. com/2009/09/05/a-few-notes-on-my-magazinearticle/.

Krugman, P. 2009b. How did economists get it so wrong? New York Times Magazine 6(September) 36-43.

Langlois, R. N. 1988. Economic change and the boundaries of the firm. J. Institutional Theoret. Econom. 144(4) 635-657.

Langlois, R. N. 1992. Transaction-cost economics in real time. Indust. Corporate Change 1(1) 99-127.

Langlois, R. N. 2006. The secret life of mundane transaction costs. Organ. Stud. 27(9) 1389-1410.

Langlois, R. N., P. L. Robertson. 1989. Explaining vertical integration: Lessons from the American automobile industry. J. Econom. Hist. 49(2) 361-375.

Langlois, R. N., P. L. Robertson. 1995. Firms, Markets, and Economic Change: A Dynamic Theory of Business Institutions. Routledge, London.

Leiblein, M. J., D. J. Miller. 2003. An empirical examination of transaction—and firm-level influences on the vertical boundaries of the firm. Strategic Management J. 24(9) 839-859.

Lee, B. 2009. Finding your place in the (organic) food chain: The effects of regulation and certification on vertical disintegration. Working paper, London Business School, London.

Levinthal, D. A. 1997. Adaptation on rugged landscapes. Management Sci. 43(7) 934-950.

Madhok, A. 2002. Reassessing the fundamentals and beyond: Ronald Coase, the transaction cost and resource-based theories of the firm and the institutional structure of production. Strategic Management J. 23(6) 535-550.

Malerba, F., R. Nelson, L. Orsenigo, S. Winter. 2008. Vertical integration and disintegration of computer firms: A history-friendly model of the coevolution of the computer and semiconductor industries. Indust. Corporate Change 17(2) 197-231.

Marschak, J., R. Radner. 1972. Economic Theory of Teams. Yale University Press, New Haven, CT.

McGrath, R. G. 2010. Business models: A discovery driven approach. Long Range Planning 43(2/3) 247-261.

Nakamoto, M., D. Wighton. 2007. Citigroup chief stays bullish on buy-out. Financial Times (July 9) http://us.ft.com/ftgateway/ superpage. ft?news_id=fto070920071725183786.

Nelson, R. R. 1991. Why do firms differ, and how does it matter? Strategic Management J. 12(S2) 61-74.

Nelson, R. R., S. G. Winter. 1973. Toward an evolutionary theory of economic capabilities. Amer. Econom. Rev. 63(May) 440-449.

Nelson, R. R., S. G. Winter. 1977. In search of useful theory of innovation. Res. Policy 6(1) 36-76.

Nelson, R. R., S. G. Winter. 1982. An Evolutionary Theory of Economic Change. Belknap Press, New York.

Parmigiani, A. 2007. Why do firms both make and buy? An investigation of concurrent sourcing. Strategic Management J. 28(3) 285-311

Penrose, E. T. 1959. The Theory of the Growth of the Firm. Oxford University Press, New York.

Pisano, G. P., D. J. Teece. 2007. How to capture value from innovation: Shaping intellectual property and industry architecture. Calif. Management Rev. 50(1) 278-296.

Porter, M. E. 1996. What is strategy? Harvard Bus. Rev. 74(6) 61-78.

Prencipe, A., A. Davies, M. Hobday, eds. 2003. The Business of Systems Integration. Oxford University Press, Oxford, UK.

Quinn, J., A. Murray. 2009. The community context of evolving industry architecture. J. Marketing Channel 16(4) 327-357.

Reitzig, M., P. Puranam. 2009. Value appropriation as an organizational capability: The case of IP protection through patents. Strategic Management J. 30(7) 765-789.

Richardson, G. B. 1972. The organisation of industry. Econom J. 82(327) 883-896.

Rosenberg, N. 1969. The direction of technological change: Inducement mechanisms and focusing devices. Econom. Development Cultural Change 18(1) 1-24.

Santos, F., A. Abrunhosa, I. Costa. 2006. How to compete in mature industries? Boundary architecture as a mechanism for strategic renewal. Strategic Management Soc. Conf., Vienna.

Santos, F. M., K. M. Eisenhardt. 2009. Constructing markets and shaping boundaries: Entrepreneurial power in Nascent Fields. Acad. Management J. 52(4) 643-671.

Schumpeter, J. 1934. The Theory of Economic Development. Translated by R. Opie. Harvard University Press, Cambridge, UK. [Orig. pub. 1911. Duncker & Humblot, Leipzig, Germany.]

Shell, G. R. 2004. Make the Rules or Your Rivals Will. Crown Business, New York.

Silver, M. 1984. Enterprise and the Scope of the Firm: The Role of Vertical Integration. Martin Robertson & Co., Oxford, UK.

Simon, H. A. 1962. The architecture of complexity. Proc. Amer. Philos. Soc. 106(6) 467-482.

Sutton, J. 1991. Sunk Costs and Market Structure: Price Competition, Advertising, and the Evolution of Concentration. MIT Press, Cambridge, MA.

Tae, C. J., M. G. Jacobides. 2011. Tracking value migration along an industry architecture: Kingpins, bottlenecks, and evolutionary dynamics. Working paper, London Business School, London.

Tee, R., A. Gawer. 2009. Industry architecture as a determinant of successful platform strategies: A case study of the i-mode mobile Internet service. Eur. Management Rev. 6(4) 217-232.

Teece, D. J. 2010. Business models, business strategy, and innovation. Long Range Planning 43(2/3) 172-194.

Tripsas, M. 2009. Technology, identity, and inertia through the lens of "The Digital Photography Company." Organ. Sci. 20(2) 441-460.

Tripsas, M., G. Gavetti. 2000. Capabilities, cognition, and inertia: Evidence from digital imaging. Strategic Management J. 21(10-11) 1147-1161.

Velkar, A. 2009. Transactions, standardisation, and competition: Establishing uniform sizes in the British wire industry. Bus. Hist. 51(2) 222-247.

von Neumann, J., O. Morgenstern. 1944. Theory of Games and Economic Behavior. Princeton University Press, Princeton, NJ.

Wigand, R. T., C. W. Steinfield, M. L. Markus. 2005. Information technology standards choices and industry structure outcomes: The case of the U.S. home mortgage industry. J. Management Inform. Systems 22(2) 165-191.

Williamson, O. E. 1999. Strategy research: Governance and competence perspectives. Strategic Management J. 20(12) 1087-1108.

Winter, S. G., G. Cattani, A. Dorsch 2007. The value of moderate obsession: Insights from a new model of organizational search. Organ. Sci. 18(3) 403-419.

Zott, C., R. Amit. 2007. Business model design and the performance of entrepreneurial firms. Organ. Sci. 18(2) 181-199.

Zott, C., R. Amit, L. Massa. 2012. The business model: Theoretical roots, recent developments and future research. J. Management Stud. Forthcoming.

Chapter 10

Prologue
Walter W. Powell
Professor of Sociology, Organizational Behavior, Management Science and Engineering, and Communication
Stanford University

Microfoundations of Institutional Theory

Walter W. Powell and Jeannette A. Colyvas

Prologue:[18]

Walter W. Powell

We wrote the paper republished in this volume to bring more attention to the micro processes of institutions, networks, and organizations. I believe this chapter came about because there is widespread recognition that work in macro institutional research could benefit from what we call a micro motor. I think most people understand that institutions are sustained, altered, and diminished as individuals enact their everyday social worlds. There has been very little thinking, however, about how to study these dynamics or what a theory of the micro foundations of institutions would look like. So the editors of the *Sage Handbook of Organizational Institutionalism* asked me and others who had been working on these issues to contribute chapters. Steve Barley has a nice chapter in the volume that examines the older school of Chicago Sociology and how it might be revitalized for such purposes.

Many of the ideas in our paper have their origins in work I had been doing for some time. There were elements in the introduction (DiMaggio & Powell, 1991) to Paul DiMaggio's and my so-called "orange book," *The New Institutionalism in Organizational Analysis.* There we outlined a theory of practical action that was in part a response to people who had read earlier works (DiMaggio & Powell, 1983; Meyer & Rowan, 1977) and thought that mimetic and normative isomorphism involves mere copying and replication. Paul and I, in our introductory essay, tried to emphasize that practical consciousness involves a lot of energy, effort, and reflection and that habit isn't simply passivity. Habits are a skilled means of directing attention and everyday reasoning that requires individuals to negotiate rules and manage procedures in a flexible and reflexive way. We are constantly trying to assure ourselves, and people all around us,

---

[18] This prologue is a rendering of an interview with Woody Powell on June 19, 2013

that our behaviors are in some ways sensible. I think this is an important, albeit somewhat subterranean, area of work in organization studies. There are some elements in Nelson and Winter's (1982) discussion of routines, as well as in Sid Winter's more recent work on capabilities, which is also part of this commemorative volume. Herb Simon's writing on habits and premises in his *Administrative Behavior* is clearly foundational. I think in some way all of these writings reflect an interest in how the routines of organizational life are sustained, and view such routines as more than mere replications.

Theorizing the challenges of making replication successful was part of what motivated this paper. While writing it, it also happened that both Jeannette and I were working on research projects in which we observed individuals who were responsible for managing lines of work in specific organizations that were later seen as quite remarkable and entrepreneurial, and subsequently touted as great efforts of change. We were familiar enough with the cases to know that when those accounts of entrepreneurial acumen were championed, they were quite different from the facts on the ground. In both cases, the individuals in question thought they were doing rather routine work in hewing to the values of their respective organizations. It just so happened that momentous changes grew out of their routine actions. We have to be careful in our studies not to replace the emergence of change from everyday actions with veneration of a "muscular, instrumental change agent." Many times people celebrate "heroes" by sampling on the dependent variable and only picking cases that are successful examples.

I have been interested in the concept of micro translation since Ron Jepperson's thoughtful chapter in *The New Institutionalism in Organizational Analysis*. It spoke to how people pull down, from the larger social order, forms of justification for their actions, and how larger rituals get instantiated and extended in day-to-day interactions. At that time, however, he did not have much to say about a social psychology of institutions.

In our view, there are at least two good social psychologies that can help us with explaining multi-level phenomena and social reproduction. One is Karl Weick's (1995) concept of sensemaking and his ideas of retrospective accounting and post hoc dissidence reduction. Also useful are his beautiful writings on the Mann Gulch incident, and human intuition and expertise. In addition, we drew a good bit on ethnomethodology, a stream of work that is quite rich and doesn't get sufficient attention today. This work includes remarkable empirical organizational studies—particularly analyses of how people make sense of their experiences in courts of law, juvenile detention centers, and psychiatric hospitals. These studies represent various ways of acting in organizations as a form of giving accounts. These accounts not only narrate what people are doing, but also justify what they are doing.

Moreover, I think some of the imagery in Goffman's (1974) front-stage and back-stage frames as a way in which the self and the organization is presented to the exterior world is extremely useful in regards to understanding how institutions present their public "selves". It is interesting that we have this rich social psychological theory from the 1960s era, and part of the effort in our chapter was to recapture strands of that work and try to bring it forward to help develop ideas about how institutions get inhabited and how people live inside institutions and engage in everyday reasoning.

One of the toughest questions I ever received about this paper was from my good friend and colleague John Meyer, who, as everyone knows, is a very macro-oriented theorist. He sees Weber's spirit of rationalization spreading around the world at a pretty rapid clip. After reading the paper, he said, "This is interesting—but wouldn't any old social psychology do? Don't you just need something to start turning the wheels?" That question or provocation has stayed with me for a very long time. I think his challenge is: Why does a micro motor of sensemaking and ethnomethodology work better than other kinds of social psychology? My answer is still not sufficiently well formed, but relates to how both those literatures view habit as an active effort involving everyday reasoning. The development of interpretative schemas and how those schemas become a repository of organizational knowledge are key to the dynamics of the micro motor and its relationship to macro institutional constructs. At least, that is my pushback to John's very good question.

Although we have received many tough questions and smart comments concerning this chapter, I don't believe we would drastically change the content. I do think there are things we would want to add— probably two key things. First, we would like to have provided more depth on methods. To a considerable extent, the research that we draw on is ethnographic, and I don't think that ethnographic methods are the only way you can study these processes. There are lots of ways you could examine micro foundations through laboratory experiments and agent-based modeling that pick up on how norms move and travel through and within communities. So I would like to have seen more methodological variety; I think that would have helped the paper.

The second feature that would have been interesting would have been to make it more prescriptive. We should try to chart the tools that students and managers would take away from these insights. What do you look for in organizations as evidence of how policies and procedures are reproduced? For example, my students and I are currently studying linguistic networks and the ways in which organizations are similar in their use of terms. We are gathering content from web pages of organizations and then characterizing organizations by their similarity or dissimilarity in language use. From this you get a sense of the ways in which communities are formed through a common language. I think developing more prescriptive ideas about how you would take these insights from the micro foundations and study them would have been helpful. I understand there was a review essay of the *Sage Handbook of Organizational Institutionalism* that indicated that this chapter has been one of the most cited from the book. So apparently people are reading it, but it would have been nice to give them more of a toolkit that they would take away from it.

Of course, one of the fun things about teaching at the GWU ELP program is you get a reflective cast of experienced professionals. These are people who have been through battles and have been around the "organizational change" block many times in a number of different organizations. The fact that they are pursuing a doctorate at this stage in their career shows there is a curiosity and a desire to make sense of these experiences. I think for these scholar-practitioners, an article like this resonates in a way that it probably doesn't for people who don't have those experiences and backgrounds.

References

DiMaggio, P. J., & Powell, W. W. (1983). "The Iron Cage Revisited: Institutional Isomorphism and Collective Rationality in Organizational Fields." 48(2): 147-60.

DiMaggio, P. J., & Powell, W. W. (1991). Introduction. In *The new institutionalism in organization analysis* (pp. 1-38), W. Powell and P. DiMaggio, eds. Chicago, IL: University of Chicago Press.

Goffman, E. (1974). *Frame analysis.* New York, NY: Anchor Books.

Meyer, J. W., & Rowan, B. (1977). Institutionalized organizations: Formal structure as myth and ceremony. *American Journal of Sociology, 83,* 340-363.

Nelson, R. R., & Winter, S. G. (1982). *An evolutionary theory of economic change.* Cambridge, MA: Belknap Press of Harvard University Press.

Weick, K. E. (1995). *Sensemaking in Organizations.* Sage Publishers.

Microfoundations of Institutional Theory[19]

Walter W. Powell and Jeannette A. Colyvas

INTRODUCTION

For almost two decades, scholars have stressed the need to make the microfoundations of institutional theory more explicit (DiMaggio and Powell, 1991; Zucker, 1991). Curiously, there has been limited progress in this effort, although Barley, Glynn, and Sahlin, in Chapters 8, 16 and 20 in this volume, also remedy this deficit. We think that much analytical purchase can be gained by developing a micro-level component of institutional analysis. Moreover, there are useful building blocks from ethnomethodology to Goffman on interaction rituals to Weick on sensemaking and social psychological research on legitimation that can be drawn upon to contribute to this effort.

We begin by making a case for the benefits of examining micro-processes. We then selectively review the terrain, cobbling together useful, albeit disparate, lines of research and theory. The thrust of this chapter is generative and by no means intended as a comprehensive survey. From these diverse sources, we contend, a viable micro-analysis of institutionalization can be developed. We apply our ideas to several contemporary issues, notably the rise of academic entrepreneurship in universities in the U.S. and the trend toward increased efforts at earned income by nonprofit organizations. These applications illustrate the analytical utility of our approach. We conclude with a discussion of research tools generated by this line of theorizing that can be used to fashion compelling, multi-level explanations.

---

[19] Originally Published as: Powell, W.W. and J.A. Colyvas (2008). Microfoundations of Institutional Theory. The Sage Handbook of Organizational Institutionalism. R. Greenwood, C. Oliver, R. Suddaby and K. Sahlin. Los Angeles, Sage: 276-298.

WHY A MICRO-LEVEL THEORY OF INSTITUTIONALIZATION?

The bulk of institutional research has focused on the sectoral, field, or global level. And properly so, as the transfer of ideas, practices, and organizational forms spans the boundaries of organizations, industries, and nations. A core insight of institutional theory is just how taken-for-granted formal organization and rationalization has become (Drori, Meyer, and Hwang, 2006). In our view these macro-lines of analysis could also profit from a micro-motor. Such a motor would involve theories that attend to enaction, interpretation, translation, and meaning. Institutions are sustained, altered, and extinguished as they are enacted by individuals in concrete social situations. We need a richer understanding of how individuals locate themselves in social relations and interpret their context. How do organizational participants maintain or transform the institutional forces that guide daily practice? From an institutional perspective, how are the passions and interests implicated in human behavior? In our view, the development of micro-level explanations will give more depth to accounts of macro-level events and relationships.

Institutional forces shape individual interests and desires, framing the possibilities for action and influencing whether behaviors result in persistence or change. Macroinstitutional effects, through processes of classification and categorization, create conventions that are the scripts for meaning making. This process is recursive and self-reinforcing. Institutional logics are instantiated in and carried by individuals through their actions, tools, and technologies. Some actions reinforce existing conventions, while others reframe or alter them. Ideas can be picked up in one setting and transposed to another, tools can be multi-purpose, and some settings are rife with multiple logics. Such situations afford considerable latitude for human agency and interpretation.

Nonetheless, the individuals that presently populate institutional analysis are portrayed as either 'cultural dopes' (Garfinkel, 1967: 68-75) or heroic 'change agents' (Strang and Sine, 2002: 503-507). The move to consider institutional entrepreneurs was motivated by a desire to replace the over-socialized individuals who seemed slavishly devoted to habit and fashion. But the celebration of entrepreneurs has perhaps gone too far, as not all change is led by entrepreneurs, and surely heroic actors and cultural dopes are a poor representation of the gamut of human behavior. Indeed, we recoil somewhat at the frequent use of 'actors' in social science writings to characterize both individuals and organizations. As Meyer (Chapter 21 in this volume) notes, such language typically implies purposive, muscular, rather free actors, unembedded in their surrounding context. Institutional theory gains little by making unleashed actors the drivers of institutional change.

Institutions are reproduced through the everyday activities of individuals. Members of organizations engage in daily practices, discover puzzles or anomalies in their work, problematize these questions and develop answers to them by theorizing them. In turn, participants ascribe meaning to these theories and, in so doing, develop and reproduce taken-for-granted understandings. Institutional transformation is often rather subtle, not particularly abrupt, and apparent only after a considerable period. Rather than perspectives that either highlight habitual replication or savvy change agents, we stress that most micro-motives are fairly mundane, aimed at interpretation, alignment, and muddling through. And, as individuals and groups engage in such actions and resist others' attempts as well, they may well trans-form logics and alter identities.

We contend that institutional analysis needs more attention to everyday processes than momentous events, to less powerful members of organizations as opposed to only leaders or champions, and to cultural and cognitive aspects as well as political ones. Research on external shocks that prompt change and on voices that catalyze transformations has been valuable in adding insight into how institutions are altered. But a more explicit focus is needed on how the local affairs of existing members of a field can both sustain and prompt shifts in practices and conventions. The ongoing activities of organizations can produce both continuity and change, as such pursuits vary across time and place.

There is presently much interest in under-standing institutional change, as attention has shifted from early concerns with persistence and convergence to growing concern with dynamics and contestation. We welcome this development, but worry that too many analyses conflate macro-factors with structural forces and assume these factors only reinforce stability and homogeneity, while associating micro-factors with entrepreneurship and agency. But individuals also play a powerful role in maintaining the social order, and organizations can serve as entrepreneurs. Moreover, macrotrends, such as globalization, can be profoundly destabilizing to local orders and individuals. It is a mistake for institutional analysts to blindly equate change with the micro-level and persistence with the macro. We need to develop multi-level explanations that account for recursive influences.

Some attention has already been paid to micro-translation, or an understanding of how macro-categories get inside the heads of individuals (Jepperson, 1991). Macro-framings or values can be `pulled down' to the everyday level of practice, as varied activities can be pursued under a common interpretation or account, or diverse practices can be pursued in the search of a common goal (Colyvas and Powell, 2006; Colyvas, 2007a). Indeed, many micro-processes represent local instantiations of macro-level trends. We need a parallel effort to link key micro-concepts, e.g., identity, sense making, typifications, frames, and categories with macro-processes of institutionalization, and show how these processes ratchet upwards. This linkage between levels holds promise to better explain institutional dynamics. Attention to the mediating role of language, interaction rituals, and categories will help explain how organizational routines and rules develop, stick, and fall into disuse.

BUILDING BLOCKS FOR MICROFOUNDATIONS

As a rough approximation, we divide the literatures we discuss below into two main groupings. The first draws on arguments that adopt a 'built-up' focus, in which micro-level rituals and negotiations aggregate over time. These local influences may bubble up and threaten or replace macro-level coherence. The second line of analysis focuses on how macro-orders are 'pulled down,' and become imbricated in local or particular cases, situating macro-effects inside organizations and individuals. Both streams of research are vital to building microfoundations for institutional theory, but it is important to attend to the different directions of the causal arrows in these research traditions.

There is, of course, an exceedingly broad literature in social psychology. Our goal is selective, that is, to cull useful work that complements the arguments that have characterized institutional theory and aid in explaining the creation, transformation, and impact of institutions. To this end, we draw on research that highlights constructivist processes. To illustrate, consider the verbs typically used in the literatures we highlight. With interactionist arguments, scholars commonly use the terms *saving face* or *affirming*. In ethnomethodology, *negotiate* and *improvise* have primacy. With sensemaking, *enact* is the standard bearer. Research on legitimation processes finds *associated with, orient towards, comply with,* and *accept,* Note that we rarely find words like *choose, plan,* or *determine* (see Weick, Sutcliffe, and Obstfeld, 2005 for a lovely discussion on this point). These verbs are more constructivist, constitutive and interpretive than calculative or purposive. The individuals in these theories *behave,* but they seldom *choose* (see discussion in DiMaggio and Powell, 1991: 7-11).

Many of the writings that provided the initial microfoundations for institutional theory date from 1967—Erving Goffman's *Interaction Ritual,* Harold Garfinkel's *Studies in Ethnomethodology,* and Berger and Luckman's *The Social Construction of Reality* were all published in that propitious year. It is notable that we continue to draw on this work that is more than four decades old. In their canonical article, Meyer and Rowan (1977) observed that much ceremonial activity, and accompanying categorical rules, generates conflict and uncertainty in day-to-day activities. They proposed that organizations resolve these tensions through

398

decoupling and a logic of confidence. Drawing on Goffman (1967: 5-45), they invoked his idea of 'maintaining face' Crafting a distinction between the public face and backstage reality, overlooking or avoiding anomalies, minimizing discordant signals, and decoupling formal procedures and structures from everyday work are all steps taken to maintain the assumption that organizations are acting appropriately and that lamer rationalized myths are sustained. This 'logic of confidence' is crucial to maintaining an illusion of consensus within schools, for ex ample.

DiMaggio and Powell's (1991) overview of the elements of a theory of practical action also drew on microfoundations, using an ensemble of ideas from Simon (1945), Garfinkel (1967), and Giddens (1984). Responding to readings of their 1983 article that contended that mimetic and normative isomorphism entailed 'mere' copying and replication, DiMaggio and Powell emphasized that practical consciousness involves energy, effort, and reflection. Drawing on Simon (1945: 79-109), they recognized that habitual action does not reflect passivity, but is a skilled means of directing attention. Garfinkel (1967) contributed the critical insight that everyday reasoning requires individuals to negotiate rules and procedures flexibly and reflexively to assure themselves and others around them that their behavior is sensible. Giddens' (1984: 54) observation that sustaining social interaction is the 'basic security system' of the self, and that control of human anxiety is the 'most generalized motivational origin of human conduct' was also influential. DiMaggio and Powell's initial outline of a theory of practical action was brief, but it clearly attempted to build on microfoundations. We seek to continue and deepen that discussion, and build on others who have made contributions in recent years (Jennings and Greenwood, 2003; Lawrence and Suddaby, 2006; Weber and Glynn, 2006; Lounsbury and Crumley, 2007).

Interaction rituals

Goffman (1967) was keenly aware that individual capability at 'face work' varied considerably, but that such variation pertained more to the efficacy than the frequency of its application' (p. 13). Skill at face-work is a distinguishing feature that differentiates individuals. He was also very cognizant of how interaction rituals connected to the larger social order. Goffman himself was a highly skilled card player, and he drew a distinction between 'the value of a hand drawn at cards and the capacity of the person who plays it' (p. 32). Not only are the rules of how cards are played highly governed, a reputation for good or bad play is a face that requires maintaining. Such micro-encounters at a card table represent sequences of coordinated understandings from, which social interaction is accomplished.

For Goffman, speech, expressive behavior, and demeanor embody intentions, but these individual instruments are 'governed' by the normative order of society. In *Asylums,* Goffman (1961) discussed how organizations instill tacit acceptance and conformity through inducements. But in his work on face-saving, he emphasized how individuals use talk, with ritual care, to present an image of self-control and dignity. While standards and rules 'are impressed upon individuals from without,' the particular rules an individual follows derive 'from requirements established in the ritual organization of social encounters' (Goffman, 1967: 45).

Ethnomethodology

While Goffman emphasized how facility at everyday interactions sustains face, Harold Garfinkel, one of Talcott Parsons' favorite students, developed a distinctive line of inquiry that stressed the skills that emerge out of everyday encounters, which generate sociability and reproduce the social order. His ethnomethodological approach has provided tantalizing insights for institutional theory, most clearly in Zucker's (1977) work, where she argues that many taken-for-granted understandings are 'built up' from the ground level by participants in interactions, and in DiMaggio and Powell's (1991: 22-27) sketch of a theory of practical action. Ethnomethodology never developed into an expansive subfield, and given both its cult-like approach and the controversies it provoked, perhaps it never had the chance.[1] Nevertheless, Garfinkel's focus on practical reasoning and the role of 'accounts' in normalizing and legitimating the social order offers considerable insight into the implicit and contested assumptions that make organizational life possible. Rather than find social order in cultural norms or social roles, ethnomethodologists examine the cognitive work that individuals do to assure both themselves and those around them that their behavior is reasonable.

There are several compelling reasons to revisit this line of work. Contemporary scholars are largely unaware of just how much of this research focused on work and organizations. Meticulous studies of record-keeping procedures in juvenile justice facilities (Cicourel, 1968), high mortality wards in hospitals (Sudnow, 1967), and psychiatric clinics (Garfinkel and Bittner, 1967) reveal how counting, reporting, and legal requirements are often highly improvised, as veteran staff draw on deep, tacit knowledge of how reports ought to be assembled. Other work examined case files, folders, and dockets to ascertain the classification schemes used in psychiatry or a public welfare agency, where documents could be treated either as 'plain facts' or the opportunity to construct an account that provides grounds for accepting the testimony of the document against the testimony of the welfare applicant (Zimmerman, 1969).

Bittner's (1967) studies of policing on skid row illuminate how officers performed complicated and demanding work with relative ease, without any real personal or peer recognition of their skills. Given that the destitute and mentally ill were often the objects of police work on skid row, perhaps the lack of high regard is to be expected. But Bittner underscored how strongly a powerful sense of craftsmanship among the police was rendered routine, even as it went unacknowledged. Similarly, Sudnow (1965) analyzed how the penal code was used by public defenders with great facility. Lawyers took into account a welter of 'facts'—the ecological characteristics of a community, the biographies of criminals and victims, and past records of criminal activity. They trans-, formed a criminal action into a shorthand representation that was intelligible to attorneys and judges. Sudnow's brilliant analysis revealed how delicate teamwork between the offices of public defender and public prosecutor in the face of a demanding organizational calendar jointly facilitated the construction of 'normal crimes,' a proverbial characterization that certain kinds of illegal actions were typically committed by particular types of people. Once such categorizations were made, plea bargaining ensued, based on unstated recipes for reducing original charges to lesser defenses to avoid the costs of trial.

In ethnomethodological studies, categories and classifications become interpretive schema that members of organizations draw on. Over time, these schemas become a repository of organizational knowledge. As particular schemas become routinized through repeated application and use, they develop a habitual, taken-for-granted character. Berger and Luckman (1967) emphasized that once joint activities are habitualized and reciprocally interpreted, patterns both harden and deepen as they are transmitted to others, particularly newcomers. When schemas become perceived as objective, exteriorized facts, their contingent origins are obscured. Organizations do have rich and varied repertoires, however, and multiple schemas are available. The possibility of mixing or combining practices in alternative or novel ways to produce different patterns is ever present.

Throughout this rich vein of research, ethnomethodologists demonstrate how classifications and categorizations are invoked on the fly by skilled actors to keep peace on the streets, in the courts, in hospital wards, and welfare agencies. Consider the contrast of this view with the conception of organization found in many other lines of organization theory. Rather than struggling with or coping with uncertainty, the practical reasoning view emphasizes how situations are rendered comprehensible, and sees such efforts as an ongoing, contingent accomplishment. In contrast, ever since Weiber, most students of organizations regard formal structures and procedures as 'ideally possible, but practically unattainable' (Bittner, 1965). Selznick (1949), for example, attributed these limitations to the recalcitrance of the tools of action; while Weber conceived of the typical bureaucracy more as a target or an idealization. For the ethnomethodologists, however, bureaucracy is neither a rarified nor lofty goal, but deeply embedded in common-sense routines of everyday life. Organization is a formula to which all sorts of problems can be brought for solution (Bittner, 1965).

This focus on practical reasoning as a routine accomplishment emphasizes how people in organizations both make and find a reasonable world.[2] Organizational life entails constant doing and achieving. For Goffman and Garfinkel, social order is created on the 'ground floor,' through situated local practices. As practices are reproduced over time and across settings, macro-categories emerge from these interactions and negotiations.

Performativity

Across the Atlantic, a companion line of work known as actor-network theory has developed in France, focusing on scientific research and practical applications of science outside the laboratory (Latour, 1987). The core assumption of these studies is that laboratory life often requires scientists to create material conditions in which theory and reality can be juxtaposed and in so doing create affordances that make science 'work' (Latour and Woolgar, 1979; Callon, 1986). Callon (1998) has recently expanded the actor-network approach to the field of economics, and analyzed how market participants think about economics and act in relation to one another and to the market through their models and artifacts.[3] This approach to 'making markets' resonates with core themes of ethnomethodology in the view that phenomena only exist in the 'doing' and social relations have to be continuously performed in order to persist.

For Callon (1998, 2006), a discourse is performative if it contributes to the construction of the reality that it describes. Callon (2006) is careful to distinguish the idea of performativity from Goffman's imagery of the presentation of self and from Merton's (1948) notion of a self-fulfilling prophecy. A self-fulfilling prophecy often has a pathological form of influence or entails a misconception of the situation. In contrast, performativity is not arbitrary, rather there are contests associated with performance. Success or failure become clear at the end of struggles, when opposition, controversy and cooperation are sorted out. The general claim of this line of study is that such diverse domains as science, technology, accounting, marketing, engineering, and even friendship are all arenas where activities, relationships, theories, and tools are both created and enhanced by their performance.

The Scottish sociologist Donald MacKenzie has been highly influential in developing and studying the idea of 'the performativity of economics.' He has, with his students, studied many of the major economic innovations of the late 20th century, viewing economists and their theories and tools not only as describers and analysts, but as participants and inventors. Mackenzie and Millo's (2003) research on options trading, which 'with its cognitive complexity and mature mathematical models has been a central driver of the marketized, mathematicized risk-evaluation culture' of modern life, shows that the famous Black, Scholes and Merton model did not describe an already existing world. When first introduced, the model's assumptions were unrealistic and prices differed systematically from it. But with its growing use and prevalence, option prices began to exhibit a near-perfect fit to the values predicted by the model.[4] Clearly, technological and computational improvements played a role in the acceptance of options, as did the elite status of the authors of the model, but options pricing came to shape the way participants thought and talked about finance, and altered the understanding of volatility and arbitrage. MacKenzie (2006) does not consider a financial model to be a camera capturing reality, but an engine that allows traders to explore and exploit economic phenomena.

Abstracting from this important case, MacKenzie (2006) argues that performativity entails transformation: an aspect of economics must be used in a way that has effects on the economic processes in question. The model or tool, he argues, must make a difference, that is economic processes that incorporate this element of economic reasoning must differ from processes where it is not used. MacKenzie takes pains not to portray modern economists as rational, calculating agents but as human beings, limited in their cognitive capacity and susceptible to social influence. Nor does he fully embrace a view that businesses in the U.S. and around the world have become 'financialized,' and attend solely to market-value maximization, even though his superb analysis of the legitimation of options pricing provides consider-able evidence for such an argument. Instead, his focus on performativity illuminates how human beings can 'achieve outcomes that go beyond their individual cognitive grasp' (MacKenzie, 2006: 268). By stressing human cognitive limits and the distributed nature of cognition in contemporary organizations, this line of research demonstrates how the 'social' and the 'technological' come together to constitute markets.

We turn now to other micro research pro-grams that also focus on how everyday practice in organizations produces meaning—whether in the form of accepted routines or legitimated models. These other approaches, we contend, emphasize more that interaction often draws on the larger social order, as well as accumulated experience, to interpret and produce organizational life. These strands of social psychology attend less to emergence and performance, and more to interpretation, appropriateness, and meaning making,

Sensemaking

Karl Weick's research program OD sensemaking addresses how people enact order and coordinate action. Individuals convert circumstances into action through the reciprocal interpretation of who they are and how they understand their environment (Weick, 1995),

Identity, the enacted world, and accepted mental models are all key to this perspective. Taken together, sensemaking is the locus of how 'meanings materialize that inform and constrain identity into action' (Weick, Sutcliffe, and Obstfeld, 2005: 409).

Weick and colleagues draw on many strands of microsociology to fashion their approach. Garfinkel's (1967) insight that rationality is constructed through common-place interactions is emphasized; so is Goffman's (1974) use of frames as providing a structure to social context. Sensemaking analyses share with ethnomethodology a methodological stance of privileging cases that reveal rather than represent.[5] But there are notable distinctions as well. While the ethnomethodologists highlight the cognitive work of individuals in creating social order, sensemaking attends to the contingent influences of nouns and role structure. For Weick, conceptions of identity and logics of action are relational, constructed not only through projections of self and others' perceptions, but also through scripted interactions in relation to what others are 'supposed to do.' Individuals are enmeshed in a structure of relationships, taking cues from both situations and others, and these guideposts provide substance for them to enact their environments.

In his analysis of the Mann Gulch fire dis-aster in Montana, Weick (1993) demonstrates how a breakdown in sensemaking explains what went wrong in a seemingly routine encounter for a highly trained crew. The disintegration of the crew's routines in the face of unexpected conditions impeded the firefighters' ability to draw on their stock of experiences to generate a novel means of survival, or to comply with their leader who did. Weick attributes the tragic deaths of these skilled men to three features, a breakdown in role structure among members of the team, a stalwart adherence to a less critical categorization of the fire, and practical challenges to their identities as firefighters. All of these features are reflected in the difficulties that the firefighters faced to make sense of who they were, the situation they encountered, and the repertoire of actions they should take. Because the stock experience of the firefighters did not match their anticipated, less critical categorization of the fire when they arrived on the scene, the situation was rendered meaningless, as 'less and less of what they saw made sense' (Weick, 1993: 635). Cues from other firefighters, e.g. stopping for dinner and taking pictures, reinforced a spurious categorization of the fire and impeded the firemen's ability to activate a different course of action. When the leader of the crew, confronted with looming disaster, lit a fire in the only escape route, lay down in its ashes, and called on his crew to drop their tools and join him, the team disintegrated. The firefighter's identified hindered their ability to comprehend an order to drop the very materials that defined who they were and comprehend the practicality of a solution that would have saved their lives. Weick's analysis demonstrates that even very effectively trained and organized teams can falter when 'the sense of what is occurring and the means to rebuild that sense collapse together' (1993: 633).

From a sensemaking view, many features of organizational life are *uncertain*, which relates to ignorance or the inability to estimate future consequences to present actions. Organizational life is also wrought with ambiguity, which reflects the inability to attribute clear, mutually exclusive categories, codes or specifications (March, 1994; Weick, 1995). These distinctions are important because while information can provide a remedy for uncertainty, it can also further *ambiguity*, as evidenced by the Mann Gulch fire when new information did not fit preconceived categories. Weick also draws on Garfinkel to emphasize that *equivocality* is present when numerous or disputed interpretations exist. As with Garfinkel's jurors, individuals may justify multiple, incompatible accounts, often with the same evidence. Weick argues that uncertainty, ambiguity, and equivocality may occasion different triggers to, and remedies for, sensemaking.

A notable feature of sensemaking studies is a focus on situations where apparently normal events go badly awry.[6] Sensemaking emphasizes interpretation and (mis)perception of the environment, especially where received wisdom is poorly aligned with current context. For example,

Scott Snook's 2000) examination of the fire' incident when US F-15 fighter pilots shot down their own Black Hawk helicopters in peacetime over the Persian Gulf, demonstrates how an organizational failure may occur without anything breaking or anyone to blame. Snook attributes this tragedy to a slow, gradual drift away from globally synchronized logics of action, encoded in written rules and procedures, to locally generated task-based routines. Such 'practical drift' is often manifested locally as adaption because individuals organize around immediate demands of work, and thus learn and adjust to their own realities. Similar to Mann Gulch, where the smokejumpers ignored cues that the fire was more serious than categorized, the F-15 fighter pilots were unable to identify that the helicopters were not the enemy. In both settings, the individuals attended to cues that fit their expectations, missing numerous contrary signals. Furthermore, like the smoke jumpers, the fighter pilots relied on each other and their team for coordination, and their responses reinforced their mistaken attribute clear, mutually exclusive categories, interpretation.

Through an analysis of the complexities of command in military missions, Snook demonstrates how meaning trumped decision making as context, identity, and the enacted environment constrained interpretation and shaped action. The F pilots had to identify 'what was going on' before taking any action, and their interpretation was constructed through who they were, prior experience, the pre-flight context, and social interactions (Snook, 2000: 81). Sadly, their inaccurate reading led them to shoot down their comrades in broad daylight.

Sensemaking provides important insights to the analysis of meaning, particularly the idea that meaning making is not only about creation but also contingent expression. For Weick, the key to identifying such instances rests on the view that sensemaking is inherently retrospective and precedes action because situations are only understood upon completion.[7] Meaning is shaped through attention to what has already occurred, and is therefore directed, not attached, to action. This contrast emphasizes the influence of what is current to perceptions of the past. Thus, anything that affects remembering will affect the sense that is made of remembering' (Weick, 1995: 26). Furthermore, since outcomes and subjective objects are implicit in interpretation, sensemaking entails a process that simultaneously enacts identity and environment. Identity is central because individuals act based on who they are, not on what choices they have, and this feature is constituted out of the process of interaction. Mead's (1934) insight that each individual is at 'parliament of selves' and that 'social processes precede the individual mind' are critical. The environment is not viewed as a fixed and stable reality, but as a co-construction of individuals' minds and their actions. Enactment represents the reciprocal interaction of the material and the cognitive world. Thus, individuals and environments are mutually constitutive.

This feature extends the process of sensemaking beyond interpretation. Weick (1995: 13-14) likens the distinction between sensemaking and interpretation as the difference between discovery and invention, Interpretation, with its focus on identification and understanding vis-à-vis a wider reality, relates to discovery, which, implies that something is evident and needs to be recognized or approximated. Features of the world are pre-given or ready-made. Sensemaking, in its focus on process and generation, relates to invention, which emphasizes how images of a wider reality are created, maintained and rendered objective. Much as action precedes sensemaking, sensemaking is a precursor to interpretation.

A sensemaking approach directs attention to the importance of language, routines, and communication for analyzing microprocesses. While emphasizing that various institutional materials are commonly 'pulled down' by individuals and translated within Organizations, these processes may differ across circumstances. Multiple modes of meaning making occur at the interface of identity and the enacted environment, and how such understandings are forged and enacted occurs through retrospection. Sensemaking is thus a key micro-mechanism of institutionalization that allows consideration of both the 'cognitive complexities' that guide organizational behavior and recognition of the varied ways that institutionalized practices operate at the micro-level (Jennings and Greenwood, 2003).

Status expectations

Research on expectation states provides a further point of discussion of how macro-categories guide micro-interactions (Berger, Ridgeway, Fisek, and Norman, 1998; Correll and Ridgeway, 2003; Zelditch, 2001, 2004). This line of research views legitimation as a process shaped by interpersonal status hierarchies, in which individuals draw on widely shared cultural beliefs concerning status and success. These referential beliefs are evoked in situations as both guides for interaction and as ready accounts, creating strong expectations as to the types of individuals who are or should be influential in specific circumstances. In this fashion, broader understandings about who and what is appropriate guide local circumstances, and these interactional processes further reinforce cultural beliefs about what characteristics and practices are perceived as appropriate.

Research on expectation states and legitimation analyzes the emergence of status within task groups, observing that power and stereotypes regarding gender, race, age, education and occupation. In turn, these characterizations shape and legitimate the manner in which group members evaluate one another (Ridgeway and Berger, 1986; Ridgeway and Walker, 1995). Thus, assignments of status draw readily on the macro stratification system, while the assignments and rewards that ensue at the group level reinforce the larger social order.

Put differently, micro-level consensus is generated through a process in which values and beliefs from the larger society are pulled down into local circumstances, creating differential expectations about the performance individuals in task groups. These expectations can become taken-for-granted features of organizations, and persist even if they are unjust or unproductive, thus giving them an 'objective' quality.

Owen-Smith (2001) analyzed a neuroscience lab and the rankings of a community of colleagues with respect to experimental and analytic ability and productivity. He found that assessments of ability and accomplishment are not neatly correlated. Instead, position in the lab's prestige order was heavily shaped by expectations that accrue with rank and discipline, and whether one was dependent on autonomous in regards to funding. In this academic research setting, gender as a status measure was less consequential than stereotyped expectations based on disciplinary affiliation.

Research on expectation states offers another lens through which to view how widely shared societal beliefs become incorporated and reinforced at the work group level. This line of work emphasizes that it is in the conduct of tasks that social objects and categories drawn from the larger society are rendered legitimate. This perspective complements sensemaking by stressing how external social statuses are manifested in everyday activities.

MICRO-PERSPECTIVES ON INSTITUTIONAL CHANGE

We turn to a discussion of two examples of recent transformations that have typically been analyzed in terms of broader social and political currents. In both settings, exogenous forces loom large in current explanations. When attention is directed to the organization level, most reports celebrate risk-taking entrepreneurs. in contrast, our aim is to demonstrate how much explanatory power can be garnered by examining the micro-level processes underpinning these changes. We underscore how the 'entrepreneurs' did not even consider that they were taking risks, but instead were responding to unanticipated situations.

Universities and academic entrepreneurship

In recent decades, U.S. universities and the profession of academic science have under-gone a profound transformation in the way science is conducted. Where university and industry were once separate domains, public and private science have become intermingled, notably in the norms and practices related to career advancement and in the development and dissemination of knowledge. Patenting and licensing academic research findings, taking equity in start-ups, and encouraging academic entrepreneurship, have become core features of how U.S. universities define success.

Most studies of this transformation stress either pecuniary interests or national policies (Lath and Shankerman, 2003).[8] Indeed, academic institutions made more than $1385 billion in gross revenues in fiscal year 2004 from technology licenses (AUTM, 2005). Before 1980, there were fewer than 25 university technology transfer offices, and today there are well over 200 (AUTM, 2005). Clearly, some universities are profiting considerably from technology licensing, and virtually every research university now has a technology transfer office. Government policy has strongly encouraged such efforts. The Bayh—Dole Act in 1980 authorized universities to take title to patents generated by federally funded research. A Supreme Court decision in the same year, *Diamond vs. Chakrabariy,* authorized the patenting of life, providing a catalyst to the emerging biotechnology industry. A few universities, namely University of Wisconsin, Stanford, MIT, and UCSF are credited for shaping the way in which technology transfer became organized (Mowery, Nelson, Sampat and Zieclonis, 2004). Many organizational accounts point to the founders and consultants to university tech transfer programs as the key institutional entrepreneurs for the new university models (Mowery et al., 2004). One of these founders, Niels Reimers, created the Stanford University Office of Technology Licensing, a highly successful operation on which other technology transfer offices have modeled their operations. Reimers went on to reorganize programs at MIT and UCSF, and consult to many other universities in Europe and Asia. The 'Stanford Model' is practically a household term in the technology licensing community, emphasizing a marketing focus, service to faculty, and a lauded 'incentive system' of a 1/3 division of licensing royalties shared equally among the department, school, and scientists.

A careful analysis of archival records and interviews with participants at Stanford University suggests an alternative account in which current practices evolved from conflicting conceptions about commercializing science. Colyvas (2007a) analyzes scientists' engagement with commercializing life science inventions at Stanford in the 1970s, long before the Bayh-Dole legislation or significant financial returns from university patents, By examining archival records of invention disclosures of biological scientists, Colyvas identifies how practices took shape in advance of external policy developments, how individual scientists pursued disparate entrepreneurial actions, and how these actions were facilitated and anchored by organizational procedures. In the performance of technology transfer, commercializing science was re-shaped and became institutionalized.

In the 1970s, commercialization efforts emerged from scientists' labs when routines for technology transfer were ambiguous and unfamiliar. Unfamiliar projects included the importation of the legal categories of inventor and invention, the problem of establishing boundaries between business and science, and the necessity to establish procedures for distributing royalties. This ambiguity created opportunities for interpretation by both scientists and administrators. Scientists, in the context of their laboratories, generated multiple accounts of who was an inventor, what kinds of science constituted an invention, as well as divergent views of how material benefits from commercial involvement could legitimately be used.

For example, within a basic life science department that eventually became a hotbed of academic entrepreneurship in the 1990s, early efforts in the 1970s were fraught with uncertainty. Three examples from this department are illustrative. One distinguished scientist, concerned with his reputation, allowed the university to license his basic biological research tool only with hesitation and declined any personal royalties, agreeing to participate only after securing agreement to donate his proceeds. 'I can accept a view that it is more reasonable for any financial benefits . . . to go to the university, rather than be treated as a windfall profit to be enjoyed by profit motivated businesses; I agreed to cooperate . . . for that reason . . .' (Colyvas, 2007a: 465). Another noted scientist, motivated by how industry development of his invention would disseminate his technology and expand his research program, reasoned that royalties should benefit his laboratory, the locus of the effort for the research. 'Many 'inventions' are really the work of a group . . . Although inventors need to be identified in the technical sense to satisfy the requirements of the patent process, in fact, the most important advances often are made by other members of the group . . .' (Colyvas, 2007a: 464). This scientist refused to patent basic biological materials, stating that patenting was neither necessary nor appropriate for their dissemination, but he believed that strong property rights for device inventions were important. A third scientist, angered at companies' lucrative exploitation of academic science, demanded remuneration to the university: 'Although many of us are not in a position to exploit our discoveries, we do feel that universities . . . should benefit from profitable applications of our findings. I had hoped that an industry so recently spawned by university research would be enlightened in its recognition of who is responsible for its existence . . .' (Colyvas, 2007a: 467) He also threatened corporate partners that he would patent 'everything in sight' in order to beat industry at their own game.

These examples provide evidence of significant variation in how scientists in one department at the same university practiced commercialization differently and ascribed meaning to what they did. In the first example, the scientist utilized an enduring vocabulary from the profession of science, stating that his contribution to a discovery was only because he was 'standing on the shoulders of giants' and could not identify himself as an inventor by profiting personally from a patent. He invoked the legitimacy that is accorded to the scientific enterprise, and the expectations that flow from it. In the second example, political and ideological references provided resources for justifying practices and generating claims of 'team effort' that the laboratory was communal and organized to benefit everyone equally. In the third example, the scientist theorized cause and effect in response to his perception of a crisis over industry exploitation, control and justice: 'I assure you that I will alert my colleagues throughout the world to guard against what I consider exploitation' (Colyvas, 2007a: 467).

The variation in responses reflects a profound tension between public and private science at the incipient stages of technology transfer. Attention to micro-processes, however, demonstrates how Much meanings were generated through practical action as local, experiential aspects of the laboratory and scientists' identities and emotions inter-acted to construct an appropriate conception of academic entrepreneurship. These scientists were neither cultural dopes nor institutional heroes. As much as they recognized the unfamiliarity of their industry ties and questioned the legitimacy of their activities, they were also aware of the opportunities and benefits of their actions. Involvement in entrepreneurial science was not simply repeated and habituated, however. As practices were executed, they were also altered and justified anew, as the same individuals and their peers tried their hand at subsequent inventions. The organization of the laboratory and the ethos embedded in it informed how technology transfer would be performed.

The organizational ambiguity attached to definitions of inventor and invention, and procedures associated with commercializing science such as royalty distribution, provided multiple opportunities for generating disparate meanings and practices. These individual approaches resonated with the faculty members because they drew on their familiar identities and ideals as scientists in meaning-making processes. As the world of

415

science came into contact with commerce, the identity associated with a university scientist expanded to include entrepreneurship. As more high-status elite scientists participated in such activities, commercial involvement transitioned from unfamiliar and unusual to plausible and appropriate, and finally to a core component of a scientific career (Colyvas and Powell, 2007). By engaging in the unfamiliar and making it plausible in the context of academia, scientists transformed what it meant to be a scientist. Their involvement helped render the older model of ivory tower science quaint and these new entrepreneurial activities indicative of engagement (Colyvas and Powell, 2007).

A parallel feature of the institutionalization of commercial science was the establishment of routines and practices that created and normalized activities. Colyvas and Powell's (2006) analysis of 31 years of technology transfer archives at Stanford University demonstrates the importance of the instantiation and codification of two core institutional features—legitimacy and taken-for-grantedness-into organizational rules and procedures. They show how the development of conventions extended academic science further into the industrial realm, and how the integration of universities and companies into a community of common interests became desirable and appropriate. Once prohibited from consulting to companies that commercialized their technologies, academic scientists became emulated for their multiple roles as founders, scientific advisory board members, and equity holders.

Conflict of interest policies and reporting requirements occasioned these opportunities, shaping and reinforcing the appropriate form that entrepreneurship would take. Social and technical categories provided windows into the core cognitive features of taken-for-grantedness. The criteria that distinguished an 'inventor' from a co-author, or an 'invention' from a research publication were transformed from points of elaborate discussion to well-understood, highly scripted routines and guidelines. The kinds of responsibilities and expectations that would be imposed on scientists in the commercialization process also underwent a similar process of elaboration and subsequent compression. Invention disclosure forms, boilerplate letters of agreement, and marketing tools were developed and revised in order to anchor and support on-going efforts at clarification. As categories became settled, roles were more defined and practices well rehearsed. Job titles, conflict-of-interest guidelines, and organizational routines developed to sustain these activities. Eventually, there was little need for articulation or explicit expositions of the premises and rationales that characterized scientists' early engagement in entrepreneurship.

Language and meaning played an important harmonizing role at the organizational level as the vocabularies utilized in this setting transformed over time. In the early years, commercializing science was pursued as an exception rather than the rule, justified for the 'benefit and use of the public.' As university technology transfer gained legitimacy and the once sharp boundaries between university and industry blurred, a more local, institutional vocabulary took form. Finally, during the later stages of institutionalization, the language of entrepreneurship and academic mission became integrated into a common identity of public benefit, profession, and practical action. The language of science and the mission of the university to benefit the public endured, yet the conventions associated with them were redefined as the institutionalization process unfolded. We see similar processes of unexpected circumstances becoming routinized, and made sensible in our second case, to which we now turn.

Earned income and nonprofit organizations

Commercialization is a much discussed topic in the nonprofit world. More and more nonprofits are pursuing commercial activities to secure funds, and turning to earned income activities to boost their budgets. The fiscal challenges faced by nonprofits are considerable and many external funding sources now demand and support more entrepreneurial approaches (Powell, Gammal, and Simard, 2005). Not only do some funding sources stipulate earned income efforts, but there are a growing array of courses, programs, and elite entrepreneurs that proselytize about importing entrepreneurship into the nonprofit sector. Moreover, many non-profits prefer to deliver goods and services in a fashion that does not create dependency, as they view extensive reliance on donors as a sign of vulnerability and weakness. There is also a widespread neo-liberal belief that market discipline is healthy, and entrepreneurial activities generate autonomy and build capabilities (Dees, 1998).

Most of the literature on earned income activities follows two themes. One argument stresses the need to augment the social non-profit sector with practices from for-profit businesses (Letts et al., 1997; Porter and Kramer, 1999), with attention focused on the individuals and organizations involved in the transfer and circulation of ideas across sectors.[9] To these analysts, entrepreneurial ventures have become the 'hallmark' of a successful nonprofit. The second theme is sung by a chorus of scholars and practitioners who worry that earned income initiatives are particularly difficult for nonprofit organizations and that responding to both financial and non-financial concerns is inevitably fraught with tension (Foster and Bradach, 2005). These discussions are healthy for theory and practice, as they not only highlight the tensions between making a profit and staying true to one's mission, but also recognize that basing decisions solely on mission can threaten financial survival, while putting business concerns ahead of organizational mission can have deleterious long-term consequences (Minkoff and Powell, 2006).

The rival metaphors of mission and business often lead to internal strife within non-profit organizations. For example, this tension is manifest in an art museum between curators—the traditional guardians of art—and museum directors and entrepreneur:[10] administrators who are responsible for the financial viability of the organization. Debates over the benefits or disadvantages of earned income activities seldom attend to evidence drawn from day-to-day operations, however. When we examine rare, successful cases of revenue generation, we see a rather different account in which local action has often emerged as necessity in response to unexpected conditions. These practical responses triggered new steps that eventually led to organizational changes, and connected with much ballyhooed larger macro-trends, but were not prompted by them. In such cases the ethnomethodological insight that mixing practices prompts surprise and novelty can be applied to illuminate how new forms are generated.

A notable case of successful nonprofit entrepreneurship is Minnesota Public Radio (MPR), one of the nation's largest and now richest public radio stations, known for award-winning documentaries, innovative programming, and extraordinary success at revenue generation.[10] Between 1986 and 2000, MPR's for-profit ventures generated $175 million in earned income for the non-profit station, including a $90 million contribution to its endowment (Phills and Chang, 2005). The origins of this success reveal how strongly organizational behavior is often constructed 'on the fly', and necessity is the mother of entrepreneurship.

In the late 1970s and early 1980s. MPR developed a satirical show called A Prairie Home Companion. They offered the show to National Public Radio, but NPR declined, saying it wasn't a show that would have nationwide appeal. It appears that MPR was peeved by National Public Radio's decision to decline the show, which fueled the desire to make the show successful. By the early 1980s, A Prairie Home Companion had generated a fairly healthy audience, and in 1981 Garrison Keillor, the show's popular host, offered listeners a free poster of his mythical sponsor, Powdermilk Biscuits. The fictitious sponsor was part of a regular ongoing gag on the show. To everyone's surprise, more than 50,000 listeners requested a copy of the poster. The station faced a $60,000 printing bill. In such circumstances of surprise, sense-making efforts often spring into action. And so MPR continued the tradition of the fictitious sponsor by turning it into a commercial product. To avert financial disaster, MPR President William Kling recalled, 'We decided to print on the back of a poster an offer for other products that you could buy, like a

Powdermilk Biscuit t-shirt. The idea worked. I think we netted off that poster, which was really our first catalog, $15,000 or $20,000' (William Kling, quoted in Phills and Chang, 2005; 65). 'It instantly became clear that there were things like that you could do' (Kling, quoted in Khan, 1995).

To tap the popularity of *A Prairie Home Companion,* MPR created the Rivertown Trading Company, a mail order catalog business that sold mugs, t-shirts, novelties, and eventually clothing, jewelry and items related to Keillor's radio show. The new entity grew rapidly and by 1986 was reorganized as a separate for-profit subsidiary of MPR to remove any legitimacy and tax issues related to a nonprofit organization owning a highly profitable business. By 1994, Rivertown Trading distributed five catalogs, including *Wireless, Signals, Seasons, Circa* and *Classica.* It also ran the US Golf Association's catalog. Moreover, the product selection in its catalogs extended well beyond its original focus on gifts associated with the Keillor show.

The origins of Minnesota Public Radio also had a similar 'creation in the wild' flavor. Back in the 1960s, the president of a small Benedictine college in Minnesota asked a young college graduate, William. Kling, to start a college radio station to honor the Benedictine tradition of providing artistic and cultural enrichment to their local communities. Kling viewed this opportunity in a simple manner: 1 was doing what I really liked to do, building something that hadn't been done before:[11] He likened building the radio station to his childhood fascination with assembling ham radio sets and listening to distant stations.

In December 1995, MPR asked a handful of employees to assist Rivertown Trading on a voluntary basis to fulfill backlogged holiday orders. MPR employees were told that Rivertown would make donations to their favorite charities or contribute to a holiday party for those who volunteered. Nine employees pitched in, working two to three hours each, earning $350 each for their favorite charities. The expectation. at MPR was that employees at the radio station and the catalog company should be from common backgrounds. Indeed, Kling, the general counsel and other key staff were executives at both companies. 'We didn't want to hire people who worked for Lands End or Williams Sonoma,' William Kling commented, 'we wanted people who held the values of the nonprofit.[12] This decision also led to a firestorm of protest and controversy.

Politicians in Minnesota, newspaper reporters, and other public broadcasting officials were highly critical that employees of the nonprofit radio station also received compensation for their work with for-profit Rivertown Trading, and considerably higher wages to boot. Instead of seeing routines and organizational continuity, critics saw a pattern of insider dealing, conflict of interest, and public funding for an entrepreneurial effort, and raised concerns of unfair compensation and lack of transparency. It is not our task here to assess the merits of these criticisms. We note instead that Kling and colleagues' response was to stress that the interests of the radio station and the catalog company were indistinguishable. Kling emphasized that the $4 million in annual support given by Rivertown to MPR over two decades exceeded the budgets of the great majority of public radio stations in the U.S., and the $90 million endowment that the sale of Rivertown produced, secured MPR's future: 'We could have done a lot of good things with MPR, but suffice to say the $175 million contribution made it possible to do things we would not have been able to otherwise.' Rather than engage with or respond to critics, or assume the role of entrepreneurial champion, Kling focused on the daily activities of a radio broadcaster: more reporters, better signal coverage, more investigative journalism, and the ability to acquire struggling public radio stations in other parts of the country.

MPR is not the only nonprofit that has generated earned income through new or alternative means in recent years. The chapters in Weisbrod (1998) chronicle an array of activities pursued by organizations as diverse as the Girl Scouts, zoos and aquaria, and art museums. As government support has declined or stagnated, nonprofits have increasingly turned to revenue generation. But such efforts are most likely to be successful-financially, organizationally, and politically—when they flow from existing operations, In the MPR context, success at the catalog business built upon Garrison Keillor's performances. While critics opined that 'if Garrison Keillor ever gets laryngitis, Bill Kling is out of business![13] Kling commented, 'My fear is that there are too many nonprofits seeking the holy grail . . . if it doesn't come naturally to you, you shouldn't do it.[14]

In response to growing public criticisms in the late 1990s over the large sums generated by the for-profit operation and the hand-some financial rewards that Kling and colleagues reaped from the sale of the catalog business, Kling invoked a political justification for the activity: that entrepreneurial efforts with Riverside Trading were enhanced by the 'imprimatur from the Reagan administration that it is OK to go out and think that way, indeed we encourage you to think this way.' [15] Interestingly, however, none of the dozens of reports, newspaper columns, and magazine articles written about the situation in the 1980s or early 1990s employed a political mandate as a rationale. More than a decade after the fact, the signature of the Reagan era was 'pulled down' to retrospectively explain the entrepreneurial effort.

The story of MPR is notable for both accomplishment and controversy. Few other nonprofits have been so successful at revenue generation or as agile in securing a sizeable endowment to guarantee a sustainable future. But rather than linking their efforts to broader trends at social entrepreneurship, MPR's leadership has responded modestly to critics, emphasizing how earned income activities were initially a response to an unexpected emergency. One might say that MPR learned to perform as entrepreneurs, rather than 'strategize' about this performance. Moreover, actions that critics interpreted as inherently conflictual and questionable stemmed from an organizational practice that executives should oversee the actions of both the station and the company in order to ensure values-based continuity between them, This choice clearly reflected a managerial desire to routinize the efforts of both branches of the organization, and to engage in sensemaking around for-profit activities in service of nonprofit goals.

These two cases of university and non-profit entrepreneurship illuminate how activities take form through micro-processes of development and institutionalization. Archival records, interviews, and vestiges of organizational routines provide tools that reveal instances of practical reason and the attribution of meanings to such efforts. In the same manner as studies address the adoption and spread of organizational forms, these examples underscore how practices and their attendant meanings and identities develop and crystallize into a form that later becomes adopted.

The two cases we have used are admittedly unusual in several respects. They both involve organizations that eventually became highly successful at activities which were initially regarded as novel and unusual, even questionable. As the new practices and identities became institutionalized, the organizations were held up for scrutiny and debate, and then veneration and emulation (Colyvas and Powell, 2007). One advantage of studying these hallmark cases is there is a rich documentary trail that can be analyzed. Studies of how institutional practices are formed should recognize the tradeoffs that are entailed in the choice of cases. Nevertheless, we think that fine-grained attention to enterprising organizations can be instructive, as well as analysis of how activities do or do not spread to other venues and are interpreted at other sites.

RESEARCH METHODS FOR STUDYING MICROFOUNDATIONS

In this last section, we discuss various tools that researchers can use to study the emergence and sustainability of institutions. Instead of assuming that institutions reproduce themselves, we examine efforts that lead to institutional creation and maintenance, and ways of capturing these processes.

Language and vocabulary are a first step. These are the protocols that people use to engage in dialogue and achieve mutual understanding and inter-subjective awareness. The next step is to see what aspects of language become codified into formal measures of performance and accomplishment. These constructed definitions become metrics by which people evaluate one another. As these 'accounts' of performance or activity take hold, they become reified, that is received and accepted as normal by their participants and adopted and emulated by others who were not a part of their initial creation. In this sense, local measures become 'natural.' Once natural, they become public, as the measures redefine and reinterpret history, and evolve into models that others aspire to, and are recognized as guideposts of accomplishment.

Consider how start-up companies as university spin-offs were once objects of contestation and debate, when the idea of universities engaging in commercial ventures was nascent and questionable (Colyvas, 2007a). Eventually, debate was resolved through the creation of formal conflict of interest forms and procedures. Today, the number of spin-off companies has become a metric by which universities are assessed for their contribution to local economic development. With earned income efforts by nonprofits, donors look less at the programs they fund and which audiences they reach, and more at the percentage of administrative costs that are allocated to program development. Administrative overhead has become a key, but rather orthogonal, criteria for assessing the effectiveness of nonprofits. Such categories and metrics have become not only tools of evaluation, but the accounts by which organizational leaders justify their activities.

Following the insights of ethnomethodology, organizational record-keeping can provide a longitudinal conversation about how daily activities are rendered intelligible, affirming that organizational practices are comprehensible to others. Close examination of organizational archives and correspondence, as well as newer electronic forms such as websites, blogs and e-mail, afford the opportunity to witness organizational performance, and see social reproduction at the micro-level, as daily accounts culminate into ongoing conversations and larger stories about organizational purposes and goals. One could, for example, listen to older broadcasts of *Prairie Home Companion* to assess how often references were made on the air to the burgeoning catalog business to discern how earned income efforts permeated programming.

A sensemaking approach directs us to follow organizational actions—the efforts of individuals as they *engage* in the routines of regular operations. This naturalistic focus on work as skill offers insights into how social meanings become attached to routine conduct. Status expectations research alerts us to how standards of legitimacy in the broader society inform group practice. In contrast to other approaches, this line of work alerts us to look for how social categories and expectations in the wider environment are utilized at the local level. Recall, for example, how in the early stages of academic entrepreneurship, faculty used both the norms of science and statements about the proper organization of their labs to communicate and interpret their experience with a novel activity.

Sensemaking is most salient when surprises happen or events are perceived to be dissonant with past experience (Weick, Sutcliffe, and Obstfeld, 2005). in such instances, individuals reach into their repertoire of experience to make a situation fit the immediate circumstances and allow them to resume their actions.[16] Weick suggests a repertoire of vocabularies that direct attention and shape action. 'Words approximate the territory' and reflect resources for individuals to convert ongoing cues into meaning by 4editling) continuity into discrete categories and observations into interpretations (Weick, 1995: 107). Weick identifies both the content (as words) and resources (as frames) that vocabularies take. Individuals often draw on the vocabularies of professions and occupations to understand organizational actions, and cope with their consequences. At MPR, for example, the organization consistently used the language of radio broadcasting to explain their commercial success in the catalog business. In this respect, their discourse was performative, as it enacted and enhanced the commercial enterprise. Since sensemaking is primarily a retrospective process, individuals make sense of traditions by drawing on the language of predecessors and use narratives to account for sequence and experience. Language and communication are central, as they provide filters and constraints on what can be said, how expressions are categorized, and conclusions retained.

Members of organizations expend considerable effort at communication through codes, categories, and metaphors. Categories serve as boxes or bins that people, problems, and tools get assigned to. Bowker and Star (1999: 38) recount a lovely story from sociologist Howard Becker who learned that airline reservations staff have a category called an `irate' to characterize disgruntled customers. When Becker was having a difficult interaction with a reservation clerk, he calmly said to the person, 'I am an irate,' and the operator responded by asking him, 'how did you know that word?' and immediately sped up his reservation. The creation, resilience, and transmission of categories offer a particularly useful window into organizational life as they not only reflect daily practice but connect organizations to the wider society as they render the mundane generalizable. Categories also contain either latent or explicit rules for action, as they invoke scripts that are associated with people or problems. Studying the formation of categories in organizations is an excellent way to connect micro-level processes with the larger social order.

Metaphors are another topic for examination, as they provide a means of shaping the understanding of a new experience by defining one domain in terms of another. Lakoff and Johnson (1980: 142). suggest that metaphors . . . sanction actions, justify inferences, and help us set goals 'In doing so, metaphors offer meaning to daily activity, often retrospectively by locating the past in present beliefs, values, and daily tasks. The ubiquity of metaphors renders them taken-for-granted-in many respects invisible, yet very salient in terms of generating and transmitting meaning.

As one illustration, Colyvas (2007b) examined the language used to explain the recombinant DNA breakthrough, tracing the thematic content in newspaper articles and campus documents regarding breakthroughs in genetic engineering in the 1970s. The vocabulary of the time drew on the metaphors of factories, hazards, and contamination, which transcended both bacteria and university. She traced the application and flow of common language in both public media and private, university correspondence, following the metaphors of factory and production in formal announcements about the development of rDNA science. The factory image was first introduced in the popular press as a way to describe this basic research tool and explain its linkage to curing disease. Concerns over biohazards in the popular press, however, quickly amplified fears of contamination and images of 'Frankenstein genes.' Eventually, the production metaphor triumphed, capturing a theme of therapeutic and commercial promise. The same images quickly transposed into the university setting through marketing discussions over patenting and licensing the breakthrough. Becoming a 'factory' or 'contaminating' the academy became exemplars for contesting commercial efforts at the university.

Viewed more abstractly, metaphor played a comparable role of reducing ambiguity and mitigating uncertainty in both science and university settings. The application and normative tone of the same imagery, however, differed as factory language extolled science and technology, but simultaneously disparaged universities, By analyzing the two-way flow of metaphors in science and society, Colyvas highlighted the ways in which understandings are conveyed, developed, and transmitted through metaphor, and how those metaphors morph as they are transferred.

Such work suggests that when metaphors become generalized in their use, they render some features of social life 'objective,' but deflect attention to other aspects. As a result, metaphors shape perceptions of situations, problems, and analogues for solving them. One might regard institutionalization as making metaphor dead. If the surprise of metaphor is in its novel application, then language may be understood as a reef of 'dead' metaphors—that is, no longer unfamiliar, but routine and taken-for-granted.

The ongoing relationship between meaning and action is another key area for inquiry. These core features of social life are not proxies for one another, but distinctive institutional elements to investigate. Attention to what individuals or organizations do, separately from what they mean by doing it, should be central to the study of micro-processes. Our earlier analysis of scientists' engagement in entrepreneurship offers an example. Colyvas (2007a) coded practices and premises separately for each invention over the first 12 years of the Stanford technology licensing program. She identified core areas in technology transfer where institutions and resources intersected, notably in the definitions of social and technical categories and in how revenues from inventions were disbursed. Through analysis of correspondence archives, she discerned bow conventions developed and transformed as scientists were introduced to the emerging field of biotechnology. Laboratory-level models of technology transfer that were once coherent became fragmented. The convergence and harmonization of entrepreneurial logics was characterized by the re-attachment of practices from some labs to the meanings generated by other labs. She found that the modern interpretation of an incentive system for successful entrepreneurship was the outcome of the process of institutionalization, rather than an input to it. Thus, actions shape meanings as much as meanings shapes practices (Mohr, 1998). This recursive process has a dynamic of variation and change, much like the mutation of a virus that transforms as it spreads or comes into contact with others. The meaning behind patenting a scientific research finding is quite different today from 30 years ago, and what was once an exception for technological necessity or currency for a career transition out of academia has become a core component of an academic identity in the life sciences.

Tradition and stories offer insight into the retrospective aspects of organization (Weick, 1995). Tradition necessarily invokes the vocabularies of predecessors, reinforcing patterns of action that have been reproduced or believed to have existed across generations. A notable feature of traditions is that they must become symbolic in order to persist or be transmitted. Stories draw on vocabularies of sequence and experience. Patterns such as beginning, middle, end, or situation, transformation, and situation often provide the basis for constructing narratives, drawing analogies and causal linkages, integrating what is present to what is absent, and what is known to what is conjecture. When pressed about the entrepreneurial success of MPR, William Kling turned to childhood memories of ham radios and the history of outreach of the Benedictine church, and 'rat to a celebration of business acumen.

This discussion was offered as an entry into methods for studying processes of micro-institutionalization. As a next step, an analysis could distinguish between meanings and practices in cross-case comparisons over time, particularly in tracing institutional change as the product of micro-level efforts at enactment, interpretation, and compliance.

SUMMARY

We have argued that institutional research can benefit from complementary attention to the micro-order and the macro-level. We urge more examination of the genesis of organizational practices and the resulting meanings that are attached to these routines. Such attention will not only provide a fuller account of institutionalization processes, but will also enable much clearer parsing of endogenous and exogenous influences. Our aim is to trace how efforts on the ground, so to speak, may prompt macro-level changes and responses. A multi-level view will offer more purchase to the question of why institutional practices and structures take the form they do. Rather than focus only on the diffusion or success of a form, we can better explain the nature of what becomes regarded as appropriate or venerable. The results of such inquiry will lead to more compelling and integrative analyses.

Acknowledgments

We are grateful to Marisa Buena, Gili Drori, Mary Ann Glynn, Royston Greenwood, Tricia Martin, John Meyer, David Suarez and Megan Tompkins for helpful comments on an earlier draft. Research support for Powell provided by the Center for Social Innovation at the Stanford. Graduate School of Business, and for Colyvas by the Columbia-Stanford Consortium on Biomedical Innovation.

Endnotes

1. See, for example, the review symposium on Garfinkel's Studies in Ethnomethodology in the January 1968 American Sociological Review, notably Coleman's (1968) blistering critique, or Coser's (1974) presidential address where he used the bully pulpit of the annual ASA meetings to argue that ethnornethodology was a—method in search of a theory.

2. Garfinkel (1968) describes this accomplishment aptly 'how jurors know what they are doing when they do the work of jurors.'

3. We do not take up the fascination of the actor network approach with artifacts and their politics. Simply stated, studies demonstrate that economic technologies—trading screens, stock tickers, calculators, etc. do not simply represent the market's ups and downs, but are very much involved in shaping market behavior (Knorr-Cetina and Bruegger, 2002; Buenza and Stark, 2004; Callon and Muniesa, 2005).

4. In 1970, there was no financial trading in 'futures,' but by 2004, financial derivative contracts totaling $273 trillion were outstanding worldwide.

5. Sensemaking's insight lies in the ways it 'captures the realities of agency, flow, equivocality, transience, reaccomplishment, unfolding, and emergence . . . , that are often obscured by the language of variables, nouns, quantities, and structures' (Weick, Sutcliffe, and Obstfeld, 2005).

6. In contrast to ethnornethodology, where Garfinkel's (1967) clever studies of breaching transform mundane encounters into unfamiliar controversies, sensemaking studies tend to analyze how skillful routines can result in terrible tragedy.

7. Charles Perrow often makes a very Weickian remark, 'how do I know what I think until I say It?'

8. See Sampat, 2006 and Rothaermel, Agung, and Jiang, 2007 for excellent reviews of the debates around university technology policies.

9. Pressures on nonprofits to become more 'business-like' are certainly not new Indeed, such urging has been common throughout the sector's history (Hall, 2006). In the early twentieth century, religious charities were criticized by progressive 'scientific' charity providers. who urged the rationalization of services for the poor (Lubove, 1965; Mohr and Duquenne, 1997). In the 1970s and 1980s, leading management consultancies persuaded many large nonprofit organizations to develop strategic plans in order to 'enhance' their operations (DiMaggio and Powell, 1983; Mintzberg, 1994; McKenna, 2006).

10. The Center for Social innovation at the Stanford Graduate School of Business and National Arts Strategies, a nonprofit consultancy for the arts, jointly developed the case on Minnesota Public Radio for classroom use. We have taught this case numerous times in MBA classes and executive education courses. James Phills and Ed Martenson were the primary contributors. to the case's development. We draw on it for this extended example.

11. Interview with William Kling by Ed Martenson of National Arts Strategies, 2004.

12. Interview with William Kling by Ed Martenson, ibid.

13. Ron Russell, 'Public Radio's Darth Vader invades L.A. by gobbling up a sleepy Pasadena college station.' New Times Los Angeles, June 29, 2000.

14. Interview with William Kling by Ed Martenson, 2004.

15. Interview with William Kling by Ed Martenson, ibid.

16. The guide points to sensemaking are found in 'institutional constraints, organizational premises, plans, expectations, acceptable justifications, and traditions inherited from predecessors' (Weick et al, 2005: 414). Furthermore, these guide points do not have to be accurate. What matters is that they are plausible from the point of view of enacted identities and context (Weick, 1995: 55-56).

References

Association of University Technology Managers (AUTM) 2005. U.S. Licensing Survey, http://www.autm.net

Berger, PL., and T. Ludcman. 1967. The Social *Construction of Reality.* Garden City, NJ: Doubleday. Berger, J., C. Ridgeway, M.H. Fisek, and R. Norman. 1998. 'The legitimation and delegitimation of power and prestige orders.' *American Sociological Review,* 63 (3): 379-405.

Bittner, E. 1965. 'The concept of organization.' *Social Research,* 32: 239-255.

Bittner; E. 1967. 'The police on skid row: A study in peacekeeping,' *American Sociological Review,* 32 (5): 699-715.

Bowker, G., and L. Star. 1999. *Sorting Things Out.* Cambridge, MA: MIT Press.

Buenza, D., and D. Stark. 2004. 'Tools of the trade: The socio-technology of arbitrage in a Wall Street trading room.' *Industrial and Corporate Change,* 13: 369-400.

Callon, M. 1986. 'Some elements of a sociology of translation: Domestication of the scallops and the fishermen of St. Brieuc Bay.' Pp. 196-233 in J. Law (ed.), *Power; Action and Belief. A New Sociology of Knowledge?* London: Routiecige & Kegan Paul.

Callon, M. (ed_) 1998. *The Laws of the* Markets. Oxford: Blackwell.

Callon, M. 2006. 'What does it mean to say that economics is performative?' Working paper, Ecole des Mines, Paris.

Callon, M. and F Muniesa. 2005. 'Peripheral vision: Economic markets as calculative collective devices.' *Organization Studies,* 26 (8): 1229-1250.

Cicourel, A. 1968. *The Social Organization of Juvenile Justice.* New York: John Wiley. Coleman, J.S. 1968. 'Review symposium of *Studies in Ethnomethodology.' American Sociological Review,* 33 (1): 126-130.

Colyvas, J.A. 2007a. 'From divergent meanings to common practices; The early institutionalization of technology transfer in the life sciences at Stanford University.' *Research Policy,* 36 (4): 456-476.

Colyvas, Jeannette A. 2007b. 'Factories, Hazards, and Contamination: Metaphors and Recombinant DNA in University and Biotechnology.' *Minerva,* 45 (2): 143-159. Colyvas, 1.A., and W.W. Powell. 2006. 'Roads to institutionalization: The remaking of boundaries between public and private science.' *Research in Organizational Behavior,* 27: 305-153.

Colyvas, J.A., and W.W. Powell. 2007. 'From vulnerable to venerated: The institutionalization of academic entrepreneurship in the life sciences.' *Research in the Sociology of Organizations,* M. Ruef and M. Lounsbury, (eds.), 25: 223-266.

Correll, S.J. and C.L. Ridgeway. 2003. 'Expectation states theory.' Pp. 29-51 in John Delamater (ed.), *The Handbook of Social Psychology.* New York, NY: Kluwer Academic Press.

Coser, L.A. 1974. 'Two methods in search of a substance.' *American Sociological Review,* 40 (6): 691-700.

Dees, J. Gregory. 1998. 'Enterprising Nonprofits.' *Harvard Business Review,* 76, (1): 54-67.

DiMaggio, PI, and W.W. Powell. 1983. 'The iron cage revisited: Institutional isomorphism and collective rationality in organizational fields.' *American Sociological Review,* 48(2): 147-160.

DiMaggio, P.J., and W.W. Powell_ 1991. 'Introduction,' Pp. 1-38 in W.W. Powell and P.J.

DiMaggio (eds.), The New Institutionalism in Organization Analysis. Chicago: University of Chicago Press.

Drori, G.S., J.W. Meyer, and H. Hwang (eds.) 2006. *Globalization and Organization: World Society and Organizational Change.* New York: Oxford University Press.

Foster, W. and J. Bradach. 2005, 'Should non-profits seek profits?' *Harvard Business Review,* 83 (2): 92-100.

Garfinkel, H. 1967. *Studies in Ethnomethodology,* Englewood Cliffs, NJ: Prentice Hall. Garfinkel, H. 1968. 'The origins of the term 'ethnomethodology: Pp. 15-18 in R. Turner (ed.), *Ethnomethodology.* Middlesex, England: Penguin Books, 1974.

Garfinkel, H. and E. Bittner. 1967. 'Good organizational reasons for bad clinic records.' Pp. 186-207 in H. Garfinkel (ed.), *Studies in Ethnomethodology.* Englewood Cliffs, NJ: Prentice-Hall.

Giddens, A. 1984, *The Constitution of Society.* Berkeley: University of California Press.

Goffman, E. 1961. *Asylums.* New York: Anchor Books.

Goff man, E. 1967. *Interaction Ritual: Essays on Face-to-Face Behavior,* New York: Pantheon Books.

Goffman, E. 1974. *Frame Analysis.* Cambridge, MA: Harvard University Press.

Hall, PD. 2006. 'A historical overview of philanthropy, voluntary associations, and nonprofit organizations in the United States, 1600-2.000: Pp. 32-65 in W.W. Powell and R. Steinberg (eds.), *The Nonprofit Sector,* 2nd end. New Haven, CT: Yale University Press.

Jennings, P.D., and R. Greenwood. 2003. 'Constructing the iron cage: Institutional theory and enactment.' Pp. 195-207 in R. Westwood and S. Clegg (eds.), *Debating Organization,* Malden, MA: Blackwell.

Jepperson, Ronald L. 1991. 'Institutions, institutional effects, and institutionalization.' Pp. 143-63 in W.W. Powell and P.J. DiMaggio (eds.), *The New Institutionalism in Organizational Analysis.* Chicago: University of Chicago Press.

Khan, A. 1995. 'MPR successful. raising money: Its for-profit sister is even better.' *St. Paul Pioneer Press,* February 26, 1995.

Knorr-Cetina, K., and U. Bruegger. 2002.'Global microstructures: The virtual societies of financial markets.' *American Journal of Sociology,* 107: 905-951.

Lach, S. and M. Schankerman. 2003. 'Incentives and invention in universities.' NBER Working Paper No. W9727.

Lakoff, G., and M. Johnson. 1980. *Metaphors We Live By.* Chicago: University of Chicago Press.

Letts, C., W. Ryan and A. Grossman.1997.Virtuous *Capital: What Foundations Can Learn from Venture Capitalists. Harvard Business Review* Mar-April: 36-44.

Lubove, R. 1965. *The Professional Altruist.* Cambridge, MA: Harvard University Press.

Latour, B. 1987. *Science in Action.* Cambridge, MA: Harvard University Press.

Latour, B. & S. Woolgar. 1979. *Laboratory Life: The Construction of Scientific Facts.* Thousand Oaks: CA: Sage.

Lawrence, T.B., and R. Suddaby. 2006. 'Institutions and institutional work.' Pp. 215-54 in S.R. Clegg et al. (eds.), *The Sage Handbook of Organization Studies,* London: Sage Publications.

Michael Lounsbury and Ellen T. Crumley 2007. 'New Practice Creation: An Institutional Perspective on Innovation.' *Organization Studies,* 28 (7): 993-1012.

MacKenzie, D. 2006. *An Engine, Not* a Carrara: *How Financial Models Shape Markets.* Cambridge, MA: MIT Press.

MacKenzie, D., and Y. Millo. 2003. 'Constructing a market, performing theory: The historical sociology of a financial derivatives exchange.' *American Journal of Sociology,* 109(1): 107-145.

March, J.G. 1994. *A Primer on Decisionmaking,* New York, NY: Free Pres.

McKenna, C. 2006. *The World's Newest Profession*. Cambridge, UK: Cambridge University Press.

Mead, G.H. 1934. *Mind, Self, and Society*. Chicago, IL: Chicago University Press.

Merton, R.K. 1948. 'The self-fulfilling prophecy.' *Antioch Review*, 8: 193-210.

Meyer, J.W., and B. Rowan. 1977. 'Institutionalized organizations: Formal structure as myth and ceremony.' *American Journal of Sociology*, 83(2): 340-363.

Minkoff, D. and *W.W.* Powell. 2006. 'Nonprofit mission: Constancy, responsiveness, or deflection?' Pp. 591-611 in W.W. Powell and R. Steinberg (eds.), *The Nonprofit Sector: A Research Handbook*, 2nd edn. New Haven, CT: Yale University Press Mintzberg, H.' 1994. The *Rise and Fall of Strategic Planning*. New York: Free Press.

Mohr, J., and V. Duquenne. 1997. 'The duality of culture and practice: Poverty relief in New York City, 1888-1977.' *Theory and Society*, 26 (2/3): 305-356.

Mohr, J. W. 1998. Measuring meaning structures. *Annual Review of Sociology*, 24:345-370.

Mowery, D., R. Nelson, B. Sampat and A. Ziedonis. 2004. *Ivory Tower and industrial Innovation*. Stanford, CA: Stanford University Press.

Owen-Smith, J. 2001. 'Managing laboratory work through skepticism: Processes of evaluation and control.' *American Sociological Review*, 66 (3): 427-452.

Phills, J. and V. Chang. 2005. 'The price of. commercial success.' *Stanford Social Innovation Review*, (Spring): 65-72.

Powell, W.W., D. Gamma and C. Simard. 2005. 'Close encounters: The circulation and reception of managerial practices in the San Francisco Bay area nonprofit community.' Pp. 233-58 in B. Czarniawska and G. Sevon (eds.), *Global Ideas*, Herndon, VA: Copenhagen Business School Books.

Porter, M. and M. Kramer. 1999. 'Philanthropy's new agenda: Creating value'. *Harvard Business Review,* Nov-Dec: 121-130.

Ridgeway, C. and J. Berger. 1986. 'Expectations, legitimation, and dominance behavior in task groups.' *American Sociological Review,* 51: 603-617.

Ridgeway, C. and H.A. Walker. 1995. 'Status structures.' Pp. 281-310 in K.S. Cook et al. (eds.), *Sociological Perspectives in Social Psychology.* Boston: Allyn and Bacon.

Rothaermel, ET., S.D. Agung and L. Jiang. 2007. 'University entrepreneurship: A taxonomy of the literature.' *Industrial and Corporate* Change, (4):691-791.

Sampat, B.N. 2006. 'Patenting and U.S. academic research in the 20th century: The world before and after Bayh-Dole.' *Research Policy,* 35 (6): 772-789.

Scott, W.R. 'Approaching Adulthood: The Maturing of Institutional Theory.' *Working Paper.*

Selznick, P. 1949. *TVA and the Grass Roots.* Berkeley: University of California Press.

Simon, H. 1945. *Administrative Behavior.* Glencoe, IL: The Free Press.

Snook, S.A. 2000. *Friendly Fire.* Princeton, NJ: Princeton University Press.

Strang, D. and W. Sine. 2002. 'Interorganizational institutions.' Pp, 497-519 in J.A.C, Baum (ed.), *Companion to Organizations.* Malden, MA: Blackwell.

Sudnow, D. 1965. 'Normal crimes: Sociological features of the penal code in a public defender's office,' *Social Problems,* 12 (3): 255-276.

Sudnow, D. 1967. *Passing On: The Social Organization of Dying.* Englewood Cliffs, NJ: Prentice-Hall.

Weber, K. and M.A. Glynn. 2006. 'Making sense with institutions: Context, thought, and action in Karl Weick's theory.' *Organization Studies,* 27 (11): 1639-1660.

Weick, K. 1993. 'The collapse of sensemaking in organizations: The Mann Gulch disaster.' *Administrative Science Quarterly,* 38 (4): 628-652.

Weick, K. 1995. *Sensemaking in Organizations.* Thousand Oaks, CA: Sage Publications.

Weick, K., K. Sutcliffe, and D. Obstfeld. 2005. 'Organizing and the process of sense-making.' *Organization Science* 16 (4): 409-421.

Weisbrod, B. (ed.) 1998. *To Profit or Not: The Commercial Transformation of the Nonprofit* Sector. New York: Cambridge University Press.

Zelditch, M., Jr. 2001. 'Theories of legitimacy.' Pp. 33-53 in J.T. Jost and B. Major (eds.), *The Psychology of Legitimacy.* Cambridge, UK: Cambridge University Press.

Zelditch, M., Jr. 2004. 'Institutional effects on the stability of organizational authority.' *Research in the Sociology of Organizations,* 22: 25-48.

Zimmerman, D.H. 1969. 'Record-keeping and the intake process in a public welfare agency.' Pp. 319-54 in S. Wheeler (ed.), *On Record: Files and Dossiers in American Life.* New York: Russell Sage.

Zucker, L.G. 1977. 'The role of institutionalization in cultural persistence.' *American Journal of Sociology,* 42: 726-743.

Zucker, L.G. 1991. 'Postscript: Microfoundations of. institutional thought.' Pp. 103-6 in W.W. Powell and P.J. DiMaggio (eds.), *The New Institutionalism in Organizational Analysis.* Chicago: University of Chicago Press.

Part IV
Moving to the Future

Chapter 11

Prologue
W. Warner Burke
Edward Lee Thorndike Professor of Psychology & Education
Teachers College, Columbia University

A Perspective on the Field of Organization Development and Change: The Zeigarnik Effect

W. Warner Burke

Prologue:

W. Warner Burke[20]

I selected my 2011 paper for inclusion in the ELP commemorative book because it addressed four areas—loosely coupled organizations, human resistance, organizational cultures, and leadership development—that I thought we really needed to tackle (the royal "we") in the field of organizational change and development (OD). We could not continue to assume that innovation in OD was over because I didn't really think much innovation had occurred in these areas for quite a long time. That's the postulate that started my thinking. The publishing of the paper came about because I was asked to write a commissioned paper for the *Journal of Applied Behavioral Science* marking the final year of Dick Woodman's service as editor. He wanted me to write a perspective piece on the OD field. I had been thinking about these areas for some time, so I quickly agreed to do it and in fact wrote the paper fairly quickly (for me). I didn't labor over it a whole lot. It just kind of rolled out.

I hadn't thought about it, but I think the motivation to write this article came not only from the invitation, but also from a combination of thinking about our field and some passionate feelings on my part that have resulted in impatience and frustration, if not anger. Of the four areas of unfinished business, I feel strongest about my perspectives on loosely coupled organizations. The loosely coupled systems area was emotional because of my embarrassment about it all.

Much of my process of personal introspection on the OD field came about because of a paper I had coauthored a year before with Noumair and Winderman on trying to change the A. K. Rice Institute (Noumair, Winderman, & Burke, 2010). It was a case report of a short-term success and a long-term failure. In other words, the change that we brought about

[20] This prologue is a rendering of an interview with Warner Burke conducted June 14, 2013.

440

didn't last, and I couldn't figure out why. When I can't figure something out, I have to sit down and write about it to understand what is going on. In retrospect, it now seems pretty obvious. I felt rather naïve, to tell you the truth, in that I had missed the fundamentals about how different it is to work with a loosely coupled system than with a tightly coupled system.

I approached the engagement from an OD standpoint as opposed to a change management perspective because one of the things that we concentrated on early was the organization's mission. I am not sure in change management you would start there. You always start, as far as I am concerned, with the external environment and then you jump immediately to mission. That is where we started with the A. K. Rice Institute. Looking back, there wasn't necessarily anything wrong with that point of departure; it was how I went about it that turned out to be inappropriate. We only worked with the board and top teams in team building and things like that, and I now understand that such an approach was not appropriate for the A. K. Rice Institute. I should have been working more with the centers and the nodes of the loosely coupled network rather than just the top group.

I grew up in the field of OD working with tightly coupled systems. The whole world of OD is primarily about "loosening up" organizations. That is how I had learned my craft. I had not learned how to bring about change in loosely coupled organizations as networks—although I find there is a certain personal irony in this. I was head of the Organizational Development Network for 8 years and ran it pretty well. Of course, the only change that occurred in that whole time was growth. (When I took over it was 40 people, and when I left it was 2000.) Growth is change; however, it is different from trying to change something fundamental about an organization.

So it is not as if I didn't know anything about a network, but I didn't know how to change it. It became clear that you do not work as a change agent in an institution like A. K. Rice as you would, or try to, in General Motors. It was that realization that hit me between the eyes. Of course I went to the source on all of this, and that is Karl Weick (Weick, 1989; Orton & Weick, 1990). I liberally brought in his thinking and then applied it to understanding today's organizations that are moving more in the direction of loosely coupling. Let me be clear, and I say this in the article, that an organization can be both loose and tight at the same time. Therefore, you need to really understand, as clearly as you can, what aspects of the organization need to remain loose and what aspects of the organization need to be tightened. The big learning for me was understanding how you tighten up a loosely coupled system. That is what we were actually trying to do with the A. K. Rice Institute, but I was using normal OD techniques, and they don't work for a loosely coupled system.

I believe the paper can speak to the importance of the other three areas of unfinished business: organizational culture, leadership development, and our understanding of resistance to change. Jeffery Ford (Ford, Ford, & d'Amelio, 2008), Piderit (2000), and Dent and Goldberg (1999) have done some nice work, and their articles are a contribution to loosening up our thinking about resistance. We have been stuck in our ways of thinking about resistance and leadership development. We have to stop this nonsense of thinking that we can take people out into the woods for a 4-day retreat and train them to be leaders. How ridiculous that kind of thing is in today's complex world.

Reflecting back on my experience with this article, two things occur to me that I would add. I would try to elaborate in a little more detail how you work with, and consult with, loosely coupled systems. Most OD people don't have a good understanding of the dynamics of the micro interactions in the context of networks. I need to write about how to do it. I have only called our attention to the problem, as noted in Table 1 in the paper. These ideas were built on Weick's work. That is a good start, but he doesn't tell us how to do it; he just says you should approach it in an improvisational way rather than in a planned change way. Well, what does improvisational mean? We know what planned change is—following Lewin's three steps and so forth. We know all of that like the back of

442

our hands, but how do you bring about change in an improvisational way? That is like sitting down at the feet of Frank Barrett and listening to him play the jazz piano. What can we learn from that about how you sit down with a loosely coupled system and work with them? In the future, I want to take that simple table (maybe not so simple) and write the whole thing out in terms of how you would do this at a local level rather than a cosmopolitan level.

Secondly, I would now add a fifth area. It would be learning agility (not ability). I think we are on the cusp of trying to understand what learning agility is and how important it is for organizations. I know I am giving talks on it and people appear to be excited about this kind of thinking. It started for me a little over 4 years ago when I read an article about a learning agility questionnaire created by the Lominger consulting firm. They claimed there was evidence of a relationship between learning agility and leadership effectiveness—and that caught my eye. I thought that made intuitive sense and was worth pursuing. I looked more carefully at how they measured it and was not happy. The questionnaire was a consulting firm product, and I didn't think they had done sufficient homework in terms of test construction steps such as ensuring reliability and validity. I looked and looked and didn't find any indices that measured up. I talked to my doctoral students at the time and asked if they would be willing to work with me on trying to create our own instrument. So here we are some 4 or 5 years later, and I am still not quite there yet, but am getting very close to having a reliable measure of learning agility. We have rewritten items and have done the statistical analysis and have rewritten the items again. Now we are close and have an arrangement with the Center for Creative Leadership to gather a large amount of data this summer. I think by the fall I am going to be as close as possible to having a reliable measurement. Eventually, I want to work on using it with respect to selection of high potentials in organizations for leadership.

References

Dent, E. B., & Goldberg, S. G. (1999). Challenging "resistance to change." *Journal of Applied Behavioral Science, 35,* 25-41.

Ford, J. D., Ford, L. W., & d'Amelio, A. (2008). Resistance to change: The rest of the story. *Academy of Management Review, 33,* 362-377.

Noumair, D. A., Winderman, B. B., & Burke, W. W. (2010). Transforming the A. K. Rice Institute: From club to organization. *Journal of Applied Behavioral Science, 46,* 473-499.

Orton, J. D., & Weick, K. E. (1990). Loosely coupled systems: A reconceptualization. *Academy of Management Review, 15,* 203-223.

Piderit, S. K. (2000). Rethinking resistance and recognizing ambivalence: A multidimensional view of attitudes toward an organizational change. *Academy of Management Review, 25,* 783-794.

Weick, K. E. (1989). Organized improvisation: 20 years of organizing. *Communication Studies, 40,* 241-248.

A Perspective on the Field of Organization Development and Change: The Zeigarnik Effect[21]

W. Warner Burke

Abstract. Essentially, and perhaps arguably, there has been no innovation in the social technology of organization development (OD) since appreciative inquiry originated in 1987. It is *as if* the creative work of OD is done. Moreover, it is *as if* the mission of OD—to loosen tightly coupled systems, think large bureaucracies—has largely been achieved. Decentralization, involvement, and autonomy on the job are commonplace in many organizations. There is a paradox, however. The need for expertise in organization change has never been greater, and OD has so much to contribute, yet the failure rate for organization change efforts is around 70%, and for mergers and acquisitions the failure rate is even larger. The premise of this article is that there is much work yet to be done. We who identify ourselves with the field of OD have unfinished business. As research on the Zeigarnik effect showed, we tend to remember things undone more than we remember things that have been completed. A purpose of this article is to create a Zeigarnik effect. Four domains of unfinished business in the field are identified and explored. There are no doubt many other domains, but these four definitely need attention. We need to know much more than we now know about how to (a) work with loosely coupled systems, (b) change the culture of an organization, (c) identify and deal with *perceived* resistance to change more effectively, and (d) get leadership development right—it is not about training.

Keywords: organization development and change, loosely coupled systems, culture change, resistance, leadership development

It is *as if* organization development (OD), and now in some circles, for example, Academy of Management, referred to as organization

---

[21] Originally Published as: Burke, W. (2010). "A perspective on the field of organization development and change: The Zeigarnik effect." Journal of Applied Behavorial Science **47**(2): 143-167.

development and change (ODC), practitioners believe that the bulk of the creative work for the field has been done. Arguably, there has been little or no new social technology since appreciative inquiry (Cooperrider & Srivastva, 1987). Some would contend that the large group intervention (Bunker & Alban, 1997) represents new social technology, and in some respects that is a reasonable argument, yet what is new is an expansion and improvement of a former creation—Beckhard's (1967) confrontation meeting.

It is *as if* the mission of early OD has been largely achieved. Whether stated in these specific terms or not, the mission of OD has been to loosen tight, bureaucratic organizations. Early work particularly in the 1960s and into the 1970s was with large corporations (General Mills, Esso, TRW Systems, Union Carbide, Pillsbury, Digital Equipment Corporation, Proctor & Gamble, General Foods, Westinghouse, Kaiser Permanente, and General Motors in the United States and organizations such as Volvo and Norsk Hydro in Europe, to name a few), with the Episcopal Church, and in the 1970s with the U.S. Army, where the initiative was labeled *organizational effectiveness* (OE). In other words, the practice of OD was largely with huge, bureaucratic systems. Although spotty, some degrees of success were accomplished (see, e.g., French & Bell, 1995; Golembiewski, 2003; Macy & Izumi, 1993; Mirvis & Macy, 1983; Porras & Robertson, 1992; Woodman, Bingham, & Yuan, 2008).

Thus, OD emerged in the late 1950s, grew rapidly, particularly in the 1960s and 1970s, and to some extent has become established with a body of literature, university and professional programs, and acceptance in many organizations in the United States (Wirtenburg, Abrams, & Ott, 2004) and a number of other countries (Fagenson-Eland, Ensher & Burke, 2004). At present, however, OD is somewhat stagnant with growth leveled and new technology sparse (Bradford & Burke, 2005). With such promise from the 1960s and 1970s and with the need for competence in the world of organization change greater than ever before, it is somewhat puzzling and paradoxical that OD is not more prolific and influential than it is. (Burke, 2008, p. 14)

The purpose of this article, then, is to address the puzzlement and paradox by arguing that the field of OD/ODC has considerable unfinished business. Bluma Zeigarnik, a Russian-born psychologist working with Kurt Lewin in Germany at the time, 1927, found in her research that we tend to remember better those tasks that are incomplete. Not having closure in some matter can even nag us until we do complete it, or at least, try to. Thus, a purpose for this article is to attempt to instill a Zeigarnik effect. To be more specific, innovative work is needed especially in four areas of practice: *loosely coupled systems, culture change, resistance*, and *leadership development.*

First, a case will be made that the work of OD has been to loosen tight organizations, and some headway has been achieved; at least, we have some knowledge and experience of how to deal with tight systems. But the majority of these large systems are still too tight. Control-oriented leaders seem to like it that way.

The second case to be made is to identify where innovation is needed, that is, the four areas mentioned above, and to explore these areas in terms of clarifying what we need to know, where the unfinished business exists.

We will conclude with an admonition about lifelong learning and that without it OD/ODC will remain stagnant.

Before moving on, let me clarify one more point. Although I have cast the two labels, OD and ODC, together they should not be considered as exactly the same. Historically, of course, OD preceded ODC. Some would perhaps like to see ODC as the modern version of OD. But that would mean that the two, except for chronology, are the same and that would not be quite accurate. OD is about *planned* change, and there is a phased way of practice. Those who classify themselves more with the ODC rubric, and even though there is significant overlap, would nevertheless tend to be more aligned with the academic world than with practice, and they would more likely view ODC as organization change *writ large*, planned or unplanned. And whereas OD practitioners have typically avoided incorporating such interventions as Six Sigma, reengineering, and work out into their consultative efforts, ODC folks would be more likely to include any and all change interventions into their work.

What the Practice of OD/ODC Has Been

As stated before, whether articulated specifically or not the mission of OD along with the field's value system has been for the most part to loosen tight organizations. This loosening process has emphasized involvement and participation with the mantra being "involvement leads to commitment." Bureaucracy was choking the life out of organizations. The beginnings of OD, circa 1959, were about "bottom-up management" with Douglas McGregor and Richard Beckhard at General Mills (Beckhard, 1997), and the use of T-Group methodology and the early stages of the Managerial Grid to "open up" Esso, Humble Oil and related companies and refineries (now Exxon-Mobil) by Herb Shepard, Robert R. Blake, and Jane S. Mouton (French & Bell, 1995).

This loosening process was also about humanizing the work place. Maslow's (1954) self-actualization, Herzberg's (1966) job enrichment, Hackman and Oldham's (1980) job redesign for more meaningful work, Dyer's (1987) teamwork, Hackman's (1992) self-directed groups, Blake and Mouton's (1968) 9/9 (participative) management, and Likert's (1967) System 4-consensus management were all contributions to the movement. Also, learning about and confronting issues of authority from a psycho-analytic perspective were part of this humanizing and democratizing process (Bion, 1961; Rioch, 1970).

Putting *life* into organizations, then, concerned the humanizing of work and OD was essentially an all-out attack on bureaucracy. A primary general leading the attack was Warren Bennis. In fact, he declared at the time "the coming death of bureaucracy" (Bennis, 1966). Bureaucracy, according to Bennis, was vulnerable because of (a) its inability to cope with the growing pace of change, (b) the sheer size of most bureaucracies, (c) the fact that the workplace was becoming more diverse and highly specialized, and (d) the newer philosophy promoted by OD of humanizing the workplace. Bennis was not alone. Tannenbaum and Davis (1969) were similar in their beliefs about bureaucracies and the need for changing values more toward humanistic aims.

But a few years later, Bennis (1970) was more pessimistic. His experience of trying to run two different universities caused him to doubt what he had stated earlier regarding the death of bureaucracy. Yet others took up the clarion call. V. E. Schein and Greiner (1977), for example, discussed "behavioral diseases" of bureaucracies such as functional myopia and suboptimization, top-down information flow and problem insensitivity, and routine jobs and dissatisfaction, and how OD served as an antidote, if not cure, for these diseases. And although not in the OD field per se, others were also on the attack regarding the inefficiencies, if not oppression, of bureaucracy—see, for example, Ackoff (1974), Freire (1970), and Thompson (1967). Later in 1980, a special issue of *The Journal of Applied Behavioral Science* was devoted to "Bureaucracy in the Eighties" (Littrell & Sjoberg, 1980). Littrell (1980) in the introduction pointed out that the contributors for this issue identified four urgently important themes . . . that will benefit from addressing the changes in power relations that affect:

1. the openness of organizational structure
2. the nature of participative management
3. the responsibility of social and welfare problems, and
4. the impact of organizational relations upon economic problems. (p. 273)

Littrell went on to suggest that research and action for the coming decade would benefit from following these four themes. In my article for this special issue (Burke, 1980), I was rather pessimistic about changing bureaucracies and that "tinkering" with change would not fundamentally change anything. The organization's culture had to be tackled, and I recommended three types of interventions: (a) *group*, for example, promoting more self-directed groups; (b) *participative management* as a way of decentralizing power; and (c) installing *flexible reward systems* that were based more on intrinsic than extrinsic rewards.

In spite of pessimism, OD practitioners in the late 1970s and 1980s continued to chip away at bureaucracy, and their underlying values of openness, confronting issues instead of sweeping them under the rug, and humanistic interventions in general provided direction and motivation. One way that bureaucracy was confronted was to "invent" a parallel organization. An example was the work of Howard Carlson at General Motors (Miller, 1978). He created a "time out" process whereby members of an organization would suspend for a day all rules, norms, and hierarchy of how the company normally operated. During this suspended time, open discussions with everyone having a voice would be conducted, and problems, even "sacred cows," would be confronted and often solved. Interpersonal issues would also be dealt with in an open manner. The role of Carlson was to facilitate these meetings and help ensure a "safety net" for organizational members so that they could feel free to express themselves. Stein and Kanter (1980) also experimented with such processes, and the U.S. Army's "After Action Review" is another form of a similar process.

Innovation in the practice of OD continued with prime examples being the advent of appreciative inquiry (Cooperrider & Srivastva, 1987) and large group interventions (Bunker & Alban, 1997).

Coming now to the second decade of the 21st century, it is rather clear that organizations, certainly in the corporate sector, are not as bureaucratic as was true in the 1960s and 1970s. Decentralization has been the bias for a number of years now. I know of at least one *Fortune* 100 company that has upward of 100 separate businesses with each business head operating quite autonomously. Yet with growth now stagnant and cost containment paramount, the change effort being launched is one of tightening and centralizing. Assuming that this change is diligently pursued, things will be difficult, to say the least. Once autonomy has been given, taking even some of it back will cause heavy resistance and strong feelings.

Can OD/ODC practitioners help here? Loosening a tight system is one thing; tightening it is quite another. So new learning for the field is required. The innovative work is not done. From my perspective, the new learning is required in at least four areas, as noted above. We begin the four with loosely coupled systems.

Have We Become Too Loose?

The primary premise of this section is to argue that we ODC practitioners have paid insufficient attention to the nature of loosely coupled systems by concentrating most of the practice work on attempting to loosen tightly coupled systems. First, let us consider a summary of what constitutes a loosely coupled system and then address what we as ODC practitioners need to know about how to work with these kinds of organizations.

Loosely Coupled Systems

It is natural and often useful in our attempt to understand something to consider its opposite; in this case, a loosely coupled versus a tightly coupled system. Comparatively speaking, a university is a loosely coupled system— see Weick's (1976) classic article as illustrative—and the U.S. Army is a tightly coupled system. Two concepts easily come to mind to help understand "looseness" versus "tightness": hierarchy and interdependence. Both a university and the U.S. Army have hierarchies, but in a university it is rather flat and decentralized with a major constituency, the faculty, largely ignoring the "chain of command." A long-standing debate has been about who is actually in charge—the faculty or the administration. In the U.S. Army, the hierarchy is steep, centralized, and extremely clear about who is in charge. The chain of command is sacrosanct. With respect to interdependence, the more units within the organization depend on one another for accomplishing the organization's mission and its goals, the more tightly coupled the system is considered to be. Accomplishing the mission in the Army is a strongly interdependent process. In the university, departments rarely cross boundaries much less cooperate with one another. Interdisciplinary efforts are sometimes discussed but almost never realized. Independence is much more the name of the game than interdependence.

Describing these two organizations in this bifurcated way causes us to think unidimensionally with loose on one end and tight on the other. But according to Orton and Weick (1990), a dialectical way of thinking about loose versus tight is a more realistic and accurate mode for considering these two concepts. In other words, a system can simultaneously be both loose and tight. It is like asking the question of whether an organization should be centralized or decentralized. The answer to this question is both. The better question to pose is which organizational functions should be centralized, such as finance, and which ones decentralized, such as human resources.

In an effort to understand the dialectical nature or quality of loosely and tightly coupled systems, Orton and Weick (1990) considered more than 100 studies and then summarized them into five categories: (a) causation, (b) typology, (c) effects, (d) compensations, and (e) outcomes.

Causation. The question here is what causes loose coupling. According to Orton and Weick's (1990) study, there are at least three factors: (a) Causal indeterminacy—unclear means—end connections; for example, improving product and service quality do not appear to lead to higher customer satisfaction. (b) Fragmental external environment—increased complexity of the marketplace; for example, new competitors who seem to come from out of nowhere. (c) Fragmented internal environment—high differentiation of functions with little integration. The point with causation is that the more organizational elements that differentiate an organization, the more there are differentiated responses and, in turn, loose coupling.

Typology. All loose couplings are not the same. From their study of the literature, Orton and Weick (1990) identified at least eight different types—individuals, sub-units, organizations, hierarchical levels, organizational external environments, ideas, activities, and intentions and actions. With this category, Orton and Weick are simply meaning that loose coupling can take many forms ranging from among and between individuals to ideas and activities, and so on. *Direct effects.* This category refers to the fact that loose coupling can be advocated by certain organizational members, that is, loosening the way we do this or that aspect of our work is a good thing. The "work-out" initiative at General Electric a number of years ago is an example: "We do not need to do this procedure anymore; it does not contribute to the overall effort." In this example, it is more a process of "de-coupling" that usually leads to "loosening."

Compensations. This category can be considered the opposite of direct effects, that is, loose coupling is not a good thing. "We need to tighten things." Managerial strategies to tighten too much looseness include (a) enhanced leadership, (b) focused effort, and (c) shared values. To compensate for too much looseness, then, would be to provide a stronger and more direct leadership, by emphasizing, say, greater efficiency and cost effectiveness, that is, more control of key variables in the organization, and to focus on values that organizational members share. Orton and Weick (1990) summarize this category of compensation by stating that it "preserves a dialectical interpretation when it builds on the premise that looseness on some dimensions should be complemented by coupling on other dimensions" (p. 213).

Organizational outcomes. This fifth and final category from Orton and Weick's work refers to the effect that loose coupling has on organizational performance. At the organizational level (as opposed to individual or subunit levels), things get more complicated. In other words, the causal factors on outcomes are more varied and distant; therefore, the looser the coupling, the more difficult it is to determine what causes what. Orton and Weick (1990) point to evidence (Firestone, 1985; Wilson & Corbett, 1983) in support of this statement, that is, "tightly coupled systems are more conducive to systemwide change than loosely coupled systems" (p. 213). Returning to the example of the university compared with the U.S. Army and the dialectical interpretation of loose-tight, we know that the university and the Army can have both these qualities at the same time. Within the university, departments can be tightly coupled and fight to keep it that way by insisting on the larger system's being loosely coupled. And with respect to the Army, it is well known that loosely coupled is a much more accurate description of reality during combat conditions than when soldiers are back on the post.

This loose-tight dialectic, of course, falls within other organizational forces that contribute to conflict and consternation such as freedom and constraint, autonomy and relationships, differentiation and integration. For the purpose of organization change, the loose-tight dialectic is particularly important, however. Weick (2001) has continued to help us understand loosely coupled systems when he has focused on change. He has stated that when attempting to change loosely coupled systems the practitioner should

- focus more on change as a continuous process rather than episodic,
- assume that change will most likely occur on a small rather than large scale,
- emphasize improvisational initiatives more than planned ones,
- be more accommodative than constrained, and
- operate more locally than in a cosmopolitan manner.

What We Need to Know

To be honest, when consulting with organizations to bring about change, I have tended to emphasize the opposite of these five admonitions from Weick (2001), that is, to focus on episodic, large-scale, planned, constrained, and to be more cosmopolitan than local. See Table 1 for a summary comparison of these two processes: changing a loosely coupled system and changing a tightly coupled system.

Table 1. A Comparison of Changing a Loosely Coupled System (LCS) With a Tightly Coupled System (TCS)

Dimension for Comparison	Process for Changing an LCS	Process for Changing a TCS
Focus	Continuous	Episodic
Scale	Small	Large
Type of initiative	Improvisational	Planned
Consulting process	Accommodative	Constrained
Locus of change	Local	Cosmopolitan

Note. Weick (2001).

For the most part, my approach, differing from Weick's (2001) points about working with loosely coupled systems, has not been inappropriate. My work, after all, has been more with tightly coupled systems. Recently, however, I worked with a very loosely coupled system in an attempt to bring about a significant organization change. The need was to tighten the system, and I relied on typical ODC techniques. The change effort over a span of 2 to 3 years was successful—but only temporarily. The change did not last; in fact, the organization reverted to its previous state. I realized that I have a lot to learn about how to change a loosely coupled system. The story is more complicated that these few statements convey—see Noumair, Winderman, and Burke (2010) for the full report—yet what was simple for me to understand was my need to learn more about loosely coupled systems.

The fact that the work of ODC practitioners since the 1960s has been more with tightly than loosely coupled systems means that we, at least speaking for myself, are deficient in our knowledge of and how to work with loosely coupled systems. Consulting (a) in a continuous manner, (b) on a small scale, (c) improvisationally, (d) accomodatively, and (e) locally all seem to demand that we move away from our comfort zones and create new approaches and techniques for changing those organizations that are largely loosely coupled, such as a network, a consortium, strategic alliance, partnership, university, or a cooperative, to name just a few examples. Kaplan (1982) described a situation where using a large group intervention could have possibly helped with his work in a loosely coupled system. Also applying concepts and techniques from the field of network analysis might help our work with loosely coupled systems.

Whether loosely or tightly coupled, all organizations have a culture. If we are serious about changing an organization fundamentally, we must sooner or later tackle its culture—the norms, deeply held beliefs, and eventually the collective unconscious. We need to know more about how to address and make these kinds of changes that lie deep inside the organization. The following section considers these kinds of changes.

You Don't Change Organizational Culture by Trying to Change the Culture

Suppose I ask you to rank order the following three concepts from most difficult to change to least difficult to change:

- values
- attitudes
- behavior

You would no doubt agree that the order in which the three are listed is the answer to my ranking request. This is not to say that *behavior* is easy to change. Among these three, behavior is comparatively the least difficult with *values* being the most difficult. Values are fundamental to culture. In trying to change organizational culture, then, why would you begin with the most difficult aspect? The point is that you would start with behavior change to have an impact-eventually-on the fundamentals of organizational culture.

Not so fast you might think. Don't you need to define what the desired culture should be? Absolutely. And this defining should be incorporated into the organizational vision for the future. In the case of culture change at British Airways (BA; Burke, 2011; Goodstein & Burke, 1991), it was a matter of defining the desired culture as one that was more responsive to the marketplace and in particular to the passenger who purchased a ticket to travel in their airplanes. The intention was for the new culture to be more market driven and less operations driven, as had been true from the origination of BA, without sacrificing the importance of and attention to safety. So it is a matter of determining the right set of behaviors, in this case, for example, to manage the BA frontline employees in a more open, considerate, and participative manner so that they, in turn, would be more attentive and considerate of the customer.

But determining the right behaviors is only half of the change effort. It is also a matter of getting beneath the surface of day-to-day behavior, attempting to understand the unspoken, the deep structure (Gersick, 1991); in other words, E. H. Schein's (2004) third level of organizational culture-basic underlying assumptions. Yet during the initial stages of an organization change effort, we do not know what these unspoken, beneath-the-surface concerns and factors are. Much if not most qualities and dimensions of the culture are difficult to identify and to define and therefore difficult to anticipate. They do not emerge very readily until challenged and questioned by change initiatives. Thus, reactions to these initiatives (interventions), sometimes in the form of resistance, become significant and directional, with respect to subsequent steps in the change process. Not surprisingly, Kurt Lewin told us about this reactive quality a long time ago when he said something like, "If you really want to understand (diagnose in more depth) an organization, try to change it." These reactions to intervening into the system give us clues about the unspoken, what is hard to articulate, and what may be sacred and perhaps untouchable. My favorite metaphor for this phenomenon that Lewin identified is the scene of a young child throwing a pebble into a shallow, clear pond. Instead of following the pebble to the bottom to see where it lands, it is more important to follow the ripples across the pond's surface. These ripples are the clues about where to look deeper into the personality of the organization. In BA, it was about power and authority, and to some extent, obvious. After all, BA originated from the Royal Air Force of World War II. But in civilian clothes, the BA culture in the 1980s was more about what represented power and how authority was exercised than power and authority per se and in a traditional sense— the hierarchy, command and control, and obedience. It was more about information—who had it and how it was disseminated if shared at all. Wielding influence via information was not obvious at the outset of the BA culture change effort.

In summary, organizational culture change begins with identifying the desired culture, its characteristics and relevant values, but then moving quickly to determining what the primary behaviors are that will lead to these new, desired qualities. The emphasis needs to be on these key behaviors not so much on the values and the desired culture per se. In other words, it is a movement first particularly with managers "walking" in a new direction. The focus in not on mangers' "mental sets"; it is more about overt behavior than cognition. This process and way of initiating change is consistent with and follows the principles of the James-Lange theory rather than concentrating initially on attitudes and values. Cognitive change follows behavior change—see Burke (2011) for more details on these principles of change.

The second half of organizational culture change, therefore, is a process of getting at and attempting to discern as clearly as possible underlying assumptions that organizational members hold about the "way things are done around here." But these members usually are not that consciously aware of these deeply held beliefs and assumptions. Interviewing them is not likely to be all that useful but observing their reactions to change initiatives and interventions can be very diagnostic. We need new tools or the revision of old tools to help us get at the underbelly of an organization's culture—a segue to the closing part of this section.

Innovation Needed

At least 70% of organization change efforts fail, failure meaning not attaining the goals for change or accomplishing change but the attainment does not last. The failure rate is even higher for mergers and acquisitions (Burke & Biggart, 1997), and I suspect the same to be true for attempts at culture change. The message is clear: This rate of failure is unacceptable. We need new or revised social technology. There are at least three categories of need here: (a) overt techniques, (b) covert tools and techniques, and (c) the same need for sustaining change efforts, that is, techniques for maintaining momentum.

Overt. By overt I mean primarily behavior that we can see and hear. Referring earlier to the premise that culture change begins with behavior, what we need to know more about is how to *translate* the vision (future state), mission, and values that represent the goals for the organization culture change efforts into the behavioral practices that will lead to the desired future state. I tell our doctoral students that they must learn how to be "translators." In essence, it is about measurement—composing behavioral statements that can be used as a Likert-type scale for ratings and in turn provide feedback for managers who are in key change roles.

I have found over the years when supervising students for their doctoral dissertation research that more often than not, the central problem for their studies is one of measurement—are we measuring what we say we are measuring? This is a validity question, of course, yet not all that apparent until the data have been collected, and then we have a difficult time understanding what the numbers mean particularly when those numerical outcomes did not support the hypotheses for the research.

459

Perhaps I am not addressing innovative needs as much as I am harping on the importance of devoting the time, energy, and effort to composing effective behavioral statements that will reveal the realities of an organization's culture and how to change it. Purchasing an instrument over the Internet purporting to measure an organization's culture is not likely to do the job. Besides, we must craft our own so that it is tailored to the organization's change goals. Innovation and hard work in the translation thereof is the need.

Covert. By covert I mean getting beneath the surface of an organization's culture, finding ways to go beyond what E. H. Schein (2004) refers to as the first level, cultural artifacts, and the second level, espoused beliefs and values, to his third level of culture—the basic underlying assumptions that organizational members hold. These basic assumptions are (a) rarely if ever discussed; (b) taken for granted, that is, assumed; and (c) based on beliefs and behaviors that have over time contributed to the success of the organization; beliefs about what to embrace and support, and beliefs about what to avoid. According to E. H. Schein (2004), these assumptions "tend to be non-confrontable and non-debatable, and hence are extremely difficult to change" (p. 31). To change ultimately the organization's culture, we must nevertheless get to those matters that "are extremely difficult to change" which helps explain why the change failure rate is so high.

Moreover, to change the culture means that organizational leaders and consultants must devote considerable time and energy to the effort—time spent on building openness and trust so that organizational members will talk and feel safe in doing so. After all, the culture change at BA took at least 5 years.

In using the terms *getting at* the underlying assumptions, what do we mean? We mean things such as trying to understand *why* organizational members interact with one another as they do day in and day out, what is ok to say openly and what is not, and why not? Also, trying to understand how the history of the organization affects today's behavioral patterns, for example, what is cherished and held onto from the past—at BA it was things such as their enviable safety record that needed to remain if not strengthened and that the long-haul pilots and crew had more status than the shorthaul members. The highest status of all were the pilots and crew for the former Concorde flights. These status factors were a hindrance to the changes that were desired, that is, they contributed to elitism, which in turn worked against the attempts to instill participative management and involvement processes.

We need new thinking about and development of ways to help organizational members feel safe during times of upheaval. Attempting to address basic underlying assumptions means that emotions will be front and center, and resistance may loom large. Encouraging people to talk about their feelings of fear and resistance can be helpful in (a) understanding what's underneath the surface and (b) moving the organization toward the change goals.

Perhaps this need for new thinking and methods should focus on techniques that are nondirect. In other words, such approaches might be more beneficial than a more direct approach of asking people to talk about the past, their feelings and fears, and so on. Role-play and simplified versions of psychodrama come to mind, or depicting the culture in art form—painting or sculpting.

The point is that innovation is needed to access culture in many ways that will surface the "undiscussables" as well as feelings and impressions that are difficult to articulate, to put into words, and to simplify.

Sustaining, maintaining momentum. Although most any attempt to change an organization is difficult, it is easier to initiate a change effort than to sustain it once underway. When change is underway and movement is occurring, the process is typically messy if not chaotic, and things do not actualize as planned. The new software that we were counting on is not working, and some people are simply not doing what they said they would do, and so on. During such times and tribulations, change recipients in particular begin to get weary and say things such as "I

461

knew this whole thing wouldn't work; it's simply too much," or "Things are a mess, nobody seems to know what to do, and the boss is no where to be found." In other words, people begin to give up, and the change dies a slow but sure death. It is likely that the primary cause of organization change failure is the experience of having to deal with the consequences of initiatives and interventions that were unanticipated, surprising, and unpredictable. We plan change in a linear manner, Step 1 (unfreeze), Step 2 (movement), Step 3, and so on, but the implementation of change is nonlinear, and we are having to spend most of our time on dealing with unanticipated consequences not what we thought the change was going to be or look like.

To maintain momentum, there is at least one clear and extremely important action to take. When something occurs that was not anticipated, and this something, for example, software problem, creates a significant barrier to the success of the overall change effort, it is critical that the problem be tackled immediately and be solved as soon as humanly possible. Otherwise, the process, the movement toward the change goals gets bogged down, and momentum is lost, and discouragement ensues.

Other steps and activities are needed as well to sustain the change process such as celebrating events when milestones are reached or recognizing certain individuals who have contributed to the effort significantly.

In human affairs, momentum can be rather ephemeral and not obvious. Yet in sports we can tell when one team changes the tide and begins to outperform the other team, or even a single individual against an opponent as in tennis or boxing. With respect to an organization change effort, it is probably more important to concentrate on teamwork and create supportive activities, such as appreciative inquiry, and provide resources that help team members work together well. Good teamwork can be contagious for other teams and thereby contribute to momentum. In any case, the need for innovation in this category of momentum is enormous since the lack of sustainment may be the greatest cause of organization change failure.

Changing an organization's culture is a long-term endeavor. Persistence is key because from time to time and at whatever stage of the change process, resistance on the part of organizational members is highly likely. For us ODC practitioners, and again, at least speaking for myself, there has been a tendency to assume that organizational members will either resist the change or embrace it. It is not that simple, as we shall see in the next section.

Resistance Isn't What It Used to Be

First, allow me to own up to my contribution to the problem discussed in this section. Second, the issues will be explored combined with an admonition to modernize our thinking and practice.

On occasions when I am wearing my organization change consultant hat, I have been known to advise my clients when they are planning a change effort for their organization to categorize their organizational members, that is, the change recipients and eventual implementers of the change, into two groups—the champions camp, those who are likely to be supportive of the proposed change, and the resistance camp, those who are likely to be opposed to the proposed change. Then I advise my change leaders to plan their strategy and tactics accordingly. This advice stems from my training and education in the field. I grew up on Coch and French (1948), and luminaries such as Goodwin Watson (1967) and Paul Lawrence (1969), all of whom emphasized the term *overcome* in dealing with resistance. I tended to think in "we—they" terms "You are either for or against us!"

But I also learned later that all resistance is not the same. O'Toole (1995) in his book *Leading Change* devoted an entire chapter to "Change Resisted: Thirty-Three Hypotheses Why." Resistance can not only be forceful but can also take a variety of forms. Hambrick and Cannella (1989) boiled it down to three kinds—blind, ideological, and political.

They defined each one, and then I took their distinctions a step further and suggested different ways of dealing with each of the three types (Burke, 2011). In other words, resistance is real, to be expected, and should be dealt with quite deliberately.

Piderit's (2000) work, however, began to turn me around. She pointed out that responses to change are "neither consistently negative nor consistently positive" (p. 783). Ambivalence may be the more dominant reaction. Thoughtful people may see the positive outcomes of change yet at the same time be wary of potentially adverse consequences. At about the same time, Dent and Goldberg (1999) challenged our thinking (certainly my thinking) about the nature of resistance, that is, the idea, or mental model, as they referred to it, that there is consistently resistance to change and leaders and managers must overcome it. These authors then showed us how management textbooks have perpetuated the mental model that resistance is a given, without defining it, and strategies must be developed for overcoming it. Dent and Goldberg (1999) also traced the emergence of the term resistance starting with Kurt Lewin. He, of course, embedded resistance within an energy field of forces, that is, the person within context. The Coch and French (1948) study exemplified Lewin's theoretical approach. Yet in the tracing of the resistance concept, Dent and Goldberg argued that many have strayed from Lewin's origins and made resistance more psychological, a force within the individual rather than a combination of the individual and the context. They argued further that managers have been brainwashed (my term not theirs) about resistance, that is, it is to be expected on the part of employees and managers must overcome this resistance to make organization change work. This mental model has therefore exacerbated the problem not unlike a self-fulfilling prophecy, and what must be overcome according to Dent and Goldberg is this mode of thinking not resistance per se. Moreover, they argued that resistance since Lewin's time has been narrowed to a psychological phenomenon instead of a systemic one and located within change recipients—the "others" who have to be overcome. The implication by Dent and Goldberg (1999) was that resistance has become an inappropriate if not outmoded term.

Ford, Ford, and D'Amelio (2008) more recently picked up the banner, but moved from narrowing to broadening when they declared in the opening statement of their article that "It is time to expand our understanding of resistance to change, including its sources and its potential contribution to effective change management" (p. 362). Change agents (leaders and managers of change and their consultants whether internal or external) act as if what they perceive to be resistance actually *is* resistance. "There is no consideration assigned by change agents to the behaviors and communications of change recipients, or that these interpretations are either self-serving or self-fulfilling" (p. 362). Perceived resistance is rarely seen by change agents as rational, thoughtful, or reflective. The perspective of change agents concerning resistance to organization change is therefore quite limited. Ford and his colleagues provide three ways of expanding our understanding of resistance and in so doing they have helped us improve our practice:

Sensemaking. Borrowing terminology from Weick (1995), Ford et al. depicted the interaction between change agents and change recipients as a matter of problem solving that leads to an attempt to make sense out of the change situation, or vice versa, that is, trying to make sense can lead to solving a problem. The problem for change agents is one of determining how best to implement change, and for change recipients, it is more personal—what does this mean for me? Instead of assuming automatic resistance and acting accordingly thereby enacting the self-fulfilling prophecy, change agents can alternatively assume that two different problems exist. One problem is theirs, and there is another problem for the recipients. Proceeding down a path of problem clarification, making sense of the situation, and then problem solving is not the same as assuming resistance and then acting in such a way as to evoke it.

Change agent contributions to resistance. Ford et al. (2008) cite several studies (and we know from accounts in the media) that demonstrate how resistance can be generated from change agents' breaking agreements and violating trust. Evidence also shows, on the other hand, that when change agents work to repair damaged relationships and restore trust resistance decreases. Communication breakdowns can also contribute to resistance when change agents (a) fail to legitimize change, that is, not to make the case, explain the reasons, show the need adequately; (b) misrepresent the chances of success, for example, change agents attempting to make themselves look good; and (c) resist perceived resistance, that is, to ignore change recipients ideas, proposals, or counteroffers. Change agents can come across to recipients as defensive, highly stubborn, and seeing the change to be done in only one way.

Resistance as a resource. Worse than resistance is apathy. At least with resistance there is energy, and the recipients care about something. Resistance can help keep discussion going and potentially moving in a problem-solving direction. Moreover, resistance when expressed is, after all, a form of engagement and can eventually move some recipients from ambivalence to acceptance. With such movement on the part of some, others may join in albeit perhaps slowly. This is when patience on the part of change agents can be a virtue.

Ford et al. (2008) also pointed out that resistance is a form of conflict, yet as we know, when differences among people are surfaced, confronted, and debated, improved decision making can occur. In other words, the organization change effort can progress just perhaps not quite in the same way as change agents may have planned or thought that the process might proceed. These authors concluded their article with a "reconstruction" of resistance by stating that it "can be more appropriately understood as a dynamic among three elements" (Ford et al., 2008, p. 370). These elements are (a) recipient action, (b) change agent sensemaking, and (c) the change agent-recipient relationship. *Recipient action* refers to attempts to shift private and internal feelings about organizational change to more public behaviors. The more such attempts are successful, the more change agents have actual "data" to work with rather than, say, interpreting silence and lack of affect as resistance. Change agent *sensemaking* means that none of the recipients' actions and behaviors "are, in and of themselves, resistance, and they do not become resistance unless and until change agents assign the label *resistance* to them as part of their sensemaking" (p. 371). Thus, some behaviors may reflect resistance and some may not. The third element, *change agent—recipient relationship*, constitutes the interaction between the two parties. This means that resistance should be considered as a two-way street—that both parties may indeed contribute to the problem.

To *summarize*, let me provide a brief anecdote about organization change and perceived resistance.

Several years ago in my role as director of our graduate programs in social organizational psychology I (read "change agent/leader") proposed that we initiate a new MA program in addition to the two programs (MA and PhD) that we had been providing for well more than 20 years. I explained (I thought patiently) the market, the need, and our capabilities of delivering such a program successfully. When I finished, there was a long silence followed finally by a faculty member's raising questions rather than cheering me on. I perceived the questions to be resistance, and I became rather belligerent and withdrawn. A rather heated debate then ensued. I later learned that my colleague was not necessarily opposed to the idea; her behavior could more accurately be labeled as ambivalent (Piderit, 2000). In fact, we as a faculty did decide to proceed with the new program. As the change agent, I came close by my own behavior to fulfilling a prophecy about my colleague who was not necessarily resistant, only questioning. As the change agent, I needed to have treated these questions as important concerns, reasons to explore in more depth the rationale and potential hazards for such a program.

This short story captures and illustrates the primary points that Ford et al. (2008) make—the role and behavior of the change agent, the change recipient, and the interaction between the two. It is this dynamic, to use

Ford and his colleagues' term, that needs to be understood in more depth and used as a framework for learning and skill development.

Innovation Needed

As noted above, we practitioners in the world of OD and organization change, in general, need more skill in understanding (a) resistance when it is real, (b) how we may contribute to the problem, and (c) what to do to get beyond resistance and solve the actual problem. Moreover, as Ford et al. (2008) note,

> There are few tools, for example, that help change agents (1) repair damaged trust resulting from broken agreements (Tomlinson, Dineen, & Lewicki, 2004), (2) address and resolve issues of mistreatment or injustice (Folger & Skarlicki,1999), (3) admit mistakes or take other actions that restore credibility (Kouzes & Posner, 1993; Reichers, Wanous, & Austin, 1997), or (4) complete and bring closure to the past (Albert, 1983; Ford, Ford, & McNamara, 2002). (p. 370)

Reading the references noted by Ford et al. (2008) can help and so can reading a popular-press book such as *Difficult Conversations* (Stone, Patton, & Heen, 1999). But there is no substitute for experiential learning, reminding me of T-groups and sensitivity training. Yet learning can occur from role-playing and getting feedback, from Gestalt methods, and from negotiation and conflict management exercises.

The final section of this article continues with the theme of learning, particularly experientially and in this case about leadership and leadership development.

Getting Leadership Development
Right Is Long Overdue

One of every two individuals who fills a position of leadership fails (Hogan, Curphy, & Hogan, 1994)—failure being defined as a lack of goal accomplishment. We either have a selection or a development problem. Evidence would suggest that it is both.

Selection

With respect to selection, at least three biases dominate: (a) Even though we have been warned about the dangers (e.g., Bennis & O'Toole, 2000; Levinson, 1974), the tendency to clone ourselves is strong. (b) The big five factors of personality are attractive. We like people for leadership roles who are reasonably stable mentally and emotionally, agreeable, conscientious, more extroverted than introverted, and open to new experiences and learning. And throw in the additional factor that if the candidate is a man who is 6 feet 2 inches tall, the choice is all but made (Schwartz, 2010). (c) And if not prone to cloning and if we know nothing about the big five factors, we nevertheless have some kind of bias regarding selection of our leaders. In a word, we carry around in our heads an "implicit theory" about what a leader should be and look like. The individual differences regarding these implicit theories are remarkable. Take, for example, the "experiment" that I have conducted many times.

When giving a presentation on leadership to a group of executives and managers, I begin by asking them to write down the five most important qualities or characteristics of a successful leader; just a word or two for each of the five—and not four, and not six, but five. Once everyone has completed the task, I pull cash out of my pocket and propose two bets of two dollars each. (Now with inflation, I have increased the wager to five dollars each.) The first bet is that there will not be any two people who will have the same list. And the second bet is that there will not be one characteristic that is common for all, that is, the same single quality or characteristic that is on everyone's list, such as "effective communicator" or "visionary." Having done this "experiment" with hundreds of executives and managers over many years, and I almost always have takers in my sessions for each of the two bets, I have never lost either of the two wagers. And I take their money; I don't fool around. You can conduct my experiment too, of course, but a word of advice. If the group is more than 40 people, you increase the risk of losing the first bet—two individuals having the same list—and if the group is less than 20, you may lose the second bet. Within that range, however, you will make money.

The point is that we all have "implicit theories" about what a successful leader looks like, and they are different from one another, idiosyncratic to the person making the list. Thus, when we are serving on a search committee for the new leader, we as a group have a difficult time of it when trying to agree on our choice.

To compound the selection problem, we may from time to time become involved in working with people responsible for talent management in their organizations. Typically, one of their primary responsibilities is to select "high potentials" for leadership development. To avoid the bias problems noted above, we in a consultant role may suggest criteria for selecting these "hi-pots." In the end, however, we often find that bosses nominate hi-pots from among their array of subordinates, and the criteria that they use for nomination are not exactly objective. In working with a client not too long ago to improve their multirater feedback system, my doctoral students and I found rather serendipitously that executives who were selecting hi-pots from their ranks were choosing those who looked remarkably like themselves when comparing their self-ratings with those who were selected. Cloning appears to remain alive and well. To avoid this problem of bias, we gave them a set of 10 criteria for selection to use instead, but it has not been clear subsequently that this company's executives have put them to use.

We do know some things about selection. One clear example is that our criteria for selection must fit the culture and the future vision for the organization. We ignore context at our peril. However, we sometimes face the problem of an organization's vision for the future not being congruent with the current culture that needs to change. Thus, our selection criteria must be forward thinking. So, yes, we know some things but we have a long way to go with respect to selection of people for leadership. For a review about identifying potential, see Silzer and Church (2009).

Development

Regardless of how effective or flawed our selection process may be, development of potential leaders is more difficult and complicated. Many more variables are involved. One thing does seem clear: We can train managers more easily than we can train leaders. It is easier, for example, to teach people about how to analyze a financial statement than it is to teach them about how to inspire followers. Leadership is so much more personal such that training, as compared with development and education, can be quite limited and problematical.

Considerable clarification about this problem of leadership development has recently been provided by McCall (2010). He points out that to the extent that leadership is learned, experience remains the best teacher. This declaration is no doubt obvious, but some experiences are more important than others. McCall notes that many studies show that

> successful managers describe similar experiences that shaped their development. These experiences can be classified roughly as early work experiences, short-term assignments, other people (almost always very good and very bad bosses or supervisors), hardships of various kinds, and some miscellaneous events like training programs. (p. 4)

Although debatable as to the exact proportions, the "70-20-10 rule" appears to be apropos, that is, 70% challenging assignments, 20% other people—especially good and bad bosses, good and bad mentors, and good and bad coaches—and 10% programs. An important caveat about programs (mentoring, coaching, skill training) is that the more stand-alone they are, the less effective they turn out to be. Programs work best when they are directly in support of on-the-job developmental experiences. The 70%, developmental experiences, need to be "challenging—the unexpected, high stakes, complexity, pressure, novelty, and so on—is what makes it a potentially powerful learning experience" (McCall, 2010, p. 4). Helping these executives reflect on their experiences particularly with the assistance of a competent coach adds to the potential for the learning to stay with them and transfer to other situations.

Much of the original work that provided the basis for the 70-20-10 rule was conducted a number of years ago by McCall, Lombardo, and Morrison (1988) and since that time additional studies have been consistent about the significance of learned experience (e.g., Yost & Plunkett, 2009).

The process for leadership development is now clear-providing challenging job assignments from which potential leaders can learn. But what in particular should they be learning? The huge number of lessons learned as reported by executives in the studies over the years by McCall and his colleagues (and reported in McCall, 2010) can be summarized in terms of the five basic demands of the leadership role:

1. Setting and communicating direction—determining purpose, vision, goals, and establishing support for these endeavors
2. Aligning critical constituencies—making sure that those who need to support these endeavors are "on board"
3. Developing an executive temperament—being able to cope with complexity, ambiguity, and the pressures of the leadership role
4. Setting and living values—clarifying what to believe in and stand for, and making sure that as leader one's words match one's actions
5. Growth of self and others—practicing and supporting in others' lifelong learning, growth, and change

A way of thinking about the overall process of leadership development is to conceptualize it as a set of stages or phases. *First,* we have to select those who have high potential using appropriate criteria and avoiding cloning. *Second,* we need to provide opportunities for learning via challenging job assignments. *Third,* we must understand that having a challenging experience alone does not guarantee learning. A program of personal reflection is key. Most of us need assistance with this reflective process, someone to discuss our experience with—a mentor and a coach, preferably two different people. *Fourth,* and finally, we need to establish procedures for evaluating the effectiveness of the previous three phases, that is, a set of measures (such as multirater

Table 2. A Phased Program of Leadership Development

Phase I. Selection	Phase II. Job Assignments	Phase III. Reflection	Phase IV. Evaluation
• Based on the criteria that are grounded in the organization's current or future, desired state • Avoid cloning of bosses • Emphasize diversity—heterogeneous executives outperform homogeneous executives	• Provide challenging assignments such as • Turn around, fix-it jobs • A leap in scope, e.g., from middle manager to general manager • Line to staff switch • Start from scratch, e.g., new business line • Task force and project management	• Provide support for learning via • Mentoring • Coaching with emphasis on learning and introspection • Specific skill-based training, e.g., public speaking	• Before and after assessments based on multirater systems • Performance appraisal • Promotion rate • Extent to which a person is selected for further challenging assignments

feedback, job performance indicators, rate of promotion, and extent to which one is selected for additional challenging assignments) that can help us improve if not significantly change our overall program of leadership development. See Table 2 for a summary of such a phased program of leadership development.

It is one thing to conceptualize an overall phased program of leadership development and quite another to implement such an elaborate and complex process. A significant problem lies at the outset, which can be characterized as an issue of performance versus development. To what extent are top executives committed to development of leaders, which requires deliberate placement of a high potential individual into a job that is new, the person has no previous experience with such an assignment, and it is perhaps risky, as opposed to a placement decision based on tried-and-true experience already by the individual and the possibility of failure being remote. With the pressures that executives face in our rapidly changing world putting an inexperienced person, regardless of how bright and able the individual may be, into a tough, risky assignment requires a strong commitment to development, a commitment that most executives are unwilling to make. McCall (2010) addressed this issue and suggested, among other ideas, to "embed development seamlessly in the business strategy" (p. 11). In short, he argued that it is better to "join with" executives than to confront them about the development versus performance issue. Whether to fight or join, we as change consultants nevertheless have a lot to learn about how to ensure that evidence—based knowledge regarding leadership development gets used appropriately in the organizations we serve.

Summary and Conclusions

Arguably, the field of ODC has been stagnant for at least the past two decades with respect to innovation and new social technology. The fact, however, that the field has existed for half a century and continues to the present day may mean for some that ODC is here to stay and has proved itself. The job of creation is done, and it is a matter of practicing well what we know how to do. With this article, my argument, on the other hand, has been that there is considerable unfinished business at hand. Two points: *First*, we must face the reality that well above the majority of organization change efforts fail. To assume that we know a lot about organization change and how to manage change effectively is a matter of unwarranted hubris. *Second*, the strengths of ODC have been largely based on loosening tight systems. Our expertise regarding the opposite, tightening loose systems, is sparse at best.

So we must learn to work with loosely coupled and highly decentralized systems and help them operate better, that is, the work may be more about improvement not revolution. Transformational interventions are probably too powerful and overwhelming for the fragile and subtle nature of a network or a highly decentralized organization. Moreover, as noted earlier, once autonomy has been authorized and become inherent to the system you cannot "go home again." Autonomy is about freedom and liberty, precious commodities in our society and way of life, so tightening the system may generate massive resistance if not rebellion. With a loosely coupled system, a large group intervention might need to focus on how to keep the organization together rather than change it into something else that would result in tightening (see, e.g., Kaplan, 1982). Or perhaps the initiative should be on what to keep loose and what to tighten. Working in this kind of dialectical manner is where learning and innovation are needed.

At the risk of overstating the point, it is as if the work of ODC is complete. By declaring the opposite and stating that there is unfinished business, I am attempting to instill a Zeigarnik effect, and as we know, when this effect is established, we seek closure. Achieving closure, then, is to seek and conduct innovative activities and then to write about it. I have proposed four areas for such work. There are other areas, of course, but there is plenty to do just with these four. Now, please allow me to close on a personal note. Perhaps, I have been trained too well in how the traditional ways of doing the work of organizational change occur and am therefore stuck in my ways. To be the kind of the organization change practitioner, I continue to aspire to be, I must constantly learn, get out of my comfort zone, and try new approaches, such as learning how to tighten a loosely coupled system. If I do not continue to learn and change, then I will contribute to the stagnation of the ODC field.

Acknowledgments

I am grateful to Debra Noumair and Bill Pasmore for their helpful comments on an earlier draft of this article.

Declaration of Conflicting Interests

The author declared no potential conflicts of interests with respect to the authorship and/or publication of this article.

Funding

The author received no financial support for the research and/or authorship of this article.

References

Ackoff, R. L. (1974). *Redesigning the future: A systems approach to societal problems*. New York, NY: Wiley-Interscience.

Albert, S. (1983). The sense of closure. In K. Gergen & M. Gergen (Eds.), *Historical social psychology* (pp. 159-172). Hillsdale, NJ: Lawrence Erlbaum.

Beckhard, R. (1967). The confrontation meeting. *Harvard Business Review, 45*, 149-155.

Beckhard, R. (1997). *Agent of change: My life, my practice*. San Francisco, CA: Jossey-Bass.

Bennis, W. G. (1966). The coming death of bureaucracy. *Think, November-December,* 30-35.

Bennis, W. G. (1970). A funny thing happened on the way to the future. *American Psychologist, 25,* 595-608.

Bennis, W. G., & O'Toole, J. (2000). Don't hire the wrong CEO. *Harvard Business Review, 78*(5/6), 171-176.

Bion, W. R. (1961). *Experiences in groups*. New York, NY: Basic Books.

Blake, R. R., & Mouton, J. S. (1968). *Corporate excellence through grid organization development*. Houston, TX: Gulf.

Bradford, D. L., & Burke, W. W. (Eds.). (2005). *Reinventing organization development: New approaches to change in organizations.* San Francisco, CA: Pfeiffer/Wiley.

Bunker, B. B., & Alban, B. T. (1997). *Large group interventions: Engaging the whole system for rapid change.* San Francisco, CA: Jossey-Bass.

Burke, W. W. (1980). Organization development and bureaucracies in the 1980s. *Journal of Applied Behavioral Science, 16,* 423-437.

Burke, W. W. (2008). A contemporary view of organization development. In T. G. Cummings (Ed.), *Handbook of organization development* (pp. 13-38). Thousand Oaks, CA: Sage.

Burke, W. W. (2011). *Organization change: Theory and practice* (3rd ed.). Thousand Oaks, CA: Sage.

Burke, W. W., & Biggart, N. W. (1997). Interorganizational relations. In D. Druckman, J. E. Singer, & H. van Cott (Eds.), *Enhancing organizational performance* (pp. 120-149). Washington, DC: National Academies Press. Coch, L., & French, J. R. P. (1948). Overcoming resistance to change. *Human Relations, 1,* 512-532.

Cooperrider, D. L., & Srivastva, S. (1987). Appreciative inquiry in organizational life. In W. A. Pasmore & R. W. Woodman (Eds.), *Research in organizational change and development* (Vol. 1, pp. 129-169). Greenwich, CT: JAI Press.

Dent, E. B., & Goldberg, S. G. (1999). Challenging "resistance to change." *Journal of Applied Behavioral Science, 35,* 25-41.

Dyer, W. G. (1987). *Team building: Issues and alternatives* (2nd ed.). Reading, MA: Addison-Wesley.

Fagenson-Eland, E., Ensher, E. A., & Burke, W. W. (2004). Organization development and change interventions: A seven nation comparison. *Journal of Applied Behavioral Science, 40,* 432-464.

Firestone, W. A. (1985). The study of loose coupling: Problems, progress, and prospects. In A. Kerckhoff (Ed.), *Research in sociology of education and socialization* (Vol. 5, pp. 3-30). Greenwich, CT: JAI Press.

Folger, R., & Skarlicki, D. P. (1999). Unfairness and resistance to change: Hardship and mistreatment. *Journal of Organizational Change Management, 12,* 35-50.

Ford, J. D., Ford L. W., & D'Amelio, A. (2008). Resistance to change: The rest of the story. *Academy of Management Review, 33,* 362-377.

Ford, J. D., Ford, L. W., & McNamara, R. (2002). Resistance and the background conversations of change. *Journal of Organizational Change Management, 15,* 105-121.

Freire, P. (1970). *Pedagogy of the oppressed.* New York, NY: Continuum.

French, W. L., & Bell, C. H., Jr. (1995). *Organization development: Behavioral science interventions for organizational improvement* (5th ed.). Englewood Cliffs, NJ: Prentice Hall.

Gersick, C. J. G. (1991). Revolutionary change theories: A multilevel exploration of the punctuated equilibrium paradigm. *Academy of Management Review, 16,* 10-36.

Golembiewski, R. T. (2003). *Ironies in organizational development* (2nd ed.). New York, NY: Marcel Dekker.

Goodstein, L. D., & Burke, W. W. (1991). Creating successful organizational change. *Organizational Dynamics, 19*(4), 5-17.

Hackman, J. R. (1992). The psychology of self-management in organizations. In R. Glaser (Ed.), *Classic readings in self-management teamwork* (pp. 143-193). King of Prussia, PA: Organization Design and Development.

Hackman, J. R., & Oldham. G. R. (1980). *Work redesign.* Reading, MA: Addison-Wesley.

Hambrick, D. C., & Cannella, A. A., Jr. (1989). Strategy implementation as substance and selling. *Academy of Management Executive, 3,* 278-285.

Herzberg, F. B. (1966). *Work and the nature of man.* Cleveland, OH: World.

Hogan, R., Curphy, G. J., & Hogan, J. (1994). What we know about leadership. *American Psychologist, 52,* 130-139.

Kaplan, R. E. (1982). Intervention in a loosely organized system: An encounter with non-being. *Journal of Applied Behavioral Science, 18,* 415-432.

Kouzes, J., & Posner, B. (1993). *Credibility: How leaders gain and lose it, why people demand it.* San Francisco, CA: Jossey-Bass.

Lawrence, P. (1969). How to deal with resistance to change. *Harvard Business Review, 47*(1), 4-12.

Levinson, H. (1974). Don't choose your own successor. *Harvard Business Review, 52*(6), 53-62.

Likert, R. (1967). *The human organization.* New York, NY: McGraw-Hill.

Littrell, W. B. (1980). Editor's introduction. *Journal of Applied Behavioral Science, 16,* 263-277.

Littrell, W. B., & Sjoberg, G. (Eds.). (1980). Bureaucracy in the eighties [Special issue]. *Journal of Applied Behavioral Science, 16*(3).

Macy, B. A., & Izumi, H. (1993). Organization change, design, and work innovation: A meta-analysis of 131 North American field studies—1961-1991. In R. W. Woodman & W. A. Pasmore (Eds.), *Research in organizational change and development* (Vol. 7, pp. 235-313). Greenwich, CT: JAI Press.

Maslow, A. H. (1954). *Motivation and personality.* New York, NY: Harper & Brothers.

McCall, M. W., Jr. (2010). Recasting leadership development. *Industrial and Organizational Psychology, 3*(1), 3-19.

McCall, M. W., Jr., Lombardo, M. M., & Morrison, A. M. (1988). *The lessons of experience: How successful executives develop on the job.* Lexington, MA: Lexington Books.

Miller, E. C. (1978). The parallel organization structure at General Motors. *Personnel, 55*(4), 64-69.

Mirvis, P. H., & Macy, B. A. (1983). Evaluating program costs and benefits. In S. E. Seashore, E. E. Lawler III, P. H. Mirvis, & C. Cammann (Eds.), *Assessing organizational change: A guide to methods, measures, and practices* (pp. 501-527). New York, NY: Wiley-Interscience.

Noumair, D. A., Winderman, B. B., & Burke, W. W. (2010). Transforming the A.K. Rice Institute: From club to organization. *Journal of Applied Behavioral Science, 46*(4), 473 499.

Orton, J. D., & Weick, K. E. (1990). Loosely coupled systems: A reconceptualization. *Academy of Management Review, 15,* 203-223.

O'Toole, J. (1995). *Leading change: Overcoming the ideology of comfort and the tyranny of custom.* San Francisco, CA: Jossey-Bass.

Piderit, S. K. (2000). Rethinking resistance and recognizing ambivalence: A multidimensional view of attitudes toward an organizational change. *Academy of Management Review, 25,* 783-794.

Porras, J. I., & Robertson, P. J. (1992). Organizational development: Theory, practice and research. In M. D. Dunnette & L. M. Hough (Eds.), *Handbook of industrial and organizational psychology* (2nd ed., Vol. 3, pp. 719-822). Palo Alto, CA: Consulting Psychologists Press.

Reichers, A., Wanous, J., & Austin, J. (1997). Understanding and managing cynicism about organizational change. *Academy of Management Executive, 11,* 48-59.

Rioch, M. (1970). The work of Wilford Bion on groups. *Psychiatry, 33,* 56-66.

Schein, E. H. (2004). *Organizational culture and leadership* (3rd ed.). San Francisco, CA: Jossey-Bass.

Schein, V. E., & Greiner, L. E. (1977). Can organization development be fine tuned to bureaucracies? *Organizational Dynamics, 5*(3), 48-61.

Schwartz, J. (2010, August 29). The height of unfairness. *New York Times, Week in Review,* p. 2.

Silzer, R., & Church, A.H. (2009). The pearls and perils of identifying potential. *Industrial and Organizational Psychology, 2*(4), 377-412.

Stein, B. A., & Kanter, R. M. (1980). Building the parallel organization: Creating mechanisms for permanent quality of work life. *Journal of Applied Behavioral Science, 16,* 371-388.

Stone, D., Patton, B., & Heen, S. (1999). *Difficult conversations: How to discuss what matters most.* New York, NY: Penguin Books.

Tannenbaum, R., & Davis, S. A. (1969). Values, man, and organizations. *Industrial Management Review, 10*(2), 67-83.

Thompson, J. D. (1967). *Organization in action.* New York, NY: McGraw-Hill.

Tomlinson, E. C., Dineen, B. R., & Lewicki, R. J. (2004). The road to reconciliation: Antecedents of victim willingness to reconcile following a broken promise. *Journal of Management, 30,* 165-187.

Watson, G. (1967). Resistance to change. In G. Watson (Ed.), *Concepts for social change* (pp. 10-20).

Washington, DC: National Training Laboratories, National Education Association.

Weick, K. E. (1976). Educational organizations as loosely coupled systems. *Administrative Science Quarterly, 21,* 1-19.

Weick, K. E. (1995). *Sensemaking in organizations.* Beverly Hills, CA: Sage.

Weick, K. E. (2001). *Making sense of the organization.* Malden, MA: Blackwell.

Wilson, B. L., & Corbett, H. D. (1983). Organization and change: The effects of school linkages on the quantity of implementation. *Educational Administration Quarterly, 19*(4), 85-104.

Wirtenburg, J., Abrams, L., & Ott, C. (2004). Assessing the field of organization development. *Journal of Applied Behavioral Science, 40,* 465-479.

Woodman, R. W. Bingham, J. B., & Yuan, F. (2008). Assessing organization development and change interventions. In T. G. Cummings (Ed.), *Handbook of organization development* (pp. 187-215). Thousand Oaks, CA: Sage.

Yost, P., & Plunkett, M. (2009). *Real time leadership development.* London, England: Blackwell

Chapter 12

Moving to the Future and Learning

Ellen Scully-Russ
Assistant Professor of Human and Organizational Learning
The George Washington University

Michael Marquardt
Professor of Human and Organizational Learning
The George Washington University

Andrea Casey
Associate Professor of Human and Organizational Learning
The George Washington University

Introduction

Dewey, Mead, Lewin, and other seminal thinkers in human and organizational science were driven by a deep commitment to democracy and a scientific quest for knowledge that could both foster democratic institutions and develop the individual and social capacity to uphold them. These thinkers were the quintessential scholar-practitioners, for they viewed theory (thought) as an embedded part of human experience (reflective action) (Dewey, 1938). Dewey claimed we live our lives through a series of organic circles that connected past with present experience (reflective action) and changed the conditions for future experience. Dewey (1916) optimistically believed that this progressive knowledge creation cycle would make people more human and the world more humane.

As noted by many of the authors in this volume, human and organizational life has become complex and practice more ambiguous. Each author called on human and organizational science to account for the increased dynamism in late modern society and to consider age-old questions about the duality between action and knowledge and between lived experience and the theoretic models and constructs that attempt to represent it. Rather than seek new theories, several authors in this volume challenged us to revisit our intellectual roots to not only examine the efficacy of our basic theories but also reconnect with the field's motivating commitment to democracy and humanistic social change. Uhl-Bien et al. made clear that responsibility for organizational life and welfare is a distributed phenomenon that can no longer be embodied in or delegated to leaders or to organizational development professionals educated in the principles, techniques, and ethics of democratic change. Harvey, Huff, Marsick, Powell, Weick, and Winter suggested that all organizational members are a part of and therefore responsible for the dynamics that create and reinforce the collective reality that underlies organizational culture and practices. McKelvey examined the role of the CEO in creating the dynamics that make organizations work or not. He clearly articulated the implications of this more distributed scholarly practice for the field itself:

> Many introductions to complexity theory to practitioners have been on the soft side, like much of OD—translating self-organization into a modern version of empowerment, using complexity sciences as a modern-day re-legitimization of prosaic OD approaches . . . . My A-Ds [action disciplines] make it patently obvious that 'complexity in action' is very different from updated OD. Saying 'Be #1 or 2 . . .' is meaningless absent the threat of divestiture and losing one's job. Welch was tough

and had a vision . . . . Put bluntly, Welch replaced old-style top-down '*management by objectives*' by '*management by tension.*' *This is complexity leadership at its best!* (p. 29)

As educators in a professional doctorate program in its 25th year of educating and advising doctoral students in human and organizational learning, we have noticed an increased diversity of our student body. In the early years of our program, the vast majority of students identified as organizational development consultants, human resource development managers, and training and development practitioners. Today our student body consists of students who are managers and leaders from a wide range of functions and professions (C-suite leaders, medical doctors, military officers, pastors, educators, lawyers, engineers, accountants, cyber security and information technology professionals, and many more), and they are located across many organizational settings (private industry, health care, education, churches, military, government agencies, family businesses, and not-for-profits, for example). We view this shift in our student population as one manifestation of a distributed knowledge landscape. Diverse leaders at all levels and across generations now seek new knowledge to help them in their responsibility to design and lead innovative change—and they enroll in our program to build their capacity for these responsibilities.

Schwandt and Sashkin in chapter 1 noted that theorizing requires continuity of experience across context, time, and value frames (academic disciplines). How can this continuity be established in a more complex knowledge production landscape, such as we have observed through the shift in our student population, as well as the one described by Huff in her epilogue? How can continuity be achieved when actors pull from and contribute to knowledge in the micro interactions in multiple, disconnected locations where people work and learn today? And what about the democratic commitments that gave rise to the field of human and organizational learning? Who will take responsibility for reproducing and cultivating our ethics as new scholar-practitioners draw from our field to theorize and lead in complex and ambiguous organizations? In this chapter we look to the authors and our own experience as scholar-practitioners and educators to explore these questions and their implications for the future of our field and of doctoral education in human and organizational learning.

First we revisit the scholar-practitioner imperative delineated by Schwandt and Sashkin in chapter 1 and then we examine how the imperative appeared in the articles and prologues in this book. We use this discussion to develop three propositions about the future of theorizing and scholarly practice in our field:

1. The articles and prologues in this book point to new variability in the substance of human and organizational theory—specifically human interaction, process, and contexts—and this variability holds potential to shift the way change constructs (learning, leaders, culture, agency, etc.) are experienced and perceived.

2. This new variability has triggered the need for a new mode of theorizing that accounts for the reflexivity of scientific knowledge and the role of researchers' subjectivity in the research process and thus shifts the interpretive bias in social science research from a subjective to an intersubjective orientation.

3. The emergence of an intersubjective interpretive bias may reframe notions of who or what a scholar-practitioner is (a person, a role, a process).

The chapter concludes by discussing the implications of these propositions for the scholar-practice imperative and for the role of professional doctorate programs in educating scholar-practitioners.

Scholar-Practitioner Imperative

In chapter 1 of this book, Schwandt and Sashkin traced the evolution of 11 constructs that are significant in social change theory, which they called social change constructs. They noted that while these constructs have remained relatively stable at an abstract level of proposition, over time there has been great variation in the variables used to measure and observe these constructs. They made the case that the quality or nature of the change constructs and our understanding of the dynamic relations within them has shifted from an objective to a subjective orientation. Rational conceptions of social structure, norms, human nature, power, and conflict, for example, have given way to a subjective orientation wherein the constructs are socially constructed through the dynamic interaction of logics, emotions, norms, and values in situ.

This inherent variability of social theory and the specific subjective orientation that is emphasized today has implications for the process by which theory is formulated. As meaning and measures shift in situ, theory must keep up. Theory building gives way to theorizing, wherein the competing perspectives and varied experiences of the theoreticians, researchers, and practitioners are not only taken into account, but also valued in the study of the social phenomena. This opens up the paths of information flow between theory and practice and provides for the active integration of concepts in practice and practice into concepts.

In the next section we examine the articles and prologues for evidence of shifts in the variables that explained the change constructs, as well as for insight into the authors' approach to theorizing.

Theorizing and Evidence of Variability in Theory

Knowledge Creation and Learning

In the three articles in the section on knowledge creation and learning, the authors' theorizing was triggered by dichotomies in their understanding of the knowledge creation and learning processes in human systems and organizations. Their articles provide a robust lens into the processes by which they worked with and pushed through the dichotomies to develop a robust and integrated understanding of knowledge production, sensemaking, and workplace learning. Likewise, their prologues offer insight into the authors' current-day theorizing, which for two of the authors includes a shift in both their focus (i.e., new variables in the change constructs of knowledge and learning) and in the epistemologies and modes of theorizing that they employ to investigate human and organizational phenomena.

Huff (1999) in her original article was concerned about the university's continued role in knowledge production in light of the new and very active knowledge organizations that were undertaking scientific inquiry and discovery to support their mission. She suggested that the interplay between Mode 1 knowledge (traditional) and Mode 2 knowledge (created in organizations) would produce creative issues and related solutions through continuous interaction of knowledge and knowledge producers. She projected that Mode 1.5 (synthesis) would add diversity to knowledge production, as it bridged the dichotomy between academia and practice.

Huff's theorizing today aims to capture the changing problem landscape and the complexity of the multiple modes of knowledge production. New variables have emerged in her investigation: new voices (interaction), effectual logic (process), and the more complex knowledge creation landscape (context). Indeed, these variables have shifted her description of the object of her investigation from knowledge production to knowledge creation or innovation processes.

She concluded with a proposal for alternative problem-solving models based on open innovation in diversified organizations and start-ups using "effectual logic as opposed to casual logic" and with entrepreneurs discovering "means and ends rather than well defined objectives" (p. 3). So it seems that along with a shift in Huff's focus of theorizing (new variables), there may have been a shift in her approach to match her new awareness of the dynamic and complex nature of the object of her investigation. Her thinking may have moved from dialectic (seeking synthesis of opposing objects) to dialogic (ongoing communications with multiple voices/streams of thought to reflect, change, and extend one's own thinking).

Likewise, Weick's (1993) article challenged the dichotomy of ignorance and knowledge, noting that "ignorance and knowledge grow together" in a fluid and ever-changing world (p. 5). His article provided a moving analysis of the Mann Gulch tragedy in which he explored the "disintegration of role structure and sensemaking in a minimal organization" (p. 628). He suggested that the lessons learned in the Mann Gulch case are critical ones for people in organizations whose job it is to make sense of environmental changes that may be unexpected and sudden, creating change or collapse in roles and social structures. Resilience, which provides the means for sensemaking, is fostered by improvisation or bricolage, virtual role systems, wisdom, and norms that support respectful interaction.

In his prologue, Weick continued to theorize about sensemaking and the endurance of the lessons of Mann Gulch. Rather than focus on resilience, as he did in the original article, Weick dug deeper into his model to reflect on the variables that constitute it. Through this reflection he proposed that "a partial safeguard against such collapse and a durable reminder is found in . . . respectful interaction" (p. 3). Respectful interaction encompasses ongoing interactions that focus on honest reporting of observations, trusting the reports of others, and respecting our own observations as well as the reports of others. This form of interaction enables people to use their own experiences and those of others for sensemaking (i.e., creating a meaningful context within which they can act).

His theorizing was holistic; he "felt" his way into Mann Gulch and he drew new metaphors to aid in his reflection. This is an example of Dewey's thoroughgoing analysis. As a result, both Weick's and our understanding of the relationship between ignorance and knowledge has grown deeper and more robust.

Marsick (1988) also explored dichotomies in her original article, and she too highlighted the importance of reflection and informal interactions in learning processes in organizations. In advocating for "a new paradigm for understanding workplace learning in the post-industrial era" (p. 187), she noted the intense pressures on organizations to change "from both the external world of business, particularly the technological revolution and the increase in international competition and the nature of the workforce itself" (p. 189). These changes, she suggested, require a "fundamental shift in thinking" (p. 190). Marsick also proposed alternative views to inform our understanding of how knowledge is created, including interpretivism, which focuses on interaction, and she challenged other dichotomies related to learning, including personal versus work-related development, learning in the classroom versus informal workplace learning, and individual versus organizational learning.

In her prologue, Marsick offered insight into her theorizing. She considered three variables: *interaction* among the multiple roles that constitute people's work and personal lives and the processes through which they learn; *learning*, which is a complex process that integrates the experience of this complex array of activities into a coherent set of capabilities at the individual and organizational levels; and *context*, which provides meaning at the individual as well as conceptual level. Specifically she pointed to an emerging paradigm of learning that integrates dichotomous learning activities (personal and job, individual and organizational, formal and informal) to create a more holistic understanding of learning. In her theorizing, Marsick resisted the temptation to reconcile dichotomies through synthesis, and she transcended them through 'both/and' thinking and reflection on practice instead. This mode of praxis gives rise to a more complex and holistic understanding of learning.

Leadership and Complexity

In the previous section, the authors' prologues charted their path from the time they wrote their original article to today. The point of departure taken by the two authors in this section was different. Both Uhl-Bien and McKelvey began their prologues by reflecting on their broad research agenda and the dilemmas and motivations that drove them to write their articles in the first place. Their prologues contextualize their original articles in a broader research agenda as well as in the theoretical traditions that fueled their theorizing. This insight into their personal and theoretical history provides rich context to aid in our understanding of leadership through the lens of complexity. In addition, Uhl-Bien's and McKelvey's detailed description of their personal approach to building their conceptual frameworks provides rich data to explore the nature of theorizing.

In their article, "Complexity Leadership Theory: Shifting Leadership from the Industrial Age to the Knowledge Age," Uhl-Bien, Marion, and McKelvey noted that complexity leadership requires a series of practice precepts to foster adaptive leadership and entanglement, including respecting diversity, fostering internal tension, and tolerating dissent. It necessitates the ability to protect the complex adaptive system from external politics and top-down influences, to deal with crises that threaten to derail adaptive functions, and to move beyond personal power to an organization system based on innovative, complex power. This model is an example of both/and thinking for it recognizes that leadership is neither completely dynamic nor bureaucratic; rather, it is both.

In her prologue, Uhl-Bien described how her theorizing on leadership progressed from leader-member exchange theory to complexity leadership theory by way of a series of 'breakthroughs.' Her disillusionment in leader-member exchange sent her searching for new ideas, and she had a serendipitous encounter with complexity theory and the new variable of relationality (i.e., the invitation to coauthor a chapter on complexity). She took up the metaphor of complexity to think about leadership and developed a network of colleagues with whom she could theorize. She talked about being 'pushed' by others to think beyond the metaphor and develop a model that could be tested through empirical study and iterating (triangulation) with practitioners.

Uhl-Bien identified two key breakthroughs in her theorizing. The first was her exposure to the concept of relationality, which changed her worldview and provided her a broader context for theorizing about leadership. The role of relationality can also be inferred in her theorizing: her collaborators, her clients, and practitioners have "pushed" her beyond the metaphor and challenged her to acknowledge the limitations as well as the promise of complexity theory in theorizing about leadership. The second breakthrough was achieved when Uhl-Bien and colleagues adopted both/and thinking that allowed them to embrace the idea that organizations are both complex adaptive systems and bureaucratic—and this understanding became the basic premise of complexity leadership theory. Further empirical work and iteration of the findings through practice is giving rise to a third breakthrough, which Uhl-Bien believes will build out the framework and make it more applicable in practice.

In *Complexity Leadership: The Secret of Jack Welch's Success*, McKelvey observed that past leadership theory was focused on vision and charisma and was stuck at the bottom of hierarchies. He emphasized how adaptive leadership is a dynamic that emerges from tensions that arise from asymmetric power relations and/or a clash of preferences. Successful leadership, therefore, requires expertise and creative thinking on the part of the agents involved in order to create new knowledge and generate novelty. In his study of Jack Welch, McKelvey showed that leadership is built on creating creative tensions and applying the 12 action disciplines—which complexity scientists call "simple rules," although the rules are not so simple for leaders to understand and apply. These action disciplines make it obvious that complexity in action is very different from current leadership practice.

In his prologue, McKelvey summarized his 20-plus years in researching leadership and complexity science. He observed that Welch was a leader who intuitively found better ways of applying complexity science, and Welch's practices incorporated "bottom-up emergent complexity dynamics." McKelvey showed the power of studying an N of 1, for his investigation of Welch's intuitive and successful use of the 12 action disciplines helped McKelvey advance complexity leadership theory and offered other CEOs insight into how to adapt and compete efficaciously within the fractal structure of their industry.

McKelvey, like Uhl-Bien, clearly articulated his "trek" down the path of complexity leadership. His theorizing began when he read a book on complexity theory by Kauffman (1993). Also, like Uhl-Bien he partnered with others to apply complexity theory to the field of management (i.e., transdisciplinary theorizing). One way he applied the theory was through writing and publishing, which presumably provided him with rich feedback that fueled his theorizing. Over time McKelvey learned the ontology of complexity science (physics and biology), and this solid foundation provided him a better way to engage in transdisciplinary theorizing. Indeed, in the article in this volume, he aptly engaged in transdisciplinary theorizing to illustrate how the action disciplines of complexity science explain the efficacious leadership of Jack Welch. Again, writing fueled his theorizing.

Dynamics of Organizations

In the previous section, both authors were very articulate about the sequence of events of their theorizing, and there were striking similarities in theorizing. They both talked about the prominent role of colleagues. Both also referred to the importance of time and timing in the development of their research. Uhl-Bien observed that "quick and dirty" or simplistic research studies cannot capture the nature of mechanisms that are nonlinear and changeable, unpredictable in the long term, temporally based, and interactively and causally complex. Ironically, they both described a linear approach to theorizing about the dynamic nonlinearity of leadership. For example, Uhl-Bien talked about how one breakthrough built upon and extended previous ones, and McKelvey provided a chronological list of articles that represented how his thinking about complexity and its application to the field of management advanced or progressed throughout his career.

The prologues in the section on dynamics of organizations provide insight into the constraints that may lead scholars to reduce the complexity of their theorizing. Several of these authors provided rich details of their experiences navigating the tension between theory and practice, or perhaps more accurately, between the academy (Mode 1 knowledge) and practice (Mode 2 knowledge). Hatch talked about the "grueling 10 years" it took her to publish the article in this book. Harvey shared the story of the insensitive way a colleague rejected his article. Each author highlighted the importance of writing and publishing in their theorizing and thus implied a significant role of scientific standards and institutions in the theorizing of individual scholars.

The four authors in Section III (Harvey, Hatch, Winter, and Powell) vividly portrayed the complex dynamics that occur in all types of organizations, be they nonprofit, academic, banking, or family. Organizational behavior and action dynamics were examined from the multiple perspectives and disciplines of sociology (Powell), psychology (Harvey), anthropology (Hatch), and economics (Winter). The articles employed a rich array of methodologies, ranging from ethnomethodology to grounded theory to storytelling. Each of the articles described and encapsulated emerging paradigms in the research and practice of organizations as well as the intersections between individual behavior and organizational behavior. Tensions between the freedom and choice of individuals and the structures imposed by organizations were also explored in the articles.

Although "The Abilene Paradox: The Management of Agreement" was written over 35 years ago, Harvey observed that the issues that he introduced relative to "going on the road again" and being "abandoned" are present as much today as in the 1970s. Anaclitic depression, a form of depression that occurs when an individual is abandoned, still happens in the workplace. He noted that too many of us take the trip to Abilene because of the fear of taking risks and because of our desire to be liked rather than to be authentic and honest.

Harvey ended his prologue where the story of his theorizing began, with him not knowing why others liked his story of Abilene. He indicated that the story came from a talk he gave that was well received; the feedback encouraged him to write it down. He commented that he has no goals for his writing; he just writes. Harvey experienced difficulty in publishing this story. It was not academic enough, but it struck a chord in the management world, so he found ways to share it via publication and movies. But the critiques from his academic colleagues continued.

As Harvey related his thoughts and feelings about navigating the hard boundary between the academy and practice, he began to tell the story of the dynamics of the Abilene paradox in his life and career. His own reactions and fears helped him to theorize about the paradox and its dynamics. He described the touching story of his relationship with Elliott Jaques, who shared with Harvey the abandonment he experienced for refusing to board the bus to Abilene. Their relationship was a rich source of personal and intellectual support in Harvey's theorizing. Indeed, Harvey's prologue is an example of how a scholar used his theory to theorize and how his theorizing resulted in a rich relationship and deep self-knowledge and cultural awareness that can only come by relating openly to others.

Hatch, in the "Dynamics of Culture," described how organizational culture works, as defined from a point of view established within the organization. She called her model *dynamic*, not only to point out that culture is dynamic, but to show that people have to be dynamic along with the organizational processes if they want to understand how culture works and how to manage effectively within it. Hatch added the processes of realization, manifestation, symbolization, and interpretation to fill in the gaps in Schein's model of assumptions, values, and artifacts.

In her prologue, Hatch shared that her article took "a grueling 10 years" to write and publish and that it takes a good 10 years for doctoral students to learn to theorize. She described the series of events through which she developed both her theory and her way of theorizing about organizational phenomena. After her article was published, she "sat back and waited for these important ideas to be recognized by my contemporaries, but apart from the Executive Leadership Program students I met at George Washington University, hardly anyone gave the article much attention." She "stubbornly kept writing" to "establish merit" for her ideas. She built out her model by comparing it to other theories, like Weber's theory of routinization, and she applied it to other constructs, such as leadership, identity, and branding. Her writing about her cultural dynamics model gave "discipline" to her theorizing—and it also resulted in her unique, dynamic way of theorizing.

Like Harvey, Hatch's theorizing proved to be generative of many other ideas as well as of her way of theorizing about organizational phenomena. Her current approach, historicization, incorporates a temporal perspective in organizational studies to investigate how phenomena happened. This is not the first time Hatch took up a particular epistemological model to theorize; she used the hermeneutic circle to represent her cultural dynamic model. She looked to the classics, like Dewey's pragmatism, for inspiration, and these models and theories have had a generative effect on her thinking. Yet she continues to search for a method that can help her observe the dynamic phenomena of culture, and she is sensitive to questions that challenge the validity of the models she and others have developed to represent the object of their study. She talked about turning to the arts to experiment on the artistic notions of validity, like intuition and empathy—again, sharing features with Harvey's relational theorizing.

In "Capabilities: Structure, Agency, and Evolution," an article coauthored with Michael Jacobides, Winter also examined the challenges of navigating the relationship between two different conceptual and research approaches in economics, the organizational capabilities approach and the transaction cost approach. In the article they assessed recent progress toward an integration of these two approaches, primarily in the context of the analysis of vertical structure and related phenomena. Whatever the theoretical perspective at the level of the firm, analyses must reach beyond that level to grasp the important causal forces affecting capability development, firm boundaries, and structural features more generally.

Winter, like the other authors in this section, focused fundamentally on the process for building a *bottom-up* understanding of how social structures are created—and to try to make the case for the ways in which networks and the intersection of multiple networks form social structures. The coevolutionary process for the dynamic interaction among the agents, firms, and industries gives rise to the industry architecture, which in turn makes it possible for technology, organizational change, and institutional change to influence the actions of individual actors.

The structure of firms, the industry, and the niche and competitive position of various actors evolve and change through this historic process of coevolution. For economic theory, more insight is needed into the role of agency and its evolutionary significance and the role of structure, or more specifically, industry architecture, on the development of organizational capabilities. Business model research needs to become more "socialized," less focused on the heroic depictions of successful firms and individual entrepreneurs and more attuned to the dynamics of coevolution between individual business models and the industry context that supports or rejects them.

In his prologue, Winter talked about his theorizing and how it was partly fueled by a paradigm war in economics. In his article, he and Jacobides compared the organizational capability model with the transaction cost model by applying them to an analysis of the financial industry crisis. They compared and contrasted how each model would analyze the events—and the solutions that both would offer. This approach supports Winter's claim that paradigms make a difference in understanding how the world works and in the actions that can make it work better. He theorized by comparison and critique and argued that the dynamic way of theorizing leads to more effective results in the world of practice.

Powell's theorizing also focused on the micro-motor dynamics of institutions. He noted the need to make micro-foundations of institution theory more explicit to show how institutions are sustained, altered, and extinguished as individuals in concrete social situations enact them. Powell, like Winter, argued that most micro-motives of individual agents are instrumental in interpretation and too simplistic to understand the logic and dynamics of organizations. As Powell remarked, "Celebration of entrepreneurs has gone too far, as not all change is led by entrepreneurs, and surely heroic actors and cultural dopes are a poor representation of the gamut of human behavior." Thus, structures, routinization, and problem-solving processes may form and inform the organization more than a charismatic leader. Powell and Colyvas' article, "Microfoundations of Institutional Theory," illustrated the power and determination of the vertical structure, a key element that demonstrates the contrasts between mainstream and evolutionary economics. Micro-level explanations also give more depth to accounts of macro-level events and relationships. Micro-institutional forces shape individual interests and desires, frame the possibilities for action, and influence whether behaviors result in persistence or change.

In his prologue, Powell shared that his theorizing has been driven by a set of consistent questions throughout many years. In part he creates the conditions for his theorizing by provoking others to question his ideas. For example, he talked about how he theorizes by writing in response to feedback on his articles—i.e., he wrote about how isomorphism is not copying, that habits are not passive. He sought out an eclectic set of theories that could help him understand and examine micro dynamics, and he integrated them into his models and methods—all in an effort to develop a more robust theory of micro-foundations of institutions. He began with micro-translation to explain the reciprocal relationship between structure and agency, added sensemaking to account for the social-psychological dimension of the dynamic, drew on the seminal sociological work of the 1960s (ethnomethodology) that examined performance and the power of habits and routines in everyday life, and brought this line of inquiry forward into his research. Though he appeared confident in his theorizing as well as in his model, he showed that he is not yet done. He deeply considered a question from a peer, John Meyer: Why these particular theories and not others? Although he answered, he acknowledged that his answer was tentative.

Discussion

The scholars in this book have devoted their careers to theorizing by posing thought-provoking questions and exploring new variables that challenge classical social change constructs and the theories that they foster. Their work has deepened our appreciation of the dynamics of human nature and culture, and more specifically the role that human interaction, process, and context play in our ability to understand the reciprocal or coevolving relationship between individuals and their social surround. Weick talked about durable questions that drive theorizing, and the authors in this book raised many such questions. Powell perhaps best articulated one question that appeared across the articles when he wrote in his prologue: "How do institutions get inhabited and how do people live inside institutions and engage in everyday reasoning?" At its core, this question probes the relationship between and among people and society, to include relationships among people (Weick, Marsick), between people and groups (Harvey), among institutions (Huff) or processes (Uhl-Bien, McKelvey, Hatch), and across levels in a social system (Winter, Powell).

In her prologue, Uhl-Bien shared the result of her taking a more dynamic stance towards this question early in her theorizing about complexity leadership. "My world changed . . . . I read about complexity, I was introduced to a whole other dimension of relational thinking—one grounded in *relationality*, . . . the idea of interactive dynamics and a world that operates *in relation*."

Common notions of relationships, as Uhl-Bien noted, are that they involve two or more individuals, or bounded selves (Gergen, 2009), who interact, which causes an effect for the individuals and their social surround. In this light, life occurs and people and social systems change through an ongoing process of cause and effect. Gergen (2009) called into question the utility of these assumptions and invited consideration of the world in relational confluence. Traditional views of the self are not necessarily false, but they are constructs around which we build and lead our lives, and he advocated a different relational-centered view, or relationality, that he believed would enrich our potential for living.

> My attempt is to generate an account of human action that can replace the presumption of bounded selves with a vision of relationship. I do not mean relationships between otherwise separate selves, rather a process of coordination that precedes the very concept of self . . . . [V]irtually all intelligible action is born, sustained, and/or extinguished within the ongoing process of relationships . . . . We are always already emerging from relationships; we cannot step out of relationship; even in our most private moments, we are never alone. (Gergen, 2009, p. xv)

If we consider the three variables of human interaction, process, and context that emerged as significant in theorizing about the nature of human and social systems in this book in light of this relational-centered understanding, they do not stand as separate and distinct from each other, nor can they be isolated in one or more social change construct. The three emerge as a holistic dynamic underlying the ongoing "process of coordination." The process *is* the interaction, and this interaction is both the tool and result (Holzman, 2006) of human development and meaning, or context. The dynamic of relationality not only challenges us to reframe our understanding of the social change constructs; it may also shed new light on how they came to be in the first place.

> *Proposition 1.* The articles and prologues in this book point to new variability in the substance of human and organizational theory—specifically human interaction, process, and contexts—and this variability holds potential to shift the way change constructs (learning, leaders, culture, agency, etc.) are experienced and perceived.

In this book, we observed a tendency among scholars to reduce the complexity of the story of their theorizing to a linear series of events leading to the advancement of their ideas, and we noted the irony of this approach to talking about theorizing a nonlinear complexity dynamics. While we recognize the constraints imposed by the internal logic of the scientific process, we also must acknowledge the consequence of a relational-centered understanding of human nature for the ontologies, epistemologies, and ethics that drive theorizing about human and social constructs (Gergen, 1997, 2009).

In chapter 1, Schwandt and Sashkin identified how the interpretive bias in social theorizing shifted from objective to subjective, or "from a more rational conceptualization to a more subjective orientation, or one that combines both normative and rational and value orientations." The complexity of the external environment challenged the narrow, bounded rational explanations of human and organizational phenomena.

In addition to recognizing the complexity of the environment, scholars began to recognize the recursive nature of the scientific process and thus developed greater appreciation for the role of discourse and social interaction in the process of knowledge construction. Together, these two events moved the interpretive bias in social science from objective, in which theorizing represents or mirrors reality through static constructs and models, to subjective, in which theorizing actively interprets and constructs representations through social interaction, reflection, and dialogue in situ.

Powell in his article and prologue, like others (Gergen, 1997; Bruner, 1986), looked to social constructivists including Mead, Bruner, Goffman, Garfinkel, and Weick and the field of social psychology more broadly for theoretical and methodological inspiration in the shift to a subjective bias.[22] Their empirical quest was to understand the reciprocal relationship between society and the development of individual consciousness.

Mead (1962) posited that the mind and indeed humans were innately social. Human consciousness was formed as people instinctively coordinated their actions, which enabled or gave rise to individual capacity for self-reflection. People constructed and reformulated their means for meaning making as they adjusted to the influence of others. This adjustment was made possible by the ability to take the perspective of the other and reflect that onto the self in the micro-interactions of daily life and routines. Thus there is no individual consciousness without a community of others whom one depends upon for his or her sense of self (Mead, 1962).

This perspective remains a significant challenge to the idea of an individual, rational knower separated from a world of others and objects, yet some (Gergen, 1997; Holzman, 1996; Olesen & Weber, 2012) still note the remnants of the deeply ingrained perspective of the independent subject in this stream of thought. For example, there is a continued focus on the mental world of the individual that ultimately functions as the source of individual action (Gergen, 2009). There is also a tendency to theorize the self and other as separate—the self and society or culture—and developmental interaction occurs when the two come together

---

[22] Noticeably absent from the articles in this book and hence this chapter are other theoretical traditions such as critical theory, feminism, postmodernism, and poststructuralism that offer a political, cultural, and historic explanation of the shift to a subjective orientation.

(Gergen, 2009). This then leads to the tendency to explain collectives, like family or society, as influencing and having an effect on the individual (cause and effect). Olesen and Weber (2012) explained that for Mead, socialization was largely the social imprinting of individual agents, and "the role of subjectivity in history remains largely untheorized in its own right" (p. 3).

The relational-centered understanding stretches the implications of the constructivist's notion of subjectivity (Gergen, 2009) and may cause a fundamental shift in the interpretive bias in human and social theorizing. Gergen (1997) asked: "Are we prepared to address the final orientation toward relatedness, one that shifts from remote realms of social structure and individual subjectivity to the domain of the microsocial patterns, interdependent action, and the realm of the *in-between?*" (p. 217).

> *Proposition 2.* This new variability has triggered the need for a new mode of theorizing that accounts for the reflexivity of scientific knowledge and the role of researchers' subjectivity in the research process and thus shifts the interpretive bias in social science research from a subjective to an intersubjective orientation.

> Bruner (1986) defined intersubjectivity as: . . . [A] shared cognition that shapes our ideas and relations—it presupposes a shared context, an invitation to negotiate a shared context, and solidarity with another . . . . Human beings not only come equipped with the means to calibrate the working of their minds, but also to calibrate the worlds in which they live through subtle means of reference. (pp. 62, 64)

Contemporary conceptions of intersubjectivity broaden the idea of a shared cognition to include holistic ways of knowing and engaging in the relationality of the world. In fact, the shared experience is not primarily cognitive, for it also includes affect, perceptual processes, and conative engagements (Zlatev, Racine, Sinha, & Itkonen, 2008), and it is both historically and culturally constituted (Gergen, 2009).

Thus, the awareness of the relationality brings the "epistemic subject-object-relativity" (Olesen & Weber, 2012, p. 25) into focus—and this reveals the social nature of research. In other words, research is a social practice (Olesen & Weber, 2012; Alhadeff-Jones, 2013), and this understanding challenges the common understanding of the knowledge production process on epistemological, psycho-social, anthropological, and ethical grounds (Alhadeff-Jones, 2013). Not only are new tools required for reflecting the researchers' subjectivity, but we must recognize that the reflection of the researching subject (i.e., the relative) *is* an empirical issue (Olesen & Weber, 2012).

The method then is a matter of critical reflection or perhaps reflexivity in which the basic assumptions that frame the inquiry are constantly challenged by considering both the researchers' subjectivity as well as the conditions framing their interaction in the research context. In other words, the method is experiential learning (Alhadeff-Jones, 2013), but in the context of relationality one needs to ask: Who or what learns through or within the research process?

If this is so, then what is the implication for Schwandt and Sashkin's third scholar-practitioner imperative, which is that the development of the scholar-practitioner requires theorizing as practice over both time and contexts? We certainly cannot conceive this as a process of strictly individual learning and development. In relationality, we need to conceive the scholar-practitioner as a dynamic network of relationships that motivate and guide practice, to include the social practice of research and theorizing.

Proposition 3. The emergence of an intersubjective interpretive bias may reframe notions of who or what a scholar-practitioner is (a person, a role, a process).

Moving to the Future

Burke in chapter 11 focused on the future as he considered the unfinished business of organizational development. In his article he identified three areas for future theorizing: organizational culture, leadership development, and resistance to change. He shared in his prologue that his theorizing is driven by the limitations of his knowledge in practice. "So it is not as if I didn't know about a network, but I didn't know how to change it." Since he wrote the article he has continued to theorize about how to interact with and influence the micro actions of loosely coupled systems. Weick's improvisational approach is a good start, but we need to know more about what improvisation means and how to engage in improvisational change. These are questions that drive Burke's theorizing, and they also provide us a point of departure for considering the implications of this discussion for the scholar-practitioner imperative and the future of the professional doctorate in human and organizational learning.

As Huff noted, the university, traditionally the training ground of Mode 1 researchers, now also provides a steady supply of researchers for Mode 2 knowledge production—and this more distributed knowledge may also be one source of the more complex knowledge production landscape she described in her epilogue. Lee, Green, and Brennan (2000) explored the implications of the rise of Mode 2 knowledge production for the university. The socially distributed nature of Mode 2 enables "new forms of research practice carried out in places that are far flung from the university and judged by, and communicated to, communities other than academic-disciplinary ones" (p. 124). They acknowledged that Modes 1 and 2 overlap in significant ways; "both have always existed and they are mutually dependent" (p. 124). Nevertheless, the two are different, and according to Lee et al. (2000) the professional doctorate is rooted in these differences.

Professional doctorates can be seen . . . to represent an emerging form of knowledge production and practice of research within a Mode 2 environment. There is accordingly a need to engage

505

carefully in exploring the particular practices of knowledge generation in these degrees—practices that emerge as doctoral candidates in different professional doctoral programs negotiate relationships within practice sites in which their research will be carried out, and to which they are a member; with the idea of professionalism itself; and with the university, still the primary credentialing body and still the custodian of the doctoral enterprise. (p. 125)

Alhadeff-Jones (2013) extended the discussion of the complex research landscape by considering the implications of the appreciation of relationality and the shift to an intersubjective orientation. He delineated at least four subsystems that constitute the research process:

1. The authoring system, usually thought of as a single researcher but in a relational-centered perspective extending to the institutions, professions, relationships, etc., in which the author is embedded
2. The system of ideas that defines and legitimates how knowledge should be produced
3. The system of the object of the study or the practical research questions that require a solution
4. The system of methods that guide action and aid in understanding the object of the study

Though the systems are historically constructed and this history must be considered, they are also intertwined and mutually constituted in a research process in situ. These subsystems dynamically interact with each other and the research environment to calibrate the world as well as the means by which it can be known.

This approach requires the capacity to access, describe, interpret, and challenge assumptions that frame the way scientific knowledge is organized as well as the social-cultural conditions from which it emerges

(Alhadeff-Jones, 2013). It also requires deep, experiential knowledge of the research environment and the anticipated 'finalities' of the research process, such as building new knowledge, solving intractable problems, or deeply describing a phenomenon. Lee et al. (2000) suggested that scholar-practitioners in the new research landscape need multiple research literacies, including academic literacies, professional literacies, and workplace literacies—as well as the ability to draw upon the literacies in complex ways to navigate their development as a researcher and the research process.

But if we are to respond to Schwandt and Sashkin's third element of the scholar-practitioner imperative—the need for theorizing as practice over both time and contexts—then we have to conceive these literacies and the capacity to apply them in relational terms. An intersubjective orientation would reveal the historic, cultural origins of these capacities and would lead us to understand that the only way to enlist people is by engaging them holistically in the social practices that they seek to acquire. We cannot just teach and challenge doctoral students to learn the theories of the field and then leave them to figure out how to apply and integrate them into their practice settings on their own. We must help them develop the capacity to utilize the literacies and we must help them yield to the developmental demands that these literacies place on their way of thinking, acting, and relating in the world. In turn we must also ensure that our social practice of theorizing and research also yields to challenges that are sure to come from the "informed skeptic," or as Powell described our students, "people with enough experience to be immune to theoretical indoctrination."

So what might this process look like? What habits would it need to foster in the individual and the community of practice of scholar-practitioners? These are the questions that might help to move the field as well as individual professional doctoral programs to the future.

Lee et al. (2000) suggested a hybrid curriculum, one that takes seriously the intersection between the university and the organization in which doctoral research will be undertaken. In other words, universities would actually partner with the sponsoring organizations of their students to not only help individual students conduct dissertation studies, but to collaborate through these studies to investigate the new kinds of knowledge emerging in practice and new ways of producing knowledge and to explore the most appropriate ways to legitimize and represent it.

Such a move might lead us to join Hatch in her quest for new criteria for validity such as esthetics, intuition, and empathy that acknowledge the demands of the relational-centered epistemology and the subsequent understanding of the relationality. What is our role as educators to help our students engage in relational-centered research while also ensuring that they have the language or the literacies required to legitimize and defend their work? Harvey's story of his theorizing illustrates that this is not just an intellectual challenge; it is also a personal risk and political contest.

If we accept the idea of multiple literacies underlying scholarly practice, then we must also acknowledge the developmental effects of exposing people to multiple literacies. People would need to learn to think dialogically, through and within the conversation that occurs across multiple literacies, and in turn they would be required to use both reflection and reflexivity to continuously challenge the principles that govern a particular way of thinking, or literacy (Alhadeff-Jones, 2013). This process demands a disposition for ambiguity and a related habit of "permanent self-reflection" to lead scholar-practitioners, and by extension their educators, to continuously examine their doubts, ignorance, and confusion (Alhadeff-Jones, 2013).

Both Winter and Marsick examined how structure, culture, and the physical design of the learning environment affect learning, raising issues about how educators manage and are managed in the design and delivery of our courses. New forms of collaborative learning are required that help people examine the organic circle of their own learning and that of others in the process by which it unfolds. How can we help students learn from their rich life experiences and to theorize about them through the macro concepts they are exposed to in the doctoral curriculum? And what is the role of action research and challenging questions in helping them to apply knowledge to help solve real, urgent, and complex problems that they encounter in the complex world of practice?

Weick offered a framework of respectful interaction as a way of helping groups of people draw from the experience of individuals to make collective sense of and construct collective objects. What is the role of this respectful interaction in the doctoral curriculum, and can educators model it in their relationship with students and with each other?

Harvey raised concerns about the potential for anaclinic depression among doctoral students who are offered the opportunity to think differently without being prepared for the accompanying shifts that may occur in their sense of self. Learning is holistic and affects people's values, aims, careers, and intimate relationships. What is our responsibility to students who experience transitional and transformational learning in our programs? Do we take these shifts into account by providing developmental as well as intellectual support to our students, and more importantly, should we?

Finally, educators must model the skeptical and reflexive stance we encourage in our students and turn our gaze onto our own practices as scholar-practitioners and educators, continuously challenging the assumptions that drive our pedagogies and theorizing. New lines of research on the professional doctoral model itself might aid in this critical reflection. Lee et al. (2000) posed a set of questions that might provide a good start:

Who will be the new doctors? What will be their roles in the organizations they work in and for, and also in social life more generally? What are the research, pedagogical and textual practices that will produce them? What implications are there for the university and the professions, and for organizations populated by these differently trained and licensed professionals in these newly articulated relations of research and practice? (p. 133)

Powell drew on Dewey's idea of habits to think about the relationship between everyday reasoning and the interpretive schema of the collective knowledge stock. If we use Dewey's idea of the organic circle to understand the development of these habits on both the individual and collective level, then we can also understand how to establish the continuity required to realize the third element of the scholar-practitioner imperative, the need for theorizing as practice over both time and contexts. Taken together, these activities suggest that the professional doctorate take a position at the nexus of at least two organic circles—the one of the seasoned professionals who enroll in doctoral programs and develop new identities as scholar-practitioners and the other that underlies the stock knowledge of our field.

But first we may need to learn to see our students as complex representations of a historic process of development, as well as complex people. We may need to figure out how to support each of them in their personal journey to become a scholar-practitioner, while also recognizing that their motivation and need to take this journey also may manifest a broader historic process that is changing the nature of knowledge and our understanding of what it means to be human, to learn, and to theorize. Once we adopt this both/and understanding of our students, then perhaps we can become more concrete and hence more effective in our attempts to foster the scholar-practitioner imperative.

References

Alhadeff-Jones, M. (2013). Complexity, methodology and method: Crafting a critical process of research. *Complicity: An International Journal of Complexity and Education, 10*(1/2), 19-44.

Bruner, J. (1986). *Actual minds: Possible worlds.* Cambridge, MA: Harvard University Press.

Dewey, J. (1916). *Democracy and education: An introduction to the philosophy of education.* New York, NY: Macmillan.

Dewey, J. (1938). *Experience and education.* New York, NY: Kappa Delta Pi.

Gergen, K. J. (1997). *Realities and relationships: Soundings in social construction.* Cambridge, MA: Harvard University Press.

Gergen, K. J. (2009). *Relational being: Beyond self and community.* New York, NY: Oxford University Press.

Holzman, L. H. (1996). Pragmatism and dialectical materialism in language development. In H. Daniels (Ed.), *An introduction to Vygotsky* (pp. 75-98). London, UK: Routledge.

Holzman, L. (2006). Activating postmodernism. *Theory & Psychology, 16,* 109-123.

Lee, A., Green, B., & Brennan, M. (2000). Organisational knowledge, professional practice and the professional doctorate at work. In J. Garrick & C. Rhodes (Eds.), *Research and knowledge work: Perspectives, case-studies, and innovative strategies* (pp. 117-136). London, UK: Routledge.

Mead, G. H. (1962). *Mind, self, and society; from the standpoint of a social behaviorist.* Chicago, IL: University of Chicago Press.

Olesen, H. S., & Weber, K. (2012). Socialization, language, and scenic understanding. Alfred Lorenzer's contribution to a psycho-societal methodology. *Forum: Qualitative Social Research, 13*(3), Art. 22. Retrieved from http://www.qualitative-research.net/index.php/fqs/article/view/1906

Zlatev, J., Racine, T. P., Sinha, C., & Itkonen, E. (Eds.). (2008). *The shared mind: Perspectives on intersubjectivity.* Amsterdam, The Netherlands: John Benjamins.

CPSIA information can be obtained at www.ICGtesting.com
Printed in the USA
BVOW08s0810140515

400200BV00001BA/11/P